Preserving the Great Plains
& Rocky Mountains

PRESERVING THE GREAT PLAINS & ROCKY MOUNTAINS

Elaine Freed

Foreword by Clark Strickland

National Trust for Historic Preservation

UNIVERSITY OF NEW MEXICO PRESS: ALBUQUERQUE

Library of Congress Cataloging-in-Publication Date

Freed, Elaine.
    Preserving the Great Plains & Rocky Mountains / Elaine Freed :
Foreword by Clark Strickland. -- 1st ed.
        p.   cm.
    Includes bibliographical refreences and index.
    ISBN 0-8263-1304-3. -- ISBN 0-8263-1305-1 (pbk)
    1. Historic sites--Great Plains--Conservation and restoration.
2. Architecture-Great Plains--Conservation and restoration.
3. Historic sites--Rocky Mountains Region--Conservation and
restoration. 4. Architecture--Rocky Mountains Region--Conservation
and restoration. 5. Great Plains--History, Local. 6. Rocky
Mountains Region--History, Local.   I. Title. II. Title: Preserving
the Great Plains and Rocky Mountains.
F591.F85   1992
978--dc20
91-25262
CIP

Design by Susan Gutnik.
Map by Imagigraphics, Colorado Springs, Colorado.

CONTENTS

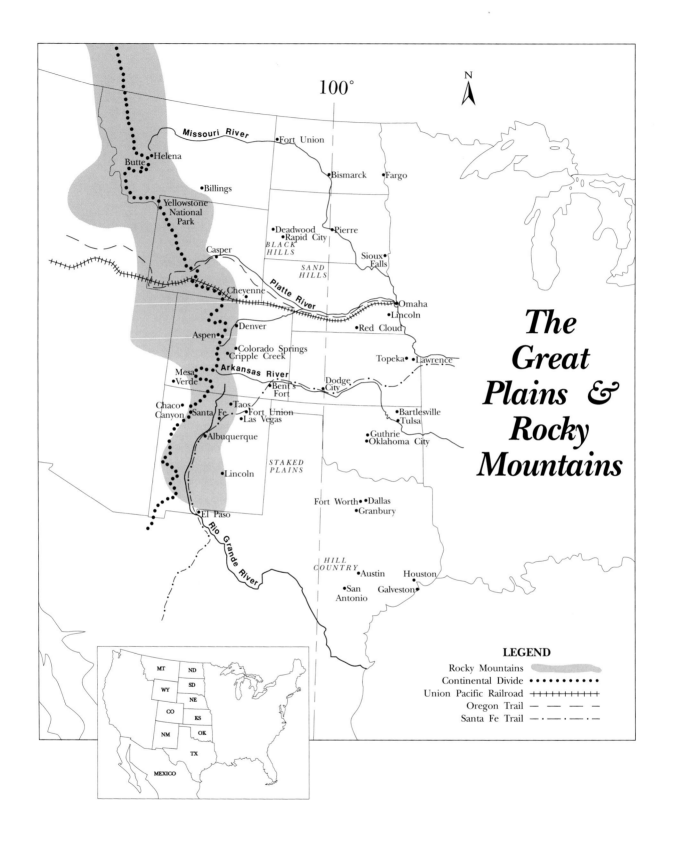

The Great Plains & Rocky Mountains

LEGEND
Rocky Mountains
Continental Divide ••••••••••
Union Pacific Railroad +++++++++++
Oregon Trail — — —
Santa Fe Trail —·—·—·—

onsider the rugged mountains and the vast plains of America. Has the hand of man wrought changes here? Carved homesteads? Created lasting and valuable public works? What were the lifeways of the first Americans, the aspirations of the pioneers, and the effects of the Industrial Revolution? Has there grown up in this region a civic spirit of pride and esthetic aspiration?

These questions are raised and answers are suggested in this volume on the preservation of the physical heritage of the mountains and plains states. The answers are not final, because adaptability and flexibility are among the requirements of life in a region where the forces of nature are so strong and changeable. This book also gives ample proof that society has matured beyond simple survival to the point where honor and respect are granted to the work of forebears, to tradition.

This maturity is seen in the growing numbers of local and state preservation organizations and agencies. It shows up in an eagerness to enjoy and promote local heritage as a basis for tourism. It can be counted in the growth of National Trust membership in this part of the country. The willingness of makers of public policy to consider the importance of heritage sites along with other values is becoming more firmly established. All of this bodes well for the future of historic preservation in the region.

Nevertheless, the preservation of our physical heritage exists within a difficult environment. Rugged and harsh terrain, a widely dispersed population, and economic control from outside characterize much of the mountains/plains region. The variety of conditions and problems, even within a single state, makes standard solutions difficult or impossible to design. There is a suspicion of government and a reliance on individual responsibility rather than on collective action. The federal government holds title to huge amounts of land in the mountain states, making access to decision-makers difficult. Population growth, always slow in this century in agricultural areas, has slowed in all of the region's states owing to tough economic times. Rural areas are losing ground even more drastically.

The successes that have been achieved are all the sweeter for the difficulty of their being accomplished. The connections of living people with many of the historic resources of the region are personal and intimate. Especially in small towns and rural areas, families can recall when commercial buildings and farmsteads were built by grandparents or great grandparents. It is only in recent years that this personal connection with the man-made environment has been translated into a larger appreciation that these buildings, districts, and sites are more than family legacies, that they are physical evidence of our nation's history.

This is not to say that all of the historic resources of the mountains and plains states are of recent construction. The Anasazi cliff dwellings (ca. 1200) at Mesa Verde National Park in southwestern Colorado were three centuries old when Columbus made his voyage of discovery. There are physical remains of settlement in the southern part of the region that are 800 years older than that. Some of the earliest evidences of the human occupation of North America are found on the plains.

The desire to save archeological sites in this region led to the first systematic involvement of the federal government in the preservation of cultural resources. The citizens of the region have extended the reach of continuing public efforts by the creation of not-for-profit organizations to achieve historic preservation goals. Some of the most sophisticated, powerful, and successful local preservation organizations in the country are to be found in Galveston, San Antonio, and Denver. Small cities and towns, too, have created innovative programs, although the lack of population and great distances between communities have made organizing groups a difficult task.

The tools and techniques that have been developed by preservation groups recognize the special challenges that face the region's historic resources. One of the most extensive archeological salvage operations in the nation was undertaken on the Dolores project in southwestern Colorado. Revolving funds to meet the need for capital for downtown and residential rehabilitation have been established in Fargo, North Dakota; Denver, Colorado; Lawrence, Kansas; and for the entire states of South Dakota and New Mexico. Community foundations in New Mexico have created targeted giving programs in historic preservation. Denver has enacted an ordinance that permits the transfer of zoning density away from historic buildings to other sites. Colorado and South Dakota have created programs to identify and honor families who have preserved historic farm and ranch buildings. Oklahoma and New Mexico engaged in efforts to promote the Route 66 corridor, an early artifact of the automobile age. Wyoming has made special efforts to document historic sites photographically. Montana has utilized coal severance tax revenues to support historic preservation activities. Nebraska has conducted detailed surveys of rural areas to locate historically significant farmsteads.

These activities suggest the variety of methods needed to deal effectively with threats to historic resources. They also suggest the variety and types of properties that have something to tell us about the history of our country. The list of important cultural properties includes ships and boats like *Elissa* and *Capt. Merriwether Lewis*. It encompasses world heritage sites like Mesa Verde and national shrines like the Alamo. Also included are exquisite places, the Church of San Jose de Gracia in Las Trampas, New Mexico, for example.

Native American sites such as the Muskogee Creek Council House, in Okmulgee, Oklahoma, and the Medicine Wheel in the Big Horn Mountains of Wyoming are found here. Ethnic districts, from Czech communities in Texas to German-Russian settlements in the Dakotas add variety and interest to the stock of historic areas. Military sites abound, and ghosts are found as well in scores of abandoned mining towns and crossroads communities in agricultural areas. The vastness of the region, and its variety, make the area difficult to categorize or summarize in a short, simple way.

This richness of heritage rewards and informs those who take time to study the fascinating history, architectural history, and archeology of the mountains and plains states. These investigations are most enjoyably conducted on site, where the evocative strength and beauty of these places can be most fully enjoyed. For those who cannot have the pleasure of visiting this diverse and challenging region, this book will provide an excellent introduction to the challenges and opportunities before the preservationists of the mountains and plains.

—CLARK STRICKLAND
DIRECTOR
NATIONAL TRUST FOR HISTORIC
PRESERVATION, MOUNTAINS/PLAINS REGION

*T*he historic sites presented in this volume constitute a small but significant sample of the whole. I regret that a great many communities did not get the attention they deserve and that special historic features, such as railroads and bridges, were neglected altogether. But other photographers and writers will tackle these important historic resources.

The amount of illustrated material being published today is encouraging to anyone interested in preservation. We are in need, however, of a popular work on the region's archeology, particularly a book that would synthesize the vast amount of archeological material excavated and studied as a result of the energy development of the 1970s and 1980s. In a related area, it would be gratifying to read a study of the region's native American architecture, particularly if the material were presented from a native American perspective. This study should also examine the continuity and discontinuity of environments in the period that spans prehistory, the era of Euroamerican settlement, and current circumstances. Finally, we need to direct to larger audiences the local and state historic sites studies now being written.

As we enter the 1990s, it is time to develop strategies for documenting and celebrating the region's twentieth-century architecture, including the post–World War II buildings that we have neglected in our zeal to record older sites. The split-level suburbs are waiting for us. So are the strip malls, drive-in theaters, and glass office towers of modern America. After twenty years of survey, we've only just begun.

The central focus of historic preservation is architecture and the environment and the people who lived in and changed that environment. The work of preservation is entirely an accomplishment of committed individuals who, alone or in concert, commit themselves to saving evidence of the past. During a period of several years, I spoke with hundreds of preservationists throughout the mountains and plains region who shared with me their excitement and concern about the protection of historic buildings, landscapes, districts, and entire communities. They include Deborah Abele, Tucker Hart Adams, John Albright, Mary Ann Anders, Nancy Arnon, Willie Atencio, Cheryl Babcock, Joe C' de Baca, Jay Bangle, Jean and John Baucus, John F. Baucus, Ellen Beasley, Mildred Bennett, Michael Birkes, Sallie Bodie, Diana Bolter, Gary Bowen, Jim Bratton, David Breed, Kent Briggs, Peter Brink, Eulene and Horace Brock, Ann Brooks, Jan Buckingham, Ann Buffington, Thomas Caperton, Nicholas Bonham Carter, Mary Ann Castleberry, Cheryl Clemmensen, Donald Coffin, Wes Colbrunn, Richard Collier, John Conron, Janet Cornish, Marty Craddock, Dana Crawford, Carla and John Cronholm, Anthony Crosby, Mary P. Davis, A. Richard Dempster, Chris Dill, David Dillon, Joanne Ditmer, Peter Dominick, Jr., Barbara Doolittle, Lesley Drew, Julia Eberhard, Roxanne Eflin, Sharon Eiseman, Ron Emrich, Don Etter, John Fey, Richard C. D. Fleming, Bernd Foerster, Paul Foster, Shirley Fredericks, Michael Gaertner, Grace Gary, Lee and Ruth Geiger, Scott Gerloff, Mary Glenski, Tom Gougeon, Todd Guenther, George Haecker, Louis Hafermehl, Martha Hagedorn-Krass, Bonnie Halda, Robert Hardy, Cheryl Hargrove, Robert Hart, Jim Hartmann, Arn Henderson, Melvena Thurman Heisch, Nora and Walter Henn, Susan Henneke, William Hochman, Mary Humstone, Goeffrey Hunt, Julia Jarrell, Hildegard Johns, Victor Johnson, Terry Jordan, Mark Junge, Donald Kerns, Helen Knecht, Kathy Kruse, Peg LaMont, William Lees, Nancy Loe, Kathleen Lyons, Thomas Marceau, Ramona Markalunas, Father Jerome Martinez, Elaine Mayo, Virginia McAlester, Sue McCafferty, Ralph McCalmont, Trish McDaniel, Mark Mercer, Thomas Merlan, Lynn Meyer, Olivia Meyer, Melanie Milam, Alice and Robert Miller, Jennifer Moulton, Robert Mitchell, W. Mitchell, Inez Morrow, John Mosty, David Murphy, Al Nichols, Barbara Norgren, Steve Obering, Patricia Osborne, Kathleen Page, Barbara Pahl, Adora Palma, Richard Pankratz, J'Nell Pate, Joanna Parrish, George Pearl, Robert Peters, Garneth Peterson, Christine Pfaff, Dean Pohlenz, Jon Pomeroy, Boone Powell, James Purdy, Lisa Purdy, Robert Puschendorf, Paul Putz, Fred Quivik, Myles Rademan, Ron Ramsey, Anice Read, Mark Reavis, Gilson Riecken, Rock Ringling, Bruce Rippeteau, Mary Roberts, David Root, Richard Ryan, Abad Sandoval, Leif Sandberg, William Saslow, Dorothy Savage, Elizabeth Schlosser, Albert Schroeder, Richard Sellers, Douglas Scott, Dennis Seibel, Ann and Michael Shaw, Marcella Sherfy, Richard Shope, Katherine and Wid Slick, Jacqueline Sluss, Morgan Smith, Beverley Spears, Jim Steely, Diana Stein, Michael Stevens, Barbara Sudler, Bernard and Noeline Sun, Richard Sutton, Pat Syring, John Tatum, Barbara and Lloyd Taylor, John Tiff, Linda Tigges, Carolyn Torma, Arthur Townsend, Conrad True, Bobbi Uecker, Mary Lou Watkins, Melody Webb, Rod Wheaton, Sherry White, Nore Winter, Ellen Work, Kay Young, Tiana Zaffuto, Barbara Zook, and Dale Zinn. My son David Freed assisted in organizing the photographs.

In addition, I am grateful for the counsel and assistance of two staff members of the National Trust for Historic Preservation: Elizabeth Barker Willis, coordinator of the Texas/New Mexico Field Office, and Clark J. Strickland, director of the Mountains/Plains Regional Office.

This project was supported by a grant from the Graham Foundation for Advanced Studies in the Fine Arts.

Preserving the Great Plains
& Rocky Mountains

1.1   *An abandoned homestead in the grasslands of western Nebraska. Courtesy R. Bruhn*

The West Perceived: Images of the Great Plains and Rocky Mountains

Two centuries ago a carpet of grass covered the Great Plains from far up in Canada down through the continent halfway into Texas. Treeless, flat, and dry, the land supported vast herds of buffalo and antelope that grazed on a pasturage reaching from the edge of the midwestern forests to the foot of the Rockies. Dozens of grass species were rooted in this soil. Big, bluestem grasses covered the eastern prairies. Farther west, short-stemmed grama grass blanketed the High Plains that spread out below the Rocky Mountains. Constantly in motion, this giant grassland was compared to the sea by all who saw it. Waving, swaying, bowing to the west winds, it was green and glossy in summer, then bleached to a burnt orange or a pale yellow under the winter sun.

The deep, open sky seemed even larger than the land. When thunderheads churned overhead, their huge shapes appeared at home in the limitless expanse of sky. Occasionally, layers of low grey clouds closed in, compressing the prairie world and cutting off its vistas. But often a bountiful sky reigned bright and blue under the sun. It was the simplest of landscapes—grass and sky, stretching to the very edge of the earth.

Indian tribes, trailing the buffalo and each other, moved lightly across these dry, flat plains. By the late eighteenth century, all the northern tribes owned horses, introduced to the continent by the Spaniards. Mounted and mobile, the Plains

1.2   Tall-grass prairie in eastern South Dakota. Courtesy State Historical Preservation Center, South Dakota Department of Education and Cultural Affairs

1.3   A ranch near the Grand Tetons, Wyoming. Courtesy Richard Collier, Wyoming Department of Archives, Museums, and History

1.4 *Indian tribes built earth lodges through-out the Missouri Basin in what is now the Dakotas, Nebraska, and Kansas. This re-construction is in the Slant Indian Village near Bismarck, North Dakota. Courtesy Signe Snortland-Coles, State Historical Society of North Dakota*

Indians prospered during a brief golden age of commerce and hunting. They moved about freely, trading fur pelts and stolen horses. As Indian wealth increased in the late 1700s, the tribes aspired to greater ceremony and visual splendor.

During this time, the Plains tribes engaged in what archeologist A. L. Kroeber describes as "gratuitous warfare," a fierce but stylized quest for honor consisting of ritual dances, showy combat, and, for some, death. Arapaho, Cheyenne, Sioux, and Assiniboin rode the northern and middle plains. Other tribes came down from the mountains: Crow, Cree, Ute, and Blackfoot. Farther south in Texas and New Mexico, in land then owned by Spain, the Apaches and Comanches reigned supreme, the greatest horsemen of them all. Around 1800 other tribes migrated onto the plains from the east, pushed out by the pressures of the fur trade and the first surge of western settlement.

The hunting tribes, and those who went often to war, carried their tentlike lodges with them as they moved across the plains. Clusters of tipis could be seen along the Powder River or the Platte, home for the Cheyenne and the Pawnee. Along the Missouri River in the north-central

1.5 *The mountains of the West rise up like a great wall. This view shows the Sangre de Cristos across the Wet Mountain Valley in Colorado. This and all subsequent uncredited photos are by the author.*

1.6 *Incoming Euroamericans found the western mountains inspiring and grand, but native peoples centuries before had already invested mountain peaks with spiritual meaning. Bear Butte in western South Dakota has long been a holy place for Cheyenne and Sioux. Courtesy State Historical Preservation Center, South Dakota Department of Education and Cultural Affairs.*

CHAPTER ONE

1.7 *Pueblo Bonito, built around* A.D. *1100, is the largest pueblo site at Chaco Canyon, New Mexico. It contained five stories and as many as 800 rooms. Courtesy National Park Service*

plains, other Indians lived in round lodges built of logs and packed earth. These tribes—Mandan, Hidatsa, Arikara—hunted game but also raised crops of corn and squash, storing them in deep cache pits dug into the earth near their lodges. They surrounded their villages with fortifications of ditches and wooden palisades.

The grasslands, then, were the heart of the plains. But along the edges, the land, and life itself, was quite different. To the east great rivers shaped the land and dictated its uses. The fur trade flourished along the Dakota Territory's Red River flowing out of Canada. Later, as settlers moved west, the valley would become rich farm country.

The eastern border of the plains territory from the Red River of the North to the Gulf of Mexico represented the last outreach of midwestern prairie and southern forest. The leafy, lush woods of east Texas and the bountiful fields of Iowa were nurtured by high humidity and heavy rains. To the west, moisture gradually lessened until, in the heart of the short-grass country of the High Plains, annual rainfall measured a meager ten to twenty inches, too sparse to nourish the woodlands and greenery of the East.

The plains, seemingly endless in their stretch westward, stopped abruptly at the high wall of mountains that reached down from Canada, cut-

1.8   *These ruins at Mesa Verde, Colorado, were built in the 1200s and deserted a century later. Angloamericans rediscovered the site in 1888. Courtesy National Park Service*

ting through Montana, Wyoming, Colorado, and New Mexico. Compared to the plains, the mountains were high, cold, and wet, and as formidable as they were glorious. Deer, elk, and buffalo grazed in high meadows and on grasslands that spread between the mountain ranges. Beaver swam the streams, hunted by white trappers and the mountain tribes.

South of the mountains and plains, along the valleys of the Rio Grande in what was to become Mexican territory, Pueblo Indians for centuries had nurtured a culture distinct from that of the nomadic hunting and warring tribes of the central and northern grasslands. The landscape, too, was different. Bare rock mesas loomed above cottonwood-lined riverbanks. Scattered forests of piñon and juniper covered the lower mountain slopes, which gave way to brush-filled desert flats below. In this spare, sunny region, the native tribes built pueblos of stone and adobe. They survived by foraging and farming, and through trade with other Indians.

In the sixteenth century, Spanish clergy and soldiers invaded this quiet land. By the early 1600s, they were building churches in the pueblo villages and establishing agriculture along the rivers. During the course of the next 200 years, while nomadic Indians and buffalo freely crossed the grasslands of the Great Plains, the Southwest was absorbed into the colonial frontier world of Spain and Mexico, a remote outpost governed by the rigid precepts of church and state.

1.9   *Colonizing Spaniards were building in Texas and New Mexico by the 1600s. Great adobe churches became part of the culture and the landscape in New Mexico. Here a mountain snowstorm shrouds San Jose de Gracia de Las Trampas (ca. 1775) north of Santa Fe. Courtesy Myron Wood*

Exploration: The Romantic Vision

By the early nineteenth century, all of the West, including the Mexican territory, was poised at the edge of a new stage of history. America's expansion westward was proceeding at an astonishing pace. Less than fifty years after purchase of the Louisiana Territory from France in 1803, the wilderness boundary had been extended all the way to the Pacific coast. The Great Plains, the Rocky Mountains, the Oregon Territory, the former Republic of Texas, the deserts

of the Southwest, and the Great Basin—all were annexed by the United States by 1850. Within another fifty years this great western frontier was comfortably assimilated into the new American nation.

But first, the territory had to be explored. In 1805 the Lewis and Clark Expedition mapped and recorded the upper plains and northern Rockies while searching for a passage to the Pacific. Other survey parties followed. Their discoveries, when added to the firsthand knowledge of the fur trappers who guided them, gave welcome form to the almost incomprehensible territory of mountain and plains that lay beyond the Mississippi.

Artists and writers soon added their impressions to the expanding lore of the West. In 1805

1.10 *From Montana down through New Mexico, mountains challenged all explorers and travelers. This rocky terrain is southwest of Colorado Springs.*

1.11   Isolated landforms took on awesome proportions to travelers on horseback and wagon. Sites such as Chimney Rock along the Oregon Trail in Nebraska would have been visible during several days of travel. Courtesy D. Murphy

Lewis and Clark had no documentary artist with them, nor did Zebulon Pike a year later, but the Rocky Mountain survey led by Stephen Long in 1820 produced landscape sketches by Samuel Seymour. They were the first pictures of the mountain West to be circulated in the East. From such evidence, Americans gleaned their initial notions of the frontier.

The grandeur of the landscape enthralled the earliest western painters. In the 1830s, three exceptional artists traveled toward the Rockies: Carl Bodmer, accompanying the scientific survey of Prince Maximilian of Germany; Alfred Jacob Miller, recording the Oregon Trail under the auspices of a Scottish nobleman, William Drummond Stewart; and George Catlin, joining the American Fur Company for a voyage up the Missouri aboard the steamboat *Yellowstone*.

Easterners were unfamiliar with the landforms these artists depicted. Paintings of flat, barren buttes and fantastic rock formations graphically established the great expanses of the West and emphasized its lack of human scale. These landscape portraits revealed splendid mountain ranges and the immense spaces of the plains. Vast, varied, larger-than-life, the West enchanted and overwhelmed its visitors.

Against this awesome background, Indians

1.12   The photographer William Henry Jackson recorded these unusual rock formations in 1870 while on Hayden's Expedition. The same scene, near the Chugwater River in Wyoming, was painted by artist Sanford Robinson Gifford, a noted Hudson River landscape painter who was also part of the Hayden group. Courtesy Richard Collier, Wyoming Department of Archives, Museums, and History

1.13 *Early trails across the prairies were life-lines to the Far West. Ruts of the Santa Fe Trail are still visible in Ford County, Kansas. Courtesy Kansas State Historical Society*

appeared in ceremonial dress, hunting, dancing, warring, and riding. The artists presented mundane domestic details as well: early lodge villages and great camps of nomadic Sioux, where children played and women bathed in the river. These scenes were to become permanent records of a disappearing way of life. The Mandans of the Dakota Territories, for example, whom Catlin painted in 1832, were nearly destroyed by smallpox three years later.

More immediately, the Indian paintings captivated a large eastern audience. Here were exotic savages in colorful costumes—the regalia of ritual and war—and primitive rites of passage: dances of endurance, scaffolds for the dead. Later, as conflict

between white settlers and the Indians intensified, the natives, formerly romanticized, became simply enemies, hunted and reviled.

Thus, Catlin, Bodmer, and Miller defined the early frontier through their documentary painting. They were among the first illustrators to recreate the West for eastern and European viewers. Seeing an unspoiled wilderness, the artists glorified its innocence and romance. Washington Irving, Francis Parkman, and other writers strengthened that image. Their personal travel accounts were widely read in the eastern press at mid-century.

Later expeditions were more practical, setting the stage for the taming of the West. By mid-

1.14   *A smokehouse of fieldstone, German-Russian settlement, Emmons County, North Dakota. Courtesy J. Sluss, State Historical Society of North Dakota*

century a half-dozen surveys had been sent out to find rail routes to the Pacific Coast. Other expeditions had military aims, such as John C. Frémont's journeys in the 1840s that anticipated America's eventual dominance of the Southwest. In 1848, following war with Mexico and the annexation of Texas, the remaining portions of Colorado, Wyoming, New Mexico, Kansas, and Oklahoma were added to the United States, along with all the far western lands. What had been either wild territory or the foreign soil of the Spanish Southwest was now part of the American nation.

The early interpretations of the western landscape, of necessity, were from the vantage of a journey. That paradigm of travel and transience remained part of the western myth well beyond the era of exploration and soon infused the practical realities of western life. People were always on the move. Transportation, mining, and trade at the outset demanded independence and separation. Even agriculture, that most settled of industries, exploded in a peripatetic drama of cattle drives from deep in Texas to the mountain pastures of Montana.

1.15   Susan Magoffin, traveling over Raton Pass, New Mexico, in 1846, saw a view like this—little changed today except for the small town at the foot of the mountain. Courtesy Myron Wood

At this stage there was precious little architecture throughout most of the West, only a network of trails along which Americans hastened west toward the mountains or southward into lands formerly held by Spain and Mexico. Traders streamed out of Missouri toward New Mexico along the Santa Fe Trail. Farther north, wagons carried pioneers along the Oregon Trail to claim free lands in the Pacific Northwest. The discovery of gold in California in 1849 sent a rush of prospectors across the mountains and deserts. Suddenly, a romantic wasteland became the Golden West—free land and a chance for easy money. Constant talk of America's Manifest Destiny fired up expansionist fever. The press, meanwhile, kept the public's attention on western images and events.

But the land was more than a picture or a dream. To produce a livelihood for the hundreds of thousands of immigrants who headed west, the land had to be settled and worked. Cheap land—some of it free—provided opportunities under the right conditions, but often the conditions were disappointing. It seemed that for every

1.16 Taos Pueblo, New Mexico. Courtesy Myron Wood

main chance—gold strikes or good crops or abundant grazing lands—a set of hazards appeared alongside, negating the hard work and destroying the bounty. Without enough wood or water, and faced with dangerous extremes in weather, pioneer families struggled to survive. Hail and drought destroyed crops. Livestock froze in freak winter storms. Grasshoppers ate every green leaf in sight. Prairie fires raced across the huge expanses of dry grass. The sod itself defied familiar tools, requiring a new steel plow to cut through

it. The earliest settlers had to make do with subsistence farming because, until the railroads came, it was nearly impossible to move equipment in or ship produce out. Cattle had to take themselves to market, herded along by the cowboy, the new western professional.

The memoirs of a young Nebraska woman, Mollie Dorsey, reveal clearly the changes and adjustments faced by a single family moving west in the nineteenth century. In the late 1850s, Mollie Dorsey Sanford, age eighteen, came by steamer with her family from Indianapolis to eastern Nebraska. Three years later, she traveled by wagon train across the Great Plains to a mining camp in Colorado. When the Civil War broke out in 1861, Mollie's young husband joined a volunteer army poised to head off a Confederate threat coming up from Texas. For several months, Mollie Dorsey followed her soldier husband from post to post in southern Colorado and New Mexico. Then, after a brief stint of ranching along the front range of the Colorado Rockies, the young family settled in Denver, becoming permanent residents in that rapidly growing western city.

Throughout this nine-year itinerancy, Mollie Dorsey held a variety of jobs, from teaching in a Nebraska country school to cooking for twenty gold miners in Colorado. There was an easy flow from farm to town and back again, and a ubiquitous jack-of-all-trades approach to working. During her nine-year pilgrimage, Mollie lived in at least thirty-five different homes, most of them makeshift. Her account suggests that nearly everyone else was living the same way—flexibly and open to opportunity. Mobility was the region's *modus operandi*.

Another young woman's memoir, Susan Magoffin's *Along the Santa Fe Trail*, tells of a similar journey across the Great Plains followed by an encounter with the traditional village culture of what is now New Mexico. Mexico's Spanish rulers had prohibited trade with foreigners and thereby created a restrictively insular culture. At Santa Fe in 1846, after several months on the trail, Magoffin describes adobe churches, the portal-lined plaza in the center of town, and her own temporary quarters in a typical adobe house. These structures were part of a building tradition already two centuries old and one that would outlive the influence of Anglos coming into the country.

In many parts of the West, American settlers and European immigrants either brought architectural solutions with them as they moved west, or invented new ones. But in New Spain, where they found an architecture already in place, they adopted it, adapted it, and only temporarily overshadowed it when the railroad swept through with a plethora of Victoriana in 1880. The indigenous adobe tradition survived, incorporating changes in technology and form introduced by the Anglos—innovations such as pitched metal roofs and glass door surrounds—but remaining true to its Indian and Spanish origins.

2.1   Life's ephemeral quality in much of the mountains and plains is borne out by the frequency of abandoned buildings, such as these structures in western Nebraska's Box Butte County. Only in the Southwest have architectural traditions and actual settlements prevailed for centuries, and many have undergone great change in the past 100 years. Courtesy D. Murphy

Buildings of the Early West

A s a land of passages, the West attracted from the beginning a miscellany of roaming, restless individuals. Long before the plains and mountains were settled, they had been crossed again and again by Indians and then by trappers, soldiers, and surveyors. Energized by the promise of the West, Americans attempted to experience all of it. Even after they had settled in a place, building homes and businesses, they were likely to leave again, uprooting themselves and their families in pursuit of brighter opportunities. Crises and constraints, too, added to the transient character of the region. Failed crops, long distances to markets, and exhausted mines drove people to seek a better life somewhere else. Little wonder that the buildings left behind seem tentative, half-formed, sometimes half-finished.

In the southwestern portion of the region, in what we know today as New Mexico, Texas, and southern Colorado, this model of perpetual motion came head-on against an established tradition evolved centuries earlier by the native Pueblo Indians and later joined by colonizing Spaniards who had come up through Mexico. They created an architecture of multistoried houses, churches, plazas, and modest, flat-roofed adobe dwellings. In the early nineteenth century, when the Mexican people drove their exclusionary Spanish rulers out of the country, and entrepreneurial Americans, arriving first as traders, invaded this insular Hispanic and Indian world, the indigenous stone and earth building legacy held fast. As the century

2.2 *Earth lodges once were common along the Missouri River and its tributaries. These lodges have been reconstructed at the Slant Indian Village, Mandan, North Dakota, near Bismarck. Courtesy Signe Snortland-Coles, State Historical Society of North Dakota*

wore on, at least in the urban areas, the Spanish colonial and Pueblo building forms began to incorporate features from American and European architecture, but the adobe tradition continued to dominate.

Whether in the Great Plains, Rocky Mountains, or Southwest, most of the building of the early western frontier was a folk architecture, a vernacular expression of simple traditional building done in a certain way out of necessity and because it had always been done that way, with skills and techniques passed along by neighbors or families from one generation to another. Builders used the materials at hand: earth, stone, grass,

and wood. Often these folk structures reflected particular conditions of an area—the scarcity of timber and water, or the prevalence of high winds and extreme temperatures. A low sod house, for example, offered protection from both winter winds and searing summer heat.

The first white explorers in the West found a rich building tradition among the native Americans. In 1832, when artist George Catlin visited Fort Union on the Upper Missouri, he depicted Mandan earth lodge villages, moundlike timber and earth structures erected behind defensive palisades. None survive today, although they were once common along the rivers of the Dakotas,

2.3   *This tipi was photographed on the Sioux Reservation near Sisseton, South Dakota, in August of 1886. Courtesy W. H. Over State Museum, Vermillion, South Dakota*

Nebraska, and Kansas. Catlin also painted Plains Indian tipis belonging to the migratory Sioux, Crow, and Comanche. These decorated conical shelters of buffalo hides stretched around pine lodge poles were to become popular symbols of Plains Indian life.

Early in the nineteenth century, in order to free up more land for white settlement, the United States government began to remove Indians from the East, resettling them in Oklahoma Territory. More than sixty different tribes eventually migrated there, bringing with them building traditions that ranged from log cabins to thatched lodges and tipis. Grass and bark-covered houses,

especially suited to the dry southern plains, were common throughout the territory. Some tribes over the course of a year lived in several different dwellings: a winter house of log or earth, a thatched summer lodge, and a portable tipi for the hunting season. Even sedentary agricultural Indians depended in part on hunting and foraging and therefore required movable homes. During the latter half of the nineteenth century, Oklahoma Territory became a sampler of native American shelter.

Only in the Southwest along the Rio Grande in New Mexico and on the mesas farther west did a permanent Indian architecture evolve, an

2.4   *Pueblo Pintado, termed an "outlier,"*
is one of many Chacoan sites scattered across
the San Juan Basin in the Four Corners area.
Some of these masonry buildings were as high as
three stories when they were constructed around
1100. Courtesy National Park Service

architecture that in some instances survived the societies that built it. By A.D. 1100, four centuries before the Spaniards invaded, the Indian farmers of the Southwest had produced a complex, stable life of agriculture. These prehistoric Indians are known today as the Anasazi. Their civilization supported water-control systems as well as elaborate buildings and roads (even though they had no wheeled vehicles or draft animals).

Before A.D. 500 these Indians lived in shallow, excavated pithouses and later in square shelters of mud and wood attached to one another in gently curving rows. By A.D. 1000 they were building multistoried aboveground stone houses, forming large villages. The spectacular ruins of Chaco Canyon in New Mexico and at Mesa Verde in Colorado are evidence of the Anasazi achievement. Around A.D. 1300, seemingly at the height of their power, they fell victim to a mysterious force. Conjecture has it that an extended drought left the land uninhabitable. For whatever reason, the Anasazi abandoned their urban dwellings and migrated east to the Rio Grande Valley and perhaps west and south to the Hopi Mesas and

2.5 *Taos Pueblo, northern New Mexico. This site was occupied by the 1300s; portions of these buildings date to at least the sixteenth century. This remarkable complex of adobe homes has had an enormous influence on the course of architecture in New Mexico. Courtesy Myron Wood*

2.6 *Adobe brick—earth, sand, water, and straw—is the basic building block in the South-west. Native peoples had built with earth and stone for centuries when Spanish colonizers introduced sunbaked adobe bricks to the region in the very late sixteenth century.*

2.7   Beginning in the seventeenth century, Catholic priests from Spain and Mexico guided Pueblo Indians in the construction of adobe and timber churches. Through time, similar churches were built in Hispanic villages such as Las Trampas, north of Santa Fe. This simple wooden and iron cross rests on the entry gate to the Church of San Jose de Gracia (ca. 1775).

2.8   The sanctuary wall and buttresses of San Jose de Gracia in Las Trampas. The earliest churches had flat roofs of vigas, or beams, which spanned the adobe walls. Canales, or spouts, carried water from the roof.

2.9 *After the expulsion of the Spaniards from Mexico in 1821, the clergy withdrew, leaving Catholics in the northern frontier without an active, formal church. Villagers developed a folk Catholic religion called the Penitente Brotherhood and built* moradas—*meeting houses—throughout what is now New Mexico and southern Colorado. This restored morada is in Taos.*

Zuni lands. Their descendents farmed along the river, raising crops of corn, beans, and squash. From these settlements, modern Pueblo society developed.

The tribes along the Rio Grande built houses of puddled adobe, thick walls of built-up mud layers finished off with flat roofs of timber and earth. These small cubic dwellings were sometimes attached to one another or stacked in huge apartment clusters. One of the oldest multistoried pueblos is at Taos, north of Santa Fe. It has been continuously occupied for nearly 700 years.

When the Spaniards came into New Mexico in the late sixteenth century, they introduced adobe brick-making. Finding an architecture of mud and log houses when they arrived, the Spaniards added mission churches and occasional forts, or *presidios*. The mission churches were long and narrow. The span of the *vigas* (logs placed horizontally to form the roof) determined a building's width. Most churches were constructed of adobe brick plastered with mud inside and out. Spanish priests, aided by Indian laborers, shaped the mission churches with hand tools brought 1500 miles from Mexico City along the Camino Real (Royal Road) and through the perilous Jornada del Muerto (Journey of Death) far south of Santa Fe. Limited by technology and materials, the Franciscans developed simple structures that bore only slight resemblance to their own heritage, the rich baroque stone architecture of Mexico and Spain. Their labors resulted in the unique, sculptured churches that form a treasured folk architecture in New Mexico and Colorado.

After Mexico gained independence from Spain in 1821, the church administration virtually withdrew from the New Mexico frontier. Secular priests replaced the Franciscans. No more religious supplies or artifacts were sent up from the south. As a result, folk Catholicism flourished among the people, producing a rich expression of religious art, particularly paintings and wood carvings. The men in the villages established a religious fraternity, Los Hermanos Penitentes (Penitent Brothers), to fill the void left by the exodus of the priests. They built small, windowless meeting houses, called *moradas,* close to the village church and *campo santo* (cemetery). From this sudden shift in international power and politics, a new religious organization evolved and a new building form with it. From the outside, many moradas resemble a family chapel, a familiar enough form, but internally the space is organized into an area for worship, another for meeting, and a third for storage of the paraphernalia used in ceremonies. The Penitente Brotherhood, as its name implies, chose penance and self-flagellation as means of religious expression and were sometimes in conflict with the Catholic church hierarchy because of their devotional extremes. Despite controversy, moradas continued to be built throughout the nineteenth century in New Mexico and Colorado, and many are in use today.

During the early 1700s, as part of the colonization of Texas, the Spaniards built a line of mission outposts along the San Antonio River. Two of these missions, San Jose and Mission Concepcion, were built with large bell towers and elaborately carved doors, emulating the religious architecture of Central America and Spain. The mission compounds, built of limestone, typically included living quarters, courtyards, farm outbuildings, and irrigation systems in response to frontier circumstances, which required that they be self-sufficient.

One of the peculiarities of the Spanish Southwest was its paucity of institutional or commercial building forms. Aside from the distinctive architectural massing of the churches and the easily recognized form of the *torreon* (the round watchtowers built for defense), there was little variety to the buildings constructed for dwellings, trade, or governance. Most were modest variations on the small, adobe box, often joined one to another in a row. Individual rooms of these extended buildings were sometimes inherited separately by family heirs, creating problems in use and maintenance.

The conservative approach to design resulting in this continuity of existing forms can be attributed in part to the confining characteristics of adobe, particularly the thickness of walls. Size limitations were dictated as well by the length of the tree trunks used for vigas to support the roof. The fortresslike adobe buildings offered the Spanish settlers and Pueblo Indians protection from the tribes of the Plains who, throughout the eighteenth century and until after the American Civil War, regularly raided settlements along the Rio Grande and the mountain valleys to the east. To protect themselves, wealthy landowners built large rectilinear adobe compounds centered around two enclosed courts, one a dwelling and the other a combination of barn and corral. The thick, windowless walls were impenetrable.

Less affluent farmers and ranchers in the sparsely populated valleys of New Mexico had the option of banding together in closed compounds—again with windowless, adobe walls to the outside. The individual dwellings, joined together, faced a large plaza that might contain an irrigation ditch, gardens, corrals for animals, and perhaps an orchard. The village of Chimayo in northern New Mexico is the only extant example of this ancient, defensive community enclave.

In the mountains of the Southwest, the Spaniards built with logs, particularly for outbuild-

2.10   Mission San Jose y Miguel de Aguayo, founded in 1720. In Texas along the San Antonio River, Spanish priests supervised construction of stone missions that were more directly identified with the baroque churches of Mexico and Spain than were the adobe churches of New Mexico. Courtesy San Antonio Convention and Visitors Bureau

2.11   The Mission San Antonio de Valero, founded in 1718 and known as The Alamo, was the scene of a bloody battle between Texas soldiers and Mexican troops during the Texas War of Independence in 1836. Courtesy San Antonio Convention and Visitors Bureau

2.12 The Plaza del Cerro in the village of Chimayo in northern New Mexico is the only surviving example of a defensive plaza in which contiguous adobe houses were built around a square. The outer walls were originally constructed without entries or windows as protection against the Indian attacks that were common until the mid-nineteenth century. Courtesy Historic Preservation Division, Office of Cultural Affairs, State of New Mexico

ings. But wood—even when readily available—was never as popular as adobe. Often mud plaster was applied over logs, filling the spaces between the logs or covering the wood entirely.

In *jacal* construction, an old southwestern building technique, vertical logs are held together to form a wall. In the late nineteenth century, builders positioned logs vertically in trenches, capped their tapered tops with a horizontal log, and plastered the whole with mud. The result was a sturdy wall capable of supporting a traditional roof of earth and vigas. Architectural historian Bainbridge Bunting tells of prehistoric Pueblo Indians weaving poles together to form a fence-like enclosure. It was this practice that very likely influenced the Spaniards.

North of Texas and New Mexico, beyond the Spanish frontier, settlement came late. Build-

2.13 The Gingras House and Trading Post (1801) State Historic Site near Walhalla in northeastern North Dakota. Fur trading was the heart of the western economy in the first part of the nineteenth century. Trading posts, often little more than log cabins, were the region's first commercial enterprises. Courtesy Bonnie J. Halda, State Historical Society of North Dakota

2.14 This stone rubble and log cabin, still standing near Brookings, South Dakota, was the site of one of the state's last fur trading operations. Courtesy State Historical Preservation Center, South Dakota Department of Education and Cultural Affairs

2.15   Bent's Fort (1833), a large adobe bastion along the Arkansas River in Colorado, catered to the western fur trade and also to the growing commerce between the United States and Mexico, which opened up after the Spaniards were driven from Mexico in 1821. Courtesy Catherine Taylor

ings were few and far between until the mid-nineteenth century. Before then, in the quiet of the early 1800s, Indians ruled the mountains and plains. When white traders and trappers came into the West searching for beaver along mountain streams, they lived near or among the Indians and imitated their adaptable shelters. The fur industry brought a new building form, the trading post, which became a center for nascent white cultures and for the neighboring Indian tribes as well.

Arrival at a trading post meant more than fresh supplies and a place to sleep—it was a social event to be anticipated and savored. The historian Francis Parkman, approaching Bent's Fort in Colorado with his companions, thought the occasion important enough to require a bit of special grooming: "we arrived within three or four miles," he wrote in *The Oregon Trail*, "pitched our tent under a tree, hung our looking glasses against its trunk, and having made our primitive toilet, rode towards the fort." They were not disappointed. Although General Kearney's troops, enroute to Mexico, had cleaned the post of supplies, the resident trader graciously entertained Parkman's small party. Parkman expressed pleasure at finding regular chairs and a proper table laid with a white cloth.

Susan Magoffin, the well-born young wife of a Santa Fe trader, recorded in her diary a similar reaction to Bent's Fort during her visit there in

2.16   The house of the "bourgeois"—the chief
trader—at Fort Union in what is now North
Dakota was an oasis of urbanity on the frontier.
Recently the National Park Service reconstructed the fort. The house is surrounded by
wooden palisade walls fortified with stone towers
at the corners. Courtesy National Park Service

1846 enroute to Mexico along the Santa Fe Trail.
Magoffin was the first white woman to visit this
fortified trading post along the Arkansas River.
She praised her dinner of buffalo rib soup as
equal to anything served at the finest hotels in
Philadelphia and New York. Romantic expectations may have fired her imagination: "the outside
exactly fills my idea of an ancient castle," she remarked of the fort's high, thick adobe walls and
corner bastions. Not everyone had such pleasant
memories of the fort—one of Parkman's traveling companions complained of a convalesence
spent on a buffalo robe spread on the floor of a
small mud room. Still, frontier Americans took
their pleasures where they could and welcomed

civilization's signs whenever they appeared.

Fort Union, a northern counterpart of Bent's
Fort, was built in 1829 for John Jacob Astor and
his American Fur Company at the juncture of the
Yellowstone and Missouri rivers on what is now
the border between Montana and North Dakota.
The largest trading post on the Missouri River,
Fort Union was made of logs. Although the surrounding plains were bare of timber, the river
bottomlands held a heavy growth of cottonwood,
ash, and elm. Logs formed the palisade walls of
the fort. Only the corner bastions were built of
stone. Inside the protective palisades, the chief
trader, Kenneth McKenzie, built a stylish and
formal two-story house of white-painted planks.

2.17 Captains' and first lieutenants' quarters at Fort Totten (1867) near Devil's Lake in North Dakota, one of hundreds of military posts established in the West during the last half of the nineteenth century, primarily to protect settlers against Indian attack and to direct the relocation of Indians to reservations. Courtesy Bonnie J. Halda, State Historical Society of North Dakota

Here, McKenzie entertained his guests in grand style, offering them wine, wild game, and freshly baked bread. They dined at a formal table set with silver and china. In this remote outpost, just as at Bent's Fort, the men in charge enjoyed occasional luxury.

Traders at these privately owned fur-trading posts tried to maintain neutrality among the warring Indian tribes. Later, as the fur trade declined and white settlement increased, the trading disappeared and military forts took their places along the major trails and rivers. By the late nineteenth century, to prevent Indian attacks on white settlers

and wagon trains, nearly 200 forts had been built in the mountain and plains region. The forts were most heavily garrisoned during and immediately after the Civil War period of the 1860s.

Fort Larned, built in Kansas Territory in 1859 to protect travelers along the Santa Fe Trail, presents a well-preserved example of a western fort. Fort Larned became a key post in the campaign against the Indians in the late 1860s. Colonel George Custer led the 7th Cavalry from this fort to a battle along the Washita River, an encounter that permanently crushed the Southern Cheyenne.

2.18   The stone prison at Fort Union (1851) in New Mexico, one of the region's largest military forts; its adobe buildings are now in ruins. Courtesy National Park Service

The first Fort Larned was made of small adobe buildings constructed in the dry, treeless country along the Pawnee River. Journalist Henry Stanley described the compound as a collection of "shabby, vermin-breeding adobe and wooden houses." After eight years the army replaced the adobe fort with new construction of local sandstone and pine timbers shipped from the East. Because soldiers were garrisoned at the military forts, these encampments were much larger than the earlier fur-trading posts. At Fort Larned, stone barracks and commissaries were built around a square parade ground. The buildings were of a simple shed style with long, low porches along the front. The commanding officer's quarters were slightly more decorative: wooden gingerbread trimmed the front porches.

South along the Santa Fe Trail in northern New Mexico, the United States Army in 1851 established a second Fort Union as the southwestern command center for the Indian Wars. New Mexico had only recently become a United States territory. Trade grew rapidly as American settlers arrived, but clearly the newcomers could never really prosper until hostile Indians in the area were subdued. For more than two centuries Coman-

2.19   The officers' quarters at Fort Union were built of adobe, with brick chimneys and stone foundations. Courtesy National Park Service

2.20   Classical lines and ornamentation were combined with traditional adobe architecture in the Territorial style of the Southwest. These officers' quarters, now in ruins, are at Fort Union, New Mexico. Courtesy J. R. Riddle, photographer, Museum of New Mexico, No. 38218

ches and Kiowas from the plains had raided Indian pueblos and Spanish villages along the Rio Grande. Apaches and Navajos threatened from the south and west. Fort Union would soon change all that. Its commanders would not only wage war against neighboring Indians, they would supply and equip all the military forts throughout New Mexico and Arizona.

Fort Union's giant facilities included barracks for soldiers and a depot for storing weapons and ammunition. Officers lived in private rooms or apartments. The post functioned much like a well-supplied frontier town. It had a bakery, a laundry, a blacksmith, a machine shop, and a telegraph office. Local ranchers and farmers sold beef and produce to the fort. Other supplies came by wagon along the Santa Fe Trail from Fort Leavenworth in Kansas.

Despite its size and diversity, Fort Union was very much a frontier post, geographically remote and socially cut off from the civilian world. Undoubtedly, an army post was as tiresome for a soldier stationed there as it was diverting for the occasional traveler who came to spend a day or two. On duty, mounted troops fanned out into three neighboring states, Oklahoma, Texas, and Colorado, searching for Indians. The risk of battle was always present: sudden skirmishes, chance encounters, an occasional full-scale fight. But at the fort, the soldiers performed laborious drills and chores and amused themselves with cards, or they rode and hunted in the nearby Turkey Mountains under clear and brilliant skies. Officers expected and received more amenities and perquisites than the common soldiers. Most important, they were allowed to have their families with them. Their wives organized formal dinners, dances, and amateur theatricals, keeping a semblance of civilian society in the privileged world of officers' row.

Soldiers stationed at Fort Union and other army posts, particularly those in command, brought bits and pieces of their culture with them from the East—social rituals, such as balls and birthday parties, and material objects, such as books, parasols, and silverware. They also brought

an architecture and imposed it as far as they could on the existing regional styles. The resulting buildings suggested an improbable marriage of the new dynamic, expanding American Republic with the static, culturally insulated world of Spanish New Mexico. This peculiar union produced the Territorial style, native materials combined with Greek Revival decoration imported by the invading Americans.

The Greek Revival style had reached its zenith in America at mid-century, about the time Fort Union was built. For more than fifty years, starting around 1800, American buildings had emulated Greek temples—large porch columns, a low ridge roof running front to back, rectangular openings for windows and doors, everything arranged in perfect balance. The Greek Revival moved from the East into the Middle West and South, where it appeared as romantic antebellum plantation architecture.

The style then moved west with the United States Army. But on the High Plains, which lacked the usual eastern building materials of stone, brick, and wood, certain compromises were necessary. In New Mexico, with few sawmills and only limited timber, the traditional material was adobe. Builders in the Territorial style, therefore, used adobe brick. And they continued to use the low, flat-roofed, one-story building form that had existed in the Southwest for more than two centuries. A few details, drastically changed—such as a row of bricks, their ends facing out at the roof line to suggest dentils—expressed the "new" taste for classicism.

As the Indian threat waned, it became possible to install windows in what had earlier been fortress adobe walls, and traders traveling the Santa Fe Trail began to bring in glass along with other household goods shipped from the East. Large windows made of small rectangular panes illuminated the once-dark interiors. Panes of glass were placed as well in the framework around entry doors, very much in the Greek Revival tradition.

This opening up of buildings to the outdoors represented a major change from earlier Spanish patterns of retreat and enclosure. The total effect of a Territorial style building—adobe brick, large windows, brick coping, a front porch or portal, and wood trim—only slightly resembled a Greek temple, but these stylistic additions made easterners feel at home. Required to live for a time on the frontier, they chose the practical course of adapting an existing Spanish adobe architecture to make it meet their own expectation of what was orderly, elegant, and open. The symmetry of the buildings and their exacting arrangement on the post grounds acted as a balance to the casualness of the rough, native materials. But the Territorial style did more than dress up an otherwise modest building—it lent a stamp of authority and legitimacy to a frontier outpost.

Western Mining Towns

During the latter half of the nineteenth century, while the United States Cavalry was taking hold in the new territories, a second army, less deliberate and orderly, arrived in the plains and mountain West. These invading troops—gold and silver miners—defied the traditional frontier pattern of East flowing toward the West. The California gold rush of 1849 had first attracted prospectors both overland and by sea around Cape Horn. A decade later, searching for new strikes, these gold seekers turned east again, fanning out over the Great Basin in Nevada on into the Montana and Colorado Rockies and later reaching the Black Hills of South Dakota. At each venue, they were joined by streams of immigrants from the American East and Europe.

The haphazard, hazardous world of mining set off an erratic boom-and-bust economic cycle that marks western industry to this day. The waste and depletion of resources reflected a rampant opportunism. Minerals were there for the taking, the land itself seemed limitless, and the social

problems could solve themselves. Each bonanza ended, slow or sudden, when the minerals gave out or when demand or prices collapsed. Labor disputes sometimes closed the mines, as happened at Cripple Creek, Colorado, in 1903 when the Western Federation of Miners called a general strike that lasted nearly a year.

Gold and silver seekers would go anywhere, and did, taking their new technology with them from the Pacific Coast into the interior. If their wanderings were to produce more than a literal "flash in the pan," they required what all new westerners required—a lifeline to civilization. Freight wagons, the telegraph, and eventually the railroad kept mining alive. For money and equipment, mine owners relied on eastern and European investors. For basic supplies, they looked closer to home. Mormon farmers in Utah hauled produce all the way to the Montana "diggings" in the early 1860s; ranchers in eastern Colorado packed beef in snow and then hauled it 200 miles through the mountains to the mines in Leadville.

While they waited impatiently for railroads, the mining districts generated a huge freighting business that had important economic effects. During the Black Hills gold rush of the 1870s in the Dakota Territory, the town of Bismarck, 200 miles north of the mines, underwent a lively boom as a result of its supply line to the gold camps. A regular stagecoach and freight line ran from Bismarck to Deadwood, in what is now South Dakota, with stations set up every twenty miles along the way. The Northern Pacific Railroad had just completed tracks to Bismarck a year before, augmenting supplies that came by steamer up the Missouri River. These important trade networks servicing widely scattered mining camps greatly hastened western settlement.

Nineteenth-century gold and silver mining created entire towns and facilitated a new industrial architecture. During the earliest mining stages, prospectors looked for "placer" deposits, concentrations of pure metal near the surface, often exposed in gullies or creek beds. The romantic image of a prospector with his pick, shovel,

2.21   *South Dakota's Black Hills were the setting for a gold rush in the 1870s. The Stand By Mill is typical of a building type developed by the mining industry. The processing of ores depended on the work of gravity; the raw ore was moved from one level to another, while various processes extracted the precious metal. This technology resulted in large slant-roofed mills built along a mountain slope and enclosing several stories. Courtesy State Historical Preservation Center, South Dakota Department of Education and Cultural Affairs*

pan, and burro is part of the placer mining story. Compared to what came later in underground mining, placer technology was exceedingly simple. For surface mining, prospectors built flumes (wooden chutes) near rushing mountain streams, filled the flumes with coarse "pay dirt," and let water flow over it. The gravelly soil surrounding the precious metal washed away, leaving the heavier particles of gold and silver. Flat metal pans or simple structures of wood—toms, sluices, and riffle boxes—demonstrated the same principle of removing extraneous soil with running water.

Most metals, however, remained buried underground, mixed with other materials in rocky substances called ores. To remove them, mining companies dug a vertical shaft and then covered it with a headframe that supported cables and a platform by which equipment and workers could be gotten in and out of the mine. At first miners made primitive headframes from the timber at hand, building a simple hoist system run by hand or horsepower. Later, mechanized headframes that were operated like modern elevators carried miners and equipment up and down and removed ore to the surface.

Each large underground mine had a network of horizontal tunnels following the veins of ore. A honeycomb system of timber framing prevented collapse of the tunnels. Miners gradually constructed this timber framework as they dug and blasted new rock faces.

Western hardrock miners in the nineteenth century devised new methods and tools, and even a new vocabulary, just as cowboys had done out on the plains during the same period. In *Western Mining*, Otis F. Young offers a glossary of mining terms reprinted from an 1878 book by Richard J. Hinton on Arizona mining. Among miners, small heaps of ore were "squats" or "chats." Rubbish piles were dismissed as "deads." Miners found new words to describe the myriad extractive treatments to which the ore was subjected: it might be buddled, chimmed, tozed, jugged, or riffled. Tools, as well, had special names: gads, gurts, kibbles, flangs, and slukes. Underground in musty

dank mines, shapes and cavities carved into the tunnels were called by equally peculiar names: sumps, stopes, vuggs, winzes, gulphs, or zawns. Although these words sound strangely right for murky diggings beneath a mountain, they seem more a language of trolls and troglodytes than the talk of men at work.

At the surface, miners dumped buckets of ore into stamp mill chutes, beginning an uncertain process of extracting the metal. To take advantage of the pull of gravity, mine owners built their mills on the sloping mountainsides just below the mine exits. The earliest mills were built by hand with materials hauled in by burros; later, in the established districts, mining companies used manufactured equipment brought in by the railroads. The slanted multilevel design of the mills enabled ore to move from one processing stage to the next in a step-down construction that followed the mountain's slope. Ores were shoveled in at the top, crushed and "stamped" by vertical rod shafts with iron hammerheads, and then washed and jiggled until the heavier metal particles dropped away from the wastes.

Larger mills built later in the nineteenth century became part of the American industrial mainstream, but the early mining camps constituted a true regional vernacular—traditional construction adapted to a particular locale with whatever materials could be found. A typical hardrock mining camp was a jumble of headframes and smokestacks towering over shafts, mills, office headquarters, and storage sheds, all tied together with a network of roads and train tracks. A large pile of "tailings," the waste materials from processed ore, collected next to each mill. Alongside each mine entrance a smaller heap of earth marked the initial shaft diggings.

When the ore played out, everyone abandoned camp in search of the next rumored bonanza, taking with them what could be carried and leaving the rest to rot under the typically heavy winter snows. The lifespan of some camps was short. South Pass City in Wyoming and Alder Gulch in Montana were exhausted and abandoned

2.22 *Headframes and attendant sheds and shacks form the unusual industrial skyline in Butte, Montana, for years the copper capital of the world. The Anselmo Mine is close to Uptown Butte and surrounded by the homes of men who worked in the mine. Courtesy Jet Lowe, Historic American Engineering Record, National Park Service*

in little more than a year. It was hard to predict a mining district's future. A camp might die early, with only a few empty shafts remaining as evidence of high hopes, or it might grow quickly into a large city, as happened to Leadville, Colorado, and Butte, Montana.

Duane A. Smith in *Rocky Mountain Mining Camps* describes the evolution of a typical western mining town. First, a chaotic sprawl of wagons, tents, and shanties was built close to the mining operations. Trash accumulated everywhere—garbage heaps of bottles and tin cans, piles of manure left by horses and mules. After a snowfall or rain shower, a camp's mired roads would be nearly impassable. No amenities eased this early stage, no laws or government, no cultural trappings—only

2.23   *St. Elmo, a mining camp in the Rocky Mountains of Colorado. After the first rush, in which people lived in wagons, tents, or lean-tos, simple wooden buildings were erected to bring more order, efficiency, and comfort to the emerging town.*

a make-do life far from supplies and civilization.

Freighters hauled goods over steep mountain passes, setting up shop directly from wagons until frame or log stores could be built—modest sheds with pitched roofs, their gable ends facing the street. False fronts covered many of these early frame buildings, adding a touch of urbanity to an otherwise primitive street scene. If the nearby "diggings" were successful, crowds of people poured into the camps, including tradesmen whose new buildings filled in the early straggle of false fronts.

With time, a bonanza district evolved into a stable, mature town. Although devastating fires leveled many mining boomtowns, a sweeping blaze was usually followed by a more sophisticated architecture. Permanent buildings of stone, brick, and iron replaced burned-out wooden false fronts. A well-established mining town had banks, a mining exchange where company stocks were traded, large hotels, law offices, and an assay office to test ore for metal content. On the edge of downtown, there might be a city hall, certainly a jail, and at least one railroad station. As families moved in, they joined together to build churches and schools. The miners' homes were modest, although porch brackets and sawn-wood trim decorated workers' cottages and boarding houses.

2.24   *If mining camps survived for any length of time, they typically moved from frame to masonry building. This stone structure is in Westcliffe, Colorado.*

2.25   *A fading but graceful wooden fan under the keystone lightens the effect of a ponderous arch.*

2.26 *A few large and long-lived mining towns developed urban cores. In the 1890s a row of commercial properties was built along Bennett Avenue in Cripple Creek, Colorado. Courtesy Myron Wood*

When the mines produced, everybody prospered. Money flowed freely in restaurants, hotels, dance halls, and saloons. With sufficient resources and a healthy market, mining towns evolved quickly into major cities. Leadville, Cripple Creek, and Victor, all in Colorado, had business districts of several square blocks. Butte, Montana, which started out as a small silver and gold mining district in the 1860s, mushroomed into the nation's copper capital after the turn of the century, eventually reaching a population of 80,000 during a

boom period around World War I. Helena, Montana, built a large downtown district around Last Chance Gulch, its original gold camp, and remained a prosperous governmental and financial center long after the rush for gold had passed. These large mining districts were surprisingly cosmopolitan, populated by Americans from all over the country as well as by Europeans, Chinese, and Mexicans. In the expansive, boom years, a mining city offered financial opportunity and excitement.

Most mining districts, however, dwindled and

2.27   Circumstances changed quickly in the West, especially in mining towns. Bannack, Montana, which had a gold boom in the early 1860s, was important enough to be declared the seat of Beaverhead County. This brick courthouse was later converted to a hotel. Courtesy Montana Department of Fish, Wildlife, and Recreation

2.28   A home in the mining town of Silverton, Colorado.

died. The entire mountain West is pockmarked with abandoned mining towns. A few caved-in, buckling log cabins are all that remain of the town of Independence near Aspen, Colorado. New Mexico's nineteenth-century mines produced copper as well as gold and silver. For the most part, these enterprises were short-lived. Elizabethtown, north of Santa Fe, enjoyed a gold boom after the Civil War but then suffered a lasting slump. Farther south, near the border with Mexico, Silver City and Lordsburg shifted their energies to agriculture after a brief burst of silver mining in the late nineteenth century. In west Texas, the town of Shafter grew to a population of 2000 as a silver-mining district during the 1880s. The last mine closed in 1952, leaving the town nearly empty.

There is a peculiar hiatus in America's romance with western mining. Several of the mountain and plains states, famous for their silver and gold, also had rich deposits of coal. Coke processed from Colorado's coal deposits heated the furnaces of Pueblo's steel mills and fueled the smelters that processed gold from Cripple Creek. Until after World War II, coal was commonly used for home heating, and it continues to be an important fuel for the production of power. Despite their large numbers and economic importance, coal towns never attained the romantic aura of gold and silver camps. Crested Butte, Colorado, now a popular ski town high in the Rocky Mountains, is a notable exception. For the most part, coal towns lacked glamour and were readily forgotten.

Western Ranches and Cow Towns

The fitful, episodic character of early western settlement was borne out in agriculture as it was in mining. While prospectors scoured the mountains, ranchers on the Texas plains were enacting an equally fascinating drama, driving large herds of cattle north along trails toward the railheads of Kansas. Spaniards had introduced cattle to the Southwest in the seventeenth century. By the late 1860s, shortly after the American Civil War, cattlemen had begun rounding up wild longhorns in southern Texas. The problem was getting them to the North and East where there was a growing demand for beef. Several cattle trails soon stretched up from Texas. The first, in 1866, brought cattle into Sedalia, Missouri. A year later, Texas cattleman John Chisholm routed a second trail into Abilene, Kansas, with a spur into Ellsworth to the west. A third trail, the Western, passed through Dodge City and then veered northwest to the small town of Julesburg on the Platte River between Nebraska and Colorado. The Goodnight–Loving Trail cut west along the Pecos River from the Staked Plains of Texas, north through New Mexico and Colorado along the front range of the Rockies, then up to Wyoming.

Cattlemen hired a crew for the long drive north—a trail boss and perhaps a dozen cowboys to handle a herd of 2000 cattle. For up to two months, cowboys prodded the animals along the trail, moving at a rate of ten to fifteen miles a day. The operation was alternately tedious and terrifying, with dangerous river crossings, and the possibility of a stampede always present. The men slept in tents or outside in bedrolls. They took their meals from a chuckwagon, a portable kitchen and pantry first devised by one of the West's most prominent cattlemen, Charles Goodnight, who founded the trail bearing his name and who owned the million-acre JA Ranch in the Texas Panhandle. Goodnight's chuckwagon, a converted army field kitchen left over from the Civil War, is an example of a portable building adapted successfully to the West's peculiar needs.

In their evolution, cow towns were much the same as mining camps. Both were boom towns filled with restless men with money to spend, resulting in a disproportionate number of hotels, restaurants, saloons, and brothels. Like mining camps, cow towns began as sorry collections of

2.29 *The different kinds of livestock and crops raised in the West generated a great variety of buildings and facilities: gates, fences, corrals and pens for livestock, and storage sheds of all shapes and sizes for grains. The buildings at the Grant-Kohrs Ranch in Montana reflect more than a century of ranching.*

tents and shanties, only later becoming orderly towns with commercial buildings of substance lined up along the main street. Both went through a transition stage of modest frame structures, simple one-storied buildings covered either with horizontal wooden clapboards or with vertical board-and-batten siding. A modest cornice might extend out from a false front. Plank signs were either nailed to the building's exterior siding or extended across the boardwalk, the better to be read by passers-by.

In the famous Kansas cow town of Dodge City, Front Street in the late 1870s had three general stores, a gunsmith, a drugstore, a restaurant, two barber shops, and a U.S. post office. With fewer than 1000 residents, Dodge City had sixteen saloons, mostly simple whiskey bars but a few pretentious places like the Long Branch, which advertised an orchestra and gambling rooms. Front Street burned down in 1885, just as Dodge's cow town days were ending.

Away from their main streets, cow towns and at least the larger mining towns had significant differences. Miners shaped the residential patterns of their towns; cowboys did not. Cowboys lived in railhead destinations like Dodge City for only a short time, staying in hotels and transient boarding houses. Miners, on the other hand,

2.30 *Dugouts, log and earth shelters, usually built into a slope, were common throughout the plains. The Mayfield dugout in Briscoe County, Texas, was built in 1889. Courtesy Texas Historical Commission*

were permanent, full-time workers who lived in small cottages and resident boarding houses as close to the mines as they could get, creating a high-density, industrial pattern of residential life quite at odds with the more spread-out configuration of other late nineteenth century western communities.

Between 1866 and 1886, trail drivers escorted in the neighborhood of 5 million cattle to Kansas railroad towns, then shipped them east to new packing houses in Chicago, St. Louis, and Kansas City. But not all the trails converged on the Kansas cow towns. Large herds were driven north to the high meadows of the Rockies where they were fattened for market or delivered for slaughter to nearby military forts and mining camps. Ranchers near Fort Union and Fort Sumner in New Mexico sold beef to the United States government to feed soldiers as well as the Indian tribes newly confined to reservations. Conrad Kohrs, who became a Montana cattle baron in the 1870s, started out as

a butcher selling meat to gold miners in Helena's Last Chance Gulch. Enterprising cattlemen accumulated their fortunes by keeping the new West supplied with beef.

By the late 1880s ranching had changed. Killer blizzards in 1886–87 destroyed entire herds. Overgrazing ruined the land, while droughts and lowered prices ruined profits. Many of the big cattle companies went bankrupt or reorganized as smaller, fenced ranches, with more attention being given to improved stock breeding. As railroads spread everywhere across the West, the long trail drives became unnecessary. Instead, ranchers took their cattle to local terminals, such as Miles City, Montana; Lusk, Wyoming; Ogallala, Nebraska; Roswell, New Mexico; or Medora, North Dakota. Dozens of markets throughout the West replaced Dodge City and the other notorious cow towns.

When ranchers started fencing their lands, they became more serious about building. Their herds and hired hands stayed in one place, or two

2.31   A ranch east of Sheridan, Wyoming. Courtesy Richard Collier, Wyoming Department of Archives, Museums, and History

at the most, assuming that the cattle were moved to high country for grazing during the summer. Ranchers began to invest in sheds and hay barns, and they added to existing corrals and bunkhouses. Mountain ranchers built summer "cow camps" of simple log cabins, where cowboys lived while managing herds in the high meadows. On the edges of the big spreads in the Southwest, ranchers built "line camps"—dugouts of adobe or fieldstone or, if there was timber nearby, small jacal shacks made of unpeeled logs placed upright and then chinked with adobe. Cowboys moved from one line camp to the next, guiding the herds to grass and rounding up strays.

The closing of the range in the 1880s opened the modern era of ranching. Though architectural changes took place throughout the twentieth century, the basic configuration of ranch building was set during the final years of the nineteenth century after the fences went up. After World War I, automobiles and trucks were commonplace on ranches; tractors arrived a short time later. Garages and machine sheds were built to house them. Indoor plumbing and electricity brought bathrooms, lighting, and appliances, adding a great deal of convenience and comfort to ranch life but resulting in only minor alterations to building exteriors.

The Western Farmer

On the eastern prairies, before the invention of barbed wire in the 1870s, farmers planted hedges, usually of osage orange or honey locust, to contain their livestock and to keep out their neighbors' animals. Hedges appeared along field boundaries, typically set on the straight lines and right angles that followed the pattern established by the General Land Survey.

No single decision by the federal government had as overriding an impact on the visual quality of America's western landscape as the grid system of square-mile land parcels imposed by the General Land Survey in the nineteenth century. The square parcels, called *sections,* contained 640 acres of land each. When divided into rectilinear fields separated by fences and bordered by groves and hedges, these square-mile sections were powerful man-made interventions that brought a regular, geometric, and orderly aspect to the land. Contours of hills and of creek and river beds interrupted this grand scheme but failed to overpower it. Only on the high, drier plains farther west, where few plowed fields and farmsteads occupied the land, did the open range defy the square-mile grid system.

The General Land Survey prepared the way for a second revolutionary piece of legislation. During the 1860s, just as mining and ranching were getting underway in the West, the United States Congress passed the Homestead Act of 1862, entitling any adult to 160 acres of free land for a $10 filing fee. The law required five years of occupancy and certain improvements, including a modest amount of building. Or a settler might choose to buy a 160-acre parcel outright at $1.25 an acre. The railroads, awarded large tracts of public land by the federal government, vigorously promoted land sales to new settlers, charging the highest prices for those acres closest to the tracks. As a means of selling the land, the first step in generating farm produce for shipping, railroad agents offered European immigrants free passage to the western states.

Cheap and plentiful land drew immigrants west by the hundreds of thousands. But the promise of plenty had its limits, for the land that stretched before these new settlers, seemingly without end, lacked sufficient rainfall to sustain customary farming. Only on the eastern edges of the prairie country was there enough rain for crops, roughly in the third portion of those states that lay east of the 100th meridian, an imaginary line that runs from Bismarck, North Dakota, straight south to Laredo, Texas.

Rainfall was meager on the plains—ten to twenty inches per year, and even lower in some patches of desert. Only the high mountain meadows received a "normal" annual rainfall of twenty inches or more. The dry climate caused immediate problems for farmers accustomed to the humid conditions of Europe or the eastern half of the United States. During a normal year, it was nearly impossible without irrigation to harvest a decent crop; after a drought, the fields yielded nothing at all. Through trial and error, farmers learned dry farming methods—deep plowing followed by mulching to stop evaporation—and turned to hardy, drought-resistant crops. After a few bad seasons, farmers on the plains stopped growing corn—a thirsty crop—and planted oats and wheat instead. German–Russian immigrants who settled in the Dakotas, Nebraska, Kansas, Oklahoma, and Colorado introduced Turkey red wheat, a highly productive strain suited to the dry plains.

Western farmers who worked the land soon learned its limits, but others who stood to gain from farm productivity—bankers, newspaper editors, land agents, and railroad owners—took their time acknowledging the scarcity of water. The continued immigration of homesteaders served the interests of these land promoters. Ignorance, foolishness, and even fraud contributed to the illusion of a garden in the desert. Westerners needed water. They hoped against odds for water. Finally, they convinced themselves that water was there

2.32 *The Hedwig Hill cabin is chinked with stone rubble and mortar and has a stone shed addition. The cabin is now part of the Ranching Heritage Center in Lubbock, Texas. Courtesy the Museum of Texas Tech University*

and more was coming. An astonishing theory circulated in the late nineteenth century claimed that cultivation of the land increased rainfall. Water evaporating and rising from the turned soil supposedly created new moisture-laden clouds that emptied back onto planted fields. Promoters consistently exaggerated the "lushness" of western land, and a few wet years in the 1880s further heightened expectations. It took years of drought and depression in the 1890s to convince farmers of the West's fundamental physical harshness. By then, many settlers had already given the best years of their lives to a disappointing dream.

In the meantime, farmers on the plains had established an architecture of sorts. Beginning in the 1860s, the first homesteaders arrived by wagon, later by train. Most only had money enough to plant a first year's crop. Few had anything left over for building. Consequently, they used whatever the land had to offer. In the mountains and on the eastern prairies, settlers built log cabins using nearby stands of timber. In parts of Kansas, Oklahoma, and Texas, surface quarries yielded stone for the taking. On the dry plains between these two regions, newcomers depended on sod or adobe.

Of the estimated one million sod houses that once occupied the plains, few survived long. Un-

2.33 Many of the large frame barns associated with rural America were not built until well into the twentieth century. Barns like this one held hay in the loft. Today, hay is rolled, stacked, or baled, but no longer hoisted into barn lofts. This frame barn and log shed north of Billings, Montana, are abandoned.

less they were covered with protective stucco or with wood siding, they lasted only five to ten years. A "soddie" cost almost nothing, its greatest recommendation. Homesteaders helped each other to build, giving newcomers the advantage of having old hands teach them the tricks of sod construction.

While they lived temporarily in dugouts or tents, homesteaders built sod houses of one or two rooms. They cut sod strips with a plow, then used a spade to chop the strips into bricks one

and one-half feet wide and three feet long. A small house required an acre of sod. Builders stacked the bricks two rows thick to make walls; each new layer of sod was placed to cover the seams of the layer underneath. A layer of sod also covered the roof, a low framework made of rafters or cottonwood poles. The earthen walls might then be plastered inside and out, making them cleaner and stronger. Soddies were cheap, quick to build, and well-insulated, but they were dirty and dark. Heavy rains left them sodden. Rodents, snakes,

2.34   *German-Russian immigrants around the turn of the century settled in large numbers on the North Dakota prairie, building fieldstone or adobe houses identical to homes built generations earlier in Russia and before that in Germany. This typical long house is in McIntosh County south of Bismarck. The small enclosed porch in front was a standard feature. Courtesy J. Sluss, State Historical Society of North Dakota*

2.35   *German-Russians in North Dakota used earth construction in a number of ways, including "puddled" clay built up in layers between wooden studs. The location is Emmons County. Courtesy J. Sluss, State Historical Society of North Dakota*

2.36 *Now a garage, this earth structure was formerly a chicken house. Several other buildings on this North Dakota farm are made of fieldstone. Courtesy J. Sluss, State Historical Society of North Dakota*

and insects burrowed into the walls and sometimes dropped from the ceiling. Without a doubt, soddies were the poor relations among frontier dwellings.

Log construction was a popular choice in the mountains or wherever sufficient timber stands allowed it. Just as wood was often paired with adobe in the Southwest, on the plains it was used together with earth construction to roof a soddie or to form the front portion of a dugout, for example. A small log building that served as a house or barn during the earliest years of homesteading and was then replaced was usually saved for use as a tool shed or other outbuilding. Occasionally, a larger house was built around a log cabin. Wood offered great flexibility to settlers with limited resources.

Of the tens of thousands of log structures that existed a hundred years ago, most have dis-

appeared. Geographer Terry Jordan estimates that Texas has lost the largest portion of its once-rich inventory of log buildings. Because of the variety of notching and chinking techniques used, log buildings express ties to particular ethnic traditions that were frequently traceable back across the eastern part of the United States and into Europe.

German settlers building in the Texas Hill Country west of Austin in the 1840s combined logs and stone in their native tradition of *fachwerk*, half-timbered framing enclosed with stone or stuccoed adobe brick. Other Hill Country buildings were made entirely of native limestone. Seamed metal roofs were common to all houses and outbuildings in this Texas region.

German farmers in the Hill Country town of Fredericksburg, wanting to take full advantage of village life, created a unique version of the

CHAPTER TWO

2.37　A "Sunday house" in Fredericksburg, Texas. Courtesy Myron Wood

2.38　A stone livery stable in the ranching country of Springer, New Mexico. Courtesy Myron Wood

townhouse. The rhythm of farmwork kept families home during the work week and sent them to town at week's end. Every Saturday, families would arrive by wagon in Fredericksburg to sell produce and buy supplies. On Sunday morning they went to church, and then spent the afternoon visiting with friends. To avoid two trips to town, these farmers needed a place for their families to stay during the weekend. The solution was to buy small lots in town and build "Sunday houses," small cottages of stone or fachwerk just large enough for sleeping, eating, and modest socializing after church. Each Sunday house had a loft entered by a wooden stairway on one of the gable ends. Stairs to the loft were placed on the outside so the small interior would not be crowded.

Twentieth-Century Settlements

Although vernacular buildings represent a first stage of settlement, often to be replaced with something more stylish and modern, folk buildings common during the early periods continued to be constructed into the twentieth century. When the last wave of homesteaders came to Colorado's eastern plains around World War I, they built dugouts and houses of sod and adobe as thousands had done before them. A group of these farmers settled near Tructon, thirty miles east of Colorado Springs, on land that had sup-

2.40   Of the region's many architectural
legacies, the most pure is the heritage of folk
churches. Isolated examples in the vastness of
the Great Plains are particularly evocative. The
Eastern Orthodox church in Calhan, Colorado, sixty miles east of Colorado Springs, was
built around 1930 but looks older than its years
because of its weathered wooden surfaces.

2.41   The spire of Calhan's Eastern Orthodox Church. This area of the High Plains is
extremely dry. During the growing season, a
prayer for rain is part of each Sunday's service.

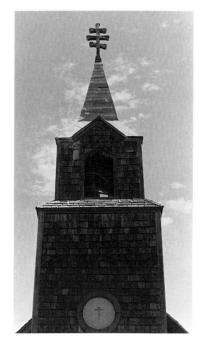

2.42   *The Vinland Presbyterian Church in Douglas County, Kansas, near Lawrence, was built in 1878–79 and used by its congregation until the late 1940s. Courtesy Douglas County (Kansas) Historical Society*

2.43   *In western Nebraska, the Keystone Community Church (1908) serves two congregations—and was built for that purpose. Catholics use the altar at the north end, Protestants the lectern opposite. Hinged seating can be reversed to accommodate either group. Courtesy Janet Jeffries Spencer, Nebraska State Historical Society*

ported sheep in the 1870s and was later used for cattle grazing.

The flat, treeless plains surrounding Tructon stretched to the far horizon. Only Pikes Peak, forty miles distant, broke the landscape. "You could see as far as you pleased," one pioneer woman remarked. After plowing under the native grama and buffalo grasses, as well as soapweed and cactus, Tructon homesteaders planted corn, millet, and pinto beans. They dug wells, installed windmills, and built dugouts or soddies. The Tructon community grew rapidly from 1910 until the mid-1920s when the beginnings of the national farm depression brought prices down. Periodic drought made life worse, and soon people began to leave.

Because the area declined quickly, little more than a decade after its founding, few homesteads got beyond the first stage of primitive earth and frame buildings, but for a brief time there was a family and farmstead on every 160-acre parcel. Today, most of the farm buildings are gone and

2.44   *The builders of this small church in east Texas added a porch with twin towers and protruding gable, which suggests a Greek pediment. Courtesy Myron Wood*

the town is a deserted crossroads. Only a consolidated school remains, used later as a church by a small number of ranching families in the area.

Small churches and schools were commonplace in the country. The schools were built with government funds, the churches with volunteer labor, donated materials, and the small amount of cash that homesteaders could afford. Not all country people were poor, of course, and when enough money was available, they would hire carpenters to build their churches. Frequently, churches were built in the nearest town, ensuring a larger con-

gregation to share the responsibility of building and maintenance. With few exceptions, the little school buildings were functional and spare—the school itself, two outhouses, a storm cellar, and a pump for water. The village and country churches of this era—the very late nineteenth and early twentieth centuries—were equally unpretentious but designed with a bit more elaboration, if only for such small features as a bell tower, Gothic windows, or a wooden cross over the front door. Churches were an important part of country life, socially as well as spiritually.

2.45 *Pleasing proportions and the crispness of outlining wooden trim have created a graceful frame church in Throckmorton, Texas. Courtesy Myron Wood*

In the agricultural communities of the Southwest, churches were an equally dominant part of the culture. There were two community strongholds in the Spanish village: the church and the irrigation system that sustained the orchards and crops. Each of these institutions was governed by an elected mayordomo who was charged with organizing maintenance and repair, all of which was accomplished communally. Water rights were, and are, extremely complex. Landowners are accorded certain amounts of water depending on availability and location, among other variables, and are required to participate in the expense and labor of maintaining the system.

Much of New Mexico's early Indian and Spanish settlement was confined to the Rio Grande Valley, but as the population grew in the nineteenth century, family groups of Hispanos began fanning outward into other river valleys where they established defensive villages organized around a plaza and, later, linear villages along a life-giving stream or river. They raised corn, chilis, squash, beans, and fruit.

In addition to individual irrigated parcels,

2.46   *The Hispanic farm villages of New Mexico depend on irrigation systems maintained by the community. This ditch, or* acequia, *is near Holman in the Mora Valley. Courtesy Nancy Hunter Warren*

the entire community by tradition controlled the shared grazing lands, typically higher grasslands less suited to raising crops. Here, farmers raised sheep for their meat and wool and to use as barter for other necessities. Sheep were the primary livestock, but farmers might also have pigs and horses.

Each family had a small, flat-roofed adobe house and perhaps an orchard and a corral fenced with poles. The community properties would include the church, cemetery, morada, a threshing floor, and a dance hall. With few exceptions, the architecture was adobe.

Later in the century, with the American military occupation of 1846, modest neoclassical features began to appear in new buildings. After the railroads arrived around 1880 in northern New Mexico, milled lumber was available for carpentry trim, glass for windows, and flat metal sheeting for roofs. Architecture in the villages incorporated these materials, which in turn gave rise to new forms, such as pitched roofs. These nineteenth-century staples, combined with Spanish and Indian building traditions from centuries earlier, prevailed well into the 1900s. Much of this heritage is evident today.

*3.1   Jefferson, Texas, prospered in the middle
of the nineteenth century as supplies moved
through it from the Gulf into the heart of
Texas. Later, railroad competition from other
towns killed its economy, but not before a wealth
of Greek Revival buildings filled Jefferson's
streets. Courtesy Texas Historical Commission*

CHAPTER THREE

Railroads, Automobiles, and the Rise of the Urban West

Before the railroads enveloped the West, an urban fabric of sorts had already existed there. In Texas and New Mexico, the cities of San Antonio and Santa Fe had been regional capitals for a long time—San Antonio since the early 1700s, Santa Fe a century earlier. Throughout New Mexico, traditional Spanish villages, arranged around a central plaza, offered religious, social, and commercial activities for visitors as well as for the permanent residents of surrounding farms and ranches.

But even the venerable Spanish town system was not the first in the region: more than a millennium earlier Indian tribes had organized themselves into permanent communal settlements in Colorado and New Mexico and had built apart-mentlike dwellings of slab stone in the Texas Panhandle region. Village cultures had established themselves on the central and northern plains as well, particularly along the Missouri River and its tributaries. These indigenous peoples had a long tradition of community settlements and, in some instances, of high-density urban living.

By the mid-1800s, to serve the growing number of migrants and traders as the American nation expanded westward, a vast network of stopping-off places began to develop along the major trails. Some of these supply stations—hostelries, ranches, farms, and trading posts—developed into towns. On the region's very eastern edge, river towns had developed well before the Civil War, becoming important local markets while offering a supply line to points west—Jefferson, Texas;

*3.2   Another Greek Revival building in
Jefferson, Texas. Courtesy Texas Historical
Commission*

Brownville, Nebraska; Vermillion, South Dakota; and Fort Benton, high up the Missouri River in Montana. Along the Gulf Coast, several ports, particularly Galveston, were well established by mid-century.

By 1860, then, the plains and mountain states had a nascent urban fabric and a population of 480,000. There were not many people—yet—but enough to fuel the aspirations of railroad developers who saw the West's vast resources and envisioned the migration that was to come.

The Civil War, and the years of conflict leading up to it, had delayed extension of the railroads beyond the Mississippi Valley. When the guns were finally silenced in the spring of 1865, Americans turned their attention again to the West, eager to complete a transcontinental railroad all the way to

the Pacific coast. To the awakening heartland, the railroads brought people and prosperity and, in so doing, created the modern urban West. Trains carrying manufactured goods from the industrial East sent back riches from western farms and mines. Built on a grand scale and heavily subsidized by the federal government, the railroads were a match for the region's daunting size.

Railroads coming into the country threw the settlers of the mountains and plains into a frenzy of building. During the period beginning in the early 1870s and lasting until well past World War I, towns appeared everywhere in the West, growing up around the new train stations, which anchored thousands of miles of track splayed across the grasslands.

Throughout this giant landscape, railroad

3.3   Railroads were the lifeline that tied late nineteenth century western towns to the rest of the world. Haswell, Colorado, shipped grain out and brought in goods and produce for area farmers and its own small town population. Typically, the grain elevator was the largest and most important structure in town. Courtesy Myron Wood

3.4   The former Northern Pacific/Burlington Northern station (1902; architects: Reed and Stem, St. Paul) at Livingston, Montana, where passengers alighted for the final leg of the journey to Yellowstone Park. Most western depots were small, frame structures, but large cities and special destinations were awarded costly "High Style" stations. This building now houses a special collection from the Buffalo Bill Historical Center in Cody, Wyoming. Courtesy Livingston Depot Foundation

companies built stations at intervals of five to twenty miles. As construction of roadbeds and tracks proceeded, each new town would become a temporary terminus, enjoying a lively but brief boom period as entrepreneurs rushed to get their goods and services operating in the still-virgin territory that lay ahead. There was an uneasy balance between the need to settle new towns and the persistent pressures to keep moving west with the railway line. At the railroad construction sites, it was not unusual for several thousand workers to converge as they built road beds and laid new track. To serve this army of laborers, enterprising tradesmen established new businesses, operating out of tents or hastily built frame structures. In the midst of this frenetic building activity, stage-coaches and freighting wagons arrived to carry goods and passengers into the frontier beyond the terminus. Thus, for many of the new arrivals, these towns were a way station, not a destination.

As building commenced, the towns took form. The storage of goods required warehouses; the conduct of business required banks and managers. The boom might foster newspapers and hotels. Certainly there would be saloons, dance halls, and brothels. After a few weeks of laying track, the construction gangs moved west, leaving empty buildings and streets. In 1867, when the Union Pacific moved into North Platte, Nebraska, the population rose from almost none to more than 3000. By fall, most of these people had moved on to Julesburg on Nebraska's western border. Julesburg repeated the cycle, as did scores of other instant towns along the rail line. These towns survived the sudden departure of workers, but usually in much reduced circumstances compared to their explosive and optimistic foundings. A traveler writing in 1871 described Cheyenne, Wyoming, as a "Magic City" because it grew rapidly out of the wilderness when the Union Pacific first arrived. The same observer described the town of Kit Carson in eastern Colorado as a booming terminus along the Kansas Pacific track, full of warehouses and shippers. Shortly, booming Denver claimed the railroad's business, and Kit Carson became a quiet country town.

Certain early towns faded because the railroad passed them by altogether. In the late 1860s, when the Fort Worth and Denver City railroad went around Quanah, Texas, residents voted to move the entire town the few miles necessary to place it next to the new tracks. Railroad companies sometimes chose to bypass existing towns because of the fortunes to be made on land sales for new townsites. When William Jackson Palmer built his Denver and Rio Grande Western railroad along the front range of the Colorado Rockies in 1871, he founded new towns a stone's throw away from struggling towns already near the route, greatly increasing his company's income and its control over the new territory.

When the established towns of New Mexico were circumvented, the result was a permanently split community, the Hispanos remaining in flat-roofed adobe shops and homes around the old plaza and the Anglos building a new town of brick and glass near the railroad line. The Atchison, Topeka, and Santa Fe railroad entered New Mexico in 1880, building new towns in both Las Vegas and Albuquerque about a mile from the existing centers. In *Historic Albuquerque Today*, Susan DeWit describes the railroad's impact on that city as one in which essentially two towns were created, separated in space and style and, most important, segregated culturally—even after the two entities became physically and legally one.

Promoters, typically agents of the railroads, laid out the new towns along familiar and accepted grid plans—square blocks and straight streets. These featureless grids made the survey and sale of land a simple matter, and except for courthouse squares, there seemed to be little demand for grassy commons, parks, or landscaping. Often, the railroad tracks were placed along the edge of the commercial district with the main street at a right angle to the tracks, terminated by the station at one end and, in county seats, the courthouse at the other.

Speculators and enterprising town founders wanted every new place to look as much like an

3.5   Often a railroad would bypass an existing town to start a new one on land that it controlled. In 1880, the Santa Fe Railroad ignored what is now called Old Town in Albuquerque and built a depot a mile away, which soon became the urban center. The largely Hispanic population remained in their adobe buildings around the plaza and near the church of San Felipe de Neri (1793, with nineteenth-century modifications).

3.6   *With the railroads came riches from the East, including all manner of materials and products for fashionable homes. This stylish French Second Empire house was built in Seward, Nebraska, in 1885. Courtesy R. Bruhn*

eastern town as possible. The buildings of brick and stone were constructed by professional craftsmen and skilled contractors who could add the proper trimming of wood moldings, cornices, brass interior hardware, and colored glass. Before the railroads, these luxuries were inaccessible to the plains and mountain towns. Only coastal cities, such as Galveston, or inland ports, such as Jefferson, Texas, high up on the Big Cypress Bayou, or Nebraska City and Brownville, Nebraska, along the great Missouri, could claim the architectural

finery sent from the East. The railroads quickly changed all that. Spreading across the West, railroads brought milled lumber, pressed tin, cast iron, electric fixtures, cut glass, hardware, stoves, and plumbing to every small town. Even middle-class homes and workers' cottages exhibited the machine-made features that were equated in that era with style and civility.

With the materials and tastes of fashionable eastern architecture at their disposal, new towns began to look more and more like each

3.7   For dwellings, the most visible change wrought by the railroad era came with the turned and sawn wood ornaments that decorated porches, windows, and gables. The porches of this Nacogdoches, Texas, home are lavishly trimmed with the fruits of carpentry. *Courtesy Myron Wood*

3.8   With the advent of the railroads, workers' cottages, too, were graced with decorative cornices and columns, as these modest homes in Omaha demonstrate. *Courtesy Lynn Meyer*

3.9 By the 1880s, eastern architects were seeking commissions in the West, and some were establishing practices there. In Cheyenne, Wyoming, the firm of Van Brunt and Howe (Boston, Kansas City) designed the Union Pacific Depot (1887) in the Romanesque style made famous by H. H. Richardson. Courtesy Wyoming Department of Archives, Museums, and History

other. From the early 1870s until the Panic of 1893, town builders exhausted several architectural styles. Heavily decorated Second Empire facades, with elaborate curvilinear cornices of pressed metal, introduced a tone of grandeur to the main streets. Italianate details were common for several decades, sometimes presented simply with small cornice brackets and modest window surrounds, but also used lavishly and ostentatiously when expressed in cast iron.

By the 1880s architects had begun to establish professional practices in the growing cities of the West: Daniels and Proctor in Fargo, North Dakota; William DuBois in Cheyenne, Wyoming; Henry Trost in Pueblo, Colorado; and Frank Edbrooke in Denver, to name a few. At the

3.10   *The Minnehaha County Courthouse
(1888–90; architect: Wallace Dow) in Sioux
Falls, South Dakota, was one of many major
commercial and institutional buildings constructed in the 1880s after the railroad invasion
of the plains and mountain states had made
itself felt. The courthouse is built of South
Dakota quartzite. Courtesy State Historical
Preservation Center, South Dakota Department of Education and Cultural Affairs*

3.11 *The main streets of western small towns developed a standard building pattern: boxy buildings one to three stories high and joined in a row. The storefronts were built with glass display windows and recessed entries. The protective canopies were added later. This view is Valley Mills, Texas, west of Waco. Courtesy Myron Wood*

same time, architects from the East and Midwest were accepting commissions throughout the region: Omaha's New York Life Building (1889) by McKim, Mead, and White of New York, and Cheyenne's Union Pacific Depot (1887) by Van-Brunt and Howe of Kansas City are two distinguished examples. To support this architectural boom, capital flowed in from the East and from England. This fortuitous pairing of talent and money produced expressive designs and grand buildings. By the late nineteenth century, architectural news traveled fast and the latest designs were disseminated quickly. Through catalogs, competitions, and magazines, architects learned what was being built everywhere in America, and in Europe and England as well.

The American architect H. H. Richardson had a great influence on the large institutional and commercial buildings in western towns and cities. His designs introduced large entry arches, towers, columns, and gable ornaments, often presented in romantic, theatrical combinations. Architects under Richardson's spell used a great deal of stone, sometimes including several colors in a single building. Rusticated stone became especially popular, its rough, hand-hewn surfaces reminiscent of the fortresses of Europe. The Great Plains states were well endowed with stone, supplying their own building needs and those of much of the rest of the country. The Richardsonian Romanesque stone buildings of this era formed a happy blend of regional texture and urbane design.

On most western main streets, a standard commercial building type prevailed in the late nineteenth century regardless of the architectural style in vogue at any given time. Once past the initial tent and shack stage, a typical commercial structure was one of several built in a row, contiguous, two or three stories high, and the windows at each level evenly spaced and in line with their neighbors. At street level, the main entry was recessed and large panes of glass gave visual access to a display or to the building's interior.

The Southwest: A Path of Its Own

The wholesale adaptation of eastern architectural styles in the plains and mountain states penetrated the Indian and Spanish Southwest as well, despite the region's indigenous building traditions. Bainbridge Bunting, in *Early Architecture in New Mexico*, refers to this sudden transformation as a flood of new American architectural fashion, observing that new styles that had evolved serially in the East—first Italianate, then Queen Anne

and Richardsonian Romanesque—were embraced simultaneously and with undifferentiated enthusiasm in the new railroad towns of Albuquerque and Las Vegas. In and around the plaza area of old Santa Fe, these imported eastern styles were built among and sometimes over existing traditional adobes.

The familiar Spanish and Pueblo forms were not discarded, however, and within a short time their premier place was reaffirmed in the building choices of New Mexicans, particularly in Santa Fe. (In the more remote villages, the continuity of the adobe tradition had remained unbroken and largely untouched by outside influences.) By the turn of the century, Santa Fe as well as Taos, sixty miles to the north, had become a haven for artists and their patrons from the East, who sought a frontier life in a romantic new environment but one that offered the stimulation of cosmopolitan, talented peers. This influential group regretted the displacement of indigenous buildings by foreign styles, and they started a movement to strengthen the place of Spanish and Pueblo architecture.

This deliberate and very self-conscious revival led, for example, to an extraordinary remodeling of a major building on the University of New Mexico campus in Albuquerque in 1909. Hodgin Hall, a Richardsonian Romanesque brick and sandstone classroom building, had been a campus showcase when it was built in 1890, a perfect example of prestigious and fashionable architecture from the American East. Barely a dozen years later, Hodgin was deemed a misfit by university president William Tight, who considered it his mission to establish a distinctive regional identity for the university. For this task, he chose an interpretive version of Spanish and Pueblo architecture, using materials and features long associated with this mode: adobe, vigas, plastered surfaces, portals, and recessed windows and doors. Having set the proper tone with four new buildings in this revival style, President Tight ordered Hodgin Hall stripped of its "foreign" Richardsonian finery and reformed as an indigenous earth-and-timber structure reminiscent of earlier days along

3.12   Urban New Mexicans embraced the late
nineteenth century architectural styles coming
in from the East, but in a change of heart, a
significant number of civic and artistic leaders
began reviving the traditional adobe forms.
In one of the strangest building transforma-
tions, this 1890 stone and brick Richardsonian
hall at the University of New Mexico was redesigned along Pueblo and Spanish colonial
lines, including an adobelike surface, projecting viga ends, and sawn corbels. Courtesy
Albuquerque Museum Photoarchives Neg.
No. 78.50.701, UNM Special Collection,
Albuquerque Museum Joint Collection

3.13   Hodgin Hall redone in 1909 within
New Mexico's adobe tradition. Courtesy Albuquerque Museum Photoarchives Neg. No.
80.159.1, UNM Architecture Dept.

3.14　*The Palace of the Governors on the main square in Santa Fe has undergone substantial changes since it was first built in 1610. It was recast along Territorial lines in the late nineteenth century and was then returned to a more traditional Spanish appearance in a remodeling completed in 1913, a time of strong interest in the revival and preservation of Pueblo and Spanish colonial architecture. Courtesy Historic Preservation Division, Office of Cultural Affairs, State of New Mexico*

3.15　*The Museum of Fine Arts (1917; architect: Isaac Hamilton Rapp), a major Santa Fe building constructed during the height of revival interest, is modeled after the church at Acoma Pueblo.*

*3.16   The seventeenth-century Church of
San Esteban del Rey at Acoma Pueblo. Cour-
tesy Historic Preservation Division, Office of
Cultural Affairs, State of New Mexico*

the Rio Grande. Hodgin Hall gained an old face but a startling new look.

In Santa Fe and Taos, where the revival movement had begun, artists and architects began to build homes in what became known as the Santa Fe style, tilting what Bainbridge Bunting calls the "puebloid forms" toward a heavier emphasis on Hispanic influences, particularly the early churches. Two public buildings on the plaza in Santa Fe soon became models for those seeking an architectural redefinition of the Spanish heritage. Under the direction of anthropologist Jesse L. Nusbaum, the portal of the Palace of the Governors, which had gone through several renovations since the seventeenth century, was rebuilt in the Spanish–Pueblo Revival style, its

nineteenth century Territorial features removed in favor of a sculptured plaster surface, columns of round logs supporting an extensive porch, and protruding log ends at the roofline. Across the street the new Museum of New Mexico, designed by architect Isaac Rapp and built in 1917, stood as a loosely interpreted salute to the seventeenth-century church at Acoma Pueblo southwest of Albuquerque. These buildings offered a strong counterstatement to the influence of American architectural styles but did not obviate them.

These alternating displacements, fusions, and imitations occurring between indigenous Southwest forms and the architectural imports brought in by invading Anglos—well underway by the mid-1800s, when the Territorial style was first invented—were revitalized as a result of the railroads' capacity for making wholesale changes in the way people built their towns. In the rest of the mountains and plains, the experience was quite different. Away from the Southwest in the new frontier territories, the dominating architectural styles of the American East came and stayed, and when buildings were demolished for whatever reason, they were replaced by others in the style that was considered to be the modern American mainstream.

From Town to City: Denver, Dallas, and Omaha

From the time of the late 1860s as railroad tracks stretched from Omaha to Cheyenne and, later, south to Dallas, western towns grew quickly. Only a few were destined to become important centers of trade and culture. Even now, there are few large cities in the West. Hundreds of miles of desert separate El Paso from Albuquerque. Hundreds of miles of prairie lie between the cities of Bismarck, Topeka, and Oklahoma City.

As each city grew, it set a pace for itself, succumbing at times to conditions beyond its control and emerging with its separate image and story. Still, most cities of the West share common threads and circumstances. A look at Dallas, Denver, and Omaha reveals how forces shaped these separate cities to be much alike, and how their citizens wanted their cities to be alike. Although eager to conform to the urban standard of the day, these cities were in competition, taking each other's measure and boosting their own attributes.

Here are Denver, Dallas, and Omaha as they first took form in the 1860s: Denver poised at the edge of the Rockies, prospering from nearby gold and silver mines; Dallas hardly more than a country town at a river crossing; and Omaha, outfitting the West from the steamers and barges that plied the Missouri. Different dreams, different circumstances—Dallas and Denver flat as a board, Omaha hilly and pushed against the Missouri River bluffs—but the three were tied together by the energy of America's westward expansion.

The Union Pacific Railroad guaranteed Omaha's rise in 1869 when it chose the city as its eastern terminus for the nation's first transcontinental railroad. Heading west, the Union Pacific bypassed Denver, going through Cheyenne, Wyoming, instead. Ambitious, visionary leaders in Denver, recognizing the potential of the "iron horse," quickly formed a connecting rail line to Cheyenne. By 1870, trains were coming into Denver, transforming a mining and cattle town into a major city. Dallas in those years, at the edge of the southern plains, hustled to get railroads, and when the first track brought the Houston and Texas Central Railway to town in 1872, Dallas took off.

Western cities had few factories. Their industries were of the processing sort that took raw products from surrounding farmlands or nearby mines and readied them for sale or shipping. Instead of factories, Dallas had mills, smelters, cotton gins, canneries, leather works, and packing plants. Local lumberyards, brick works, and iron foundries met the building demands of these new cities and the smaller towns around them. If a city had several railroad lines and no central terminal, the mills and plants were spread out along the tracks. Otherwise, they were close to downtown, concentrated at one end of the commercial area with access to the main rail yards.

Alongside these industrial compounds the warehouse districts grew—rows of big square buildings, two to eight stories high, processing local produce for shipping or temporarily housing the manufactured and processed goods coming in from the East or Midwest. By 1900, Dallas, Denver, and Omaha were building a mature stage of downtown warehouses, having become major supply centers for their own regions.

Many of these practical, no-nonsense buildings, set apart from the more expensive and stylish commercial properties of downtown, have survived into our own time. Utilitarian warehouses were spared the architectural vicissitudes that brought demolition to downtown stores, offices, and hotels—buildings that were in the public eye and at the center of the business day, and therefore subject to the whims of fashion.

Denver's wholesale area hung on for years around Union Station, a collection of candy factories, warehouses, farm implement showrooms, and loading docks for produce and groceries. From its West End warehouse district, Dallas supplied nearly all of Texas and much of the nation with farm implements at the turn of the century. The city's large wholesale houses were influenced by the Chicago commercial style, their expansive windows segmented and the overall design one of simplicity and uniformity.

Omaha, a major supply station to the West, built row after row of warehouses along brick streets near the railroad yards that skirted the Missouri River. These buildings ranged in style from delicate, decorative Italianate buildings of the 1870s to Sullivanesque commercial styles coming out of Chicago before World War I. In the city's produce market district, wide canopies reached out over the sidewalks to protect goods as they were unloaded from wagons or trucks. The warehouse enclaves were at the heart of the region's commerce, and their very presence was a sure sign of economic health.

While the railroads infused cities with wealth and power, concentrating people and buildings in downtown districts, a new form of transportation—streetcars and trolleys—began to disperse them. Streetcars, abetted by land developers and speculators, created the first flight to the suburbs.

In Dallas, the earliest residential subdivisions appeared along streetcar lines to the east and south of downtown. Laborers, to be close to work, lived in shanties along the tracks or in boarding houses near downtown. People of means chose to get away from the seamier areas of the city. The Cedars, Dallas's first elegant suburb, started out as a collection of small, decorative Victorian cottages, but it soon flowered into an extravagant world of Queen Anne mansions built by such powerful and prominent citizens as Alex Sanger, founder of the city's first large department store.

In 1871 Denver's horse-drawn streetcars linked downtown to Curtis Park, a residential addition northwest of the main business district. Other neighborhoods soon clustered nearby, each serviced by a different streetcar line. For a time it looked as if North Denver would emerge as the city's most prestigious area, but the real estate market, volatile and highly speculative, determined otherwise. By 1874, competitors succeeded in laying another streetcar line running south and east to Capitol Hill, which remained Denver's grandest neighborhood for decades to come.

Families moved to the suburbs for good reason. The rapidly growing downtowns existed in a confusion of carriages, wagons, and horses, all milling about on unpaved streets either mired in mud and manure or, during dry times, sending up clouds of dust into air already filled with the smoke of countless coal stoves. Mules, cows, pigs, and horses roamed the streets; dead animals caused a stench and health hazard. Fire, always an ominous threat in nineteenth-century cities, all too frequently burned out of control in crowded downtowns that lacked modern water systems. Besides dirt and foul air at the city's core, vice in the form of brothels, gambling casinos, and saloons offended the social and moral code of middle-class Victorian families.

The new garden suburbs beckoned families away from the squalor and sin of downtown. Trees, lawns, clean air, and freshwater wells proved a welcome relief from the city's grime. The suburbs had other attributes: they were fashionable and romantic, part of the national love affair with landscape gardening and country life, and an escape from the crass circumstances of industry.

The same streetcars that turned open fields

into garden estates brought homeowners and housewives back downtown to work and shop. Office buildings—the Equitable in Denver, the New York Life Insurance Building in Omaha, the Wilson Building in Dallas—turned raw frontier towns into real cities. These were high-style buildings, urbane and esteemed. The Equitable was designed by the nationally prominent Boston firm of Andrews, Jacques and Rantoul, the New York Life building by McKim, Mead, and White, and the Wilson Building by Sanguinet and Staats of Fort Worth.

A new urban phenomenon, the retail department store, joined these distinctive office towers as a centerpiece for downtown. The huge, multi-storied shopping marts carried all the "dry goods" then on the market. Jonas L. Brandeis opened his first Omaha store in 1881 and then built an eight-story Beaux Arts building in 1905 at Sixteenth and Douglas Streets in the heart of the business district. The Denver Dry Goods Store, dating from the 1880s, brought shoppers to the new center of downtown on Sixteenth Street, a few blocks from historical Larimer Street. Denver's second major department store, the May Company, originated as a dry goods outlet in the mining town of Leadville. Owner David May opened a Denver store in the 1880s, and his company eventually merged with Daniels and Fisher, whose tower remains today as one of the city's most important landmarks.

The May Company, Brandeis, and other stores like them were more than merely downtown emporiums, they were the retail heart of an entire region, drawing customers from hundreds of miles away. Wyoming ranchers shopped at The Denver, and Dallas's Sanger Brothers Store drew families from small towns all over Texas.

As they prospered, these giant department stores occupied the biggest buildings on main street, although they had started out in true frontier style as transitory, makeshift enterprises tied closely to the hectic world of the railroads. What ended up as a department store might have started as a quickly built log cabin or a canvas-covered tent. William MacDonald in his history of Dallas relates how, in 1872, the Sanger brothers, recent immigrants from Prussia, started a retail empire in a dozen successive railroad terminal towns following the Houston and Texas Central Railroad as its track was laid to Dallas from Bryan, 170 miles south. Although the Sangers ultimately made an enormous investment in Dallas, building large mansions and stores, their initial efforts were tentative and free-flowing in the opportunistic spirit of the early West. Ambitious men pushed a half-dozen different enterprises in the belief that at least one would catch hold and generate a fortune.

The 1880s were years of confidence in the urban West, a period of explosive growth and limitless prosperity. Business leaders pulled together, joining forces to make their cities modern and attractive. Water systems, transit systems, sewer lines, gas lights, electricity—one after another, modern urban amenities entered the mountains and plains cities, lifting them from squalor into an orderly world of new technology and modern invention.

In the 1880s Denver built a sewer system and installed streetlights—first gas, then electric. In the same era, Dallas added electric lighting over streets newly paved with wooden blocks. Omaha consolidated its volunteer fire departments and, by 1880, began to pave its dirt streets, lining the main thoroughfare with granite and covering the other streets with asphalt.

Enterprising men gained fortunes through these new arrangements—Dr. Samuel D. Mercer from Omaha's streetcars, Walter S. Cheesman from Denver's water system—just as Westerners a few years earlier made money on stagecoach lines and freight wagons. The typical western money baron had a finger in every financial pie—banking, cattle, transportation, perhaps an electric company, and an assortment of land investments. William MacDonald, in *Dallas Rediscovered*, describes a Texas entrepreneur with the improbable name of Col. Christopher Columbus Slaughter, who raised cattle on more than a million acres

3.17　Around the turn of the century, American cities expansively turned toward the grandeur of Greece and Rome. Topeka's majestic Memorial Building is an excellent example. Courtesy Bern Ketchum, Topeka-Shawnee County Kansas Metropolitan Planning Commission

of land and then turned to banking, the chemical industry, and real estate to increase his fortune. He shaped much of Dallas's economy during his active years. His estate left millions to the city's charities. In the same tradition, John and Frederick Wilson expanded profits in their family business with investments in cotton, oil, banks, and a streetcar company. They built the most distinguished building in downtown Dallas, which still bears the family name.

These early princes of commerce came from all walks of life, from Europe as well as the American East. Lyle Dorsett, in *The Queen City*, credits

Denver's rise to superior leaders. Some arrived with fortunes in hand; others began with nothing. Dr. John Evans came to Denver in the 1860s as a recent member of Chicago's power elite, a wealthy investor and a renowned physician. In Colorado he went on to become territorial governor and then spearheaded the acquisition of a railroad line into Denver from Cheyenne. Later, he organized a tramway system and the city's Chamber of Commerce.

Omaha's civic leaders were equally adept at keeping several balls in the air at once. The Kountze Brothers accumulated fortunes in banking in both Denver and Omaha in the 1860s. During the same years, Milton Rogers was moving beyond a modest supply store business to become involved in real estate, founding the South Omaha Land Company. He later helped to organize the Union Stockyards, which accounted for much of Omaha's prosperity.

Individualism shines forth in the histories of these successful men, but they were most powerful when they joined together in enterprises that added new dimensions to their communities, such as a tramway system or a world's fair. The vigor of nineteenth-century boosterism, which powered the collective projects, shines clearly through the literature and activity of the times. We tend to believe that our own generation invented advertising and financial speculation. But these creations of the marketplace were established American traditions by the late nineteenth century, going hand in hand with the rise and growth of cities. Handbills, newspapers, celebrations, ceremonies—all were means of promoting commerce and community. Civic boosters, bold and presumptuous, made their big moves within an atmosphere that was expectant, charged, and even frenzied. The enterprises of the eighties and nineties were often difficult, sometimes daring, and they invariably were fueled by a conviction that business opportunities were endless.

The panic of 1893 stopped it all. This serious international depression brought a collapse of business and led to widespread unemployment. Banks failed and factories closed. Farmers, already hurt by several years of drought, glumly watched prices fall. Railroads, mining, and agriculture, the financial underpinnings of the West, buckled in the aftermath. The region's cities—Omaha, Denver, and Dallas among them—felt their life's blood draining away. For the remainder of the 1890s, the building boom was over.

A new century brought prosperity and with it a vigorous round of new construction. Increased use of steel framing and the availability of elevators facilitated skyscrapers and expanded interior spaces. Investors, seeking a higher return on valu-able downtown property, pressed eagerly for these larger, taller buildings.

Architectural tastes changed in tandem with the new technology. A functional commercial style prevailed among high-rising business blocks, an elegant classicism in institutional buildings. Regal white stone and light-colored brick replaced the earthy sandstone and ruddy brick of the late Victorian era. Denver, after the turn of the century, bowed to classicism with a new Union Station. Dallas followed suit a decade later. In a similar spirit, Omaha built its massive Central High School on a hill overlooking downtown. These majestic structures were jewels of the "City Beautiful" movement, itself a part of a larger turn-of-the-century phenomenon sometimes called the American Renaissance. Public art, civic pride, and social reform marked this era of aspiration toward a higher public good, expressed tangibly by the architecture of Greece and Rome.

The region's great cities, which had flourished together in the 1880s, luxuriated a second time during this fashionable era of formalism, but by the end of World War I, classicism was in retreat. The cities of the mountains and plains would soon succumb to the waves of modern architecture rolling across America in the early decades of the twentieth century.

Automobiles and Urban Life

After World War I, following heroic architectural expressions in the classical mode, the region's cities and larger towns entered a lively era that generated new building types and new styles as well. During the 1920s, a period of general prosperity in the cities, people had more leisure, more money, and increasingly cosmopolitan expectations. They also had the automobile, an invention

3.18 *The automobile created a new set of buildings and permanently altered the lifestyles of town residents. In Cheyenne, this terra cotta and brick showroom has been operated by the Dinneen family since 1927. Courtesy Richard Collier, Wyoming Department of Archives, Museums, and History*

that changed urban life more than any single development since the railroad. Automobiles not only altered the way people moved about the city, they mandated special kinds of buildings to accommodate automobile owners as well as the machines themselves.

The automobile revolution, which eventually led to drive-in facilities of all kinds, started modestly in the 1920s with automobile showrooms and filling stations for gasoline and minor repairs. The showrooms spread across the country quickly and became standardized early as essentially functional structures but with sufficient architectural ornamentation to salute the importance of this new focus of American society. Their salient fea-

ture was a large expanse of glass at the front of the building to show off the new cars. Typically, dealer showrooms were constructed at the edges of a downtown business district close to the banking and merchant community but with sufficient room for a large, low building to showcase the automobiles.

The Dinneen Garage (1927) in Cheyenne, Wyoming, incorporated the necessary car showroom qualities: a conspicuous corner location, large display windows, and a dignified styling that harkened to tradition, yet evoked a modern image. Two large towers frame the entry, suggesting an English Renaissance palace. This regal showroom first housed Buicks, then the Essex

3.19   Although gas stations serve a mundane purpose, they often have been housed in buildings more atuned to fantasy than to practical need. In Moody, Texas, futuristic gas pumps are sheltered by a Greek temple canopy. *Courtesy Myron Wood*

3.20   No aspiration was too lofty for gas station design. This crenellated stone fortress in Glen Elder, Kansas, might have housed kings and queens. *Courtesy Kansas State Historical Society*

along with Hudsons and Reos, still later Plymouths and DeSotos, and finally, Lincolns and Mercurys. The building's original owners, the Dinneen family, were still operating a Lincoln and Mercury dealership in 1989.

As the popularity of automobiles increased, filling stations became common in every city, town, and crossroads in America. Like the auto showrooms, gas stations invaded conspicuous locations, occupying choice corner lots close to downtown. As such, they were disruptive of established business districts and neighborhoods, sometimes replacing a community's largest older homes.

Filling stations achieved architectural distinction of their own, well documented by Daniel I. Vieyra in *"Fill'er Up"*, an illustrated history of American gas stations. The early stations of the twenties and thirties were often built in purely fantastic styles—castles, lighthouses, tipis, and pagodas. Others were built as miniature Elizabethan cottages or in similar quaint domestic modes. Any tradition could be borrowed for gas retailing, including Neoclassical stations to remind travelers of tradition and authority, and streamlined Art Deco stations that were up-to-date and urbane. Filling stations existed as microcosms of American building tastes. As the years passed and the automobile became less of a novelty, gas stations adopted a no-nonsense, functional appearance that bypassed fantasy to offer motorists gas, oil, and clean windshields.

With automobiles to speed them along, people traveled more. They went to races, restaurants, dances, and nightclubs (illegal ones during Prohibition). They drove downtown to see movies in theaters that were even more glittering and fantastic than the gas stations.

At night, downtown streets were aglow with lighted signs. Neon restaurant signs and flashing theater marquees beckoned with brilliant hues of red, green, and cool blue. Blinking lights, appearing to be in motion, sent messages out from huge billboards and from building facades. A hotel might have a lighted corner sign ten stories high.

By the 1920s, night life had become respectable and popular. Everyone wanted to eat dinner in a downtown restaurant, dance in a hotel ballroom, or take in the latest movie at theaters with such names as Fox, Majestic, Paramount, and Royale.

Although classicism dominated design through World War I, several widely divergent styles shared the architectural stage, including scattered examples of the Prairie School, exemplified by the early work of Frank Lloyd Wright. Prairie style buildings never attained the popularity on the plains that they enjoyed in the upper Midwest, but they captured public attention for their bold departure from familiar traditional designs. Wright himself designed a Prairie house for clients in McCook, Nebraska, in 1905. For his own home (1909) in El Paso, Texas, architect Henry Trost used the dramatic projecting eaves and imposing brick piers introduced by Wright. A dozen years later, architect Frederick Stott executed a Prairie style church—buff brick trimmed with horizontal bands of concrete—for a black congregation in North Omaha, Nebraska.

Traditionalists held their ground. British influences, melded together in a style named Jacobethan, offered new hope to a public tired of classicism but wary of Wright's modern lines. Red brick accented with white crenellated towers satisfied this taste for tradition; rows of large windows met modern requirements for light. These distinctive but highly functional structures were ideal for schools, showrooms, and factories as well. Tulsa and Albuquerque chose this style for their central high schools. Augustana College in Sioux Falls, South Dakota, added a similar Jacobethan building to its campus in 1920.

During this period, architects and builders often combined what seemed to be the best of the new and the old by using decorative brick or tile within an overall trimmed-down, modern design. Fancifully placed brick created lively ornamental patterns on an otherwise spare facade, offering decorative elegance together with a modern, progressive look.

Before the stock market crash of 1929 ended

3.21   Movie theaters were one of the glamour
items of early twentieth century architecture.
Like gas stations, they tended toward fantasy or
highly romanticized history. The Paramount
(1915) in Austin, Texas, is rather formal and
decorous compared to many of the region's movie
houses. It was originally the Majestic, another
popular theater name, and began life as a
legitimate theater, then switched to film, and
later to the performing arts. Courtesy David
Glover/Camerawork

3.22   Westerners embraced the film industry's
high-stepping style with enthusiasm. The Fox
Theater in Hutchinson, Kansas, is a handsome
and well-preserved example of Art Deco theater
architecture. Courtesy Kansas State Historical
Society

3.23   Modern architecture developed in the West alongside the more derivative styles. Frank Lloyd Wright's Prairie School influence appears here in architect Henry C. Trost's home (1909) in El Paso, Texas. Courtesy Texas Historical Commission

3.24   Frank Lloyd Wright's influence is evident again in St. John's African Methodist Episcopal Church in Omaha, designed by Frederick Stott and built in 1921. The church serves a black community in North Omaha. Courtesy Lynn Meyer

3.25　After World War I, classicism faded and enthusiasm grew for English derivatives usually done in brick trimmed with contrasting light stone or terra cotta. The Public Service Company of Oklahoma has remodeled Tulsa's Central High School for its corporate head-quarters. Courtesy Public Service Company of Oklahoma

3.26　Albuquerque's high school grew in stages, the first designed by Trost and Trost in 1914. Like similar buildings of this era, it suggests an English palace or country house. Courtesy David Gunning, City of Albuquerque Planning Department

3.27 *Augustana College in Sioux Falls,*
South Dakota, built this hall in 1920, used
now for administration. Courtesy Joel Strasser
for Augustana College

most new construction, the West's booming cities experienced a last, lively round of building in the emerging styles of Art Deco and other modernistic themes. The principles of modernism required regularity, simplicity of form and material, and abstracted rather than pictorial decoration.

Art Deco design in architecture proceeded in two directions: the glossy streamliner look of modern technology and the zigzag lines expressed in such famous structures as the Chrysler Building in Manhattan and Bullock's Department Store in Los Angeles. Zigzag Art Deco grew directly out of the 1925 Exposition of Decorative Arts in Paris, which brought together in one exhibi-

tion a quarter-century of modern industrial and decorative design from the studios of Europe.

The zigzag school of Art Deco served admirably as a style for skyscrapers, while streamline modern was well suited for small buildings or interiors, such as cocktail lounges, elegant stores, and homes. Jewelry, expensive automobiles, and other luxury items were a perfect fit for Art Deco design. The highly stylized lines of Deco, although sparely presented, achieved striking images. Contrasting colors and shiny, metallic surfaces further enriched its strong visual effects.

Just as Richardsonian design had triumphed in the great public building of the 1890s, fol-

3.28   Repeating arches and multicolored brick create a rich pattern on the Spanish-styled Kresge Store (1926) in Topeka, Kansas. During this era architects began moderniz-ing lines but added color and texture by using a variety of brick. Courtesy Bern Ketchum, Topeka-Shawnee County Kansas Metropolitan Planning Commission

3.29   Brickwork on a fire station in Rapid City, South Dakota. Courtesy The Rapid City Journal.

3.30 Moderne in style, with Art Deco details, Omaha's Union Station (1931) brought passengers a sophisticated and streamlined world. Closed in 1972, the station is now the home of the Western Heritage Museum, a gift to the city from Union Pacific. Courtesy Lynn Meyer

lowed by Neoclassicism in the early twentieth century, so did Art Deco and Moderne dominate the 1920s and early 1930s. Omaha built a new Union Station and the Joslyn Art Museum, Oklahoma City built the imposing First National Bank, and Fort Worth built the Sinclair Building. Two western states—North Dakota and Nebraska—constructed new capitols during the 1930s, each different from the other, but both monuments to modernism.

Of all the heartland cities, none is as exceptionally endowed with Art Deco and Moderne buildings as Tulsa, Oklahoma, a city that came of age in the 1920s following the discovery of oil in nearby Redfork. The city's growth was expressed

in an explosion of building as newly-rich oil men consolidated power and fortunes. By the early 1930s, Tulsa's modernistic building inventory included a department store, several office towers, a utilities building, a hotel, two large churches, the municipal airport, a bus depot, a fairgrounds pavilion, and several distinctive private homes.

Among Tulsa's most opulent modern downtown buildings is the Philcaide Building, completed in 1930 for oil tycoon Waite Phillips. Plain brick twin towers rise over a two-story entry level decorated with incised stonework reminiscent of England's Aesthetic Movement with its debt to nature and handcrafts. The distinctive Philcaide interior combines a rich assortment of colors and

3.31   In 1936, the city of Dallas erected the largest collection of Moderne and Art Deco buildings anywhere in the West to house the Texas Centennial Exposition celebrating the state's first 100 years. As in most world's fairs, many of the buildings were intended to be temporary, but their construction was substantial enough to keep them going well beyond the period of the exposition. The Hall of State, one of the avowedly permanent buildings, celebrates the natural and social history of Texas. Courtesy Doug Tomlinson

3.32   Towering above the prairie, Nebraska's State Capitol is one of the region's most architecturally significant buildings. Designed by Bertram Grosvenor Goodhue of New York, the capitol was built between 1922 and 1932 of luxurious, carefully crafted materials. The building has strong graphic and narrative qualities, integrating symbols and shapes to illustrate a story of life in Nebraska that begins with the Indians and proceeds through the historical period of settlement and consolidation. Courtesy D. Murphy

3.33 *Polychrome tile and marble surface the vaults in the capitol vestibule in Lincoln, Nebraska. Marble mosaics cover the floor. The bronze light fixtures contain symbols of Indian arrows, corn, and birds. This vestibule leads to the rotunda and its 112-foot dome. Courtesy Photo by Richard Hufnagle, Elinor Brown Collection, Nebraska State Historical Society*

3.34   Terra cotta and wrought iron carry the animal, plant, and geometric decorations of the Philcaide Building (1930) in downtown Tulsa, a city well-endowed with finely crafted modernistic buildings.

3.35   Colorful terra cotta tiles accentuate the verticality of the Gillette-Tyrrell Building (1930), which had originally been designed as a thirteen-floor tower (not realized because of the economic hardship of the Great Depression). The lobby is tiled in vibrant shades of blue, green, and rusty red.

3.36   Tulsa's Christ the King Church (1927; architect: Barry Byrne). Sculptor Alfonso Ianelli designed the terra cotta spire pinnacles and many other features of the church.

3.37   Verticality was the rule when Bruce Goff designed Boston Avenue Methodist Church (1929) in Tulsa. The church has neither front nor back and in that way presages recent office towers that are as much sculpture as building.

3.38   The Boston Avenue church was built of limestone with terra cotta decoration. The figures here are circuit riders, assigned to bring the gospel to isolated western communities that lacked a preacher. Intricate patterns of stylized flowers and leaves elaborate the building's interior.

textures in a harmony of pattern. The lobby and hallway surfaces—polished stone floors, gold leaf ceilings, and walls lined with marble pilasters and burnished metal panels—glisten with jewellike intensity. These spaces are richly appointed, yet functional—a compelling blend of elegance and vitality.

Tulsa's modern buildings made abundant use of terra cotta for exterior ornamentation. Architects had been using this material at the turn of the century in Neoclassical structures and in Tudor-inspired institutional and commercial buildings. Tulsa's terra cotta facades are notable for their rich

colors. Vivid relief murals at Tulsa's fairground pavilion depict animals and flowers. Downtown, at the Gilette-Tyrrel Building, bright geometric tiles cover the walls inside and out. Coming on the heels of two decades of white, formal, Neoclassical architecture, these bright hues—raspberry, royal blue, orange, red, gold, and green—added a giddy, exuberant touch to commercial and institutional buildings. Between its zestful neon lights at night and the vibrant terra cotta tiles evident in the daylight hours, Tulsa radiated color and life.

Tulsa's modernistic architecture extended to religious buildings as well, including two of

3.39   *South Omaha, Nebraska. The commercial fabric of most western communities, developed in the late nineteenth and early twentieth centuries, was executed with a sense of the whole. Materials used in common, bands of windows, and similar heights were the ingredients of harmony. Beginning in the 1930s, the aging buildings of main streets underwent remodelings, and this enthusiasm for change continued through the 1960s. Plastic, metal, and glass (and, often, thick wooden shingles) covered up the old lines, at least on the first floor. Upper floors became alienated from their foundation in a kind of architectural divorce. One of the great achievements of historic preservation has been the return of historic storefronts to the downtowns of America. Courtesy Lynn Meyer*

America's most significant churches since Frank Lloyd Wright's design of Unity Temple (1904) in Oak Park, Illinois. These extraordinary designs represented a breaking away from traditional church architecture. Christ the King Church (1927) was designed by Barry Byrne, who had apprenticed to Frank Lloyd Wright twenty years earlier. Alfonso Ianelli, a sculptor and designer who had worked with Wright, assisted Byrne with major decorative features, including the terra cotta pinnacles of the brick spires. As Christ the King was nearing completion, architect Bruce Goff, collaborating with artist Adah Robinson, began designs for Boston Avenue Methodist Church, a monumental building and a masterpiece of modernistic form and decoration.

Although Moderne and Art Deco buildings were concentrated in a few large cities, many smaller cities and even modest-sized towns caught the twentieth-century spirit and did what they could to keep up. A few county seats built Art Deco courthouses, and many towns built modernistic schools and post offices, some of them with splendid murals commissioned by the Roosevelt administration (by the 1930s very little building was completed with private funds). In small towns, twentieth-century touches were likely to be found in movie theater marquees and filling stations.

The Great Depression and World War II were hard on the entire country. It became more and more difficult to build a new building. People who wanted a new look turned to remodeling instead. Downtown merchants expanded the size of their windows, added signs made with sans-serif metal lettering, and faced the lower portion of their entries and showcase windows with carrera glass—black and green were the common colors. Many of these new facades are so handsome that preservationists are in a quandary over whether to restore remodeled buildings to their original nineteenth or early twentieth century state or to uphold the daring, sophisticated surfaces that were added before World War II.

In any case, the new faces on old buildings created a bizarre architectural situation on American main streets. They resulted in a stylistic divorce of the bottom floor from the ones above it. The bottom level with its streamlined glass and metal surfaces moved headlong through the twentieth century; the floors above kept their brick ornaments and elaborate window surrounds, true to their Victorian or Edwardian origins. After World War II, merchants went on a second remodeling spree, this time adding metal sheathing to the entire facade or an aluminum awning to cut off the upper stories. By mid-century, many of the region's downtowns and main streets were likely to be far removed from the architecture of their founding.

4.1   *The Western architectural heritage includes vast numbers of vernacular buildings,
such as this lumber and feed store in the small
mining town of Westcliffe, Colorado.*

CHAPTER FOUR

Survey: The Search for the Tangible Past

The Hidden West

Exploration and discovery have always been central to the mystique of the West. The out-sized landscape combined with the transient nature of life within it leave one with a sense that this land can never be completely known or mastered. Who lived on this expanse of grasslands and mountains? What did they leave? How do we know?

With passage of the National Historic Preservation Act in 1966, the federal government created a means of discovering America's tangible past. The National Register of Historic Places was established as a central record of significant sites, and historic preservation offices were set up by

each state to survey existing historic resources—architectural, industrial, natural, and archeological. The variety of eligible sites is enormous. The surveys identify architectural sites ranging from modest, vernacular examples, such as sod houses, to stylish institutional buildings, such as Greek Revival post offices. Industrial sites encompass windmills as well as mining camps. Natural features include Chimney Rock along the Oregon Trail, the native American shrine of Bear Butte in South Dakota, and a stretch of the San Antonio River in Texas. Archeological sites of all sizes are considered, from the famous ruins of Mesa Verde in Colorado to scattered surface deposits of flint arrow points in western North Dakota. Together, these disparate sites tell a story of Indian, Spanish, and American life on the Great Plains and Rocky

4.2   Beaux Arts and Neoclassical styles swept
the West in the first years of the twentieth century. Fort Worth's post office (1933; architect:
Wyatt C. Hedrick) incorporates the heads of
longhorn cattle into its column capitals. This
important building was an obvious candidate
for Tarrant County's survey of historic architecture, but 100,000 other structures also have
been mapped and recorded in the Fort Worth
area. Courtesy Historic Preservation Council
for Tarrant County, Texas

4.3   Close-up of the Fort Worth post office.
Courtesy Historic Preservation Council for
Tarrant County, Texas

4.4   *A shingle and clapboard frame house
in the West Boulevard Historic District of
Rapid City, South Dakota. Courtesy State
Historical Preservation Center, South Dakota
Department of Education and Cultural Affairs*

Mountains beginning several thousand years ago.

Today, the region's long-hidden heritage is gaining recognition. Before, because much of the area's architectural legacy came from the East, and came late at that, western sites were often regarded as too new to document or too imitative to be significant. Away from the cities, whether in the mountains or on the plains, no one even knew what remained from the past. For most western preservation offices, searching out the unknown became their special charge.

The results have been surprising in both scope and substance. An extraordinary abundance of new archeological evidence is certain to change our understanding of the prehistoric inhabitants of this continent. (Thomas Merlan, who heads

New Mexico's historic preservation office, estimates that prehistoric Chacoan sites alone from approximately a thousand years ago are spread over 50 million acres of the Southwest.) The existence of this archeological material is now known, and a significant portion has been excavated or examined in the field. Much of it has yet to be recorded, evaluated, and interpreted, however.

For the next generation of preservationists in the West, archeology is likely to be the most exciting arena of historical study. The lessons learned will not only inform the interpretation of past cultures but will direct attention to the conditions required to survive and prevail in the difficult terrain of the mountains and plains. In the more immediate future, the recent discovery of a rich lode of rural vernacular—immigrant enclaves, irrigation systems, frame houses and barns, hand-hewn structures of stone and earth—is emerging as one of the most intriguing contributions of this region to the American legacy.

Surveying the Mountains and Plains

When Paul Putz, head of South Dakota's preservation office, began in 1972 to record the state's historic resources, he approached the job with what he now regards as a naive assumption about popular regard for evidence from the past. "When you discover historic architecture, as I had several years earlier, you really start living on another planet. Your environment is permanently altered by your awareness of the buildings and the history they represent. But twenty years ago in this part of the country, almost nobody cared or even noticed. People thought we were odd because we valued these old places and wanted to learn more about them."

Putz and his two staff members got underway, working first with county governments and methodically carrying out surveys across the state. One of his colleagues had recently gone east to Nantucket Island to attend a preservation conference on historic districts and the value of documenting a number of related sites together. He came back a believer. The South Dakota survey switched its emphasis to historic districts. They surveyed and recorded West Boulevard in Rapid City (a turn-of-the-century residential area); the entire downtowns of Hot Springs and Lead; and the St. Joseph's Cathedral District in Sioux Falls. All of these districts are listed on the National Register of Historic Places.

In the meantime, the survey staff was growing, as was the interest of South Dakota citizens in their history. Perhaps the attention accorded the new districts made a difference. Perhaps the American bicentennial celebrations in 1976 reminded South Dakotans that their own history was part of a sweeping western heritage. By the late 1970s, Paul Putz saw that the idea of preservation was taking off: "I think the American people began to think about the quality of life and where they were headed. All of a sudden they made it clear that they *wanted* historic buildings and neighborhoods in their future. A few years earlier, they didn't even dream of that. It was a big switch. Now, all towns have at least one National Register site, and nearly all of them have restored or renovated or adapted some of their old buildings. And people all over South Dakota today *know* what they have."

Carolyn Torma, who coordinates the South Dakota survey, has taken the process well beyond the first tentative forays into the field, which had been marked by puzzlement and guesswork. She has composed a lengthy field guide to serve as a bible for all South Dakota surveyors. The guide, amply illustrated with examples, outlines in detail the materials, building types, and architectural styles found throughout the state. Each survey season, she takes every fieldworker through the manual and an accompanying slide show and then step by step through the inventory process.

Each significant site recorded in the field requires black-and-white photographs, color slides, hand-drawn maps showing how each feature or building relates to its surroundings, a listing and description of all building materials and forms, and anything that can be gleaned about the site's use and history. These materials are organized and coded at the end of each week and then entered into the statewide computerized survey at the end of the season. The overall aim of the survey, in addition to recording specific information accurately and clearly, is to create a consistent, informed body of data about South Dakota's historic sites.

Torma sees the field documentation process as an opportunity to reinforce a preservation ethic

4.5   *The Buell Building, Rapid City. Beginning in the 1980s, the nomination of commercial buildings and districts to the National Register of Historic Places made building owners eligible for federal tax credits for approved renovations. This legislation resulted in thousands of successful building rehabilitations, which greatly improved the appearance and economic vitality of main streets throughout the region. Courtesy State Historical Preservation Center, South Dakota Department of Education and Cultural Affairs*

among South Dakota residents. She instructs surveyors to make the most of their contacts with historic site owners, expressing enthusiasm for the buildings and underscoring the importance of preserving South Dakota's tangible past. A positive attitude on the part of the survey team usually elicits valuable information about the sites, which then becomes part of the permanent recorded history.

To help South Dakotans to appreciate their past, the University of South Dakota and the State Historical Preservation Center jointly published an illustrated guide to the state's historic sites. A brief text about the state's history is followed by a listing, with photographs, of nearly a hundred of South Dakota's most important buildings. The book offers a broad range of structures from Aberdeen's handsome Renaissance Revival

4.6 The Brown County Courthouse (1904) in Aberdeen, South Dakota. Courtesy State Historical Preservation Center, South Dakota Department of Education and Cultural Affairs

courthouse to a prairie homestead near the Badlands and the Colonial Revival Fishback home in Brookings. Organized into six districts, with each section introduced by a map, the guide helps travelers to find historic sites and lists which ones are open to the public.

All state preservation offices are obligated by law to carry out extensive surveys, but they do not accomplish all the work themselves by any means. Public and private agencies often band together to get the job done, as they have in Fort Worth, Texas, where the Historic Preservation Council for Tarrant County coordinates the interests of forty-one organizations and neighborhoods. Marty Craddock helped to organize the council, which grew out of a Junior League

preservation project she headed, and serves as its executive director. Surveys have been their central project. When they started in 1980, their best guess on time and cost was one year and $36,000. Eight years and $371,000 later they had mapped and recorded more than 100,000 properties, completed thirteen separate reports, and published five illustrated volumes of material for general distribution. The Texas Historical Commission (the state's preservation arm) awards a grant each year to the Forth Worth project, but a large part of the survey budget has been raised privately from foundations and corporations. The Tarrant County survey is considered one of the best and most thorough in the state.

Under Marty Craddock's leadership, the Tar-

4.7　*The Tarrant County Courthouse (1893–95) in Fort Worth, Texas, is probably the city's premier historic public building.*

4.8 The Dulaney House (1923) in the Elizabeth Boulevard Historic District, one of the first neighborhoods in Fort Worth to be recognized for significant architectural and historic value. Courtesy Historic Preservation Council for Tarrant County, Texas

rant County Historic Preservation Council has been visible, vocal, and active. They produced a seventeen-minute video tape on historic preservation and economic development through tourism. Television has served them well. Station KTXA in nearby Arlington regularly produces and broadcasts public service announcements about preservation. As a result of these outlets, the council is able to recycle continually—and in a lively, popular form—the knowledge gained through the surveys of Fort Worth and its environs. Their comprehensive survey is the foundation on which other historic preservation activity depends.

Craddock sees the city's successful neighborhood movement as being strongly tied to the survey. She cites the Elizabeth Boulevard neighborhood and its influence as an example. By the 1970s the economy of the area had begun to slide. Single-family residences were being broken up into apartments, a sure sign of decline. Concerned residents rallied to form the Ryan Place Improvement Association, which then initiated National Register designation for the neighborhood. National Register nomination in turn sparked further commitment. The next step was the successful lobbying of local government for a protective preservation ordinance. As a result of all this activity, the quality of the area steadily improved. The neighborhood has maintained vigorous programs, including a newsletter, house

4.9 *Victorian cottages, like this one in Fort Worth's Southside area, were common nearly everywhere in the country during the late nineteenth century, but few have survived with carpentry ornamentation as beautifully intact as this example. The house was built around 1898 for the family of a tobacco executive, Meredith Benton, and is still held by the family. Publicity for Tarrant County's surveys of historic architecture has underscored the importance of Fort Worth's older homes.*

tours, an annual race, and a Fourth of July parade.

When the preservation council for Tarrant County organized in 1980, it was able to follow up on the Ryan Place Association's pioneer efforts in the Elizabeth Boulevard district by proceeding with a survey of the entire South Side. Recently, Fort Worth's largest historic district—Fairmount, a 100-square-block area contiguous to Elizabeth Boulevard—was nominated to the National Register. Were it not for the council's umbrella opera-

tions, districts like Elizabeth Boulevard might have remained isolated success stories.

Few of the region's cities and towns have been successful at forming and maintaining preservation organizations as strong as Tarrant County's Historic Preservation Council. Often, the business of surveys, National Register nominations, and even neighborhood organization falls on city planning offices, many of which now have a historic preservation officer. Omaha's historic preservation staff has carried out impressive surveys

4.10   Albuquerque's wide-ranging architecture includes early Spanish and Indian adobe traditions as well as twentieth-century buildings. Recent citywide surveys have helped to trace the evolution of construction methods. This abandoned house combines several diverse influences: the adobe walls, which are basic to Albuquerque's heritage; the courses of decorative brickwork suggestive of the nineteenth-century Territorial style; and finally, the Victorian fishscale shingles and carpentry detailing made popular in the late nineteenth century.

4.11   Albuquerque's preliminary building survey in the late 1970s enabled preservationists and planners to take an overall view of the city's historic architecture, which includes distinctive examples of twentieth-century structures, such as the Occidental Life Building (1917; architect: Henry Trost), modeled after the Doge's Palace in Venice. The building is faced with molded terra cotta.

4.12   Close-up of the Corinthian capitals of the Occidental Life Building

4.13   Architectural surveys in the region have recognized the importance of twentieth-century buildings. In Albuquerque, preservationists took steps in the late seventies to save and refurbish the KiMo Theater (1927), which the city's surveyors describe as "Hopi Revival." Colorful terra cotta tiles brighten the facade; inside, Indian motifs and decorations of all kinds carry the Southwest theme further. Carl Boller was the original designer, Conron and Lent of Santa Fe the restoration architects.

of the city's older areas. In 1980, the city published its first comprehensive survey report, which traced Omaha's architectural heritage for roughly a hundred-year period beginning in the mid-nineteenth century. Four years later, the planning department issued a second illustrated volume, which concentrated on the history and architecture of North Omaha, a section of the city that had housed a series of incoming immigrant groups around the turn of the century and then became home for Omaha's black community. The published report includes a preservation plan for North Omaha as well as an illustrated typology of the area's buildings.

Albuquerque, founded in 1706, is now a rapidly growing modern city that depends heavily on its historic preservation planners to identify and publicize historic landmarks. In 1983 the city's planning department completed a building-by-building survey of Albuquerque's older areas. An earlier reconnaissance survey by the city's arts board produced an illustrated history and guide, which generated an intense interest in Albuquerque's architecture. The book will be brought up to date with the newer survey material and reissued. Keeping a survey current and its results before the public is one of the best tools planners have for reaffirming the importance of a city's historic buildings.

Even in communities with little preservation commitment, a survey can mean the beginning of awareness and action. By directing federal funds into a city or county planning department, the state historic preservation office gets the ball rolling. In 1984 the National Park Service, the source of federal funds for state preservation operations, began a program with each state to establish Certified Local Governments, which can take over responsibilities for site identification. To qualify, communities must enforce local and state preservation laws, conduct surveys, maintain an inventory of sites, and establish a landmarks commission staffed by a historic preservation planner. By the end of 1988, fifty-eight Certified Local Governments had been named in the ten moun-

tain and plains states. North Dakota had none; all others had at least two. Participating communities must match the state's funding.

Through the Certified Local Government program, the Montana preservation office assisted Bozeman with funding for a survey—its first—in 1983. A local architect, Don McLaughlin, encouraged the city to fund the survey and helped with its direction. During several months of work, eighty volunteers identified 3000 historically significant buildings. As a result, eight separate districts were nominated to the National Register of Historic Places, and forty individual properties as well, including many of the buildings on Bozeman's main street. With an additional grant from the State Historic Preservation Office, the Bozeman planning office was able to produce an illustrated brochure depicting and describing more than 100 of the area's most important historical sites. Bozeman preservationists organize occasional special tours of the town, and they hope that the city will eventually adopt an ordinance to protect historic buildings. These first steps are tentative, but at the very least Bozeman preservationists have begun to build an appreciation for the city's architectural heritage.

As time goes on, research on the region's architecture becomes more sophisticated and increasingly integrated into the larger body of American cultural history. Recently the University of Iowa published *The Spirit of H. H. Richardson on the Midland Prairies*, which served as a catalog for an exhibition. The book explores the popularity of Richardson's work in the heartland, particularly notable in county courthouses and railroad stations, and traces the adaptability of the region's stone as a building material for a nationally prominent style. Many of the buildings shown in the book are now demolished, but a sizable number remain. The Richardsonian focus offers a unifying theme for evaluating and enjoying the institutional buildings of the midlands and plains and at the same time links them with national and European influences.

In 1980, Tulsa's Junior League published a

4.14   *Bozeman, Montana's Bon Ton neighborhood was one of several surveyed by the city's preservation office and a corps of volunteers in 1983. The district includes classic vine-covered cottages, shown here, as well as substantial homes belonging to Bozeman's nineteenth-century merchant princes.*

4.15   *One of the upper-class homes in the Bon Ton neighborhood of Bozeman, Montana.*

4.16   Tulsa's twentieth-century buildings were showcased by the Junior League in a stunning book, Tulsa Art Deco, published in 1980. The Public Service Building (1929) joins Gothic arches with Deco styling in a streamlining of traditional motifs. The office buildings to the left display bands of bright terra cotta, used widely in Tulsa during this era.

4.17   The Oklahoma Natural Gas Building (1928), constructed during Tulsa's rise as an energy capital, makes the best of both worlds. Traditional materials and rich patterns arranged in a worldly, vertical pattern identify this structure as an up-to-date urbane building that has stood the test of time.

4.18 *Individual scholars, architects, and laymen have contributed a wealth of information on historic buildings through research and publications. A recent exhibition and book,* The Spirit of H. H. Richardson on the Midland Prairies, *presents the influence of the Boston architect on such buildings as the Minnehaha County Courthouse in Sioux Falls and on this commercial building of sandstone in Hot Springs, South Dakota. Courtesy James L. Ballard, National Trust for Historic Preservation*

well-documented and beautifully illustrated history and survey of the city's Deco and Moderne buildings, a book entitled *Tulsa Art Deco: An Architectural Era, 1925–1942*. Using the slick, sophisticated graphics made famous by *Vogue* and other elegant magazines of the thirties, the league produced a book as eye-catching as Tulsa's twentieth-century architecture, rich in color and detail. Carefully researched and photographed, the city's modern architecture is being "seen" for the first time by many Tulsans who live with it, as well as by students of architecture across the country. By producing this exceptional volume on Tulsa's modern architectural heritage, the Junior League has elevated the importance of these buildings within the city and placed them within a national

context. The book is a celebration as well as a survey, and it serves as an uncommon tribute to Tulsa's distinctive architectural heritage.

Another important player in historic survey work has been the federal government, which owns vast percentages of land in the mountain states: 37 percent of Montana, 33 percent of Colorado, 51 percent of Wyoming, and 34 percent of New Mexico. The largest landholding agencies—the Bureau of Land Management, National Park Service, Forest Service, and Bureau of Reclamation—regularly conduct surveys, primarily of archeological material but of historic sites as well. The National Park Service also is heavily involved in researching, maintaining, and interpreting sites for the public.

4.19 Formerly the First National Bank of Montana (1886; architects: Hodgson, Wallingford and Stem of St. Paul), this polychromatic granite and sandstone building on Last Chance Gulch in Helena is one of the finest Richardsonian structures in the West.

With all of these operations in motion, funded by government agencies at all levels as well as by private organizations, surveys in the West have produced a staggering amount of material that can be used by preservationists to protect and promote historic sites. The state historic preservation offices draw upon the surveys to identify significant sites for nomination to the National Register of Historic Places, a status that accords national recognition and a degree of protection. Listing on the register often brings a great political advantage locally to historic districts, and particularly to residential neighborhoods. Many older neighborhoods suffered through repeated zoning battles in the 1960s and 1970s, when commercial interests started creeping beyond the confines of downtown. Historic district designation gives neighborhoods something to rally around, a stamp of approval and importance that has helped to stabilize them.

State preservation offices act as a watchdog on projects directed, funded, or licensed by federal agencies that might have an adverse effect on historic sites, including archeological material. The agencies themselves have the responsibility for identification of the resources and assessment of effects. If, for example, the Bureau of Reclamation intends to build a dam, or a state highway department proposes construction of a road using federal funds, the agency is required to review all available information about nationally significant historic sites in the vicinity of the project. Often, additional survey work is required. This compliance process is known as "a Section 106," referring to Section 106 of the amended National Historic Preservation Act passed by Congress in 1966. In each instance, the state preservation officers work with the agencies to make certain that important historic sites are not overlooked, damaged, or destroyed.

Beginning in the late 1970s, listing on the National Register enabled income-producing properties to become eligible for generous federal tax incentives. This program, too, is administered by the state preservation offices. Owners with qualifying buildings who follow U.S. Department of the Interior guidelines for renovation are allowed tax credits of up to 20 percent (25 percent before the legislation was amended in 1986), an incentive that generated a great deal of preservation activity in the West's downtowns during the early 1980s. To encourage rehabilitation of historic properties, state preservation offices assist individual owners and municipal governments in listing single buildings as well as entire downtown districts on the National Register. All told, the improvements in residential neighborhoods and commercial buildings over the past decade or more have provided state preservation offices with satisfying hands-on results for their survey work and successful National Register nominations.

Until the 1970s, preservation activity tended to concentrate on single landmarks. As the surveys got underway and attention began to focus on entire historic districts and communities, an important critical mass began to develop. Designation of a district enlarges a community's thinking about historic architecture, making people realize that a tangible legacy from the past can include the ordinary as well as the exceptional. Because the intact districts are likely to include examples of twentieth-century buildings (much of the nineteenth-century architecture is already lost or exists as separated, scattered sites), a greater enthusiasm for relatively recent buildings has begun to develop. For many people, the connections with the past are growing and strengthening because of this broader scope.

For the survey teams, and the public as well, looking at large, collective areas resulted in an increasingly sophisticated understanding of context, scale, and the continuum of history. Recording the tangible evidence of community life and preserving it as a coherent whole became one of the goals of preservation. Studying and saving a neighborhood was accepted as a greater good than singling out a Queen Anne mansion or a Greek Revival bank. The research tended to be more revealing of a region's history, and the preservation process benefited a larger constituency.

4.20   J. Riely Gordon designed many court-houses in Texas, including this one for Wise County in Decatur. Built in 1895, the pink granite structure followed the Romanesque Revival style associated with Richardson. Courtesy Myron Wood

4.21   The late nineteenth century was a magnificent era for courthouses. This brick and stone county seat in Marysville, Kansas, also reflects H. H. Richardson's influence. Courtesy Kansas State Historical Society

4.22 *Ethnic groups from northern and east-ern Europe immigrated to Nebraska and the Dakotas in waves during the last two decades of the nineteenth century and the early years of the twentieth. They created their own commu-nities and enclaves, many of which have now been studied and surveyed by state historic pres-ervation offices. The Kounovsky House in rural Knox County is a traditional Czech house from that period. Courtesy D. Murphy*

The Vernacular Legacy

In the West, and particularly on the Great Plains, the lessons learned in the cities about multiple sites—residential neighborhoods, indus-trial areas, downtowns, and warehouse districts—were put to good use out in the countryside. The state preservation survey teams began to en-counter settlement clusters over large areas, some-times entire counties and beyond, which had been founded by immigrant groups. These people had adapted the buildings of their countries of origin to the circumstances of the isolated mountains and plains of North America.

By the late 1970s, South Dakota's preserva-tion surveyors were coming upon a unique legacy of German Russians and Czechs who had settled a century earlier in the eastern portion of the state.

4.23   Immigrant groups built churches that expressed their special traditions. This Czech church in rural Colfax County, Nebraska, Our Lady of Perpetual Help (1918), was constructed by Rudy Basta, a local Czech carpenter. The church is one of many Czech buildings recorded by Nebraska's historic preservation office. Courtesy D. Murphy

As these immigrants built houses and outbuildings on the prairie, they replicated the familiar forms of their homeland, using the materials at hand. The Czechs built with chalk rock cut from deposits along the Missouri River and with earth materials, including puddled clay. The German Russians employed puddled clay built up in layers, rammed earth (puddled clay poured and packed into vertical forms), and a variation of adobe called "batsa,"

which was substantially laced with vegetation and manure. Typically, the earthen bricks were used to form the top level of a puddled clay wall. These earth and stone structures, whose origins are in medieval Europe, are found throughout the Dakotas, Nebraska, Kansas, and Oklahoma.

The German–Russian settlements in southeastern South Dakota resembled the Czech enclaves in many respects. Most dwellings were

4.24 *This rammed earth house in Hutchinson County, South Dakota, was part of a German-Russian settlement documented by the state's historic preservation office. Courtesy State Historical Preservation Center, South Dakota Department of Education and Cultural Affairs*

built of rammed earth, but some were made of kiln-dried or adobe brick. The German Russians covered the walls inside and out with stucco made from ground limestone or clay mixed with manure. Thatched roofs sheltered the earliest homes.

In the southeastern South Dakota homes built by Mennonites, a separate religious group within the German–Russian immigrant population, a large oven occupied the center of the house. Made of brick and built directly into the partition walls, the large oven narrowed at the top to form a chimney. Fueled with straw or manure, the ovens were used for heating and for smoking meats

and baking bread. When they could afford it, most settlers substituted enclosed manufactured cookstoves for these "Russian ovens."

By tracing the origins of these buildings and trading information with colleagues from adjoining states, the South Dakota surveyors have established a history of German–Russian and Czech settlement. When the field teams first began to record rammed earth and chalk rock and adobe houses and barns nearly twenty years ago, however, they had little published information to rely on. They recorded what they found, talked with the people who lived in the buildings (some buildings were abandoned), and then examined the

4.25   *Immigrant groups built with the materials at hand. This chalk rock house was constructed by German-Russian immigrants in the Sunshine Bottom settlement of Boyd County, Nebraska. Courtesy D. Murphy*

4.26 *German-Russians settled in several counties south of Bismarck, North Dakota, where they built farmsteads of adobe, wood, and stone. This home is a variation of a "long house" commonly seen in this region. The little porch in front—a* vorhausel—*has decorative shingle siding and a chamfered roof and walls. The North Dakota preservation office began studying German-Russian settlements in the late 1970s as part of the state's survey. Courtesy J. Sluss, State Historical Society of North Dakota*

4.27 *A vorhausel with multicolored siding in McIntosh County, North Dakota. Courtesy J. Sluss, State Historical Society of North Dakota*

4.28 *A second and larger building type used by German-Russians was the square house, which usually had dormerlike caps over the windows at the roof's edge. Here the vorhausel has been removed, exposing the stone construction. Courtesy J. Sluss, State Historical Society of North Dakota*

4.29 *A sun-dried earth-brick house in Emmons County, North Dakota. Rather than using a mud plaster or stucco covering, German-Russians sometimes overlaid the bricks with wooden siding. Courtesy J. Sluss, State Historical Society of North Dakota*

4.30 *These abandoned fieldstone outbuild-*
ings in rural North Dakota appear to have had
roofs of packed earth. Courtesy State Historical
Society of North Dakota

printed histories of these immigrant groups. For these research projects, the surveyors themselves were pioneers.

In Nebraska, late in the nineteenth century, incoming German–Russian immigrants initially remained loyal to traditional building methods when they settled in Sunshine Bottom along the flats of the Missouri River near the South Dakota border. When David Murphy, historical architect for Nebraska's preservation office, surveyed this German–Russian settlement in 1977, he found that the immigrant homesteaders had attempted to recreate a traditional European linear village, concentrating their farm buildings at the narrow end of long 160-acre homestead tracts. At Sunshine Bottom, Murphy found several long houses—multiple rooms built in a row—of adobe brick, chalk rock, or limestone, similar to the German–Russian dwellings of the Dakotas. He

uncovered no rammed earth buildings, however, nor any evidence of grass-burning Russian ovens. These Nebraska settlers, after a first stage of construction using native materials and traditional forms, turned to frame construction of milled lumber, the dominant midwestern and plains farm vernacular by the late nineteenth century.

In North Dakota, the German–Russian settlement came later—between 1890 and 1920—and still exists, although many of the homesteads are now abandoned. These settlers, too, followed traditional building forms, using a variety of local materials. Their dwellings generally were of two simple types: long houses and square houses. Typically, the long house had three rooms, with the kitchen in the center and a living room and bedroom on either side. A loft above was entered through an outside stairway on the gable end, similar to the little "Sunday houses" in Fredericksburg, Texas, which also have German origins. The chimney was placed in the center of the house, servicing the kitchen. Builders sometimes doubled the size of the long houses by adding a parallel set of rooms alongside the first row and then enlarging the loft accordingly.

Adobe dwellings and outbuildings have long been at the heart of New Mexico's folk architecture, a tradition going back many hundreds of years. A recent survey of Mora Valley in northeastern New Mexico by the state preservation office reveals an interesting similarity to houses built by German–Russian settlers on the northern plains. Originally organized around defensive plazas, the Mora settlement was later rebuilt as a linear village running parallel to the Mora River, which supplied water to the *acequias,* or irrigation ditches. A common dwelling type during the late nineteenth century was a single-room house built of adobe brick and covered with a pitched metal roof. The attic was accessed from the outside by a wooden ladder. This similarity to German–Russian house types may be merely coincidence, it may connect to a common origin in European folk architecture, or it may result from the appearance in the Mora Valley in the 1870s of German merchants who adapted the Hispanic folk building tradition to meet their own commercial needs in a way customary to them. As more field evidence is compared by state preservation offices and is studied by the growing number of experts in plains vernacular building, the evolution of traditional forms will be revealed along with the cumulative and collective experiences of the builders.

The states with fertile prairie farmland, from eastern North Dakota to Texas, have a rich legacy of frame construction in addition to the folk expressions of earth, log, and stone that have intrigued the survey teams. Even on the High Plains and in the Rockies, frame barns and houses were occasional if not common, especially on the larger ranches. These more familiar building types form an equally important part of the region's rural vernacular architecture.

The eastern portion of the plains states, an area with timber stands or access to them, supported a tradition of log building, as did the tree-covered Rocky Mountains. During a historic preservation survey of southeastern Wyoming ranches in the late 1980s, architectural historian Eileen Starr discovered several large log barns quite markedly different from the long, low, log buildings typically found in Wyoming. Her research revealed them to be *piece sur piece* construction, a French method consisting of horizontally stacked square-hewn logs held in place by a vertical corner or connecting log. A flange on the end of each horizontal log fits into a channel cut into the corner post. These substantial buildings, reaching 150 feet in length and a height of two stories, were crafted by Scandinavian "tie hacks" who cut wooden ties for the railroads. The seven barns in this Wyoming cluster were erected between 1880 and 1910 and were commissioned by wealthy ranchers from England or the American East.

Because much of the nineteenth-century western architectural heritage is fragile, surveyors have taken pains to document it, but the more recent examples of the West's historic handiwork are now getting the attention they deserve. Oklahoma preservationists are looking at twentieth-century oil sites as well as WPA projects from the 1930s. Kansas architectural historian Martha Hagedorn-Krass has surveyed Depression Era post office art and will publish an illustrated book on the subject. In Oklahoma and New Mexico, preservationists are working with government agencies and private citizens to study and promote the material culture along "Route 66," the celebrated mid-century highway that carried Americans to California and back, a sort of modern alternative to the Santa Fe and Escalante trails.

Surveying historic resources and nominating the most significant sites to the National Register has occupied the states' historic preservation offices for the past two decades. To the degree that budgets and schedules allow, they share their discoveries through regular and occasional publications. The bimonthly newsletter *Kansas Preserva-*

4.31　*Wyoming surveyors found several un-usually large log barns in the southeastern corner of the state. The construction technique is the French* piece sur piece, *in which a flange is cut on the horizontal log and then inserted into a channel cut into the vertical corner and connecting logs. Courtesy Richard Collier, Wyoming Department of ARchives, Museums, and History*

4.32　*Close-up of log barn construction. Courtesy Richard Collier; Wyoming Department of Archives, Museums, and History*

4.33   *Art of the depression era has been studied by architectural historian Martha Hagedorn-Krass for the Kansas survey. This threshing scene, painted by Iowa artist Dorothea Tomlinson in 1938, is in the U.S. Post Office in Hoisington, Kansas. Courtesy Kansas State Historical Society*

tion brings information about the state's historical and archeological sites to more than 2500 readers. Nebraska's preservation office produces *Cornerstone*, an illustrated quarterly newsletter mailed to about 7000 individuals and organizations, most of them within the state. Nebraska also publishes illustrated reports of its ongoing survey, which by 1989 had documented 37,000 properties in more than two-thirds of the state's ninety-three counties. Cherry County—ranch and cattle country—in the Sand Hills region is the subject of a 230-page report issued in 1989. The report describes the region's history and presents the most significant examples of sites and structures, which are organized around "historic contexts," such as education, government, transportation, and agriculture. The illustrations include nine handsome hay barns, a ca. 1950 drive-in theater, five iron-truss bridges, and a two-story stone bank built in 1887 in the town of Valentine. These reconnaissance reports are sent to policy and opinion makers throughout the state: libraries, legislators, government agencies, chambers of commerce, historical societies, and individuals who are consid-

4.34   *Because of the sharp decline in the farm population during the past thirty years, many abandoned country buildings, such as this store east of Helena, Montana, have little chance of survival. The federally funded state surveys have made a vitally important record of these fragile structures, which may be all that remains of many of them in the long run.*

ered part of the preservation constituency.

David Murphy, deputy preservation officer for Nebraska, believes his department is reaching a substantially larger audience each year, primarily through its publications. He considers this communications work a strong beginning. "We've only been at this for about fifteen years. Compared to the East, we've only gotten started. But there aren't enough people here yet who are working on preservation. We have too few professionals in the field and too few academics doing research." Murphy's observation—that the staffs are spread

thin and the geographical scope is daunting—is shared by other mountains and plains preservation officers.

The Texas Historical Commission, too, issues a newsletter—*The Medallion*, a monthly preservation publication with feature articles on thematic topics, such as the state's restored movie palaces, as well as news briefs and announcements. The commission mails about 1500 copies each month to subscribers and distributes several hundred more to legislators, state agencies, and others who determine or carry out public policy related to preservation. Texas historic sites reach a larger audience indirectly through publications of the departments of tourism, highways, and parks.

Getting more information about historic sites off the shelves and into the hands of the public is the next big challenge for historic preservation offices. Increased media attention, especially television, can quickly build audience numbers from thousands to millions.

Searching Out the Past

Historic buildings capture attention whether or not an official survey is in place. Many people independently set out to study the architectural legacy of an area, and they are usually inclined to share what they learn with others. Some of the most revealing material available on the West's historic buildings has come from individual writers and photographers who have gone out on their own to document the past.

Photographer Robert Adams traveled through eastern Colorado during the 1960s, recording vernacular churches. Presented in *White Churches of the Plains*, his photographs portray dazzlingly bright little frame churches seen against the brilliance of the sky and the starkness of the land. Traveling through a region where homesteading had failed, Adams was well aware that these fragile buildings had only a tenuous hold on the present. What does the future hold? Without sufficiently large congregations to sustain them, they will be burned or scavanged or, at best, sold and moved. There may come a time when Adams's book is the only reminder we have of a pioneer era of church building in eastern Colorado. Adams pulls together scattered, isolated houses of worship and shows us how they reflect early twentieth century life on these high, dry plains. Two goals are

achieved: he shares his discovery and he makes a permanent record of it.

Working within a larger area but with similar material, Arn Henderson, professor of architecture at the University of Oklahoma, has undertaken a field study of vernacular architecture on the southern Great Plains. Beginning in the early 1980s during vacations and a sabbatical leave, Henderson has driven through the rural landscape of western Oklahoma, Kansas, and Texas, and eastern New Mexico and Colorado looking for structures associated with nineteenth-century settlement and on through the early part of the twentieth century.

Having been stymied in his first attempts in the field by not being able to find many buildings in the deserted expanses of the Great Plains, Henderson developed a pattern of stopping in the nearest town and talking with those residents who regularly drive out in the countryside, such as the veterinarian, county extension agent, sheriff, mailcarrier, or propane delivery man. In many communities, Henderson is referred to the local historian, someone who has become interested in geneology, or someone who collects material about the area and who, perhaps, has written a thin volume of anectdotal history. In an hour or two of conversation, Henderson learns who settled the area and finds out where the interesting and important buildings can be found.

Henderson approaches the plains from the perspective of a cultural geographer, mindful of the area's economic circumstances, transporation modes, climate, landscape, and the ethnic origins of the settlers. While examining examples of vernacular architecture, he tries to decipher which cultural variables determine the actual form of the building. Does a particular barn express the creative legacy of the builder or does it reflect the special circumstances of the area, or both? Henderson will publish his findings in an illustrated book on Great Plains vernacular.

Another Southwest architect, Beverley Spears, authored a recent book on adobe houses in northern New Mexico, a tradition that combines Span-

4.35   Searching out old buildings in the isolation of the Great Plains has its rewards, and one of them is the sudden discovery of gracefully styled buildings when something far less elegant would have done the job. Architect Arn Henderson found this barn in Osborne County, Kansas. Courtesy Arn Henderson

4.36   In the great wheatlands of the West, elevators and storage bins are found in every little town and sometimes far out in the country. For his study of southern plains architecture, Arn Henderson photographed this grain elevator in Silica, Kansas. Courtesy Arn Henderson

4.37 *This simple adobe house in Llano, New Mexico, was one of many vernacular houses studied recently by Santa Fe architect Beverley Spears. The pitched roof is covered with metal, a material commonly used on buildings in northern New Mexico. Courtesy Beverley Spears*

ish colonial and American influences to produce a unique regional building form. These folk expressions, although they appear timeless and lasting, constitute a fragile heritage that is disappearing. Spears's book depicts the common house types of northern New Mexico and examines the evolution and diffusion of their important features—portals, dormers, and doors—as well as the decorative details, such as post brackets, that give them individual character.

The material culture and customs of Hispanic villages in New Mexico are subjects for study by photographer Nancy Hunter Warren. Her recent book, *Villages of Hispanic New Mexico*, includes architecture, cultural landscape, and patterns of work and domestic life. Warren successfully illustrates the integration of environment and community life in Hispanic villages—the chopping of wood for fuel, the celebration of Catholic feast days, the maintenance of communal irrigation systems, and other activities both daily and special.

The exemplar of field research, study, and writing on the subject of New Mexico's folk architecture is the late Bainbridge Bunting, whose highly readable works, *Early Architecture in New*

4.38 *Architect Beverley Spears's survey of dwellings in northern New Mexico includes this symmetrical Territorial style house in the Mora Valley. Her research reveals the house to be more than 100 years old; the pitched metal roof was added in the 1970s. Courtesy Beverley Spears*

Mexico and *Taos Adobes: Spanish Colonial and Territorial Architecture of the Taos Valley* have become classics for all students of historic architecture in the Southwest. He has inspired others to go into the field to make a record of the region's buildings, particularly those isolated and vernacular structures that are rapidly disappearing.

A similar result has been achieved by cultural geographer Terry Jordan in *Texas Log Buildings*, which traces the evolution of log construction in Texas from its European and American beginnings. His observations are organized around five different cultural regions in the state, each ex-

hibiting great variety in roof types, chimneys, log notching, and porches. By examining one simple feature of log construction—"chinking"—he discovered fascinating variety. A chink is the space between logs; filling it makes a building snug and dry. In east Texas, chinks were filled with wedged boards. In northeast Texas they were plastered. The German settlers of the Texas Hill Country left unusually wide chinks to be filled with stone and mortar. To the south, in a German settlement with influences from France and Switzerland, buildings had no chinks at all; the logs were perfectly joined.

4.39 Scholars working independently have added a great wealth of material to the ongoing survey of western historic sites. Cultural geographer Terry Jordan of Texas University has studied the state's endangered and disappearing log structures. An example of this threatened legacy is the Asa Hoxey Home (1833) in Washington County, Texas, one of the largest log buildings in the state. Courtesy Texas Historical Commission

Jordan observed that log dwellings were often built in stages: first, a primitive cabin of logs, covered with bark—small, windowless, and hastily built. Later, with more time and money to spend, an owner constructed a proper house of hewn (square-cut) logs with plank floors, windows, and a masonry chimney. Jordan notes that these houses were usually built by itinerant carpenters and masons, not by amateur owners, a reminder that our commonly held view of the self-sufficent pioneer may be a romantic, erroneous notion.

Jordan has found that the rich variety of Texas log construction techniques extended to public buildings as well as houses. Texans built courthouses, schools, jails, stores, and churches of logs. Farm log outbuildings included corncribs, smokehouses, sheds, granaries, barns, chicken coops, and summer kitchens. In west Texas, ranchers built low log buildings with gently sloping sod roofs, a type commonly found as well throughout the Rocky Mountain ranch country.

Noting that log buildings are fast disappear-

4.40   *The El Capote Cabin (ca. 1838) is typical of log structures erected while Texas was a republic. The cabin was originally located in Gonzales County in south Texas and is now part of the Ranching Heritage Center at Texas Tech University. Courtesy Texas Tech University Museum*

ing from the Texas countryside, Jordan calls for a restoration program of selected log structures. The fieldwork that he and others have compiled in the Texas Log Cabin Register provides the documentation needed to stabilize and restore what he considers to be "a priceless and beautiful legacy of folk architecture."

A plea for preservation has been similarly made by two women in central Kansas writing about the heritage of stone buildings and features in that region. Grace Mullenburg and Ada Swineford in

Land of the Post Rock examine the extensive use of limestone in the Kansas Smoky Hills. Blessed with readily available stone quarries and outcroppings, the Kansas countryside holds a treasure trove of simple stone buildings that complement a quiet landscape dominated by wooded creek bottoms and grass-covered hills whose colors change with the seasons. Throughout rural Kansas are churches, stores, post offices, homes, barns, sheds, and schools made of stone. There are stone bridges and walls, and even fences made of stone, hence

4.41   *When nineteenth-century settlers ar-*
rived in central Kansas, surface quarries of
limestone were abundant and timber was
scarce. Enterprising homesteaders and ranchers
made posts of rock instead of wood to hold barbed
wire. Preservation-minded Kansans have been
identifying and documenting this heritage.
Courtesy Kansas State Historical Society

the "post rock" name given the territory. Early examples of stone architecture in the post rock country include the simplest of farm sheds as well as the elaborate Cathedral of the Plains in Victoria near Hays in the north-central part of the state. This large Romanesque-style church was built by Germans from Russia who settled on nearby farms. British and Czech immigrants joined the large German colony in central Kansas, bringing with them impressive masonry skills.

Because they are aware that the Kansas stone heritage is a valuable regional resource, several county historical societies have organized museums and are collecting local materials on early settlers and their stone buildings. The University of Kansas in the mid-seventies sponsored a survey, printed an illustrated catalog, and mounted an exhibition entitled "Architecture of the Great American Desert," presenting a geographical analysis of the environment and buildings. Students in the preservation program at Kansas State University in Manhattan have also done surveys of the region's stone buildings.

One cannot study rural buildings without paying attention to the land. The setting, the climate, and the vegetation are all part of the collective

4.42   The limestone post office building in Ogallah, Kansas. Both limestone and sandstone deposits are common in Kansas, with colors ranging from white to a rusty brown. Courtesy Kansas State Historical Society

circumstances that give meaning to the buildings. What were the builders' hopes and purposes? What control over the land did they achieve with their buildings? Were the buildings a reprieve from the land—a shelter—or a practical means to economic gain? What did the setting dictate? What resources did the builders bring? In the long run, did it work out? Students of rural vernacular continually ask these questions, whether they are examining a house in the highlands of New Mexico or a frame barn in central Kansas.

Looking at the cultural landscape of south-central Nebraska from the perspective of a horti-culturist, professor Richard Sutton has traced the evolution of plantings and buildings, and of such features as roads and reservoirs, in the Webster County environs of Willa Cather's hometown, Red Cloud, Nebraska. The circumstances he describes are not peculiar to Webster County but could be found in large parts of the midwestern prairie. He describes subtle but significant changes through time. The introduction of gray-green russian olive trees as windbreaks, for example, has created a new form and palette on the originally treeless prairie. The replacement of large wooden barns by flat metal storage sheds and the shift

4.43   *This stone barn near Topeka, Kansas, is
believed to have been built in 1868. In addition
to stalls for cattle and bins for storage, the barn
has a large central threshing area. Courtesy
Bern Ketchum, Topeka-Shawnee County
Kansas Metropolitan Planning Commission*

from two- or three-story homes to low, ranch-style houses has gradually changed the traditional vertical lines of prairie farm buildings to a more horizontal picture, just as silos, curving highways, and center-pivot irrigation systems have moved the landscape away from the strict rectilinear patterns of the past. Field crops have replaced native prairie, and Nebraska pastureland today contains dams and reservoirs, a dramatic interruption of traditional creeks and streams.

Sutton describes these changes as the adaptation of a pastoral landscape to an industrial one, positive for the most part and inevitable in any case. But if one values the prairie landscape of Willa Cather's writings, then some interventions are in order. Sutton mentions the acquisition of scenic easements as one possibility and encourages the collaboration of landowners with state and local organizations to protect those landscape features—groves, pastures, country lanes, buildings, and hedges—that were a part of Cather's fictional accounts of life in pioneer Nebraska. Sutton is able to make these recommendations because he knows this landscape, having examined and studied it. Again, we circle back to survey—the first step in preservation.

5.1   *The Pikes Peak Grange Hall north of Colorado Springs, Colorado. The National Grange was a nineteenth-century movement of farmers who lobbied for regulation of railroads and agricultural monopolies.*

CHAPTER FIVE

Rural Preservation: Farm, Ranch, and Village Life

A s an organized effort to save buildings, the historic preservation movement in the West's rural areas is just beginning. Even during the short period of the past decade, however, many successful and gratifying projects have been launched. It has been a late start but a lively one, with promise of more to come.

Much of the mountains and plains West is now surveyed—not yet all, but a significant portion—yielding a record of rural structures that had been previously unstudied, even unknown. This gain of knowledge has helped to offset the dismal realization that the West's continuing rural population exodus spells a slow death for many homesteads, ranches, and villages on the Great Plains and for similar settlements in the valleys of the Rocky Mountains. This agricultural revolution, with its aftermath of abandonment, cannot be stopped. The strategies for preservation must therefore take into account the peculiar contradictions that exist for the rural sites that are now identified: many will be lost to the neglect of isolation, others will succumb to the pressures of urban expansion.

Today there are far fewer ranches and farms in this country, and fewer people are needed to run them. In 1950 the farm population nationwide stood at 24 million; by 1985 the number had fallen to 5 million. Agricultural statistics for the Great Plains and Rockies tell a similar story. Montana lost 17 percent of its agricultural population during the 1970s. In Nebraska at the turn of the century, 76 percent of the population lived

5.2 *A ranch near the Sangre de Cristo Mountains north of Westcliffe, Colorado.*

in a rural setting compared to 37 percent in 1980. Since the 1930s, the state has lost half of its farms. In Wyoming between 1975 and 1980, the number of hired hands riding the state's 30.2 million acres of rangeland declined from 6000 to 4000. For black farmers in the South, the changes have been devastating: Texas had nearly 86,000 black farmers in 1930; forty years later there were barely more than 3000. Farmland itself is being displaced at a rate of 1 to 2 million acres a year nationally, giving way to new highways, subdivisions, shopping malls, industry, airports, and energy development.

Why this dramatic change? In a land of plenty, where are the ranchers and farmers? Aided by machinery, a smaller number of people are doing the same amount of work, and more. Farms and ranches therefore have been getting larger as corporations combine separate properties formerly operated by several families. At the same time, "ranchettes" of five to twenty acres are becoming more common, occupied by owners who are retired or who work in nearby towns. But the mid-size, family-operated farm is fast disappearing. The original Homestead Act allotments of 160 acres, increased later to 320, were never a practical size for successful farming in the dry West, and many of these small tracts were incorporated into large ranches early in this century. Much of the nineteenth-century rural settlement was doomed from the start, and the shakeout began early.

The good news from the country emanates from two quite different approaches to preservation. One is longstanding stewardship: owners of ranches and farms taking care of their buildings over a period of decades, maintaining and repairing them as the need arises. This method is actually the more important of the two because the original form and fabric stays in place. The second approach is rehabilitation: owners of distressed buildings investing the time and money to improve both structure and appearance. With either approach, most historic property owners have had to adapt their buildings to meet technological changes in ranching and farming. An early log house, turned later into a bunkhouse, becomes a tool shed, or an obsolete and neglected hay barn is transformed into a garage for large machinery.

During the past ten or twelve years, a few rural sites have moved into the public realm, acquired by government agencies or nonprofit organizations and made accessible to visitors. Even though several of these properties are associated with a prominent person (this phase of rural preservation is much like the earlier approaches to house museums, i.e., a concentration on the homes and lives of affluent rather than ordinary citizens), they are being presented to visitors within a larger context of basic western themes. The LBJ Ranch near Austin, Texas, tells the story of settlement in the surrounding Hill Country as well as the family history of the nation's thirty-sixth president. In western Montana, the Grant-Kohrs Ranch—once the state's largest and most powerful—interprets the early trail-driving and roundup phase of western ranching and also the evolution of ranch operations throughout this century. On North Dakota's prairie, the birthplace of band leader Lawrence Welk serves as an example of the folk architecture built by German–Russian immigrants at the turn of the century. Through these agricultural sites, visitors can get a close look at a particular farm or ranch and at the same time understand its workings within a larger picture.

This insistence on context—as opposed to settling for isolated sites and historical fragments—is also reflected in the increasing interest in the cultural landscape, which is emerging as a major preservation issue of the nineties just as urban districts were the focus fifteen years ago. The move toward a comprehensive approach to rural preservation requires a sophisticated model for political action. Private owners, government agencies, and nonprofit groups are learning to work together on complicated projects. These new collaborations, in their move away from single-vision, single-ownership properties, are regenerating western history as well as invigorating the locales of the historic properties.

Private owners, however, still carry the greatest burden of preservation. Although the West is awash with ephemeral, abandoned sites, there are encouraging examples of continuity and care. To reward historic property owners and to increase awareness of the West's historic rural buildings and settings, recognition programs have been put in place. The stewards of the region's tangible agricultural legacy deserve attention, and—more and more—they are getting it.

Although great physical distances and the stasis caused by separation still tend to keep western historic enclaves isolated from the mainstream of preservation activity, the ease with which people can communicate today by telephone and facsimile machines helps to energize and organize even the most remote preservation group. No longer does anyone have to start from scratch and struggle through all the organizational steps by trial and error. The Strasburg, North Dakota, group of volunteers working on Lawrence Welk's German–Russian birthplace has been able to exchange ideas with restoration architects, historians, government agencies, foundations, fund raisers, and other preservation enablers who can help to organize a project of quality and substance. Access to this resource network doesn't mean that the project is easy, just that it's possible.

5.3   At the end of the nineteenth century, large corporate farms, tens of thousands of acres each, were established in eastern North Dakota's fertile Red River Valley. This abandoned building was the main house of the Bagg "bonanza" farm southwest of Fargo. Courtesy Susan Holland, State Historical Society of North Dakota

5.4   The hay barn and machine sheds on the Bagg Farm. Courtesy Susan Holland, State Historical Society of North Dakota

The knowledge gained from years of hands-on preservation work is being recycled as it is needed.

But the question still remains. Will we lose the ranch? There is room for hope that it can be saved. A rural strategy has yet to be conceived, but entrepreneurial and caring citizens in the mountains and plains have begun to stem the region's architectural and cultural losses.

Western Ranches: *The Private Commitment to Conservation*

WYOMING: THE TOM SUN RANCH

The Tom Sun family ranch in central Wyoming, which now stretches northwest from Rawlins for nearly a hundred miles, began as a small hunting camp along the Sweetwater River. Several historic overland routes cross the property: the Oregon Trail, the Mormon Trail, and the Pony Express. The ranch headquarters are spread out next to a famous Oregon Trail landmark, Devil's Gate, a cloven granite outcropping through which the Sweetwater River flows.

The Sun Ranch headquarters presents a three-dimensional picture of the past. For more than a century, the ranch has been worked by a single family, descendents of Tom Sun (De Beau Soleil), a young runaway born in Vermont of French Canadian parents who went west to trap furs and then, after the Civil War, became a guide to United States troops patrolling the Oregon Trail. Sun became friends with Buffalo Bill Cody, who, when he traveled around the country with his Wild West Show, sent wealthy eastern hunters back to Tom Sun's small claim along the Sweetwater. Thus, the ranch began as an outfitting headquarters for hunting parties, with Tom Sun as guide. In 1877 Sun started raising cattle. Prices

and winters both were punishing. As a sideline, Sun prospected for gold, successfully filing for and then selling a claim in the Seminole Mountains for $20,000.

In 1883, Sun met and married Mary Hellihan, a young Irish woman working for the Union Pacific Railroad in Rawlins. The newlyweds lived in a one-story, whitewashed log house, which still stands at the heart of the ranch headquarters on a large shaded lawn surrounded by a rail fence. A later wing housed a cook's kitchen and a dining room, built to accommodate the hired help. A long, low, overhanging roof, in the style of a New Mexico portal, shelters a walkway across the front of the house. In 1882 a Wyoming newspaper, *The Cheyenne Leader*, applauded Sun's log house as a showplace: ". . . planed boards, large windows, artistic effects in whitewash and deerhorn decorations have assisted in giving it a style hardly expected in that far-off region."

Many buildings on the ranch date back to the 1880s. The sod roof of a log barn from that era was replaced by a metal one years ago, but the barn still has its original dirt floor. A chicken house and blacksmith's shed—two log structures joined together—also date to the nineteenth century.

Bernard Sun, a grandson of the French Canadian guide who founded the ranch, describes its operation as "more traditional than most." The Suns have given up on cattle roundups—the last one occurred twenty years ago. "Too hard to find a cook," Sun complains. Pickup trucks have replaced saddle horses for much of the range work. There are no more teams of work horses; tractors, mowers, and automatic stackers cut and bale the hay. Wyoming ranchers keep their hay outdoors piled in stacks that look like giant bread loaves. Irrigation water runs from ditches along the Sweetwater and other streams. Windmills pump water for livestock.

Work at the ranch is much the same as it was a hundred years ago, but the Suns have found new ways of doing it. As an example, because steel posts for barbed wire fences are easy to drive into the ground, they have been substituted for

5.5 *Headquarters of the Tom Sun Ranch, one of Wyoming's oldest and largest ranches, along the Oregon Trail and the Sweetwater River near Independence Rock.*

traditional wooden posts. "Native cedar will last as long as you need," Bernard Sun says, "but it's easier to find someone to pound a post than dig a hole."

Years ago, the ranch had a meat house and two milk houses, plus an icehouse. These specialized structures, along with smokehouses and cellars, provided the only means on the frontier for food processing, storage, and refrigeration. Now the ranch uses freezers and a walk-in meat cooler.

Of all the changes during his lifetime on the family ranch, Bernard Sun minds most the loss of his neighbors. "There's no one left around here. They're all gone." Some of the small ranches in the area have been bought out by larger operations, including the Sun Ranch. On any ranch, large or small, there are fewer hired hands these days. Bernard Sun recalls that many years ago a schoolhouse stood on the property. The two older Sun children went to nearby country schools, but none remain open now. All in all, ranch life is more isolated than it once was. Although it is easier today for rural people to keep in touch with the events of the world through television, telephones, news-

5.6 *The Tom Sun Ranch cattle corrals seen against bread-loaf haystacks and Devil's Gate, a famous landmark along the Oregon Trail. The Sun family has raised cattle here for more than a hundred years.*

papers, and computers, the day-to-day life on a ranch is lonelier than ever.

The Sun family recognizes the ranch's importance to the history of Wyoming and the West. They modify buildings and change their operations when the times demand it but always with an eye to maintaining evidence of the past. Now, a new generation is taking over. After several decades of running the ranch, Bernard Sun and his three brothers are looking to several of their children to carry on the family tradition. Although there is no guarantee that the Sun Ranch will be

around for another hundred years, it is safe to say that this jewel in the crown of the Sun Land and Cattle Company is likely to survive well into the next century.

The Sun Ranch is listed on the National Register of Historic Places. As a private, working ranch, it is not open to the public. The headquarters and that portion of the ranch near Devil's Gate can be seen from a wayside overview, which is maintained by the Bureau of Land Management to acquaint the public with landmarks along the Oregon Trail.

MONTANA: THE SIEBEN SHEEP RANCH

In Montana, the Henry Sieben Ranch—like the Tom Sun in Wyoming—is a large ranch operation held by the same family for several generations and conservatively maintained. Henry Sieben bought 500 acres northeast of the capital city of Helena in 1896 and began raising sheep and cattle. Seemingly isolated, the ranch was actually a land of passages in Montana's early days. Buffalo herds grazed in the high meadows. Indians hunted and camped there—the stones of tipi rings are still evident. The Mullan Trail, which went from Fort Benton on the Missouri across the mountains to Walla Walla, Washington, cut through the ranch, as did the road that carried goods from the steamboat landing at Fort Benton to the mining districts around Helena.

A mountain ranch, the Sieben has always run more sheep than cattle. Whereas the entire live-stock industry nationwide has been erratic in recent years, problems for sheepgrowers started decades ago. John Baucus, Henry Sieben's great-grandson, estimates that there were 4 million sheep in Montana at the beginning of World War II. Now there are around 650,000. Government controls on production during the war put a permanent damper on the industry. For years, the popularity of synthetic fabrics has cut the demand for wool.

Even during good times, sheep are costly to raise. Vulnerable to weather and predators, particularly coyotes, sheep require constant watching. At the Sieben Ranch, sheepherders still live on the range, cooking and sleeping in the cylindrical wagons that have been part of western sheep ranching since the early days. The ranch provides each herder with a rifle, a horse, and a sheep dog, either an Australian shepherd or a border collie. A camp tender checks on the herders once or twice a week and brings groceries. Sieben's owners have begun to replace the old-fashioned wagons with new camper trailers, but of the eight sheepherder rigs they own, half are still the traditional originals.

Most of the frame and log buildings at the Sieben headquarters date to the 1890s and early 1900s. John Baucus lives with his family in a house that began as a one-room log cabin. A second log cabin built in the 1880s was the original ranch house. There are several other houses on the property: one for Baucus's parents, Helena residents who spend summers at the ranch; one for the foreman; one for the camp tender during the three seasons he is not up on the range looking after the sheepherders; and one for a cook. A bunkhouse is home to several hired hands.

The ranch's big hay barn, which once held 200 tons of hay, is on its last legs. Actually, it is the barn's roof rather than its underpinnings that is threatening to collapse. Designed for the days when draft horses were kept there and fed from the loft, the barn is now obsolete. "We kind of hate to see it go," John Baucus says, but he finds its repair cost—estimated at $50,000—difficult to justify. Because of their size, barns are the most troublesome of all rural structures to maintain, and they are often the least adaptable.

The ten sheep sheds of varying sizes at the Sieben Ranch headquarters are used intensively for lambing for about six weeks each spring, beginning in March. The sheds are subdivided into small pens called "jugs," where the ewe nurses her newborn. After a day or so, the new family is moved to a small pen outside and then to a larger mixing pen until they are ready to take their place in the flock.

At the Sieben Ranch, building maintenance is part of the regular rhythm of work. "We don't schedule it because we wait for rainy days when we can't be out haying. We do most of the plumbing and wiring ourselves and a lot of the roof work." The sheep sheds have metal roofs, which are the easiest to install. Some of the other buildings, such as the shop, granaries, and machine sheds, are roofed with asphalt, and the roof of the main house is shingled. "We put a new roof on something nearly every year," says Baucus.

Like all ranchers, Baucus and his family partners continually face decisions on where to invest

5.7   *This stone barn and the adjoining frame shed are part of the Frawley Ranch in western South Dakota. The ranch property was assembled from former homesteader holdings, typical of the way that many western ranches were expanded. Courtesy State Historical Preservation Center, South Dakota Department of Education and Cultural Affairs*

and what to change. A few years ago they installed a sprinkler irrigation system to guarantee their annual hay crop. Now they raise 1500 acres of alfalfa, a portion of which they sell. They are shifting to a new kind of fence post, a treated post of lodgepole pine, which is environmentally safe. Around 20 percent of their fence posts are the old cedar variety, and the rest are steel.

The entire Baucus family gets together at the ranch in the summer, usually to celebrate the Fourth of July. Whether the Sieben Ranch remains in the family cannot be guaranteed as far as John Baucus is concerned. "I have children, my brother and my sister have children. That new generation has to make their choice. It's their decision to make."

SOUTH DAKOTA: THE FRAWLEY RANCH

Henry Sieben eventually built up one of the largest ranches in Montana, significantly adding to his holdings in the 1920s when the homestead movement collapsed and settlers left their small farms in central and eastern Montana to seek other livelihoods. The Frawley Ranch in South Dakota's Black Hills grew in the same manner. Its 4750 acres were pieced together from separate purchases of seventeen homesteads, which held

5.8   The adobe house of the Watrous Ranch
near Las Vegas, New Mexico, is organized
around a courtyard. When it was built in
1851, the Watrous compound included rooms
used for storage, the drying of foods and pelts,
and shelter for animals. The pitched metal
roof, typical of northern New Mexico dwellings, would not have been added until after the
arrival of the railroads in 1880.

remains of dugouts, cabins, wells, and foundations spread throughout fields and pastureland.
The ranch has several fine barns: two large horse
barns on the original homeplace are built of cut
stone and clapboard siding encasing an interior
of lofts, stalls, and tack rooms. Another well-
preserved stone barn stands on the eastern portion
of the property.

Three generations of Frawleys have committed
themselves to the preservation of the ranch, restoring and stabilizing buildings and features from
its earliest history. The Frawley Ranch acreage
has remained the same since 1913, but its early
years exemplified the dynamic quality of western

landholdings, continually merging, dividing, or
expanding.

NEW MEXICO: THE WATROUS RANCH

One of the Southwest's most important historic ranches—the Watrous near Las Vegas, New
Mexico—was substantially rebuilt ten years ago
by new owners James and Barbara Doolittle. The
ranch had been built originally in the late 1840s
by Sam Watrous, a transplanted New Englander
who became successful on the southwestern frontier as a trader, gold miner, and merchant. He
married into a wealthy Spanish family, and when

the war with Mexico ended in 1847, making the region part of the United States, he settled with his family along the Mora River, east of the Sangre de Cristo Mountains. There, following Spanish custom, Watrous built a large adobe compound of twenty rooms opening onto a center courtyard. The compound functioned like a little village. There were granaries, a store, warehouse areas, a blacksmith's forge, and servants' quarters. Storage rooms of all kinds held food and hides for drying and housed tools and farm implements. The family apartments contained the wares of several cultures: Mexican blankets and pots, Indian baskets, and china, books, and polished walnut furniture from the East Coast. Buffalo and bear hides covered the floors.

In 1851, two years after Sam Watrous moved his family into their new adobe home, the U.S. Army began construction of Fort Union—one of the largest military posts in the West—nine miles north of the ranch. For the next forty years, Watrous and other local ranchers supplied the fort with beef and produce; it was a major market for the region.

Watrous was not only a diligent tradesman but an astute entrepreneur who understood the value of networks and new industry. He brought the telegraph and telephone to northeast New Mexico, and he donated land for the Santa Fe railroad stations and the right-of-way for the tracks. Because all of the region's wagon trails converged at Fort Union, Watrous reaped a harvest of trade at his ranch stores. His was the first ranch in the area to be fenced and intensively cultivated for crops and orchards. Although Watrous chose traditional Southwest architecture for his home, he practiced an adaptable and innovative approach to ranching and trade.

In 1971, Jim and Barbara Doolittle bought the historic Watrous place and began to restore the house, rebuilding the living quarters in the collapsed east wing and rehabilitating the remainder. The project required 20,000 adobe bricks, handmade and sun-dried at the ranch. Typical of southwestern adobe dwellings, the rooms of the Watrous house had been built in a row without any connecting corridors. One either walked through a series of rooms to get to another part of the house or crossed the courtyard. There was no central heating—every room had its own fireplace. The Doolittles converted some of the storage areas and small bedrooms to spacious bathrooms; even these rooms have fireplaces.

By the time the Doolittles acquired the house, it had been damaged seriously by more than a century of use and long periods of neglect. Lower sections of interior woodwork had been flooded repeatedly, followed by infestations of termites. Whenever possible, the Doolittles remained true to the Territorial styling of the house—stuccoed adobe, Greek Revival features, and a seamed metal roof.

Soon after the Doolittles purchased the ranch, they discovered that John Gaw Meem, a distinguished New Mexico architect and preservationist, had completed several large measured drawings of the house in 1936 as part of the Historic American Buildings Survey. The scale drawings were of particular value in the rebuilding of the destroyed wing.

Today, the old Watrous ranch house, partially hidden behind a screen of huge willows and cottonwoods, looks much as it would have a hundred years ago. Although the ranch is not open to the public, the house is easily seen from the main highway, Interstate 25.

Historic Ranches in the Public Realm

MONTANA: THE GRANT-KOHRS RANCH

The Grant-Kohrs Ranch in western Montana, now operated by the National Park Service, provides visitors with a living history lesson on the

5.9 The Grant-Kohrs Ranch, located between Flint Creek and the Deerlodge Mountains west of Helena, Montana, represents 125 years of western cattle ranching.

changes that have taken place in ranching since Civil War days. Until recently a privately held ranch, the Grant-Kohrs meets every expectation about the West's scenic, legendary cattle country. Western Montana is wild territory still; in the 1850s, when Johnny Grant, a Canadian trapper, arrived in Deerlodge Valley, he shared the land with Indians and buffalo. Within ten years, Grant owned a herd of 2000 cattle and was ready to make a home for his Bannock Indian wife and their children. He hired two carpenters to build a large ranch house in the French Canadian style of square-hewn logs covered with clapboard siding. This large two-story house, painted white and fitted with green shutters, created sufficient attention for *The Montana Post* to designate it "the

finest in the Territory," the kind of home one would expect to see in the eastern states.

In 1866 Grant sold the ranch to Conrad Kohrs, a German immigrant on his way to making a fortune selling fresh beef to gold miners in Bannack, Last Chance Gulch, Virginia City, and other mining camps. A short time later, Kohrs went east and married Augusta Kruse, a nineteen-year-old German immigrant. They journeyed to Montana via steamboat and wagon, bringing with them fine furnishings purchased in St. Louis. An exacting housekeeper, Augusta Kohrs established a grand domestic regimen in Deer Lodge that included high standards for the daily rituals of ranch life and generous, unfailing hospitality to guests. In partnership with his half brother, John

5.10　*Once the largest house in Montana, the home of Augusta and Conrad Kohrs was built in two stages: first, the 1862 frame house that Johnny Grant built for his family, and second, the large brick addition completed by Kohrs in 1890. The gingerbread porch on the left was reconstructed by the National Park Service from early photographs.*

Bielenberg, Kohrs acquired more cattle and more land, building his holdings to 25,000 acres. They grazed their cattle far beyond ranch boundaries on lands in three neighboring states and in Canada. Each year, Kohrs and Bielenberg shipped eight to ten thousand cattle to eastern markets.

Shortly after World War I, Bielenberg and Kohrs, believing they were getting too old to operate a large spread, sold off a major portion of the land, reserving 1000 acres around the home ranch. After Conrad Kohrs died in the 1920s, Augusta ran the ranch until grandson Conrad Kohrs Warren took over in the 1930s. Beginning in 1900, Augusta spent part of each year in a large home in Helena's West Side but always went to the ranch in Deerlodge Valley for the summer.

5.11 *This 1900 view of the Kohrs's dining room is virtually identical to what a visitor sees today. One of the great values of the Grant-Kohrs Ranch as a public site is its vast collection of original furnishings and household items, which were acquired with the property. Courtesy Montana Historical Society Collection*

After she died in 1945 at the age of ninety-six, the house stayed untouched. At the time the National Park Service acquired the ranch, the public rooms in the house looked much the same as they had at the turn of the century.

Besides an imposing and well-preserved home, the ranch includes a variety of outbuildings. Fifty feet from the main house stands a log bunkhouse with its own dining room, kitchen, washroom, and woodshed. A small lean-to on a nearby ice-house served as a summer bedroom for a succession of Chinese cooks. Sometimes the household help stayed in the main house, but usually they lived in the nearby town of Deer Lodge.

Corrals and barns surround the house and grounds on three sides. In the 1870s, Kohrs built a log barn for oxen. Adjacent he constructed a horse barn with a double row of stalls on a center aisle, which sheltered Clydesdales, Shires, Belgians, and Percheron-Normans. A few years later

5.12   The 1870s oxen barn had lost its
balance and most of its roof by the time the
National Park Service acquired the property in
the 1970s. Courtesy Jack E. Boucher, Historic
American Buildings Survey

5.13   The oxen barn after restoration, including a new shingle roof. Courtesy Grant-Kohrs
Ranch, National Park Service

he built a large thoroughbred horse barn and three individual stallion barns, whitewashed inside and out, each containing a hayloft, feed room, and a stall opening onto a small enclosed corral. (In the 1920s, one of these small barns was converted to an automobile garage.)

Before the turn of the century, as the era of the open range waned, Kohrs fenced his pastureland and added irrigation systems, wells, and water tanks for livestock. He built a granary for storing feed. Formerly, range cattle had fattened solely on grass, but by the end of the 1880s, most western rangeland was seriously overgrazed. Cattle that were fed mixed grain fattened faster and produced a better-tasting beef than grass-fed cattle.

Conrad Kohrs Warren took over the property in the 1930s, and he continued to add buildings— a chicken house, dairy barn, garage, blacksmith shop, and tack room—as they were needed to meet the changes in ranch life. Across the railroad tracks from his grandfather's home, Warren built a second complex of buildings, including a large arched barn, metal granaries, and a house.

The National Park Service acquired these additional buildings and adjoining land (1059 acres) in 1988, expanding the time frame of interpretation from the 1860s all the way to the present. Altogether, the properties now comprise eighty-eight buildings and related features, such as corrals, stock pens, and water tanks. Many of the furnishings and a great deal of ranch equipment were transferred to the Park Service along with the land and buildings.

The value of the ranch as a public property is enhanced by the unusual amount of documentary material that came with it, particularly the business records kept since the nineteenth century. The repair and restoration of buildings were aided by the availability of photos and drawings completed in the 1950s by the Historic American Buildings Survey (HABS), a federal program. Canadian relatives recently sent a copy of Johnny Grant's memoirs to the Park Service; material from them will be incorporated into the care and interpretation of the property. Several family members have

written articles about the experience of growing up on this Montana ranch, and Conrad Warren has edited his grandfather's autobiography. These are extraordinary resources.

Family records and the HABS photos were of great help in the rehabilitation of the buildings. Before construction work began, however, the National Park Service had to make some basic decisions on a time frame for the buildings. Most historic properties and museums wrestle with this issue, and it is not an easy one to solve. As visitors we tend to take a historic building at face value ("This is the Grant-Kohrs ranch house") rather than recognize that several different variations might be historically correct. Should this be the house that Augusta Kruse Kohrs saw as a young bride in 1868, the greatly enlarged ranch house that dazzled guests in 1900, the house that Conrad Kohrs Warren took over in the 1930s, or the house that was acquired by the National Park Service in 1972?

It was easy to discard the late nineteenth century versions because the Park Service was mandated in this instance to preserve the ranch as a place that had evolved through more than a century. They might have chosen to stabilize and interpret the property as it existed when they acquired it. Instead they decided to identify the "prime" period for each building and then improve, maintain, and interpret it accordingly. The optimal time was one that was supported by documentary evidence. The advantage to this approach is that it produces the maximum historical and architectural yield from each building, if one can look on it that way, because each structure is presented in its highest and best version. The peril of mixing the periods is that it may mislead the visitors who take a look and think to themselves, "This is the way it was." But when was it "this way"? The answer is "never." No harm is done as long as the visitor is included behind the scenes in the preservation and curatorial process and not shortchanged by viewing only the results of that process.

The recent changes made to the buildings are

5.14 *Park Service rangers at the Grant-Kohrs Ranch use this chuckwagon to demonstrate cooking out on the range. In the early days of ranching, chuckwagons enabled cowboys to move their herds hundreds of miles from ranch headquarters.*

pleasing to the eye and in some cases critical to their survival. An 1890 brick addition to the home included a gingerbread porch, which was enclosed and altered in the 1930s. A replica of the original porch is now in place. A stallion barn, the icehouse, and the oxen barn have been rebuilt with as many of the original materials as possible. To tell this restoration and rehabilitation story, an exhibit of "before and after" photographs has been mounted in the bunkhouse.

Cheryl Clemmensen, a Park Service ranger at the Grant-Kohrs Ranch, is an advocate of informing the visitor about the responsibility of operating and interpreting the ranch. On days when the crowds are thin she takes her small tours (the limit in the house is twelve) down to the basement to look at the dozens of cases and closets filled with china, silver, jewelry, clothes, and household goods. These disparate artifacts remind the visitors that a century of living is a long time and that each item is associated with ritu-als, traditions, and the daily give and take among those who once lived and worked at the ranch.

Clemmensen is quick to explain when an item on display is illustrative rather than indigenous. The chuckwagon out in the yard, for instance, was purchased years ago by Conrad Warren, who collected vehicles, and was never used to feed hired hands on the Grant-Kohrs range. In fact, it was not even a chuckwagon until the Park Service turned it into one to use for demonstrations of ranch cooking. Clemmensen's concern for this distinction enables the visitor to sort out the particular from the generic.

Located midway between Yellowstone and Glacier National Parks, the Grant-Kohrs Ranch will soon build a substantial visitor roster, far beyond its current annual number of 30,000. Two or three hours here offer a pleasurable and informative introduction to the more realistic side of ranching's golden age and to the adaptations that have taken place during the past century.

5.15　*When the Marquis de Mores and his wife built this large home on the Little Missouri in western North Dakota, they took advantage of a panoramic view of the surrounding terrain. Now a museum, the house is owned and operated by the State Historical Society of North Dakota. Courtesy Signe Snortland-Coles, State Historical Society of North Dakota*

NORTH DAKOTA: THE DE MORES RANCH

A narrower circumstance, one that is highly dramatic but admittedly more limited, is represented in the romantic riches-to-rags story surrounding the de Mores Ranch in North Dakota. In the 1880s a French nobleman, the Marquis de Mores, bought land and cattle and started a beef-packing industry, creating the town of Medora.

His vision was grand but flawed. Rather than ship live cattle east to market, de Mores built slaughterhouses near the ranch and sent dressed beef to the East in refrigerated railroad cars. His bold idea was premature; it was impossible to fatten beef cattle with only the nutriments of the open range, and the fiercely competitive Chicago packing houses left him little margin. By the late eighties, his business and the town of Medora were in ruins. Before the bust came, however, de Mores succeeded in building a 26-room home overlooking the Little Missouri. The stucco mansion with its red-tiled roof appears plain from the outside, but de Mores and his wealthy New York bride decorated the interior with fashionable and expensive furnishings and housewares.

The Chateau de Mores is hardly representative of western ranch life, but it does dramatize a corner of the cattle kingdom that was adventuresome and risky, much of it underwritten by foreign capital. Ranching sometimes had a glamorous side, and de Mores was not the only cattleman to practice conspicuous consumption by building a lavish home.

The de Mores house and several outbuildings are owned and managed by the State Historical Society of North Dakota. The property, open to the public for tours, is part of the revitalization of historic Medora.

KANSAS: THE PRATT SHEEP RANCH

The Kansas State Historical Society has acquired a new site, the Pratt Ranch, a former sheep operation owned by a British immigrant whose several close friends and relatives joined him in similar sheep-raising enterprises on the western plains. The original 160-acre parcel, typical of the homestead movement, is small by western ranch standards. The Pratt property is an important addition to the West's publicly accessible ranches in part because the sheep-raising industry has been sadly neglected. Sheep are to the cattle industry what coal is to gold mining, an overshadowed cousin, lacking glamour and generally left out of the romanticized picture of ranch life in the West.

A distinctive set of limestone buildings stand on the Pratt Ranch, another reason the property is an important preservation success. The architectural heritage of the use of stone in Kansas is outstanding, and this set of buildings is particularly handsome. The largest outbuilding, a shearing shed, is connected to two other structures by a limestone wall. Other walls of stone form corrals. The otherwise modest buildings take on greater importance because of the increased massing created by the stone walls. A privy, a granary, and a chicken house are also evident. The single-story cottage-style house, thought to be of English design, has delicate bay windows on each of its three sections. The house is stone; the bay window structures are wood. A stone bathhouse, decorated with corner quoins, stands near the house. Many of the windows contain colored glass. Even in its abandoned and deteriorating condition, the house is engaging and makes effective use of its decorative embellishments.

The earliest portion of the house dates to shortly after Pratt's arrival in 1879. He built it with a sod roof, which was later converted to a pitched and shingled roof. This change, and many others, was documented by John Pratt himself, an amateur photographer. The buildings require a great deal of rehabilitation, which will be aided by the extensive photographic record. The Kansas State Historical Society intends to develop a living history program at the Pratt Ranch, demonstrating specific sheep ranching activities within a broad sweep of western history.

COLORADO HIGH COUNTRY: THE MUELLER RANCH

The setting of the Mueller Ranch on the "back" of Pikes Peak in the Colorado Rockies could not be more dissimilar from that of the Pratt Ranch on the Great Plains, or the de Mores along the Little Missouri River. But this, too, is a western ranch. Horses and cattle have been raised here for most of this century.

Recently, the Mueller Ranch was acquired by the Colorado Department of Natural Resources. In 1990 the ranch opens to the public as a natural scenic area with ample trails and campsites, as well as an interpretive site for Colorado history and montane zone ecology. The property is maintained and operated by the Colorado Division of

5.16 *The Kansas State Historical Society recently acquired the Pratt Ranch, a small sheep operation on the plains started by an English immigrant in the late 1870s. A stone wall connected the sheep and shearing sheds, forming a corral. Courtesy Kansas State Historical Society*

Wildlife and the Colorado Division of Parks and Outdoor Recreation.

About 12,000 acres constitute this high-mountain spread, which ranges in elevation from 8200 to nearly 10,000 feet. Many of the thirty historic buildings on the property are log; most are frontier vernacular. Indians camped on this land and trappers built log shelters here. In the late nineteenth century, miners dug shafts for gold, apparently with little success despite the area's proximity to the Cripple Creek mining district. During these years the ranch was a hideout for horse thieves, and later it sheltered a secret operation for bootleggers and their stills. Although

the ranch has a diverse and interesting history, the property primarily is a preserve of natural beauty; it is quintessential Colorado wild country, which has absorbed human activity without being greatly touched by it.

W. E. (Jim) Mueller, a natural gas and oil executive based in Colorado Springs, purchased the first parcel (640 acres) of mountain property in 1955. He decided early on that this mountain ranchland should be made part of the public domain in order to preclude the kinds of development that were marring the countryside around Pikes Peak. Mueller had watched the subdivision of large land parcels in the mountain country

*5.17   A nature preserve as well as a historic
site, the Mueller Ranch, high in the mountains
near Pikes Peak, is now owned by the state of
Colorado. Courtesy Kent Mueller*

RANCHES, FARMS, AND VILLAGES

5.18   *La Hacienda de Don Antonio Severino Martinez near Taos, New Mexico, has been restored by the Kit Carson Memorial Foundation. The fortresslike adobe building has twenty-one rooms arranged around two* placitas, *or courtyards. The structure dates to the early 1800s; portions may have been built earlier.*

west of Colorado Springs, which had resulted in small acreages—neither town nor country—that were destructive of both landscape and vista. The Nature Conservancy helped to coordinate the transition of the Mueller Ranch from private to public ownership. The project has been a model of participation and planning, and it promises to be an exemplary achievement in the conservation of a cultural landscape of grand proportions.

NEW MEXICO: LA HACIENDA AT TAOS

The burden of ranch preservation typically falls on private owners or government agencies at the federal, state, and local levels. An unusual collaboration bringing together a private foundation and several hundred descendents of

a nineteenth-century Spanish landowner has rescued a traditional adobe hacienda in northern New Mexico.

In 1972 in the village of Taos, New Mexico, the Kit Carson Memorial Foundation acquired the crumbling home of Don Antonio Severino Martinez along with three and one-half acres of land along the Taos Pueblo River. The house is an excellent example of a Spanish adobe ranch house, a rectilinear one-story building organized around two interior courtyards, combining house and barn in a single enclosed space.

The descendents of Don Antonio Severino Martinez—300 strong—gave full support to the restoration project, which required a great deal of reconstruction. Early in the project they gathered in Taos for a family reunion, at which time they

5.19　*This secure entry door was reconstructed with hand tools. Sun-dried adobe brick underlies a coating of adobe plaster.*

5.20　*The roof of the Martinez house is drained with* canales, *spouts that carry water away from the adobe walls.*

formally organized themselves to support the restoration work on their ancestral home.

Although most of the Martinez house dates to the early 1800s, portions were built in the late eighteenth century. Currently, the rectangular compound has twenty-one rooms arranged around two small, enclosed courtyards called *placitas*. With no windows or doors on its perimeter, the complex originally was entered through one of two *zaguans,* passageways secured by wooden gates and just wide enough for an oxcart to pass through. For reasons of defense, most buildings in this region had neither exterior entry doors nor windows until after the middle of the nineteenth century, when army troops at nearby Fort Union made the Rio Grande settlements secure from Indian attack.

During five generations of living at the hacienda, the Martinez family made many changes. A covered walkway, or *portal,* was added along the face and around the edge of the first placita. Doorways that allowed passage from one room to the next were alternately boarded or opened up, depending on the family's needs at any given time. In addition to living areas, the adobe compound held large work and storage rooms.

After the last Martinez owner left in 1926, the house stood vacant and, for the most part, was neglected. During the 1940s a Taos artist began to restore the house, but he gave it up. Other owners came and went; by 1972, when the hacienda became part of the Kit Carson foundation, the building had been seriously vandalized and eroded. Rising ground water had turned the floors green with mold, and the adobe walls were crumbling.

Jack Boyer, director of the Kit Carson foundation, supervised every step of the hacienda's restoration. He turned frequently for advice to architectural historian Bainbridge Bunting, now deceased, who had written extensively on Spanish colonial buildings in New Mexico. One of their first decisions was to dig a drainage ditch along the exterior walls of the compound to channel damaging water away from the adobe walls.

During the restoration, Boyer struggled with the familiar problems of how to protect the building's visual and historic character while making it safe and comfortable for visitors. His solution was one that is commonly used today in restorations—to install modern, functional materials and devices, and then cover them with authentic, reproduced surfaces. For example, to provide for radiant heat, Boyer's crew buried copper tubing in the mud-packed floors, which were then painted with linseed oil, a traditional method used to harden them and to keep dust down. One of the larger rooms, thought to have been a parlor, had a wooden floor, a rare luxury in early nineteenth century New Mexico. During the restoration, workers replaced the rotted floor with boards hand-cut with an adze, an antique wood-dressing tool that looks much like a garden hoe. To replace missing or damaged woodwork, Boyer's work crew learned the art of Spanish colonial woodcrafting. They carved wooden gates and cut by hand all door sills and porch columns.

After a decade of work and delays, the hacienda opened to the public. Descendents of Don Antonio Severino Martinez gathered for the dedication and a festival of music, speeches, and traditional Spanish costumes and foods. They arranged for the village priest to bless the house. Family members continue to be involved, offering anecdotes, photographs, and historical records. They have started a fund to bring authentic furnishings to the house.

KANSAS GRASSLANDS: THE Z-BAR RANCH

In Kansas, the Audubon Society is working to establish a grasslands ranch that will combine agricultural history, the state's hallmark stone architecture, and a refuge for plant and animal life, all of it accessible to the public. The Z-Bar Ranch near Strong City, Kansas, covers nearly seventeen square miles. A stone schoolhouse, a three-story ranch house, and several stone outbuildings occupy a portion of the ranch. The rest is grass, rolling hills, and a scant growth of trees

5.21　*The small cabin on the left is constructed of pickets; the adjoining rooms are made of sotol, a tall, woody desert plant. This ranch house from west Texas has been reconstructed at the Ranching Heritage Center at Texas Tech University in Lubbock. Courtesy Museum of Texas Tech University*

along the creekbeds. It takes only a little imagination to envision Plains Indians racing their ponies bareback after herds of buffalo or to see wagon trains following rutted trails across these hills.

Proposals for the Z-Bar Ranch have encountered some resistance among area ranchers who fear the project will disrupt the existing agricultural community and foresee the danger of eventual eminent domain moves against their own properties. Organizers of the project expect to work out solutions to these problems and are attempting to provide sufficient assurances to keep the ranch preserve idea alive. The Z-Bar Ranch would offer a strong and interesting counterpoint to the 160-acre Pratt sheep ranch across the state in western Kansas.

TEXAS: THE RANCHING HERITAGE CENTER AT TEXAS TECH

Aficionados of ranch architecture have an unparalleled opportunity at Texas Tech University in Lubbock to examine remnants of some of the Southwest's most famous ranches. The Ranching Heritage Center, a nonprofit preservation group, has organized a superb outdoor museum on a landscaped 12-acre site on the edge of the university campus. The center's purposes are to locate, move, and restore ranch structures that would otherwise be lost.

The relocation of historic buildings is always subject to scrutiny by preservationists, and there are those who object to this collection of ranch buildings from west Texas and the Panhandle.

5.22 *The Masterson JY bunkhouse, now at the Ranching Heritage Center. Courtesy Museum of Texas Tech University*

Because of the quality of the installation and the accompanying interpretive material, however, and assuming that many of these buildings would otherwise be lost, many who ordinarily would criticize have been supportive instead.

Will Robinson, a restoration architect and member of the university faculty, supervised the installation and reconstruction of the nearly two dozen buildings now on the Texas Tech grounds. Necessarily in close proximity, the center's ranch buildings are placed around berms and landscaped to maintain a sense of isolation from each other and from the surrounding urban scene. Four windmills occupy the site, including an example of the popular Eclipse model first used by the transcontinental railroads. Exhibit signs and brochures explain that the XIT Ranch had more than

300 windmills spread around its 3 million acres. A headquarters building from the XIT is among the exhibits, along with a dugout from the equally famous Matador Ranch. Several cabins and ranch houses are spread among the barns, windmills, and outbuildings. From west Texas, for example, is a picket and sotol house, its walls made of upright cedar pickets and sotol cactus stalks. The exhibit also includes a stylish Victorian ranch house with a full veranda and a widow's walk.

Other typical ranch structures are represented: a blacksmith shop, granary, schoolhouse, and bunkhouse. From Charlie Goodnight's JA Ranch in the Panhandle came a small stone milk and meat house, an early form of refrigeration for the hot Plains.

5.23   Las Escarbadas Headquarters, part of
the permanent exhibition at the Texas Tech
Ranching Heritage Center. Texas, like Kansas,
has enormous deposits of limestone, a common
material in rural buildings. Courtesy Tommy
Morman, Museum of Texas Tech University

5.24   An Eclipse windmill, part of the Ranching Heritage Center. Courtesy Museum of
Texas Tech University

5.25   *The Harlow Barn in Spink County, South Dakota, was built in the 1890s (the 1879 date on the gable refers to the year the homestead was founded). The frame barn is in the English tradition of a simple two-story, gabled structure, with flanking sheds housing stalls for horses. Courtesy State Historical Preservation Center, South Dakota Department of Education and Cultural Affairs*

The Future of Ranch Preservation

What will it take in the mountain and plains West to secure a future for traditional ranch buildings? A few ranches here and there will continue to join the ranks of museums held in the public trust. There are two obvious advantages to this solution: first, the buildings are usually well cared for, and second, an open, accessible ranch offers a powerful and enjoyable means of edu-

cating visitors about ranch and western history. Separating the buildings from their home ranch, although successfully achieved at Texas Tech, is a less desirable solution because of the loss of context.

The responsibility for ranch preservation, like every other kind, will continue to fall primarily on private owners. Agriculture by its very nature is conservative, and many ranchers accept the role of stewardship as a central part of life. With encouragement and incentives, they would probably do more. Ranch buildings, because they are income-producing, are eligible for federal tax credits when they are rehabilitated. To qualify, they must be listed on the National Register of Historic Places and meet certain design requirements. Recognition programs—certificates to families that have operated a ranch for a century or more—also inspire owners to improve their historic buildings. Western livestock ranching has been a unique part of American history, and whether public or private, our collective investment in the maintenance of ranch properties is one of the most important legacies we can leave for the future.

Farmsteads and the Countryside

In the 1970s when the state historic preservation offices started their county-by-county surveys, they began to nominate farms to the National Register of Historic Places. The nomination process was slow at first. Farm property owners have tended to be wary of National Register listing because they fear it will limit their control of their property. Even when the owners are willing, the preservation offices are often too short-handed to carry it through. A fully developed farmstead with fifteen buildings can take several days for a team of surveyors to measure, describe, and photograph, besides interview the farmers and other sources. Several weeks might go into researching the property and writing the nomination. Despite these constraints, more farms are added each year to the register.

Among South Dakota's early nominees was the Harlow farmstead south of Aberdeen, a modest example of late nineteenth century American frame construction. James Harlow filed a claim on this homestead in 1879 but lived with neighbors for the next ten years while he worked the land and saved money. Then, in two stages, he built a small hipped-roof house and, in the 1890s, added

a horse barn, a simple two-story gabled structure with sheds for horse stalls on either side. Later, he built a large granary and a cow barn. Eventually, Harlow's complex of buildings included a grain storage barn, a garage, a chicken coop, an outhouse, and a windmill. In 1911 the family moved to a house in nearby Redfield, but they continued to farm the land and maintain the buildings. The farmhouse is now a summer home for succeeding generations of Harlows, who value the "home place" as a typical mid-America farmstead, simple and spare.

A second South Dakota site now on the National Register, the Anderson homestead near Vermillion, represents a more extravagant approach to farm building construction. With twenty-one outbuildings, the Anderson place is hardly typical of Great Plains rural architecture; the Harlow farmstead better fits that category. The Anderson farm, with its great variety of buildings and features constructed over a long span of time, demonstrates the evolution of a prospering farmstead adapting to a century of changes in technology and the marketplace.

Except for an old stone creamery, new silos, and a steel barn, most of the Anderson buildings are wood frame. The original farmhouse, still standing, was built in 1871 by Olaf Erickson. When his daughter married a Swedish immigrant named Solomon Anderson, the newlyweds took over the farm. In 1901 the prosperous Andersons erected a large two-story Neoclassical house with an exterior of wood clapboard siding. Its rather grand and formal facade has a Palladian entry—a large arched doorway with long, narrow windows on either side. Other notable buildings include a square wood silo constructed in 1894 and a frame chicken house with a cupola on its roof ridge. There are also several equipment sheds, a cow shelter, a privy, and two granaries.

Typically, as farmers on the eastern portion of the Plains diversified after the financial panics and grasshopper plagues of the 1870s and 1890s, they added buildings to house livestock, crops, and new equipment. Along with a wide array of

5.26 *The first Anderson Farm home (1871, Clay County, South Dakota) was a small but graceful clapboard house. The owner, a Swedish immigrant, probably relied on a transient carpenter to build this Georgian vernacular cottage, similar to what one might have found in the East. A second, larger home was added in 1901. It, too, was in the classical mode. Courtesy State Historical Preservation Center, South Dakota Department of Education and Cultural Affairs*

5.27 *The Anderson horse barn (1894) has an unusually large number of windows, houselike in their design and arrangement. Courtesy State Historical Preservation Center, South Dakota Department of Education and Cultural Affairs*

buildings, a well-equipped farm would probably have one or more wells, a windmill, a reservoir for storing water, irrigation ditches, an orchard, a windbreak of trees planted in rows, a protective grove of trees at the northwest corner of the house, food cellars, a smokehouse, and a springhouse for keeping dairy products cool. Along the way, as facilities became obsolete or structurally unsound, owners would tear them down to keep the farmstead neat and safe.

Preservationists, along with many members of the farming community, watched this gradual demolition of rural buildings with a feeling of sadness but also with a commitment to change the downward course. How could farmers be encouraged to save these aging, obsolete buildings? Too often, the buildings were a financial handicap, or they were useless. To farmers, it seemed foolish to hang on to them, and especially foolish to invest money in them at a time when farming was already financially difficult.

In 1987, the National Trust for Historic Preservation announced the beginning of BARN AGAIN!, the first nationwide program to preserve agricultural buildings. The program has had some highly visible successes and promises to open the door to other preservation activities. BARN AGAIN!, a rural conservation program, relies on lively promotion and incentives to motivate farmers to save their old buildings. The program's first phase was short-term, manageable, and widely publicized, offering recognition, resources, and rewards to farmers who fixed up their barns. Respected and credible leaders in agriculture backed the program. A major, widely read farm publication, *Successful Farming*, promoted the project with feature articles and graphics.

By recognizing farm building rehabilitations, BARN AGAIN! organizers rewarded farmers for their efforts and, through a vigorous publicity program, encouraged other farmers to do the same. Demonstration projects organized by the National Trust and publicized by *Successful Farming* caught farmers' attention and led to further preservation accomplishments.

Barns have always been a great comfort to the American psyche. With their simple lines and straightforward design, they offer an unpretentious, populist architecture born of practical need. Barns are spacious and sheltering. They stand for hard work and harvest, the tangible proof of toil. Within their tall, frame walls are granaries, hay lofts, stalls, feeding troughs, and animal pens. The sweet smell of alfalfa competes with the acrid whiff of manure. The smells and sounds inside are as rich and reassuring as the familiar sight of a big red barn standing back from a country road. The very term "barn red" signals vigor and sass.

Magnificent barns can be found from coast to coast and from the Canadian border to the Gulf of Mexico. Fifty years ago they formed an architectural bounty as rich as the harvests they held. Who could have foretold the time when these once-sturdy buildings would fall like soldiers under siege?

Since the middle of this century there has been a heavy loss of barns. Some of them simply wore out, suffering from years of use and weathering. Others, after machine-baled hay made lofts obsolete, were needlessly large and expensive to maintain. Although the barns themselves were spacious, their doors were likely to be too small for large combines and tractors. Farming changed rapidly after World War II, and as high-tech methods replaced the old ways, barns and other outbuildings became expendable. When metal sheds—supposedly care-free—came on the market after World War II, many farmers decided that replacing the old barn was the only sensible thing to do.

For the most part, the agricultural industry spurred them on. For years, county extension agents, university specialists, farm publishers, and the industry that has been dubbed "agribusiness" had been exhorting farmers to modernize their operations. New buildings and bigger machines were necessary, farmers were told, to maintain a competitive edge. It was the modern way, but the old barns took a beating.

In the late 1980s, after two years of in-

5.28   As farming became increasingly tied to technology in the twentieth century, barns became highly specialized. An expansive stock-raising operation would have had several. This stock farm near Lincoln, Nebraska, includes a show and sale barn (left), a cattle barn, and a horse barn. Courtesy D. Murphy

5.29   Although nonrectilinear barns were an exception, farmers occasionally built them. The hexagonal Uehling Barn (1918) is in Dodge County, Nebraska, northwest of Omaha. Courtesy D. Murphy

tensive background work on rural preservation, the National Trust organized a regional forum in South Dakota to talk about old farm buildings. *Successful Farming* magazine sent one of their editors, John Walter, whose interests were in conserving the farm heritage. After two days of searching for a solution, Walter hit upon the idea of using the magazine to reach out to farmers about their buildings. First of all, did farmers *want* to preserve the buildings? Second, was it practical? Walter began to work with Mary Humstone of the National Trust staff in the Denver regional office, and together they fashioned a lively project that would hit on two fronts: four well-publicized demonstration projects to provide farmers with hard figures and detailed information on the rehabilitation process, and a contest to bring recently completed barn renovations to the fore. Publicity, education, and recognition were all part of the package.

Seeking an upbeat start for the project, the preservation team named it BARN AGAIN!, making a point of the regeneration that takes place when buildings are rehabilitated. The first hurdle was to find out how much preservation activity was already going on. Rural sites are never easy to identify, and some states had barely begun to survey farms and ranches systematically. It stood to reason that farm families all over the country had already invested in repairs on their barns. Why not take BARN AGAIN! directly to the farmers and let them speak for themselves?

The program was publicly launched in the May 1987 issue of *Successful Farming* as a contest offering $1000 rewards to the best "born again" barns nationwide. Deere and Company, a farm equipment manufacturer, and Pioneer Hi-Bred International, a seed company, joined the National Trust and *Successful Farming* as underwriters, creating a $100,000 fund for awards and demonstration projects. They developed a snappy logo, a stylized frontal view of a bright red barn, which became a popular poster. The contest announcement included illustrated examples of four successfully renovated barns in the Midwest.

More than a beauty contest, BARN AGAIN! emphasized the practical advantages and financial savings of preservation. Applicants were assured that although historical and architectural merits mattered a great deal, innovative solutions based on functional needs would capture the judges' attention. To compete, a barn did not have to be fancy or even terribly old, but interested farmers were cautioned: "How well you've preserved the original appearance of the building exterior will be a factor."

Categories for entry were made sufficiently broad to include a wide variety of barns. Farm buildings that reflected ongoing conservation, modernization (as long as the exterior remained essentially intact), adaptation to a new use, or additions were all eligible. The top winners were allotted $1000 each, honorable mentions would earn $100 awards, and merit award winners were promised a recognition plaque.

More than 500 farmers responded to the contest announcement. As the entries arrived, the printed half-page application form was often accompanied by letters explaining how that particular barn was used and what it meant to the owner family. Mary Humstone remembers letters from grateful farmers that began, "We've always loved our old barn, but we felt a little foolish putting money into it until we read your announcement."

BARN AGAIN! uncovered a wealth of old barns and a cadre of interested owners. John Walter believed the interest was there from the start. The program gave farmers something to respond to and reinforced a positive attitude about conserving old buildings. Walter thought the key to success was the emphasis placed on both the practicality and the economy of keeping the barns alive. "The contest got their attention by recognizing those farmers who were already working on their barns. It was a call to action. Then the demonstration projects walked the reader through the steps of actual construction work so they could handle it themselves and not spend too much money." During the two years following the contest announcement, *Successful Farming* ran

5.30   *This 1915 barn belonging to Leon and Joe Spartz in South Dakota was converted to a hog farrowing facility, one of several demonstration projects for BARN AGAIN!, a rural program of the National Trust for Historic Preservation. Courtesy Ron VanZee and* Successful Farming

ten illustrated articles featuring BARN AGAIN! renovations.

A South Dakota family—four generations led by 90-year-old matriarch Agnes Spartz—participated in the demonstration project, converting a 1916 hay barn into a modern hog farrowing unit without sacrificing either the original lines of the building or the exterior materials. With an investment of $40,000, including $10,000 from the BARN AGAIN! program, the Spartzes scraped and painted the exterior, added insulation to the windows (they are sealed with black-painted ply-wood but appear functional from the outside), and reconstructed the bottom level to house high-tech equipment for hog farrowing.

Because they allowed their barn to be listed on the National Register of Historic Places, the Spartzes were able to take advantage of a 20 percent federal tax credit for a savings of $8000. Under South Dakota law, property assessment on a certified rehabilitation is "frozen" for eight years, providing another tax break for the project. Replacing the barn with a new facility would probably have cost an additional $10,000. By adapting the existing barn, because of the breaks on taxes and construction costs they managed to save an old friend, and money too.

A second South Dakota farmer, Lee Gatzke, earned a merit award for rehabilitating a 70-year-old horse and hay barn built by Gatzke's grandfather. The big red barn had originally held a hay loft and stalls for fifty work horses. In 1955 Gatzke's uncle removed most of the stalls, gutted the center, and installed cribbing for grain storage. By the time Lee Gatzke and his wife bought the property in 1975, the barn needed new roof shingles and exterior siding. It was in bad shape, but they valued its link to the homestead days of the Dakota Territories and did not want to tear it down. They chose an interim solution of new paint and then in 1981 started a more serious rehabilitation, which involved a new roof, new tracks and doors, and metal siding to cover the deteriorated wood of the original. Preservationists usually discourage building owners from applying metal siding, but in this instance the old wooden siding was deemed beyond repair and new wood was far too costly.

For an investment of around $20,000, the Gatzkes have stabilized this imposing barn and made it again an attractive part of the neighborhood. Gatzke grows corn and feeds cattle. Neither operation demands a barn; however, another generation might want to convert the structure to modern hog units or some other new use. When that happens, the old red barn will be ready.

The Gatzkes have enjoyed the community of response created by BARN AGAIN! They get calls and newspaper clippings from all over the country. "When I enter a contest like this," Lee Gatzke says, "it's not so much the winning that I'm after—though I hate to lose—as it is meeting the people."

The nationwide interest in preserving barns and farmsteads has been loud and clear. In 1989, after the BARN AGAIN! contest and demonstration projects were completed, the National Trust was still getting as many as fifty letters a week from farmers requesting information or simply wanting to describe their barns. National media attention accounts for much of the public's enthusiastic response. In addition to sustained coverage by *Successful Farming*, the project was publicized in hundreds of newspapers and several national magazines.

The National Trust and *Successful Farming* must now find a way of extending or modifying the program to keep farm families in touch with others who are making improvements on their historic homes and outbuildings. Mary Humstone hopes the National Trust can produce a technical video tape to serve as a "how to" manual for barn owners who are about to work on their old buildings. In the meantime, an hour-long narrative about barn preservation is being produced by Nebraska Educational Television.

Recognition and celebration of historic sites, and a salute to the owners whose stewardship has kept them going, can be powerful preservation tools and are easily brought to bear. Most of the region's states—Colorado, North Dakota, South Dakota, Oklahoma, Kansas, Nebraska, and Texas—have organized recognition programs for owners of historic farm buildings. For example, Colorado's Department of Agriculture, the State Fair Board, and the Colorado Historical Society have established a Centennial Farms Program to honor farm and ranch families who have held and worked their land for at least a hundred years. An additional historic structures award initiated by the National Trust for Historic Preservation is given to farms and ranches with buildings more than fifty years old. The Colorado program, established in 1985, generates about thirty applications a year. Award plaques are distributed during a special ceremony at the state fair by the commissioner of agriculture.

The Colorado Centennial Farms Program makes the most of the publicity opportunities for its awards. Hometown papers run feature stories on each year's award winners, gratifying to the owners and a source of inspiration for other farm families in the region. In an era that has seen relentless reportage on the problems of the American family farm, the continuity and strength reflected by the Centennial Farms Program provide a welcome, positive message.

A successful preservation activity often prompts another like it, or an ancillary project that supports the first. In 1988, agricultural engineers at North Dakota State University in Fargo published a twelve-page practical guide to farm building rehabilitation. Using diagrams and photographs, the guide describes the successful repair of sixteen North Dakota farm buildings and lists additional sources of information. The booklet encourages farmers to use federal tax credits to alleviate the costs of building preservation. The National Trust for Historic Preservation supported the North Dakota publication with one of its "critical issues" grants. Further support came from the U.S. Department of the Interior, the State Historical Society of North Dakota, and the state university.

Farmsteads and the Cultural Landscape

Historic sites are best appreciated and understood within their original context, the physical setting that gives greater meaning and visual quality to the individual building. For rural sites, a setting can occupy hundreds of square miles—mountains, fields, valleys, pastures, buttes, bluffs, and prairie—and typically includes man-made features as well as the work of nature. Agricultural environments include roads, access lanes, fences, mailboxes, windmills, silos, grain elevators, snow fences, bridges and culverts, groves, creeks, irrigation ditches, rivers, and any number of other things that form a part of that particular life. A farmstead's larger setting usually includes multiples of itself—collections of buildings of similar design, size, and materials—located on other farms. An essential part of the harmony of rural landscapes is the repetition of these patterns and forms, much as the harmony of a city neighborhood is created by streetscapes filled with lawns, rows of trees, and buildings with common setbacks.

In Nebraska, horticulturalist Richard Sutton has studied the cultural landscape surrounding Red Cloud, Willa Cather's birthplace, and has made recommendations on how to soften the intrusions of modern technology on that pastoral countryside. Near Austin, Texas, residents in the Hill Country are trying to find ways to control the development of their agricultural region, which was the boyhood home of President Lyndon Johnson. These difficult exercises require the cooperation of property owners, government agencies, business people, and private citizens. In addition to the large number of constituencies involved, attempts to preserve cultural landscapes are daunting because of their sheer size. Despite the difficulty, protection of the cultural landscape has become one of the top items on the preservation agenda regionally and nationally.

NORTH DAKOTA: THE GERMAN RUSSIANS

Action on behalf of an important cultural landscape is just beginning in two remote corners of the mountains and plains region. The first of these settings is in south-central North Dakota, on prairie farmland homesteaded in the late nineteenth century by German Russians. Settlement took place here in the valleys that converge on the Missouri River south of Bismarck, clustering around the towns of Hazelton, Linton, and Strasburg.

The flight of these German peasants to America had been years in the making. In the late eighteenth century they moved first to Russia, settling along the Volga River and near the Black Sea, part of an ambitious colonization scheme devised by Catherine the Great. Seeking to make productive a large land area seized from the Turks, and to secure it against invasion, she enticed peasants from Germany with promises of free land, religious freedom, local autonomy, and exemption from taxes and military service. Gradually these freedoms were taken away, and the transplanted Germans turned instead to the United States, lured by the railroads and promises of work and free land. More than a quarter of a million German Russians emigrated to America between 1873 and 1910. They brought with them the centuries-old architecture that had sheltered them in Germany and, later, on the steppes of the Ukraine.

Their homes usually were one of two types: simple long houses with several rooms in a row, one accessed by a *vorhausel*, or small entry porch; and square houses with dormer windows placed symmetrically on each side at the roof line. The German Russians purchased milled lumber for the large support beams in the roofs of their homes and for framing around doors and windows. For the rest, they used native materials, commonly building with fieldstone mortared with clay and then covered with stucco. Adobe bricks made of clay, water, and straw mixed to a paste and then shoveled into molds to dry in the sun were also common. These techniques were similar to those introduced in the Southwest by the Spaniards in the seventeenth century.

Some German–Russian immigrants built their houses of puddled clay packed in molds. The clay mixture was pressed between horizontal boards and allowed to dry. Then other layers were added, raising the wall in stages to prevent it from collapsing under its own weight. After the mud walls dried, they were stuccoed with a thin layer of mud plaster or covered with wooden clapboard siding. Plaster or oilcloth covered the interior walls. The settlers applied bright paints to the interior: orange on the plank floors and chartreuse, blue, or pink on the walls and ceilings. They painted the outside walls blue or white with red trim, combining the colors to form geometric patterns. Near the houses the immigrant farmers erected barns and a variety of outbuildings: icehouses, summer kitchens, food cellars, and smokehouses.

In the small towns and in solitary places out in the country, the German Russians built churches and established cemeteries. Ornate iron crosses mark the graves. The landscape here is spare: low-lying hills and meager clumps of trees. In the flat light of a gray, cloud-covered day, the abandoned homesteads appear drab, but the fading oilcloth and flakes of bright-colored paint clinging to the inside walls suggest that these vernacular European houses were once vibrant additions to the prairie terrain.

In 1960 nearly 2000 German–Russian families lived in this three-county area. Perhaps a third to a half of the original farmsteads now stand empty. Subsequent generations have moved elsewhere. Sometimes the move has simply been to the nearest town. As in other parts of the Plains, small farms are no longer viable economic units, and when farmland is consolidated, buildings are left empty. It is unlikely that circumstances will change to the degree that most of these buildings will again find a use. Their ultimate demise seems a certainty.

Fortunately, many of these farmsteads were surveyed twelve years ago by the North Dakota Office of Archeology and Historic Preservation. There is now a strong photographic record, as well as other documentation. At least one of these ethnic farmsteads is destined to be rehabilitated and opened to the public as a museum—the birthplace of Lawrence Welk, an immensely popular band leader whose televised shows were watched by millions of Americans every Saturday night for thirty years. He is surely the state's most famous native son.

The momentum to preserve the Welk farmstead grew out of planning for North Dakota's 1989 centennial commemoration. A nonprofit organization, Welk Heritage, Inc., was formed to acquire a six-acre parcel containing the Welk homestead. The group has begun the long process of repairing and furnishing the buildings as well as working up an interpretive program for the public. They have set a fund-raising goal of $750,000 to be raised over the next several years, two-thirds

5.31   Band leader Lawrence Welk's birthplace near Strasburg, North Dakota, typifies thousands of farmsteads established here around the turn of the century by German immigrants from Russia. The outside staircase to the loft and the *vorhausel, or enclosed porch*, were common features on these folk buildings. The house is adobe brick covered with wooden siding. Welk Heritage, Inc., is rehabilitating the home and outbuildings and will open them to the public. Courtesy Welk Heritage, Inc.

of which will be set aside in an endowment to underwrite maintenance, operations, and special programs. A search for original furnishings has yielded a chair and kitchen table. Other items will be sought. The Lawrence Welk Foundation, based in Los Angeles, has offered encouragement and financial support for planning and restoration.

Welk Heritage directors decided that the rejuvenated home and outbuildings should celebrate Welk and his family but should also be a means of telling the story of the German Russians who immigrated to North Dakota. The Welk farmstead is a typical example of German–Russian folk architecture in the Strasburg area. The house is small, twenty-five by twenty-eight feet, with additional space in the attic, which is entered from an outside stairway. The walls, eighteen inches thick, are made of sun-dried earth blocks covered on the outside with wooden siding. The entry porch, located toward one end of the house, is larger than the usual vorhausel on the German–Russian homes in this area.

The Welk property includes a granary, a rather recent barn, an outhouse, and a separate summer kitchen, which would have been used for cooking and laundry. The newer barn will serve as a visitors center, thereby protecting the integrity of the older buildings. The farmstead will be rehabilitated and interpreted to reflect the period of Welk's youth between 1903 and 1924.

At the Welk farmstead, visitors will learn about the entire phenomenon of the German–Russian settlement in North Dakota. The immediate countryside around Strasburg will serve as the backdrop for interpretation of the restored Welk property. Information on other German–Russian sites, such as the Saints Peter and Paul Church in Strasburg; self-guided automobile tours of the surrounding area; and announcements of local ethnic festivals will expand the experience offered to visitors at Welk's birthplace. Even though this is only one site among thousands, the fact that it is being interpreted within a large framework magnifies its importance and very likely will encourage the preservation of other German–Russian buildings in the vicinity.

The achievements of Welk Heritage, Inc., offer proof that the preservation movement today is able to assist new projects and help them along in ways unheard of twenty years ago. Preservation, like many other aspects of life in the rural sections of the plains and mountains, is handicapped by separation, distances, and insularity. Fortunately, access to resources helps people to overcome these limitations. For example, Welk Heritage receives advice from the state preservation office, particularly the restoration architect, and other government agencies and professionals. Help from the National Trust for Historic Preservation is a telephone call away, and personnel from other historic properties share their own experiences. Locating this help requires entrepreneurial skills, but assistance is there for the

asking. When the resources are tapped, the results show. A project that might have died from inertia or discouragement is energized when it becomes part of the national preservation network and is carried to completion within the framework of professional standards and procedures.

NEW MEXICO: THE MORA VALLEY

Nearly a thousand miles away in a high mountain valley of New Mexico, another historic landscape—this one, too, filled with a folk architecture of adobe block buildings—awaits a surge of renewal to enliven its threatened culture. Mora Valley, northeast of Santa Fe in the Sangre de Cristo Mountains, is one of the poorest places in America; its county government is bankrupt, its economy is at a standstill. It is also a place of consummate beauty, a traditional Spanish pastoral setting of adobe farms and villages.

In the early nineteenth century, Hispanic settlers first entered the Mora Valley and built villages organized around a defensive plaza; this type of village planning, mandated by the colonial government, offered protection from Plains Indians. The surrounding lands were organized in the traditional Spanish way, with individual parcels reserved for farming and common lands on the upslopes set aside for grazing and woodcutting. *Acequias,* or irrigation ditches, supplied water from the river for crops and orchards, although rainfall in parts of the valley is generous by western standards—from twenty to thirty inches annually.

The opening of the Santa Fe Trail in 1821 immediately to the east increased the demand for farm products and fueled prosperity in the Mora region. The economy brightened further when Fort Union was established in 1851 as a military supply depot and as a protective post along the Santa Fe Trail. At the same time, the quelling of Indian threats made the enclosed plaza arrangement of the villages in Mora Valley obsolete and encouraged the building of linear villages, some

5.32 *The Cassidy Mill in Cleveland, New Mexico, is one of four gristmills remaining in the Mora Valley. When Fort Union was established in 1851 a short distance away, a new market suddenly opened, and the insular life of the mountain valley of Mora underwent a sudden shift. Trade with outsiders created a cash economy; the barter system of the valley was altered permanently.*

5.33   *This abandoned house in the Mora Valley near Holman, New Mexico, exhibits its basic structure of adobe brick. Earlier, the house may have had a traidtional flat roof. Pitched roofs did not become common until after the railroad era began in 1880.*

of which retained a vestigial plaza. Farmsteads became dispersed throughout the valley.

At mid-century there was a considerable amount of flux within the settlements, with Hispanic immigrants continually arriving from the west and the established families sometimes moving on to found new communities or leaving the area altogether. The arrival of Anglo merchants and traders at this time introduced an entirely new cultural element and substantial changes in the economy. Increased outside trade and cash transactions moved the villages away from their former self-contained barter system.

Two military interventions wreaked havoc in the valley, first in the form of an invasion in 1843 by the Republic of Texas, repulsed after a pitched battle, and then the leveling of Mora by the U.S. Army in 1847 following a village revolt against the occupying and victorious Americans. These violent encounters undoubtedly left a permanent mark on the Hispanic villagers, who passed to future generations their suspicion of and resistance to outsiders.

The buildings in Mora Valley express the traditional adobe and wood architecture of northern New Mexico's Hispanic villages. The very first

5.34　*Square adobe houses with hipped metal roofs are common to the Mora Valley and other parts of northern New Mexico. A little ridge gable is sometimes extended out to form dormer windows, as it does here. This building is in Ojo Sarco, across the mountain range from Mora.*

buildings were of *jacal* construction, vertical posts set into grooved logs and then covered with mud plaster. Permanent buildings were made of adobe bricks, a technology introduced to the Southwest by the villagers' ancestors centuries before. Although the roofs are now pitched and covered with metal, introduced in the 1880s after the railroads arrived, the earlier structural feature was a flat earthen roof. The house plan was linear, with two or three rooms built in a row and each entered through an outside door. A variation—four rooms assembled as a square—became a popular alternative. The square cottages typically were built with hipped roofs. Territorial

styling, a regional adaptation of Greek Revival features, appeared on some buildings late in the century. "New Mexico Vernacular" is the generic description of Mora Valley folk architecture, which is within the tradition of other northern New Mexico villages.

Newly arrived German merchants built mercantile stores in Mora. Other entrepreneurs erected sawmills and flour mills. French carpenters are credited with fashioning the unusually steep roofs on many area buildings, and for equipping the hipped-roof cottages with gablets. As the economy expanded and diversified, new building types were introduced and traditional buildings

5.35   *Additions placed end to end constitute*
a common solution to the need for more space.
This large house, now abandoned, is located at
La Cueva in the Mora Valley.

were modified. The most striking visual and functional change came with the installation of pitched metal roofs. But overall, the Hispanic earth and wood heritage held firm.

Business expansion in the latter half of the nineteenth century brought prosperity to some of the people in Mora Valley, but it tended to undermine the villagers who were accustomed to a self-contained bartering economy, a system that was economically marginal but stable. An expanding cash economy led to borrowing, small land units became uncompetitive, and the often forced sale to Anglos of grazing lands previously held in common disrupted the traditional farming patterns. Even during the agricultural boom after the Civil War, some local farmers lost their lands to investors who had the support of the American territorial government in Santa Fe. Land units grew larger, and farm tenancy increased. The closing of Fort Union in 1891 left the local farm market in a shambles. The resulting agricultural decline continued into the twentieth century, accelerating during the national farm slump of the 1920s and the Great Depression of the 1930s. By 1980, the population of Mora County had dropped to 4205, compared to 5566 in 1860 and nearly 14,000 in 1920.

Today, residents of Mora County are trying to

find ways to revitalize the economy of the valley, but they have yet to agree on a direction. There are a few promising new activities in agriculture: a large raspberry ranch, in operation for around ten years, is a successful venture employing fifty to sixty workers seasonally. A lively Christmas tree industry now ships trees to several states. There is talk of food processing—of apples, for example, which grow abundantly in northern New Mexico. There is talk, too, of expanding local crafts—furniture perhaps, or weaving, a successful enterprise in nearby Chimayo. Crafts usually depend on retail markets, at least in part, and those markets do not presently exist in Mora Valley. To create them would require a thriving tourism industry, a prospect that does not appeal to many of Mora's residents. Tourism, they fear, will bring further displacement of local families. And those residents who work in tourism services, such as motels, restaurants, and shops, are likely to be paid low wages, while profits end up in the pockets of people who live elsewhere.

A new day for Mora Valley would require a majority of the residents to agree on a strategy for change, which must then be supported and acted on by elected officials. As a first step, the state's historic preservation office has completed an intensive survey of the valley and submitted a district nomination to the National Register of Historic Places. Historic designation in Mora Valley will probably have the same positive effect it has had elsewhere: residents will take pride in their community and realize that outsiders place value on their historic buildings and landscapes. National Register designation also opens the door to federal tax credits for commercial building renovation, as well as to New Mexico tax incentives for qualified rehabilitation of all historic buildings.

A new social phenomenon among the region's Hispanos also offers hope for Mora, as well as for other New Mexico villages. Young adults are beginning to return to their towns and villages. For many years, the young left for good. They took jobs in nearby cities or they went to college and then moved away. No community can withstand a continuing drain of its young generation. The prospect of educated and trained young people returning to the villages brings promise. Those who return will bring new skills and a new perspective.

In the meantime, a remarkable project coordinated by the New Mexico Community Foundation—the rehabilitation and continued maintenance of village churches—may spark further renewal in Mora Valley. Parishioners in the village of Chacon, north of Mora, have recently restored their church, La Capilla de San Antonio. A former resident of La Cueva is trying to organize a group in that village to undertake the restoration of San Rafael, an abandoned adobe church in great peril. Demonstration has always been a powerful force in preservation, and projects that actively involve local people are likely to be doubly effective in generating enthusiasm for more of the same.

The Adobe Churches of New Mexico

The repair and renovation of New Mexico's historic adobe churches during the past decade illustrates a gratifying reawakening of concern for this special American heritage. Translated into action, this concern has produced an exemplary preservation project. The adobe church achievement is a strong community preservation model for several reasons. First, it is strategic—there is a plan, a purpose, and a determination to accomplish substantial and long-term goals for the greatest number of buildings and people. Throughout, the scope and complexity of the problem have been acknowledged. Second, it is open and participatory—a large number of volunteers and parishioners are active and involved, backed up by capable administrators and knowledgeable preservation specialists. Third, it is technically and orga-

5.36   The Gothic arch is not often found on New Mexico's adobe churches, but San Rafael near La Cueva might reflect the influence of foreigners who came into the Mora Valley to trade in the latter half of the nineteenth century.

5.37   The private owner of San Rafael has stabilized the endangered back wall with cable, steel rods, and boards. A small amount of protective adobe plaster remains on the walls, but the roof has deteriorated and the walls are separating. Further restoration work will have to be done soon to save this distressed building.

5.38 *The hand-cut corrugated metal cupola and unpainted wooden cross of Santo Domingo at Cundiyo, north of Santa Fe, expresses a powerful statement of faith.*

nizationally sophisticated—high standards are set for restoration, and the best people and techniques are mobilized to meet them. Fourth, it is cumulative—the knowledge gained and the resources assembled are recorded and transmitted so others can learn and use the information in an equally productive fashion. Fifth, it is diversely funded—it includes the modest investments of parishioners as well as support from the Catholic Church, numerous government agencies, businesses, foundations, and individuals. Much of the work is contributed. Sixth, it reflects values and circumstances that speak of spiritual, esthetic, and community activity as it might be experienced anywhere in the world. Finally, it has international application because it offers solutions to people in many other countries where structures are built with adobe.

The productive work of recent years is by no means the first attempt by New Mexicans to save their churches. An appreciation for the adobe heritage emerged early in the twentieth century with a revival of interest in Pueblo and Spanish colonial architecture. In the 1920s the Society for the Preservation and Restoration of New Mexico Mission Churches furthered the cause. Then, in

1940, George Kubler published *Religious Architecture of New Mexico*, which informed and shaped a scholarly appreciation of these regional buildings within the larger context of Mexican and Spanish baroque architecture.

More recently, recognizing the urgent need to save the churches, Thomas Merlan of the New Mexico Historic Preservation Division organized a statewide survey of religious structures. Around the same time—in the mid-1980s—the New Mexico Community Foundation established a special project, "Churches: Symbols of Community," to find the ways and means to assist villages in church restoration and maintenance. Thus, when Roberto Sanchez, Archbishop of Santa Fe, appointed a select committee in 1986 to study the problems of church buildings, he was continuing a long-established tradition of concern and action.

With approximately 1500 churches, chapels, and moradas in towns and villages scattered throughout the state, New Mexico lays claim to a remarkable religious and cultural heritage. A large majority of the churches in this traditionally Hispanic region are Catholic. For centuries, the common building material for churches—and nearly all buildings—was adobe brick. Portions

5.39   *The church of Cristo Rey in Placita de Llano near Las Vegas, New Mexico.*

5.40 Nuestra Señora de Los Dolores in Bernalillo, north of Albuquerque, is now closed; a new church has been erected adjacent to it. The future of the old building is uncertain.

5.41 The church doors of Nuestra Señora de Los Dolores.

of the earliest churches, such as San Miguel in Santa Fe, date to the seventeenth century, when the Spaniards were first colonizing the Southwest.

Most of the missions from the colonial period are gone now, and even the nineteenth- and twentieth-century churches are deteriorating at a distressing rate. For the villages, these losses are irretrievable and personal. But the sense of loss extends beyond the mountain towns of New Mexico, touching people everywhere who value this vernacular legacy.

By the 1980s, the deterioration of New Mexico's churches had become a recognized crisis. As is often the case, the loss of several important structures stirred public interest. In 1985 La Iglesia de San Miguel (1850), an adobe church in the village of El Valle near Santa Fe, was demolished after parishioners became discouraged over the prospect of rehabilitating the crumbling church.

In Peña Blanca the following year, the 116-year-old Guadalupe church was razed after villagers concluded it was too far gone to save. The parishioners may have recalled the collapse of a recently restored adobe wall in the church at El Rito in 1979, which resulted in the need for major, expensive repairs far beyond the resources of the village. During this period, a fourth treasured adobe church, San Lorenzo at Picuris Pueblo, was threatening to fall in ruins after decades of water damage.

Parishioners felt defeated by this disturbing chain of events, and the preservation community was unsure about how to help. New Mexico's village churches, which had seemed as timeless as the earth itself, suddenly were slipping away.

Adobe, that most basic of materials, has been used for hundreds of years and figures prominently in the history of the American Southwest. Despite

5.42 *San Juan Nepomuceno in El Rito was nearly lost ten years ago when a wall collapsed without warning. The church has been restored. Courtesy Mark Nohl,* New Mexico Magazine

its cultural and geographical longevity as a building type, it remains a surprisingly fragile material, subject always to water and wind erosion. Unattended, left to the elements, an adobe building will return to the earth within fifteen to twenty years of its construction.

There was a time during the 1960s when a technical solution seemed at hand: a portland cement plaster was applied as a permanent coating over the adobe brick. Parishioners then could forego the periodic application of adobe plaster to the church walls. Unfortunately, this new, thin-skinned cover often makes matters worse. A web of minute cracks soon spreads across the surface, admitting almost imperceptible amounts of rain and snow. With repeated freezings the cracks enlarge and more water enters. At that point, the coating starts to spall and fall off, leaving the bricks beneath to crumble. Cracks are not the only problem; water draining down the walls seeps back up under the cement or erodes the foundation blocks supporting the walls. Leaky pipes and roofs can also let water pass into the walls, and without room to breathe under the cement plaster, the adobe bricks retain the moisture. Water-logged walls beneath a pristine stucco coating have been known to slump to the ground without warning, the adobes dissolved. Father Jerome Martinez, pastor of the stricken church in El Rito, has described the effects of sodden adobe in simple and graphic language: "And then one day, when it is thoroughly wet, it crumbles like a cookie in milk."

Father Martinez remembers a feeling of helplessness one afternoon in the fall of 1979 when he first saw the collapsed adobe wall of San Juan Nepomuceno. The church had stood in the mountain village of El Rito since early in the nineteenth century. Adding to his sense of despair was the realization that the mass of mud at his feet had been a new replacement wall built to strengthen the 150-year-old church. Faced with the imminent collapse of the entire structure, parishioners began anew, shoring up the roof with a temporary frame, removing the adobe walls altogether, pouring a new foundation, and recreating the five-foot-thick walls. Although the church was turned inside out in the repair process, much of the original building fabric remains, including all of the wooden beams and corbels hewn during the 1830s from pine trees harvested in the nearby mountains. Rehabilitation of the church required an emergency loan from the archdiocese of $500,000, an enormous obligation for a New Mexico village parish.

The El Rito drama acted out the essential irony of adobe: it is both reassuringly timeless and distressingly fragile. Protected from wind and damp, it is as solid as the earth itself, but once attacked by moisture, it weakens and falls under its own weight.

Father Martinez, now the chairman of the Commission for the Preservation of Historic New Mexico Churches, Archdiocese of Santa Fe, views the adobe church heritage as one of America's richest folk expressions. Although the parishioners were guided by church officials, Indian and Hispanic villagers built their churches with their own hands without help from architects or contractors, and often without any manufactured materials. Beginning in 1610 and continuing through two centuries of Spanish rule, local parish groups produced hundreds of churches. They continued to build after the Mexican War of Independence in 1821 and following the American occupation, which began in 1847. These early churches constituted the most extensive mission system in the country and represented a tremendous flowering of religious and artistic expression. "A touchstone with the divine," Father Martinez calls it.

The churches have always been in jeopardy. From the beginning, wind and water assailed the adobe walls. Cultural and economic forces as well added to the destruction brought by the elements. When the Spanish colonial government was abolished in 1821, many of the clergy departed, and the villagers were left to fend for themselves. They were surprisingly successful at maintaining their religious life, but some of the early churches were lost. In mid-nineteenth century a new threat emerged when newly arrived French priests, unsympathetic to the indigenous architecture, set about to dress up the churches with Gothic decoration or to demolish them altogether.

Between the 1850s and the early 1900s, New Mexico lost a major portion of its colonial churches. Of the 1500 churches that stood in 1900, approximately 300 have survived in the Archdiocese of Santa Fe because parishioners have cared for them, taking the initiative to make repairs and carry out the periodic ritual of patching and replacing the earth coating on the walls. Father Martinez regards this task as a basic regeneration for the church and its parishioners: "There is something altogether lovely and theological about the yearly replastering of the adobe

*5.43   Our Lady of Light in the town of Lamy,
south of Santa Fe, is abandoned, as is most of
the town.*

walls. They are renewing their faith and their community ties at the same time."

Political and religious upheaval threatened New Mexico's villages throughout the 1800s. In the twentieth century, the displacements of World War II weakened them further. Men of the villages went to war, and the women found jobs in town. After the war neither was inclined to settle for the traditional subsistence living of rural New Mexico. When the young people left to find wage employment, the responsibilities of maintaining the churches and the irrigation systems fell to the older generations. Some villages con-

tinued to flourish, but many shriveled up over time, their communal responsibilities falling on fewer shoulders.

Father Martinez describes the situation as one of "a plethora of churches without support." Emphatic about the need for a remedy, he deems the surviving churches as "legacies of faith." The power of this legacy prompted the New Mexico Community Foundation in 1985 to establish a new support program, "Churches: Symbols of Community." Apart from an obvious need for money, the foundation saw the nub of the problem to be one of getting people and solutions together. The villagers themselves held many of the necessary answers—they had cared for the churches for generations. How could this cumulative wisdom be shared? How could this folk wisdom be combined with the knowledge of restoration architects and other specialists who were beginning to understand more clearly the insidious and catastrophic problems caused by water damage? The New Mexico Community Foundation set about organizing the resources that would be needed by the villages.

A short time later, Roberto Sanchez, Archbishop of Santa Fe, announced his determination to help alleviate this centuries-old problem, which always has been made difficult by the poverty of the villages and the great distances between them. The churches are dispersed over 67,000 square miles, much of it isolated mountain country. To make the most of their resources, the archdiocese and the preservation community agreed to combine forces.

By this time, the dilemma of the churches was very keenly felt, but only partially understood. Through hearings and informal meetings, a select committee appointed by Archbishop Sanchez heard from parishioners, architects, contractors, historians, and anyone else involved with preserving the churches. Adding this new information to the results of a field survey of the churches completed in 1985 by the Santa Fe architectural firm of Johnson, Nestor, Mortier and Rodriguez, the commission then made crucial decisions about a procedure to save the endangered buildings. Which churches were in greatest need? Which were the most valuable to the Church? Which could be maintained by their parishioners? What could be done with the abandoned churches?

Out of the questioning came conviction and clarity. The committee named three categories of priority, based on a guiding principle that preservation of the buildings had first and foremost to serve the purposes of the living church; therefore, abandoned churches in deserted communities were weak contenders for support. In Class

One, the highest category, are the parish churches that are active and have a resident pastor. There are about seventy of these, usually in the larger communities. El Rito, where Father Martinez had struggled to rebuild San Juan Nepomuceno, is an example. These large, important churches constitute the living legacy, and the archdiocese has pledged to do everything in its power to preserve these structures.

In the second category are the networks of mission churches that are dependent on the parish churches. Typically, the church and village populations in this group are small and often there is no resident pastor. For these buildings the archdiocese will provide matching funds and loans as well as indirect aid in the form of technical services and materials.

Class Three churches, the lowest priority, are not without hope, even though the archdiocese offers little in the way of direct aid. Santa Fe's Santuario de Guadalupe, a Class Three church, has been meticulously restored by a private foundation, which received title to the church in 1974 after parish activity ceased. The building now serves as a small community and performing arts center. When appropriate uses like these can be found for abandoned churches, the archdiocese may consider a transfer of title or a long-term lease to assist in the transition.

In addition to the twelve-member commission now in place, the archdiocese depends on more than 100 advisers to guide preservation strategy and to assist the parishes directly. Historic art objects alone require a corps of experts. They have developed guidelines for the repair and care of the wooden sculptures and altar screens that typically adorn New Mexico churches. Expert conservators assist as well in the repair of paintings, fabrics, ironwork, and other metals, such as tin and silver. Structural problems, too, are often referred to technical professionals.

Father Martinez has concluded that major rehabilitation of these buildings, especially if their historical origins are respected, defies a common-sense, layman's approach. Specialized knowledge

5.44   El Santuario de Chimayo was built in
the early 1800s in the Spanish colonial style
with a flat roof and two unadorned adobe
towers. A century later, the pitched roof was
installed and gabled roofs were placed over
the corner towers. One of New Mexico's most
famous and picturesque adobe churches, the
santuario is often painted by artists.

5.45 *St. Anthony's in Chacon has recently been restored by its parishioners with assistance from the New Mexico Community Foundation. The play of light on an adobe surface is a perpetually satisfying experience associated with this hand-crafted architecture, and it is probably the cause for the style's strong appeal to artists and photographers.*

is required, along with an ability to carry out sophisticated techniques and procedures. "The *building* of one of these churches was typically a folk project, and the maintenance of it as well," Father Martinez believes. He sees the original building process as straightforward and constructive, carried out in an orderly, familiar sequence. "But *preserving* a church requires expertise. The folk faith that built the church a century or two ago would be dumbfounded by the complexity and mystery of the repair problems that we face today." The restoration of altar screens, the conservation of rotting wood, and the control of water's relentless march through adobe are matters best referred to trained and experienced experts.

As a precaution, the commission has devised rigorous preservation standards, and Father Martinez intends to carry them out. "However well meaning, much damage has been done in the past. Pastors have brought in hack restorationists, who do more harm than good, because they ruin the original fabric." Now, all major repair work done on Catholic churches within the archdiocese must be cleared with the commission.

Although expert advice is a necessary and first requirement for successful restoration, an exclusively high-tech, professional solution is a poor fit for New Mexico's adobe churches. The archdiocese and preservationists throughout the state realized this from the start. Villagers themselves and the outside volunteers who come to help must have access to the techniques and skills needed to repair and maintain the buildings. During months of restoration work at San Jose de Gracia in

5.46 A small cemetery, or campo santo, *surrounds the church at Chacon. Several of the graves are marked with metal crosses.*

Las Trampas, volunteers learned through practice how to apply mud plaster, the more skilled teaching the others. The overall preservation strategy will continue to be guided by architects and restoration specialists, but whenever possible, the hands-on work will be done by laymen. There aren't enough technicians to go around, nor is there enough money to pay them; in addition, the care of New Mexico's adobe churches is a community responsibility and an act of faith.

Father Martinez hopes that parishioners once again will take up the traditional crafts that created the church interiors, particularly the wooden *santos, bultos, reredos,* and corbels carved years ago

to glorify the important parish churches. Today, local artisans skilled anew in the traditional crafts could help to restore the churches by reviving a major folk artistic expression and at the same time create a flourishing cottage industry to bolster the economy of the villages.

Enjarrando, the art of mud plastering, is already enjoying a revival in New Mexico. This skill requires some of the same specialized techniques as sculpture or ceramics. New Mexico's talented practitioners include Anita Rodriguez and Carmen Velarde, whose territory encompasses the region surrounding Santa Fe and Taos, an area rich in adobe church architecture. They

5.47 *San Francisco de Asis in Ranchos de Taos was covered with a cement plaster in the 1960s during an extensive remodeling. A few years ago, parishioners removed the cement and have returned to the practice of a regular application of adobe plaster.*

5.48 *Side windows in the church of San Francisco de Asis.*

5.49 *The trappings of technology and comfort sometimes rest heavily on adobe churches. Stovepipes and power lines intrude on the smooth surface of the church of St. Thomas in Ojo Sarco, north of Santa Fe, but the little church is engaging nonetheless. The corrugated metal roof is repeated in the cupola cover, which rests on a wooden tower.*

have worked on restorations of San Jose de Gracia in Las Trampas and San Francisco de Asis in Ranchos de Taos. Construction contractors as well as *enjarradoras*, Rodriguez and Velarde advise church restoration committees on repair problems and instruct the volunteer crews in the application of mud plaster to adobe walls, inside and out. These women are role models for the Father Martinez approach to restoration—having learned the traditional techniques from members of the previous generations, they are revitalizing time-honored crafts and teaching young people the basic skills of adobe conservation.

Although much of New Mexico's religious wooden statuary has been lost or stolen—it is more likely to be found in private collections or museums than in a church sanctuary—there are gratifying exceptions in such churches as Holy

Cross in Santa Cruz, twenty-five miles north of Santa Fe. This beautiful *iglesia,* or parish church, dating to 1733, is being restored under the direction of Holy Family Parish priests and a five-member restoration committee, an alternative to the more traditional mayordomo role in which responsibilities for the church property are rotated annually from one parishioner to another. Formed in 1972, the committee was charged with making substantial improvements on the building while keeping its historic character at the forefront.

The committee began with research on the church's history, which provided an important chronology along with vital new information and resulted in nomination of the church to the National Register of Historic Places. Then, Nathaniel Owings, a retired architect and founding partner in the Chicago firm of Skidmore, Owings and Merrill, volunteered to prepare a master preservation plan. Owings, the owner of an adobe house near Santa Fe, had been involved in the restoration work of San Jose de Gracia in nearby Las Trampas. Santa Fe architects Robert Nestor and Victor Johnson worked with Owings and the church restoration committee to complete the usual restoration planning tasks of interviews, measurements, site testings, surveys, inspection of historical documents, and meetings with specialists. Together, they produced a master plan that could be carried out over a period of years.

With the plan completed, a first order of business was restoration of the altar paintings, which were in desperate condition, by a specialist in Alabama who had been tracked down through the local art conservation network. The subsequent transformation of the six paintings as they were cleaned and repaired heartened the parishioners, who were facing years of arduous repair work on the church itself. A low-interest loan was obtained from the archdiocese, and structural work began in earnest on the floor joists and adobe walls. Workers removed the hard plaster covering on the interior walls, enabling trapped moisture to escape from the adobe brick. Three coats of mud plaster were then applied, followed by a final coat

of *tierra blanca,* or white earth, from nearby hills. This natural coating looks appropriately "soft" and allows the underlying adobe to breathe.

By 1980, seven years into the restoration process, improvements in heating and lighting resulted in systems that were more efficient, safer, and more sightly. Additional pews and a new altar platform accommodated the mandates of Vatican II as well as increased the comfort of parishioners during services. The Santa Cruz church is, after all, a living legacy.

The most dramatic change—the restoration of the center altar screen—involved difficult decisions. Alan Vedder of the Museum of New Mexico led the restoration team. The screen had been overpainted twice, and attribution was uncertain. Restorers tried as much as possible to recapture the original work of Jose Rafael Aragon, a prominent *santero,* a painter of saints, who created much of New Mexico's religious statuary during the nineteenth century. His bright and richly patterned screen, which holds the six paintings restored earlier, is the focal point of the church. Two other screens, one in the south chapel, the second in the nave, are also attributed to Aragon.

Pride in the renewal of Holy Cross runs deep in Santa Cruz. Willie Atencio, a restoration committee member, describes the accomplishments, and the compromises, with proprietary deference and a respectful understanding of the problems involved. He points out "modern" realistic statuary given to the church in the 1930s and relegated now to a side altar. He explains the anomaly of plastic-coated concrete on the side chapel floor, which will remain because the disturbance created by its removal would threaten the church walls. There have been other accommodations to necessity in this large, evolving house of worship. Atencio patiently explains this or that compelling reason for the choices made. But his overriding concentration remains on the triumphs, the integration of centuries-old materials and forms with the lives of parishioners in the late twentieth century.

Through his stewardship at Holy Cross in

5.50 The church of the Holy Cross in Santa Cruz—along the Rio Grande, twenty-five miles north of Santa Fe—dates to 1733 and is supported by families who trace their own history in the area back at least that far. The church was built with a flat roof. Toward the end of the nineteenth century, the twin towers at the front were heightened and a metal-surfaced pitched roof was added. Santa Cruz is a madre iglesia, or mother church, embracing some twenty mission churches within its parish community.

Santa Cruz, Atencio personifies the meaning of preservation, which is continuity and regeneration. His life has been rooted in the Rio Grande Valley, where he can trace ancestors back for two centuries. The church in Santa Cruz serves perhaps 1500 families, long-term residents for the most part whose ties in the valley go back for decades and occasionally reach back to the earliest Spanish settlements.

To many Hispanos, strengthening these cultural links is as important as the architecture. The two are seen as one and the same. Abad Sandoval, whose family settled in New Mexico as early as the 1600s, joined the preservation cause in 1985 when he learned that the El Valle church was in jeopardy. Sandoval's ancestors had lived nearby. His great-grandfather is buried in the campo santo of La Cueva church near Mora in the mountains east of Taos. Sandoval was distressed to think that these deep roots might, after all, prove too weak to last.

A public meeting was called in Santa Fe to deal with the problem of El Valle and other threatened churches. Sharing the program were an architect, a preservationist, a historian, and a villager whose church was in real trouble. Sandoval looked around the packed auditorium. More than 90 percent of the audience was Anglo. They were being warned that an American treasure was imperiled. Sandoval agreed totally, but from his point of view, the loss was much greater for Hispanos, who stood to lose an important part of their culture and personal identity.

Agitated and energized, Sandoval looked for a solution. The villages needed help, and yet they easily could be overwhelmed by outside interference. How could the necessary money be raised in a state that has great need and few resources? Without adequate financial support or a strategy for tackling these distressed and dispersed churches, preservation was likely to be piecemeal at best. A friend sent Sandoval to enlist the aid of Susan Herter, then president of the New Mexico Community Foundation. Herter responded with enthusiasm, and before long, Sandoval was on the foundation's board, organizing support for the churches.

The New Mexico Community Foundation recognizes the historic adobe church as the traditional center of village life, albeit weakened by modern economic stresses. Working in concert with parishioners, the state's three archdioceses, and Protestant leaders, the foundation has created an encompassing but flexible program to strengthen the churches and the village fabric as well.

Like most preservation successes, the adobe church project has depended on key individuals guiding hundreds of volunteers and at the same time making efficient use of enabling organizations. The New Mexico Historic Preservation Division, with a strong push from Director Thomas Merlan, organized a statewide survey of the churches, partially funded by the National Endowment for the Arts. Within four years, a majority of the state churches had been examined, measured, described, and photographed by architects Johnson, Nestor, Mortier and Rodriguez of Santa Fe. The survey, in turn, aided the archdiocese in devising the three-class categorization of churches to determine levels of financial support for preservation.

The logical step after survey is to produce a plan for preservation of particular buildings. A Critical Issues Fund grant from the National Trust for Historic Preservation underwrote the cost of hiring architects to work with local mayordomos and restoration committees to develop recommendations and cost estimates for each of nine significant churches determined by the New Mexico Community Foundation and the archdiocese to have the highest priority. The Skaggs Foundation awarded a major grant to continue the work on the preservation plan started with National Trust funds and to enable the New Mexico Community Foundation to assist the churches with materials, technical services, and training programs. From time to time, special preservation plans will be required for churches in distress that need emergency repairs.

5.51 *The church of San Jose de Gracia de Las Trampas, completed around 1775, is considered by many to be the best extant example of New Mexico's Spanish colonial ecclesiastical architecture. The wooden belfries are believed to have been added in the 1860s.*

Although the survey was judged to be an important conservation tool for the long run, many churches were already in critical need of help and a significant number were exhausting village resources. As the need became known, volunteers from outside the villages offered to help. Thus, one of New Mexico's most famous adobe churches, San Jose de Gracia in the village of Las Trampas, was rehabilitated within a two-month period in a heartening show of hands-on help from people all over the mountain region near Santa Fe. Mayordomos Frank and Bernie Lopez organized twenty-five village families to work on the 1780s church, regarded by many as the best extant example of Spanish colonial style in the country. Responding to publicity, forty outside volunteers arrived the first weekend to chip off the cracked top layer of plaster and then to apply a fresh coating of mud. A second weekend of work, again well staffed by volunteers, ensured the repair of the roof. Area firms donated materials, and several professional roofers gave their time. By summer's end, the venerable Las Trampas church was renewed, again a source of pride for its parishioners and a secured architectural treasure for all who revere it. In recognition of the accomplishments at Las Trampas, the National Trust for Historic Preservation presented an Honor Award to church parishioners in 1988.

Realizing that isolated villages were likely to be unaware of the help available, the New Mexico Community Foundation looked for a way to reach them. What good does it do to have resources unless people know about them? Again with funds from the National Trust for Historic Preservation, the foundation prepared two video tapes. The first presents interviews of people who have successfully repaired churches, and its intent is to inspire others to do the same. The second tape demonstrates basic techniques required to recognize problems and make the necessary repairs. Showing people how to handle a problem is the usual approach of the New Mexico Community Foundation. They act almost as a broker, putting mayordomos and building committees in touch with contractors or specialists who can advise them on a solution. Once a church is repaired and dried out, proper maintenance will keep it standing indefinitely. Again, the foundation offers assistance. For example, they have hired Anita Rodriguez, the Taos enjarradora, to teach high school students how to apply mud plaster to the adobe walls. When these skills are learned by the young people, ongoing conservation of the churches is made possible.

The economics of church preservation remain troublesome despite all the resources that have been energetically mobilized and applied in New Mexico. Father Martinez estimates that a minimum of $10 million will need to be spent on church repair by the end of this century in the Archdiocese of Santa Fe alone, a sum that has yet to be raised. Moreover, a successfully restored church is no guarantee that the surrounding village will be "saved" as well. Without parishioners, the churches are doomed. Architect Victor Johnson, who has seen more New Mexico churches at first hand than anyone else in the state, maintains an optimistic view. Although granting that preservation is expensive, he argues that these vernacular buildings can often be repaired for the cost of materials. Johnson insists, "Compared to what Chicago or Detroit faces, where the restoration of *one* church might run $10 million, we're lucky that we can get a lot done at very little cost. Often, $2000 or $3000 is all it takes. I find that gratifying, and I'm hopeful about the future. It's worth whatever investment we have to make. These buildings represent a major Hispanic contribution to the body of American architecture."

6.1   *Granbury's civic and commercial center—a courthouse square—is classic Texas.*
Courtesy Texas Historical Commission

CHAPTER SIX

Getting Back to Main Street

As the drama of western expansion unfolded in the late nineteenth century, cow towns and mining camps dominated center stage. Their ephemeral and often fugitive moments of glory left participants spent and observers breathless, creating legends that still dominate the American consciousness of the West.

By the turn of the century, and with considerably less fanfare, thousands of more ordinary towns had become part of the Great Plains landscape. Though they appeared stable compared to their boisterous mining and cow town cousins, most of these small urban enclaves had an equally dim economic future.

Historically, agriculture fueled the small-town world of the plains. When crops failed, when prices fell, nothing remained to tide people over, and they left for greener pastures, abandoning the crossroads settlements and towns that had served them. Remnants survive of once-thriving commercial centers, perhaps a grain elevator, a church, or an isolated false-front grocery store, but only traces remain of their vigorous, optimistic frontier beginnings. The buildings are empty, the trees dying, the land reclaimed by field or pasture. While the mining ghost towns of the mountains evoke a romantic nostalgia for a fleeting, rowdy moment in history, these dying villages of the plains are saddening to come upon. There is a sense of disappointment about them, and betrayal, as though everyone had believed at the start that this pastoral life was meant to last.

There were too many towns to begin with, thanks mainly to the railroads and their aggressive promotion of town building and land sales. Painting a bright picture, the railroads and their allied land companies assumed an optimism about climate that was soon proven wrong. All too often the expectation of progress and growth was realized only in the booster language of commerce, and many towns had a hard time hanging onto their original stores and services. Expansion was out of the question.

After World War I, when farmers started to buy automobiles, times got even tougher for small towns because everyone could drive to larger towns farther away to shop and do business. Towns with added attractions, such as a courthouse, might start to grow, but only at the expense of the small towns around them. The disruptions of the Great Depression and World War II tended to exaggerate these differences. Farm populations continued to shift downward, accelerating into a slide by the 1970s. Today, as the twentieth century nears its close, many thousands of small western towns are receding into the shadows.

Scattered across the plains, however, are towns that are now marshaling their historic resources to create a lively new era. The spotlight of Red Cloud, Nebraska, has been on its Willa Cather heritage. Granbury, Texas, once a vital farmers' market, now attracts residents of Dallas and Fort Worth. In New Mexico, travelers go out of their way to visit Lincoln, the site of a bloody frontier conflict in the late 1870s. And in Guthrie, Oklahoma, the territorial capital, residents are recapturing the town's turn-of-the-century architecture and style. All four of these communities are endowed with handsome, historic architecture. In each instance, the preservationists who work on these ambitious renewals are striving to revive the excitement and character of the towns as they first existed.

Who are they, these far-flung town savers? And what are their secrets? There is no formula, nor are there miracle workers in any of these town sagas, although Granbury has been blessed with an energetic individual who sparked a complete economic turnaround. What makes a difference are leadership, persistence, and momentum. In each of these communities, the leadership was able to identify the town's distinctive qualities.

For Red Cloud, the prairie world of writer Willa Cather emerges as the major theme. In Granbury, a courthouse square provides the focus and the surrounding countryside the context. In Lincoln, a violent moment in history supplies drama, while a harmonious adobe architecture sets the stage. And in Guthrie, all bombast and bustle, the grand era as territorial capital enlivens the present. These towns have strong personalities. Their vitality and character come out at you. But none of this happened overnight, and none of it happened by itself.

For an ailing small town to come to life again, money and support must be found to shore up its special qualities. At the same time, an audience must be cultivated to enjoy them. Money and markets. This equation is not new; it is how all towns survive. The new ingredient today is the increased interest in historic sites as tourist destinations. Learning how to protect a town's integrity and at the same time attract visitors is a perplexing puzzle that communities rich in history must learn to solve.

Granbury, Texas

The wasting away of a small town sometimes is barely perceptible to those living in it. A single main street store might close, and then another. Standing empty but still intact, the buildings look much the same as before. Then, by accident or design, a storefront window is shattered. The owner responds by covering the windows with sheets of plywood. What was merely forlorn now becomes ominously moribund. Boarding up a window is a kind of death knell for a building, a statement of failure, an end to human activity.

This troublesome sense of loss and of things going needlessly to waste motivated a returned Texas native, Mary Lou Watkins, to begin to renovate historic buildings in her hometown of Granbury. Eventually, she led a preservation campaign for the entire community, but it all started with her work on a single building—her grandmother's house, just a short walk from Granbury's courthouse square.

Watkins had returned to Granbury in 1967 after raising a family. Married to a U.S. Army officer, she had traveled widely and had lived in several different states as well as abroad. Once resettled in her birthplace, she labored on her grandmother's abandoned home—scraping, painting, repairing, and all the while despairing over the sad, neglected building on the courthouse square that her great-uncles, Jesse and Jacob Nutt, had built in 1893. Believing that Granbury still had a role to play as an active country market, she set to work refurbishing the "Nutt House"—the family hotel and store—and, in so doing, sparked a renewal of the entire town.

Once started, the revitalization of Granbury moved along with remarkable speed. Joe Nutt, a cousin, moved from Colorado to join in the revival of the family legacy. He soon developed a successful pattern for renovating commercial buildings downtown. He organized investors to buy a piece of property on the square, renovate it, lease it, and then pay off the construction loan with rental income. The rehabilitated buildings served as collateral for similar investments, creating a revolving fund. By 1973, just three years after the Nutt House reopened for business, fifteen other buildings on the square had been purchased, repaired, refurbished, and leased for new businesses, including restaurants, a bookstore, a bakery, and a high-fashion clothing store.

Certain landmark buildings central to Granbury's history were considered essential to the town's revival. The First National Bank, the project's principal lender, had occupied an important corner property on the square since 1887. Bowing to the pleas of Mary Lou Watkins and other preservationists, the bank directors dropped a plan to demolish their historic building and replace it with a new drive-in facility. Rather than

start over, the bank adapted the first floor of the building next door to accommodate a drive-up teller window. The 1887 corner building remains unchanged.

Across the square, an attorney converted a second important bank building into law offices. In the meantime, the square's centerpiece, the white limestone Hood County Courthouse, was renovated and its clock tower was repaired. Public outcry earlier had saved the storm-damaged tower from demolition.

Another significant but derelict structure, the 1886 Opera House, faced certain destruction before Joe Nutt organized the Granbury Opera Association to restore and administer it. The Opera House, a small but stylish Renaissance building of white limestone, quickly became the town's favorite preservation project. To get the work going, seventy charter members of the Opera House Association donated $1000 each, and many of the same local citizens co-signed a $50,000 bank note. Several Texas foundations awarded a total of more than $100,000 toward the restoration, which eventually cost $200,000, a sum kept modest because of donated materials and labor, including architect's fees. Ever since its gala opening in the summer of 1975, the Opera House has offered year-round melodrama as well as professional and college theater productions under the management of a professional director.

The Opera House attracts a continuous stream of theatergoers from nearby Dallas and Fort Worth, many of whom stop first at the Nutt House dining room for a sampler of regional cooking. Diners at the Nutt House are offered such traditional favorites as chicken and dumplings, red beans, pickle relish, greens, cornbread, and home-baked pies. Mary Lou Watkins's approach to her dining room menu exemplifies a philosophy of preservation that has served Granbury well: aim to be as professional as possible while presenting a simple, authentic evocation of the region's past.

Granbury's success required unity and concerted action, never an easy achievement for independent merchants. The town's private inves-

6.2 *The Opera House on Granbury's Courthouse Square. Saving this old theater accomplished two central goals for Granbury's revitalization: first, it improved the appearance of buildings around the square, and second, it created an attraction for visitors. The combination of theater, dining, and shopping has proved to be a big draw for regional residents. Courtesy Texas Historical Commission*

tors and preservationists have formally organized whenever the situation has warranted such a step; the opera association was one of the first of these citizen groups. Others have focused attention on attracting visitors. The Chamber of Commerce promotes tourism and trade for all of Granbury's businesses, and a merchants' association deals with parking, advertising, and special events.

Long before preservation work got into full swing, volunteers from the Hood County His-

torical Commission had examined records and collected information on the area's historic buildings. This research became the basis for authentic restoration. To commemorate Granbury's noted landmarks, the Texas Historical Commission has posted permanent medallions highlighting each building's history. Other agencies take a similar interest. The Town Square Historical Committee reviews proposed structural or facade changes around the courthouse, acting as a watchdog to

6.3   *The Nutt House, like the Opera, has been a steady tourist attraction for Granbury. Both an inn and a restaurant, the Nutt House has specialized in country cooking. Mary Lou Watkins, the inn's owner and an ardent preservationist, believes that simple homemade foods are in keeping with Granbury's farmers' market tradition. Courtesy Texas Historical Commission*

maintain the town's historical integrity. The Hood County Commissioners oversee the courthouse, and the city council regulates and services the Granbury Square Historic District. In all, hundreds of Granbury's citizens have been involved in rebuilding the town. Many of them work at it full-time and invest their money as well as their energy.

Although Mary Lou Watkins has been the driving force in Granbury's revitalization, she is

the first to admit that preservation works only when the community supports it. She offers the following statement as a guiding principle: "If you can convince people that the project will be good for them and for their children, you can count on those people to participate. Communities are made of dreams, hopes, and the desires of the people to improve their lives." She continually reminds her neighbors that visitors to Granbury are likely to be looking for simple rewards, such as a first-rate home-cooked meal. Simplicity, she argues, is Granbury's greatest virtue.

A country character tangibly expressed and directly experienced has drawn visitors to Granbury for more than fifteen years. Tourism is the town's primary industry, and because of its seasonal nature, with summer and Christmas providing the peaks, income on Courthouse Square can be erratic and uneven. The Texas recession in the late 1980s cooled the real estate market and left some owners with losses. Although investment in commercial buildings has slowed, especially when compared to the boom of the seventies, there has been a rise in home restoration in the old neighborhoods surrounding the square. Despite the economic downturn, Granbury has strengthened its claim as a town that knows its history and has figured out a way to show it to anyone who will spend a day walking along the limestone sidewalks of Courthouse Square.

Granbury's successful revitalization served as a model for the National Trust for Historic Preservation as it developed its MainStreet Program in the late 1970s. Granbury's preservation work, achieved entirely with private funds, was sustained by a well-organized business community. Typically, independent merchants in small towns resist cooperating in disciplined, coordinated merchandising and joint marketing, but Granbury's store owners have worked together. Throughout the renewal process, the energetic leadership of Mary Lou Watkins has provided the necessary spark. Her vision and accomplishments in Granbury have been emulated in dozens of other small towns in the mountains and plains region.

Guthrie, Oklahoma

Guthrie was born under unique circumstances, rising overnight from the Great Plains during Oklahoma's 1889 land run. Within the next year, after it had been designated the territory's new capital, the town was thrust immediately into a marathon of construction. Had fate been kinder, Guthrie today surely would be Oklahoma's largest city, for its beginnings were auspicious.

It is commonplace to say that western towns "sprang up overnight," but Guthrie literally was built in a day by eager settlers known as "sooners" who rushed into Oklahoma Territory at noon on April 22, 1889, to claim free land. Previously, much of Oklahoma had been reserved as Indian territory. Toward the end of the nineteenth century, pressures on the United States Congress led to the opening of this large preserve to homesteaders—thus, the famous "run" that created Guthrie. As bugles sounded at noon on that historic April day in 1889, more than 100,000 sooners crossed the border into Oklahoma Territory, scrambling for townsites and homestead parcels.

A commemorative issue of the state's first newspaper, *The Oklahoma State Capital*, claims that the "Great Land Run provided Guthrie with 20,000 residents, 39 Doctors, 81 Attorneys, 3 Laundries, 40 Restaurants, 46 Grocery Stores, 5 Daily and 10 Weekly Newspapers and a place in history." First tents, then shanties, then sturdy frame buildings housed this frenetic commerce. A year later, in 1890, when Guthrie became the territorial capital, permanent building began in earnest and continued throughout two decades until the capital was moved thirty miles south to Oklahoma City.

Guthrie's early building styles ranged from late Victorian, with such features as pressed metal cornices and elaborate window surrounds, to the more formal and restrained Neoclassical designs of the early twentieth century. Contrasting colors in stone and terra cotta, and textured surfaces of rough-cut stone and patterned brick, contributed to a variegated architectural picture, more startling and expressionistic than the typical western main street. Brick streets of deep red pulled the rich building tones together. Because all of the downtown structures were erected during one short period, their window and cornice lines matched up nicely even when their overall facades did not, resulting in a great jumble of designs that produced a compatible relationship overall.

In 1889, even before the dust had settled in Guthrie, a talented and ambitious Belgian architect, Joseph Foucart, arrived in town and immediately began to bring architectural order to Oklahoma's frontier landscape. His buildings gave distinction to Guthrie's physical heritage. Working with an extensive design vocabulary, Foucart established a style that is easily recognized for its turrets, crenellations, and large round-arch windows. He highlighted these features by using rough-cut stone, often in combination with brick, the colors of the two contrasting. Typically, his facades were asymmetric.

Foucart's distinctive style is very much alive today in downtown Guthrie. In 1974, when the town's revitalization began, seven Foucart buildings were still standing, which is not surprising since 90 percent of Guthrie's historic main street area has survived intact. Fittingly, Foucart's own architectural office was to become the town's first serious preservation project.

Guthrie awoke from its long sleep in the mid-1970s when two local residents teamed up to lead an economic revival. Don Coffin, then head of the Chamber of Commerce, approached newcomer Ralph McCalmont for support in preparing a grant application to the federal Housing and Urban Development (HUD) agency, which required local matching funds. McCalmont, a Texan, had just bought the First National Bank and was highly motivated to shake Guthrie out of its long-term economic lethargy. Convinced that the town's historic architecture, long a symbol of failure, was actually its greatest asset, Coffin had rounded up three owners who were ready to renovate their buildings. With help from the federal government and backing from a local lender, Guthrie's long-awaited renaissance would finally be more than just a dream.

Coffin and McCalmont agreed on Guthrie's potential and started working on the preservation possibilities, but it would be three years before they received the federal support they were after, an Urban Development Action Grant (UDAG) with which to begin the rehabilitation of downtown buildings. They had a similar setback at the Department of Interior in 1974 when their first district nomination to the National Register of Historic Places was turned down. Two years later their application was accepted, creating one of the largest historic districts in the country, covering 1600 acres. Despite several false starts, the campaign to save historic Guthrie was on sure footing by the late seventies.

Ralph McCalmont estimates that about 100 Guthrie residents became part of the lively support group that mobilized the preservation movement and kept it going. Of these, a core of ten committed activists provided the sustained push and momentum. They promoted and schemed and organized, bringing in help from the outside whenever they could, but not without a fight. Many Guthrie citizens, including several downtown merchants, were not ready for change. The more the preservation group accomplished, the more agitated the opposition became, to the point where opponents of the revitalization project would send dissenting letters to federal agencies whose help was being solicited.

As other communities have learned, tangible support from the outside helps to win some of the internal battles. Financial help not only gets things done, it provides affirmation and recognition, offsetting the impact of local naysayers. Federal grants, a National Register listing, historic landmark plaques from the state's historical society—these achievements reminded local citizens that the rest of the world was watching and liked what it saw. From the start, the McCalmont/Coffin axis has effectively recruited writers to keep a steady flow of articles appearing in newspapers and magazines. Attracting the world to their doorsteps is essential to the growth and success of the West's isolated small towns.

Although millions of dollars were eventually spent on Guthrie's revival, mostly for construction and municipal improvements, some of the most significant projects were carried out at modest costs. A $2000 grant from the National Trust for Historic Preservation in 1978 underwrote a preservation plan for the entire downtown. Arn Henderson, a University of Oklahoma professor and an architect, directed the project. He began by asking three basic questions about Guthrie's historic architecture: What do they have? What can they do with it? How can they go about it? Henderson examined, photographed, and measured each building and then rated each one according to condition and architectural significance. After studying old photographs, he prepared street elevations that showed each building in its current state, and a second version to show what it would look like if it were restored along its original lines. This exercise was a revelation to building owners. Most of them in the day-to-day round of business no longer "saw" their buildings—they took them for granted and had stopped paying attention, and they could not envision the improvements. Seeing the possibilities through an architect's eyes and being assured that the buildings had architectural quality and value helped to persuade owners that rehabilitation was a good investment.

Henderson's final report summarized the case for adopting a historic preservation ordinance and outlined the mechanics of a preservation commission. In late 1978, following Henderson's recommendations, the city council formed the Capital Townsite Historic District Commission, which was empowered to control all architectural and visual aspects of downtown, including paint colors, signs, building materials, alterations, and new construction.

Recognizing that Guthrie's skeptical merchants needed to see a tangible example of a successfully restored building, the preservation alliance persuaded three owners to take the plunge. Two of the three renovated buildings had been designed by Foucart—one, a narrow, three-story storefront, which had been his office at the turn of the century; and the other, a spacious cor-

ner property named the Victor Block. The third building, the Goodrich, was a typical late nineteenth century commercial brick structure. Like many Guthrie buildings, it had been completely faced with a metal false front in the early 1960s. All three building owners drew on funds from a facade easement program channeled from the U.S. Department of the Interior through the state's historic preservation office. Owners relinquished control over the building facades (they were transferred to the Logan County Historical Society) in return for grants used for restoration.

In the summer of 1982, all eyes were on the Victor, purchased by Guthrie residents Pete and Donna Cole for $35,000. This imposing corner structure, designed by Joseph Foucart in 1893, was regarded as the town's most important commercial building, although it was derelict at the time of purchase. The building was in general disrepair, its upper stories filled with pigeon droppings and debris. The Coles moved ahead quickly, investing $1.5 million in the Victor's rehabilitation, creating a mall of shops on the first floor, office suites on the second, and a large gourmet restaurant on the third.

The splendidly revived Victor, as is often the case in the early stages of downtown preservation overhauls, became Guthrie's crucial demonstration project. Wary merchants and cautious store owners could see with their own eyes the transformation of a dreary liability into a sparkling asset, visually as well as financially. Along with the Goodrich Building, its coating of aluminum paint now removed, and the Foucart Building, restored by architect Arn Henderson, the resplendent Victor proved to any lingering doubting Thomas that nineteenth-century architecture was gold to Guthrie, waiting to be burnished and enjoyed.

Guthrie's preservation movement gathered momentum in the early 1980s. The town turned itself inside out, its preservation activists, now well organized and in control, moving along on several fronts. Supported by $50,000 in state funds, Guthrie invited a team of preservation

6.4   Although the Victor Block in downtown
Guthrie had deteriorated badly by 1980, the
importance of this large building was obvious
to people of vision. The Victor's size, historic
features, and corner location at a central inter-
section made it a strong candidate for renewal.
Joseph Foucart, Guthrie's master architect, had
designed the 1893 building, which added to its
importance. Courtesy Logan County Historical
Society

6.5   When the Victor Block was rehabilitated
in 1982, its bright new face and transformed
interior proved to Guthrie's skeptical merchants
that the city's tired and damaged old buildings
were still full of life. Courtesy Logan County
Historical Society

GETTING BACK TO MAIN STREET

6.6 This "before" picture of the Blue Belle Saloon illustrates the problems of disjointed, accumulated improvements made to Guthrie's old buildings over the years. Here are protruding air conditioning units, a totally out-of-character shingle overhang, and a haphazard use of paint over brick. Fortunately, most of the basic facade features were left intact. Courtesy Logan County Historical Society

architects and planners from the Historic American Engineering Record (HAER) to develop a comprehensive plan for downtown revival, essentially carrying on where Arn Henderson's preliminary plan had left off. Their work became the backbone for municipal and building improvements accomplished in 1981 with federal aid—an Urban Development Action Grant of $800,000, to which local owners pledged a match of nearly $5 million in building improvements. During this project, brickwork was repointed, stonework cleaned, metal fronts removed, windows replaced, and pressed tin cornices repaired. Inside, spaces were remodeled, sometimes totally gutted and re-

built. The city, meanwhile, installed period lighting, brick sidewalks, landscaping, parking, and other improvements along a ten-block area, all of which helped the merchants and pleased the eye of the visitor.

Of the thirty-five buildings undergoing improvements at this time, most drew on benefits offered under the federal Tax Reform Act of 1976, which granted accelerated depreciation for rehabilitated historic structures. In 1981, an expanded tax act allowed owners of National Register commercial properties tax credits of up to 25 percent of the cost of approved renovations. The incentives spurred investors in oil-rich Oklahoma

6.7 *The Blue Belle Saloon "after" takes full advantage of the building's attractive, spacious storefront windows and distinctive corner entry. The signs are much improved, and the street lighting once again matches the scale and ambience of the building. Courtesy Logan County Historical Society*

to pour capital into historic preservation. For Guthrie, the timing was perfect.

Looking back on the restoration boom, Don Coffin cites three essential ingredients for a workable revitalization: "One, a motivated building owner. Then, a bank willing to lend, and finally, a professional team to put the packages together." In 1980, after struggling to coordinate the banks, city officials, and owners with the proper state and federal agencies, the Logan County Historical Society, acting as a development corporation, hired an executive director, Susan Guthrie. She was experienced in negotiating the complex financial packages that underwrote the restoration of

the buildings. Guthrie, who had held a similar position in Arkansas, knew how to help local investors and officials to meet their goal of reviving the town's historic architecture. Ralph McCalmont, the banker who had been nursing Guthrie's renewal along for five years, recognized that they had to find a manager, someone who was skilled in finance and understood government programs. "You reach a point where you *must* have a professional who works full-time on these projects and who knows the ropes or you can never pull ahead or *stay* ahead of the problems."

Until the oil collapse came in the mid-1980s, downtown Guthrie moved surely toward its territorial beginnings. Since then, the regional economic downturn, along with historic preservation setbacks at the federal level, has slowed the pace. Ralph McCalmont, experienced in the economics of small towns, remains sanguine about Guthrie's lull. "The economy of any place has cycles. The downtime is when you plan. You create your infrastructure and get organized when things are down, because when the roll starts, you've got to be ready for it."

Despite the force of the oil-driven recession in Oklahoma, Guthrie continues to gain from a local population boom that began in the early 1970s. Logan County's population has doubled during the past twenty years, strengthening Guthrie's primary market and bringing customers to its main street. As improbable as it might have seemed years ago, Guthrie's citizens have Oklahoma City to thank for much of its continuing prosperity. Just as Granbury, Texas, depends on nearby Dallas and Fort Worth for its essential tourist trade, Guthrie looks to Oklahoma City. The manager of Guthrie's downtown historic inn, the Harrison House, notes that many weekend visitors are Oklahoma City neighbors seeking an escape, a relaxed weekend away from home that does not require a long drive or expensive air fare.

Like all history-laden small towns, Guthrie is mindful of its tourist potential and what it must do to develop and maintain it. Don Coffin believes they must get people to spend the night in Guthrie; otherwise the economic benefits are extremely limited. The Harrison House, a former bank building adapted as an inn, is part of the strategy to keep visitors in town for more than a few hours. To sweeten the pot, Coffin organized a local Arts and Humanities Council, which opened a theater next to the Harrison. The 250-seat Pollard Theater now performs year-round and employs thirteen full-time actors and staff. Guthrie also offers three museums, the country's largest indoor livestock roping arena, and a dude ranch. Coffin now is encouraging owners of historic homes to open them to visitors on a daily basis, noting that residents of Jefferson, Texas, a

Greek Revival town frozen in time when the railroad passed it by, successfully host tourists and thereby add to the town's attractions.

Guthrie celebrated its centennial in 1989 with a simulated land rush and a large enough parade to create a second chapter of history for this one-time territorial capital. With this nostalgic hoopla behind them, Guthrie's preservation leadership has begun to focus again on the future. During the past fifteen years, they have managed to save and revitalize one of the best enclaves of historic buildings in the country. Now they must find a way to expand tourism without jeopardizing the town's straightforward frontier look as an unpretentious urban remnant from the turn of the century, and one that reveals a singular story of western settlement.

Red Cloud, Nebraska

Willa Cather describes small-town life on the Nebraska prairie with the special acuity of an insider who remains always a stranger, speaking with an authentic, intimate voice but maintaining a critical distance. Tapping her own experiences in the town of Red Cloud in the late nineteenth century, Cather captures the overwhelming sense of limitless space on the flat prairie, finding it simultaneously oppressive and exhilarating, depending on the degree of punishment or promise offered at any given moment by this newly settled country.

During her adolescence, Cather lived in town but had close friends among several of the surrounding farm families. She was drawn to the immigrant settlers who homesteaded near Red Cloud—the Germans and Scandinavians, the Czechs and Slavs, whose exotic old-country ways added color as well as mystery and life to a world dominated by reserved, parochial, English-speaking newcomers from the settled regions of the American East and South. She regarded the

6.8 The Farmers' and Merchants' Bank (1888–89), an avowedly urban building, would look more at home on Chicago's Astor Street than it does here in Red Cloud, Nebraska. The bank is now home for the Willa Cather Historical Center. Courtesy D. Murphy

European "foreigners" as a welcome tonic.

Although Cather loved Red Cloud and the Nebraska prairie, she left it as a young woman to live in New York City. She acknowledged and even celebrated the grandeur of the Nebraska landscape, but she found life on the land confining and sometimes defeating. She understood how quickly the vitality and diversity of the frontier spirit gave way to conventional behavior, narrowness, and caution. Red Cloud for Willa Cather was pleasure and pain intertwined, all of it a touchstone for her writing.

Red Cloud provided Cather the raw material for many of her novels and short stories. Through her writing, she put the town on the map, and its citizens in turn have celebrated her artistry by preserving those places and buildings that appear in her work.

Visually, Red Cloud is an American classic, a typical small town in the heartland. Downtown, neat rows of two-storied commercial buildings face each other across the brick paving of Webster Street. In this parade of traditional Victorian facades, one structure stands out—the Farmers' and Merchants' Bank. The bank's first owner was a prominent Red Cloud citizen, Silas Garber, a former Nebraska governor who was the model for Captain Forrester in Cather's *A Lost Lady*. Built of bright Colorado sandstone, the bank towers over downtown as a tall, rich uncle might dominate a family reunion. Of urban design—narrow and high, as if land were too precious to be wasted—the aspiring bank reflects the fashionable Queen Anne styles popular in Boston and other eastern cities in the 1880s. The Willa Cather Historical Center now occupies the bank building as a museum for Cather memorabilia.

Beyond downtown, tree-lined streets pass along fenced yards containing white frame houses, including Willa Cather's family home, a story-and-a-half gabled cottage covered with clapboard siding set off with dark shutters. Huge elms and maples tower overhead, leafy and verdant during the growing season, black and barren against the winter sky.

The downtown ends abruptly where the residential neighborhood begins. Just as suddenly, the rows of houses give way at the edge of town to cornfields and pasture. Unlike many towns, whose borders are marred and compromised by fast-food stores and service shops, the Red Cloud townscape remains neatly self-contained.

More than thirty-five years ago, friends and family of Willa Cather began to gather the memorabilia of her life and to preserve the town and surrounding countryside as the historical setting for a literary world that is real as well as imagined. Cather's followers, many of them lifelong friends and neighbors, eventually organized themselves as the Willa Cather Pioneer Memorial Foundation. Along the way, they acquired historic buildings and sites, deeding them in 1978 to the Nebraska State Historical Society, which administers and maintains them.

Thirty historic sites in Red Cloud have been organized into a self-guided Willa Cather tour. Visitors are aided by a map and illustrated brochure identifying the settings for Cather's stories: her childhood home, described in *Song of the Lark*; the Miner house, home of the Harlings of *My Antonia*; and the Burlington depot and Catholic church, both featured in *My Antonia*.

A second self-guided tour takes visitors through the Cather countryside surrounding Red Cloud. South of town across the Republican River the Nature Conservancy now manages a 610-acre tract of prairie that is being planted and groomed to replicate its original wild state. With its ever-moving tall grasses, this patch of prairie recaptures the sights and smells of the virgin prairie that greeted Willa Cather in 1884 when she arrived in Nebraska as a child. Along with old homesteads and open fields, the tour includes cemeteries, churches, the site of an old mill, roads, and cottonwood groves. Among the most compelling places is the isolated farm home of Annie and John Pavelka, who were the Cuzacks of *My Antonia*. This simple frame house calls up images from the book: white cats curled among pumpkins on the porch steps, a shining kitchen seen

6.9 *Small frame homes like this one, the Henry C. Cutter House (1894), are typical of residential neighborhoods in the plains states. The Cutter house is in Red Cloud's Elm Street Historic District, part of the Willa Cather Thematic Group nomination to the National Register of Historic Places. Courtesy D. Murphy*

6.10 *The loft bedroom in the Magee-Cather House, Willa Cather's childhood home. Courtesy R. Bruhn*

6.11   One of the great appeals of Webster County's "Cather Country" is the happy blend of rural and town historic sites, including the pristine Dane Church north of Red Cloud, one of several area churches mentioned in Willa Cather's fiction. Courtesy R. Bruhn

through a screen door, and the food cellar from which Antonia's children "exploded" in a rush of light and life during a visit from the novel's narrator, Jim Burden.

The success of Red Cloud's renaissance emerges out of the clarity of a single, simple concept operating within a complex setting. The theme of Cather's early life on the prairie is easily grasped; the context of her literature and the region it describes are extraordinarily rich. Preservationists in Cather's Red Cloud have a clear focus for their work but an endless variety of material

to work with: no danger here of a lifeless museum freezing a moment in time.

Recognizing the appeal of Cather's writings when combined with Red Cloud's tangible past, the Willa Cather Memorial Foundation organizes a conference that attracts both amateurs and experts to Red Cloud each spring to discuss the meaning and merit of Cather's work. Every two years, along with nearby Hastings College and the University of Nebraska, the foundation offers a week-long summer seminar on some aspect of Cather studies. Participants attend daily seminars

6.12   The Pavelka Farmhouse in rural Webster County was a major setting for Cather's book, My Antonia. *Cather describes Antonia's young children bursting into the sunlight through a cellar doorway. Courtesy R. Bruhn*

and then tour the town and country sites associated with Cather and her work. These excursions include a picnic on the prairie and a church social to sample Czech kolaches (pastries) and other pioneer ethnic foods. In alternating years, the foundation joins with Kearney State College to present a prairie workshop, which examines the ecology of the natural setting as well as the life and times of Cather and her circle.

As a result of these recurring events, the Cather legend and the town of Red Cloud are continually infused with new people and fresh perspectives. During late summer, the town celebrates Streetcar Days, a salute to its late nineteenth century boom years, a time when Willa Cather was absorbing the region's pioneer drama and when the town's population at 2500 was nearly double what it is today.

Despite these happenings, Red Cloud remains Nebraska's best-kept secret. Fewer than 10,000 visitors toured the Cather sites annually during the 1980s, compared to the 125,000 people who visit the historic square each year in Granbury, Texas, or the equally large crowds who enjoy the nineteenth-century ambience of Guthrie, Oklahoma.

There are some advantages to keeping the audience small. There are no tourist traps in Red Cloud, no boutiques filled with imported country collectibles, and very few tour buses idling their engines on main street. John Nikodym still sells farm implements out on Highway 136, and farmers still take their grain to the Ely and Lewis elevators by the Burlington Northern railroad tracks. Downtown, merchants sell the necessities of life—groceries, clothing, hardware, and medicine. Red Cloud is still a farmers' market, catering to the families who live in the region.

It seems a pity that so few people are able to admire Silas Garner's elegant redstone bank or gaze at the wallpapered attic bedroom in the Cather house where young Willa slept. Only a trickle of curious visitors drive past the Dane Church on the road to Bladen or walk along the banks of the Republican River, and still fewer stop to see the food cellar on the Pavelka farm or the Cloverton cemetery, where John and Anna Pavelka are buried.

Cather's prairie world not only deserves a larger audience, it is likely to require one in order to survive. Even though the Nebraska State Historical Society owns and operates six important Cather sites in Red Cloud, which means the buildings are secured, the maintenance and staff expenses to keep them going are high, in addition to the capital costs needed when they require major repairs. Can these costs be justified when only a few thousand people each year visit the properties? What will happen when other historic buildings in Red Cloud need help? Will the historical society continue to acquire buildings?

The Red Cloud world is getting smaller every decade. During the 1970s the surrounding county lost 37 percent of its farm population. When farmers leave, so do the doctors, teachers, merchants, and business owners who keep a town alive and healthy. So far, the number of new stores has equalled the number moving out, but if Red Cloud's agricultural market is disappearing, then another has to take its place or soon the town will be a shell. Unlike Granbury, Texas, which attracts residents of Dallas and Fort Worth, the town of Red Cloud has no nearby city to draw on. A new and appreciative audience must be cultivated.

The twin achievements of the Willa Cather Memorial Foundation are impressive, both their scholarly attention to Cather's literary legacy and their preservation work with landmarks. Now the foundation, together with the Nebraska State Historical Society and other allies, must look toward the future, grooming a new generation of leaders, building a larger audience, and shaping a healthy economy for Red Cloud. It may be time for a leap rather than a step. It may be time for a bold, encompassing move—perhaps a "Willa Cather Heartland Council" to pioneer a visionary twenty-first-century plan for Red Cloud and Webster County.

Lincoln, New Mexico

Even a tiny community can become a preservation giant. In the remote village of Lincoln, New Mexico (population 65), a preservation program comprising the Lincoln County Heritage Trust, the Museum of New Mexico's State Monuments Bureau, and the town's citizens has succeeded in saving twenty-odd historic buildings, many of them now open to the public.

As a rallying point for preserving this National Historic Landmark, the town's preservationists have embraced the legend of outlaw Billy the Kid, who starred in a violent power struggle—the Lincoln County War—during the late 1870s. His name has been linked to the town ever since.

To say that Lincoln is isolated is understatement. The town occupies a narrow valley below the Capitan Peaks, a small mountain range northwest of Roswell. The flat High Plains stretch eastward. Beyond the Sierra Blancas to the west

6.13 *The Tunstall Store was owned by a young British rancher and merchant who was an early casualty of the Lincoln County War. Courtesy Museum of New Mexico*

lie white desert sands and prehistoric lava beds. The mountains above Lincoln are gentle and unassuming—rounded peaks covered in their lower reaches with New Mexico's common pine trees, bushy and widely spaced. Exposed stretches of red earth brighten this spare landscape, which despite its austerity, radiates warmth through the crisp, reassuring light of a nearly constant New Mexico sun.

Forty or so adobe buildings are strung out along the town's single street, a crooked trail that skirts the Bonito River. Lincoln's architecture—modest structures of adobe and timber decorated with features borrowed from the Greek Revival—reflects the influence of nearby Fort Stanton, which like other army posts of the period, mingled American classicism with the established traditions of the Southwest.

Lincoln's beginnings were tentative and ordi-

nary, starting as a small agricultural market tied to Fort Stanton, built in 1855. The town, first named La Placita, had been settled in the 1850s by Hispanos from the Rio Grande Valley who herded sheep, built an irrigation system, planted orchards, and constructed *jacales,* small houses with walls made of upright logs of either cedar or pine and then chinked and plastered with adobe.

By the late 1860s, as the demand for beef increased throughout the country, cattlemen established ranches, ranges, and trails east of what was then La Placita. The excellent grazing lands as well as the availability of government contracts for beef and grain attracted outsiders who were eager to capitalize on selling provisions to Fort Stanton and the nearby Mescalero Indian Agency. Instability and lawlessness marked this era of economic change.

In 1869, La Placita was renamed Lincoln and

6.14   *The Tunstall Store is one of several*
historic sites restored and operated as a New
Mexico state monument. Courtesy Museum of
New Mexico

designated the county seat. The town grew and prospered until the end of the 1870s, when rivalries over the control of frontier markets triggered an outbreak of violence. The murder in February 1878 of John Tunstall, a young rancher from England who operated a mercantile store in Lincoln, whipped the town's competing factions into open war. In mid-July, a five-day gun battle left six men dead and set loose the legend of Billy the Kid, John Tunstall's 18-year-old ranch hand who escaped from the July gun battle and reverted to his outlaw stance by rustling cattle and thieving throughout New Mexico and Texas. Late in 1880, Billy the Kid was arrested and convicted of murdering Lincoln County's sheriff. Sentenced

to hang, he was taken back to Lincoln and jailed. Less than two weeks later, using a smuggled gun, Billy the Kid shot his way to freedom, killing both the jailer and a deputy marshal. In July 1881, near old Fort Sumner, bullets from the gun of Sheriff Pat Garrett ended the life of the outlaw, but the Kid's fame as an outlaw hero was just beginning. The ingredients of the story—imperious cattlemen, scheming traders, cold-blooded murder, a shoot-out, a jail break and subsequent man hunt—now seem the stuff of romantic legend, but at the time, the town of Lincoln was traumatized.

With order restored in the 1880s, and with the general western economy fueled by the railroads, mining, and agriculture, Lincoln entered a second period of growth and prosperity. Later, during the 1890s, the town became known as a health spa. Easterners suffering from tuberculosis began to come for long periods to take "the cure," consisting of medication, rest, and New Mexico's bracing mountain air. A half-dozen doctors were soon involved in supervising the rehabilitation of the sickly new arrivals. They needed a place to stay. Several existing adobe buildings were enlarged and fitted with windows and pitched metal roofs. At the same time that doctors, their patients, and families were forming a new population in Lincoln, others were drifting away, an exodus that accelerated in the twentieth century.

In 1913, the county seat was moved to Carrizozo, thirty miles west, drying up all the jobs and businesses supported by the courthouse. Around the same time, the El Paso and Rock Island Railroad began buying up water rights along the Rio Bonito. In arid country, land stripped of its water rights loses its value and usefulness. A drought at the end of World War I left many local ranchers without income. In the 1930s, an extended drought combined with the general economic depression finished the town. By World War II, only a handful of residents claimed Lincoln as their home.

Throughout its slow demise and despite its losses, Lincoln held onto many of its most important assets—a remote mountain setting, abundant sunshine, two-dozen substantial adobe buildings, and the legend of Billy the Kid, who, through time, became increasingly heroic and fascinating. Beginning in the 1950s, artists and writers rediscovered the town. They were joined by retirees and others on independent incomes seeking a quiet retreat in New Mexico's beautiful hills. The town began to come alive again.

The large mercantile store owned by John Tunstall, whose murder marked the first round of the Lincoln County War, belongs now to the Museum of New Mexico, which also owns the courthouse, the Montaño store, San Juan Church, and the *torreon,* a small, round, stone fort built in the 1850s as a refuge against Indian raids. When the torreon was restored in 1934, it became Lincoln's first preservation project. Many years would pass before the town's other historic buildings were rehabilitated.

In 1981, the State Monuments Bureau restored San Juan Church, a small adobe structure dating from nearly a century before. Tom Caperton, director of the monuments bureau, describes the restoration plan for the church as an unusual one that incorporated aspects of the church as it had evolved since 1887. Caperton had originally intended to restore the building to the way it looked on that date, and his staff completed research and architectural plans in that direction. The townspeople objected, however; they did not like the idea of features being removed that had been a part of their experience with the building over the years, features like the tin roof from the 1940s. Caperton reconsidered and then carried out what he describes as an "interpretive" restoration, which appears to please everyone.

Caperton made use of stereophotogrammetry, a state-of-the-art recording technique, to document the church building's condition and appearance prior to restoration. With this technique, three-dimensional data can be expressed in two dimensions on a printed drawing, achieving a level of accuracy that is not otherwise possible. Previously, drawings that purported to show the building's original form have been created from standard photographs or direct observation of the building, in which case the eye and the hand tend to correct crooked lines, even if that is not the intention of the illustrator. Stereophotogrammetry provides a realistic record of the exact state of a structure as the restoration process begins.

Lincoln's buildings are folk expressions of modest scale and simple materials. As restorations go, they have not been costly. The state spent $100,000 on San Juan Church and more recently around $350,000 to restore the old courthouse, a much larger building. The Museum of New Mexico owns a total of nine buildings in Lincoln, including the church and the courthouse. Altogether, these sites form a considerable finan-

6.15 *The San Juan Church in Lincoln as it appeared in the 1930s. Courtesy Museum of New Mexico*

6.16 *San Juan Church after restoration in 1981. Courtesy Museum of New Mexico*

cial obligation for restoration, operation, and maintenance.

A similar financial load is carried by the Lincoln County Heritage Trust, a private preservation group organized in 1976 by prominent ranchers and other area residents, including Robert O. Anderson, former chairman of Atlantic Richfield and a New Mexico rancher; Paul Horgan, writer; and artist Peter Hurd. The Heritage Trust owns the Wortley Hotel, the Gallegos House, and the ruins of the Aragon Store. The home and office of Dr. Woods, one of the town's several physicians during Lincoln's days as a health resort, is also a Heritage Trust property. A new visitors' center that incorporates the historical Luna Museum Store offers an orientation to Lincoln and its history.

The New Mexico State Monuments Bureau, the Lincoln County Heritage Trust, and the Lincoln County Historical Society work together to promote and operate the town's historic buildings. The Heritage Trust, for example, owns Dr. Woods's house, but the county historical society developed its interpretive program and provides the volunteers to keep it open.

As an out-of-the-way attraction, Lincoln will never be host to hordes of tourists, but its annual visitor numbers are rising rapidly. The number of visitors for the summer season jumped from about 12,000 in 1988 to nearly 20,000 the next year. These numbers are expected to climb over the next several years. Entry fees help to defray costs of operating the buildings.

Although twice blessed with benefactors, the State Monuments Bureau and the Heritage Trust, Lincoln's long-term preservation will depend on finding additional financial sources. The Heritage Trust's board of directors intends to build an endowment, not an easy prospect considering the small size of Lincoln's constituency. Finding a means of widening the circle of support for preservation is a constant and common need in the sparsely populated West.

Volunteers as well as donors are spread thin in Lincoln. Ann Buffington, president of the Lincoln County Historical Society, points to a handful of local citizens who are called on to sit on boards and commissions for policy making and to fill all the spots where volunteers are mandatory, such as the house museum of Dr. Woods and the annual Billy the Kid pageant. "We have a continual problem with citizen overload. Everyone is burned out." Buffington regards as a positive sign the recent cooperative efforts among the historical society, the Heritage Trust, and the state monuments staff. Successful collaboration, never easy within the isolating insularity of a small town, tends to invigorate the participants. Energies flow toward accomplishing a goal together, rather than creating obstacles for each other.

Interestingly, Lincoln's obsession with Billy the Kid is abating. Legends are powerful. They tend to dominate. Not everyone welcomes an exclusive focus on Billy the Kid; some citizens want to tell a larger story about Lincoln's beginnings, including its Hispanic origins, the health retreat era, and the daily life and times of ordinary people living in a small frontier village. Increasingly, tour guides and exhibits focus on the rhythms and events that were representative of life in Lincoln, rather than the fascinating but aberrant conflict in which Billy the Kid starred.

But Billy remains a big attraction. He is notoriety embodied, a scrofulous, sharp-shooting renegade who managed to be on the right side at least some of the time, though perhaps he was only in the right place at the right time until his time ran out. At summer's end in Lincoln, Billy the Kid is king for a day when the town presents a Billy the Kid pageant, reenacting the famous jailbreak and other highlights of the Lincoln County War.

Lincoln's preservationists and historians will probably continue to emphasize Billy's outlaw fame, and he clearly offers an authentic piece of theater straight out of the mythic West. The Lincoln County War is a great yarn that warms the hearts of cowboy buffs, and it is an enviable hook for promoting the town's attractions. As further research and restoration are accomplished, the Lincoln story will take on other dimensions:

6.17 *In 1886, Lincoln, New Mexico, was an agricultural village of irrigated fields and adobe buildings. The valley appears much the same today. Courtesy Museum of New Mexico, Neg. No. 76101, photo by J. R. Riddle*

there is more to ranching than rustling, more to frontier justice than shootouts with the sheriff, and more to trade and commerce than the murder of storekeeper John Tunstall.

Lincoln offers the visitor an engaging step back in time. If not a totally realistic, authentic nineteenth-century frontier town, it comes extremely close. Both Lincoln's restored buildings and its interpretive programs meet high professional standards. Strict zoning laws preclude disruptive commercial development, to the point where visitors may actually wish there were more amenities. Lincoln has no filling stations or cafes. One hotel, open for the summer season, and a recently established bed and breakfast inn serve a handful of overnight guests. For most people, a visit to Lincoln means a few hours to enjoy a distant West highlighted by a gripping story of turbulent times.

What can other preservation-minded communities learn from Lincoln? Because of its out-of-the-ordinary financial underpinnings, Lincoln's preservation solutions do not have wide application. In most communities, preserving historic architecture is seen as a means of revitalizing the economy. In these cases, building rehabilitations are often privately funded, with the expectation that the occupying commercial enterprises will return the investments made. In Lincoln, a decision to restore was made first, as an end in itself, and

6.18 *The courthouse in Lincoln after restoration in 1989. Courtesy Museum of New Mexico*

then the funding was found to accomplish the work. The fact that the economics of the Lincoln experience are quite different than the norm does not take away from the quality of its preservation program, nor from its value to the visitor. The simplicity and purity of Lincoln's physical resources result in large part from the absence of commercialization, but the level of subsidy available here is not an option for most communities. To make a comparison, Lincoln is more like South Pass City, a small mining town rehabilitated and operated by the Wyoming Recreation Commission, than it is like Granbury, Texas, or Guthrie, Oklahoma, which rely primarily on a private market to sustain them.

A Second Life for the West's Main Streets

Concern for the vitality of America's small towns led the National Trust for Historic Preservation in 1977 to create a major new program to recapture the spirit, liveliness, and look of the nation's fading main streets. For three years, the National Trust ran a trial program with three small midwestern towns and then launched its Main-Street Program in six states, including Colorado and Texas. By 1989, more than 400 communities in thirty states were participating in the MainStreet Program.

The idea behind the program echoes traditional small-town entrepreneurship—if you have a vision of what you want to accomplish and are willing to work hard with your neighbors, you can find a way to improve both your town's appearance and its economic circumstances. The National Trust's commitment to the preservation of historic architecture in small towns goes hand in hand with the possibilities for economic gain. Within the program, a town's old main street buildings are seen as an asset—part of its unique identity, and capable of drawing residents as well as visitors to spend their time and money in local stores and businesses.

Through state governments, the MainStreet Program has formed a partnership with the towns selected to participate. Each town hires a trained, full-time MainStreet manager. Local merchants and the town's government must provide the manager's salary; in this way they make a commitment and an investment in the program. The managers are supervised by the state's MainStreet coordinator following an intensive training period. Resource teams offering counsel and technical services on everything from facade design to finance are available to individual towns through the national program. Texas, which had enrolled forty towns by the end of the 1980s, has developed its own resource teams.

The MainStreet Program teaches that each community is unique, but managers organize their work around four precepts: organization—getting townspeople to plan and to act together; promotion—building a better image and learning how to market; design—improving the appearance and appeal of buildings and townscape; and economic restructuring—enhancing and expanding existing businesses as well as recruiting new ones.

Why does a community become involved in the MainStreet Program? Fear. Dwindling incomes. Hope. A sense of competition with other communities. The most promising candidate is a small town that has hit bottom and is ready to start up again.

Most small-town merchants have had a tough time in the past ten to twenty years. They have watched neighboring businesses, one by one, close up or move out to a new mall or highway commercial strip. The moment of truth for many comes when a national discount chain comes to town and dries up business on main street. Those are dark days.

Hope comes when a portion of the downtown businesses—perhaps only a small nucleus—get together and decide that they are going to fight back, regain their market share (or find a different kind of market), and rebuild their main street as a source of pride and a center for the community. Leadership and teamwork are essential. A few motivated, visionary people make the difference.

Small-town merchants tend to be independent-minded, which is why they have their own businesses in the first place. They are also competitive, not only with each other but with other communities as well. If a nearby town has captured attention and new business by renovating its old buildings, local merchants will want to emulate that success by revitalizing their own downtown. With a goal before them and with the fear of business failure pushing from behind, MainStreet business people will work in concert. This type of cooperation is not part of the normal small-town business environment; their disinclination to work together in a common cause in the past has contributed greatly to their failure to compete successfully with suburban malls, where marketing, management, and context are all orchestrated.

MAINSTREET IN TEXAS

Libby Barker Willis was a MainStreet manager in Gainesville, Texas, in 1983 and 1984. Gainesville's program was short-lived, although the town adopted several features of the program and recently has hired an economic revitalization director to carry out much of what was started under the MainStreet Program.

From her later perspective as director of the National Trust's Texas–New Mexico field office, Willis generalized from her own experience and that of other MainStreet managers on the challenges of getting a program underway. In every MainStreet town a series of procedures must be put in place right away; each tends to generate anxiety and obstacles within the business community. Willis cites the identification of historic resources as one of the first tasks to accomplish. Conducting an architectural survey and getting the downtown nominated to the National Register of Historic Places is an essential first step because it triggers access to federal tax incentives for building rehabilitation. The general public and the press usually respond positively to National Register nomination, but building owners often shy away from this step, fearing that National Register status will jeopardize their control over their property (it does not, but the anxiety is often strong nonetheless). Because this process can be a lengthy one—first conducting a survey, then preparing an application and waiting for review—the National Register step needs to be taken early on. Foot-dragging merchants can create an obstacle to change, and delays at this point can slow up everything else.

A related problem crops up about the same time. MainStreet usually urges a community to establish low-interest loans to enable owners to fix up their building facades. All local banks are asked to participate by pledging a set amount that can be available at low interest. In Gainesville, four banks each agreed to offer loans totaling $20,000, available at 8 percent interest. The banks usually resist this program because they regard it as a poor investment, and one that sacrifices their own earnings. Merchants may not like the loans either, even though the fund is designed specifically for them and carries a low rate. Why the wariness? Perhaps because they feel they are being herded into something, or that a loan implies that their business is failing, or they don't want any part of their business controlled by the bank. For whatever reason, the whole idea of a special fund for building facades is foreign.

Once the facade improvement program gets going, however, it tends to be contagious. Some cautious merchants will then do a renovation, but pay for it out of their own funds. The bank's stamp of approval on the program lends credibility and therefore has a positive influence on facade renovation, even if the individual merchant does not apply for a loan. Some MainStreet managers have found that new business people recruited to the community are more likely than the old-time merchants to participate in the low-interest loan program. They are making a big change anyway, so a new program is not as likely to be resisted.

Despite some property owners' resistance to declaring downtown a historic district, and despite some merchants' skepticism about loan programs for building renewal, most MainStreet managers push hard for both because fixing up the old stores is tangible proof that something new is happening downtown. It makes the merchants and local residents take pride in their community's appearance, and it makes out-of-town customers take notice.

For the MainStreet Program to be effective on the financial front, merchants must learn to advertise together. Again, this idea is foreign to many small-town entrepreneurs. The job of the MainStreet manager is to promote the town, including special events. These occasions require everyone's support—through handbills, mailings, and radio and newspaper advertising. A sidewalk sale or summer flower festival offers every merchant a chance to get on board in promoting downtown.

In Gainesville, Libby Willis as MainStreet manager helped the local businesses to organize a downtown merchants' association. They adopted a formal calendar of special events: four a year, with meetings every month to work out the strategy and details. For a month-long promotion, Willis organized a weekly concert on the courthouse square using talent from the local high

6.19   When it joined the MainStreet Program in the mid-1980s, Sweetwater, Texas, was handicapped by a downtown filled with nondescript buildings, many of which had been modernized years earlier. One two-story building had already been refurbished, and it offered a strong argument for the appeal of historic architecture. Courtesy Texas MainStreet Program

6.20   With fresh paint, new awnings, highlighted features, and landscaping, Sweetwater's downtown buildings entered a new era of commercial success. Courtesy Texas MainStreet Program

6.21 In Georgetown, Texas, one of the state's most attractive and successful MainStreet towns, the former Masonic Hall was restored and adapted for use as a restaurant and for offices. In the process, the onion dome was rebuilt. The preservation of an architecturally and historically important corner building is always critical to a town. Georgetown's program of landscaping and street amenities adds to the attractiveness of the refurbished buildings. Courtesy Texas MainStreet Program

school. The concerts brought a hundred or more people downtown, many of whom stayed to shop. In the summer, the merchants hosted a three-day heritage celebration—a festival of crafts, special foods, and music.

The Gainesville MainStreet Program was phased out after two years. A newly elected city council was ambivalent towards the program, undercutting support and shifting the manager to other assignments. A changed political cli-

mate inevitably hinders or sidetracks MainStreet programs, at least temporarily. Serious community change typically takes years, and fortunately most towns that have participated in the program are willing to make that commitment. The attrition rate nationwide is low. Nearly 80 percent of the original MainStreet towns are still actively involved in the program.

Although Gainesville slipped away from the fold, the Texas MainStreet Program overall is

6.22 Georgetown's Victorian commercial buildings were in a dismal state of repair when the MainStreet Program got underway in the early 1980s. Courtesy Texas MainStreet Program

6.23 Although many improvements were made to Georgetown's commercial facades, the most dramatic was the reinstatement of second-floor windows. Windows are the eyes of a building, and when they are sealed, the facade has no life.

After considerable discussion among design consultants, the suspended canopies were retained as part of the restored facades. The canopies are not original to the buildings, but they date to the World War I period and therefore have a substantial history as part of Georgetown's streetscape.

Georgetown children are shown here during the annual Christmas parade. Courtesy Texas MainStreet Program

strong, led by Anice Read, a powerhouse admin-istrator and long-time preservation leader who watches every project like a hawk and knows Texas politics inside out. What impact has the program had on the state? "During the past ten years, the face of Texas has changed," says Read. "Before that, other than Jefferson, Granbury, and Fredericksburg, there were no intact historic towns that looked like anything. Now there are dozens, including some that aren't even in the MainStreet Program but were influenced by the others."

When a MainStreet town cannot find a local manager, Read does some screening for them and makes recommendations. "We need someone who's smart, personable, and patient and who has a sense of design and the persistence to demand it." Most MainStreet managers are young (the salary is modest and the program requires high energy) and the vast majority are female. The stress is high, and the effects of isolation can drive even the most exuberant young manager into a funk. To build team spirit, Read encourages them to maintain frequent telephone contact with each other, and she brings them all together four times a year for meetings.

The program builds a strong sense of personal service and a dedication to the public. In terms of the commitment and spirit it evokes, MainStreet can be likened to the national VISTA and Peace Corps programs. Libby Willis, who follows Main-Street closely, believes the spirit generated is a powerful force, one that cuts through intransigent problems. "The energy you feel is amazing. I'd rather go to a meeting of MainStreet managers than anything."

The MainStreet Program in Texas has produced impressive results. By 1989, the program had encouraged reinvestment totaling $181 million in some forty small towns. More than 2470 buildings had been rehabilitated, 1286 new businesses recruited, and 3917 jobs added to the marketplace. Most of this work has been accomplished with private funds leveraged with modest outlays from local governments along with technical assistance from the state. The MainStreet Program is definitely a "best buy" for Texas taxpayers.

LAS VEGAS, NEW MEXICO

Other western states have participated in the MainStreet Program, albeit at a more modest scale than Texas. New Mexico joined the program in 1985 and now has nine active MainStreet programs, including Las Vegas (population 15,000), founded in 1835 as a farming community and the Mexican port of entry on the Santa Fe Trail. Las Vegas is hardly a typical MainStreet town. Its scenic setting and remarkable historic resources offer unusual advantages. On the other hand, a history of political divisiveness and long-standing economic problems have hampered citizen efforts to revitalize downtown.

Las Vegas joined the MainStreet Program after the town had already identified its substantial historic resources and had begun to improve and promote them. Several major building rehabilitations had been completed, bringing new business into town. The advantage that the program offered, coming when it did, was a broad-based structure for economic development and a means for better marketing. Renovated buildings are an essential ingredient, but without a financial underpinning and market strategy, they cannot add much to a town other than an improved appearance.

Las Vegas has both an Old Town and a New Town, built a mile apart, the latter created when the railroad came through in 1879. Old Town was originally a Mexican settlement of low adobe buildings, and it still reflects that heritage. New Town was built in the American Victorian architectural styles popular during the 1880s and 1890s. As a rail center, the town mushroomed, becoming a rich mercantile center and a destination for travelers.

Old Town and New Town operated as separate municipalities until the 1970s, when they were united under a single government. The merger has been problematic. Long-standing feuds and proprietary attitudes color legislative decisions and civic action. Time will probably wash away

6.24 When the railroads came into New Mexico in 1880, both commerce and tourism enjoyed a great surge. Las Vegas, at the edge of scenic mountain country, became a travel destination. Its most popular and prestigious hotel was the Montezuma, built several miles out of town at the entry to Gallinas Canyon. The Montezuma offered its guests thermal waters, mud baths, trail rides, and hiking. The Chicago architectural firm of Burnham and Root designed the hotel, which was owned by the Santa Fe Railway. Courtesy New Mexico Historic Preservation Division, Office of Cultural Affairs

6.25 The Montezuma burned in 1884 and again in 1885, reopening in 1886. Despite its setting and luxurious fittings, the hotel failed to sustain itself as a successful spa and stood empty for many years. When the United World College bought the Montezuma in the early 1980s, Las Vegas preservationists were greatly relieved, but the college has found the building unsuited to its needs and has put it up for sale.

6.26 *The Santa Fe Railway chose a Mission Revival style for its station and adjoining Castaneda Hotel, even though Mission Revival was more properly associated with California. "Southwest" was becoming a generic look not always tied to the region's indigenous architecture.*

6.27 *The Castaneda Hotel (1898) was one of Fred Harvey's famed chain of railroad hotels and is one of the many Las Vegas buildings that will enjoy a revival when the town's economy improves.*

some of these differences, and the current revitalization activity, by bringing underlying conflicts out in the open, may speed up the process of reconciliation.

The region has a splendid climate—high, sunny, and dry with cool summers and manageable winters. Las Vegas is at the edge of the Great Plains and near scenic Gallinas Canyon, where the Santa Fe Railway in 1886 built the Montezuma Hotel, a huge luxury hotel and spa designed by Chicago architects Burnham and Root. Las Vegas had several large hotels of its own, including the Plaza in Old Town and the Castaneda next to the railroad station.

The town's decline began in the 1920s. Agricultural prices were low, reflecting a national depression in that part of the economy, and tourists were beginning to travel by car rather than train. Turn-of-the-century railroad hotels like the Montezuma no longer drew their traditional clients. Besides, neighboring Santa Fe and Taos were attracting the carriage trade, which had once vacationed in Las Vegas.

Government payrolls kept the town stable during its long period of commercial decline. New Mexico Highlands University is located here, as well as the New Mexico State Hospital and a district office of the state's highway department. In the commercial center of New Town and around the old plaza, however, building after building deteriorated, emptying out first on the upper stories and then closing down altogether.

During the 1970s a few episodic but important efforts were made to study and save the town's old buildings. With strong support from Thomas Merlan, the State Historic Preservation Officer, a nucleus of preservationists organized a survey. As a result of their research and field work, nine districts numbering more than 900 buildings were nominated to the National Register of Historic Places. Self-guided tour brochures and special editions of the newspaper began to celebrate the city's heritage.

In 1975 the town's first significant rehabilitation was accomplished on the Louis C. Ilfeld law office on the Old Town plaza by Joe and Diana Stein, owners of Los Artesanos Bookstore. The Steins, tenants at the time they completed the work, received an award from the state for their preservation achievements. Two years later, the New Mexico Historic Preservation Bureau (now the Historic Preservation Division) gave them a grant-in-aid to acquire the building. The Steins specialize in Western Americana and have customers all over the country. Their specialty has helped them to survive the Las Vegas economic doldrums because they rely on local retail trade for only 10 percent of their sales.

Becoming more and more interested in Las Vegas's architectural legacy, Diana Stein helped to form the Citizens Committee for Historic Preservation in 1977. They began to publish a newsletter and coordinate preservation activities, becoming an "action central" for anything having to do with the region's history and buildings. Then, in 1981, the legendary Montezuma Hotel six miles north of Las Vegas was purchased by Armand Hammer's United World College of the American West, an important cultural and economic addition to the area. Preservationists all over the state, long worried about the abandoned Montezuma, breathed a sigh of relief.

Two years later, in Old Town, another historic hotel returned to life when Lonnie and Dana Lucero, in a limited partnership with Wid and Katherine Slick, undertook the complete renovation of the 1882 Plaza Hotel, the largest building on the square. The Plaza project was a major breakthrough for Las Vegas because of the hotel's size—three stories and 30,000 square feet—and its high visibility as an example of late Victorian urban architecture.

The Slicks were newcomers in Las Vegas—young, educated, urbane, well-off—and the town regarded them with suspicion when they arrived. They had been involved in historic preservation projects in Dallas, and when they discovered Las Vegas while on a back-packing trip in the Sangre de Cristo Mountains, they decided to move from Dallas and to dedicate themselves to the re-

6.28   *Louis C. Ilfeld's law office on the plaza has adapted nicely as Los Artesanos, a book shop specializing in Western Americana. Owners Joe and Diana Stein renovated the building in 1975 and encouraged others to take the town's impressive historic buildings more seriously.*

vitalization of this history-rich town on the Santa Fe Trail.

The new partnership acquired the Plaza for what Wid Slick terms "a modest cost" and then spent around $2 million to renovate it, completing the project for around $50 a square foot, or about half of what comparable new construction would cost. The owners started work early in 1982 and opened on New Year's Eve that same year. During that time they installed new plumbing and electrical systems and upgraded other facilities to meet fire code requirements. They made major changes on the rear portion of the build-ing, enlarging the rooms and adding individual bathrooms. Soundproofing to meet modern standards was accomplished throughout the building. All surfaces—floors, ceilings, and walls—were refinished. The hotel now has thirty-seven totally refurbished rooms, a bar, and a large attractive dining room, which has developed a regional clientele.

The rehabilitated Plaza introduced a new dimension in hostelry to Las Vegas. Furnished with antiques and offering sophisticated menus in its dining room, the Plaza is more akin to an up-scale inn in Santa Fe than it is to the typical

6.29   The Plaza Hotel has always been the showcase of Old Town in Las Vegas. Now renovated and totally refurbished, the hotel has spurred other preservation work on historic buildings nearby.

motel on Interstate 25 at the edge of town. With the Plaza and other attractions to support it, Las Vegas can now appeal to visitors who will consider the town a destination, rather than a place to pass through on the way to Santa Fe or Colorado Springs.

The Slicks know that the success of the Plaza depends on the creation of a compatible and attractive setting. Their guests, especially if they stay for two or three days, will want to visit galleries and specialty shops, such as the Stein's Los Artesanos bookshop next door. Visitors will surely want to have a look at the historic architecture in both Old and New Town, particularly if the buildings

are being fixed up and recycled. For Las Vegas to attract and keep large business ventures like the Plaza Hotel, a critical mass of other highly visible renovation projects is needed.

Two years after the Plaza reopened, Wid Slick helped five local investors to create La Plaza Vieja Partnership, which was formed to rehabilitate buildings in and near Old Town. By adding capital from 52 limited partners, and then securing a federal Urban Development Action Grant and obtaining loans from local banks, the partnership had access to $2.5 million in project funding and was positioned to purchase and renovate eighteen buildings for leasing.

The Plaza Vieja project got off to a good start. By late 1988, sixteen of the eighteen chosen buildings were renovated and nearly 60 percent of the space was leased. Then, several bad breaks combined with a change in the political climate to bring the project to a halt. When one of the general partners died, funds that otherwise would have been available for investment in La Plaza Vieja were tied up instead in estate proceedings. Next, a major construction contractor pulled out of the job, leaving heavy bills to be paid by the partnership. Expense money was flowing out and revenue was only trickling in.

It may have been a case of too much too soon. The partners, in order to qualify for the 25 percent tax credits available under the 1981 federal tax act, had agreed to a fast-paced project. To meet the deadline, the partnership began to complete building renovations on speculation. Suddenly, there was a lot of rental space on the market and at a price per square foot that was high by Las Vegas standards.

At the same time, a newly elected city council, feeling its way, started to pull back on the commitments made earlier to La Plaza Vieja Partnership. Large joint public-private projects involve formal agreements but are usually based as well on shared assumptions. The partnership had assumed that the council would choose to build a new police station in one of the partnership's buildings. The new council decided instead to build a new structure and, adding insult to injury, chose a site on the Old Plaza that had previously been designated for a public parking lot considered necessary to the success of rehabilitation around the plaza. The partnership believed the council had let them down. The council, for their part, felt they were being forced into underwriting and rescuing a private venture.

In August 1989 the banks foreclosed on La Plaza Vieja Partnership. Wid Slick, owner of a structure adjacent to the proposed police center, sued the city to desist from building on the needed parking lot. As the project precariously rocked back and forth, accusations and rumors flew. Crit-

ics of the partnership considered Wid Slick to be a manipulative outsider. The partnership and their allies in turn pointed fingers at the council for closing their meetings to the public and for reneging on promises made.

As the year moved into fall, the banks began to restructure the loans, and several disinterested outsiders had urged mediation for the warring factions. By the end of December and after months of negotiations, the city of Las Vegas, La Plaza Vieja Partnership, and Wid Slick reached a settlement, which allows the city to build a new jail on the Hacienda property and to develop a city parking area on nearby Bridge Street. With the deadlock broken and a settlement reached, restoration of historic buildings will continue.

Las Vegas has too many things going for it in today's lively market for historic property development to be slowed down for long by a single distressed project. Still, the outbreak of political dissension is nothing new for Las Vegas, which has a history of in-fighting and power struggles. The negative energy required for these fights can deplete a town quickly, and once the fights start, it is difficult to keep the issues sorted out. Developer Wid Slick, accused by some of leading the town down the primrose path, brought modern real estate financial expertise to a city sadly lacking those skills. He may have pushed too fast, but without a push, the forces of inertia might well have kept Las Vegas stagnant. Without Slick's involvement, neither the banks nor private lenders would likely have participated in La Vieja Partnership.

The troubles in Las Vegas involve more than suspicions cast on "outsiders," nor is the situation merely a stand-off between Anglos and Hispanics. One of the selling points of La Vieja Partnership, which had four Hispanic principals out of five, was that it would maintain the traditional pattern of local Hispanic ownership of Old Town buildings. Around 80 percent of the population of Las Vegas is Hispanic; these numbers are reflected in the membership of both La Plaza Vieja Partnership and the Las Vegas City Council, indicating an overwhelming control held by Hispanics. What else could be feeding this controversy? It is certain that the century-old division between Old Town and New Town still rankles. In addition, Las Vegas probably suffers from a disease common to circumstances of insularity, in which residents tend to begrudge any tampering with the status quo and are particularly resentful of the good fortune of others. These attitudes are an anathema to community revitalization, and one can only hope that by continuing to open up to a larger world, townspeople will begin to take change and success in stride.

The Las Vegas MainStreet Program, chaired by Katherine Slick, continued to flourish and to earn support from the city council despite the conflicts generated over La Plaza Vieja. The strategy of the Las Vegas MainStreet Program has been to persuade residents and institutions to buy locally, rather than take their business to Santa Fe and Albuquerque, or even out of state. The merchant group now pursues markets together, mailing out an advertisement tabloid three times a year. In addition, the Plaza Hotel sends out three events schedules annually to a mailing list of 2000, including former guests and a great many other persons around the region. On the one hand, the "buy Las Vegas" campaign has been slow to gain. On the other hand, tourism—which also helps the retail market considerably—has been growing at a double-digit rate thanks in large part to vigorous promotion by the hotel and the MainStreet Program.

From the beginning of 1986 to the summer of 1989, Las Vegas enjoyed a net gain of thirty businesses and seventy-six new jobs in the MainStreet district, which includes the commercial centers of both Old Town and New Town. Investments in renovation and new construction totaled nearly $3 million during the same period; when coupled with the $2 million cost of Plaza Hotel improvements in the early 1980s, this figure reflects well on the investors' enthusiasm for the town's historic districts.

In addition to the strategy of getting residents to spend their money in Las Vegas, the MainStreet leadership is promoting the region as an alternative vacation destination, hoping to lure travelers away from Taos and Santa Fe or, at the very least, to persuade Santa Fe visitors to include Las Vegas on their itineraries, an easy choice for tourists driving in from Colorado, Oklahoma, or Texas. The Plaza Hotel finds that most of its visitors are in-state, with sizable numbers also coming from California and Texas.

In late September, when sun-burnt New Mexico is at its most dazzling, Las Vegas invites visitors to a Wildflower Festival, which links the town to its lovely scenic surroundings and shows off the region's folk art talents. Academic experts lecture on folk arts, and the folk artists themselves, such as traditional fiddler Cleo Ortiz, give performances and demonstrations. There are fiddling contests and a *biscochito* bake-off, a regional specialty seasoned with anise and recently declared the state's official cookie by the New Mexico legislature. Concerts, dancing, craft workshops, poetry readings, and walking tours fill the days and evenings around the Old Town plaza. Festival-goers are plied with homemade foods and handmade crafts sold from booths set up around the plaza.

If visitors want to see the wildflowers, they must venture up into the foothills or out onto the plains. The picking of wildflowers is no longer encouraged in most parts of the West. A spokesman for the festival sees the flowers as an apt symbol for what has been happening to the town: "In the same way that after the summer rains the wildflowers of northern New Mexico become a colorful feast for the eye, the community of Las Vegas is blossoming after a long dormant period."

PEABODY, KANSAS

Most towns in the MainStreet Program have a population of between five and fifty thousand. In 1988, the Kansas MainStreet Program elected to include a small number of towns with a population of 5000 or less. They chose three, including Peabody (population 1500) in central Kansas, forty-five minutes north of Wichita, the state's largest city.

Peabody is a good example of what can be accomplished by a lot of people working very hard but with almost no financial resources. There are no multimillion dollar renovations or street improvements in Peabody, where $5000 is regarded as a considerable investment. The town has only eleven retail businesses in its downtown. Most residents do the bulk of their shopping elsewhere.

Peabody had been on a downward slide for a long time before it joined the MainStreet Program. Residents and merchants were becoming more and more demoralized as each year passed. Even the town's traditional Fourth of July celebration was in a slump after repeated invasions by motorcycle gangs.

Fortunately, Peabody still had an intact downtown, two blocks of fine Victorian buildings from the 1880s and 1890s facing each other across Walnut Street just north of the Atchison, Topeka and Santa Fe station. Most buildings still had fanciful pressed tin cornices and decorative window surrounds on the second story. The bottom floors had been modernized—some of them more than once—and were at war with their own upper stories. Still, the harmony of their Victorian lines prevailed. Best of all, several important structures were built of native limestone, a Kansas hallmark.

It took outsiders to convince Peabody residents that their old-fashioned and neglected buildings were actually an asset. Larry and Ruth Bull had moved to Peabody from Wichita, where he worked as an engineer, and they had spent months renovating a Victorian house close to downtown. Sold on the appeal and value of old buildings and convinced that Peabody's downtown could be revitalized, Bull lobbied the local government and personally raised some of the $5000 required to join the MainStreet Program. A member of the town council, Bull also became president of the Peabody Main Street Association.

When MainStreet starts a program, it sends out a resource team to help local citizens to evaluate their town's assets and liabilities. The resource team in this instance was very taken with Peabody, and they were particularly enthusiastic about the old buildings in downtown. The word got around quickly.

There is an irony to preservation that often seems puzzling to citizens of a community who have lived with poverty and delapidated buildings for a long time. Old buildings, long a financial drain for a town, become its greatest resource and offer hope for making money and becoming a physical attraction rather than a burden. That is what happened in Peabody. By the time a market survey was completed a few months after the program began, nearly everyone identified the town's old buildings as its greatest asset and a potential that deserved attention.

The MainStreet group hired a local resident, Julie Eberhard, as its part-time manager. Her ebullient personality and entrepreneurial skills have moved the program along quickly. Eberhard grew up in Albion, Nebraska, and majored in languages at the state university before living in Europe for several years. She came to Peabody in the mid-1970s to teach and later opened and operated a bed and breakfast inn. Her work history included public relations and fund raising.

Eberhard reached back into her European experience to create an unusual special event for Peabody—a *son et lumière*, a sound and light show—as a focus for the town's Fourth of July celebration. A local writer produced a script, a fictional "slice of life" approach rather than a literal history of Peabody. Other volunteers came forward to direct the complicated light show and to provide entertainment. An elderly woman who had once played the piano for silent movies in Peabody's theater was recruited to play several ragtime pieces, and a band performed as well. As the script reading and music moved along, colored lights played in an alternating pattern on the historic building facades of the main street. An ice cream social, with homemade ice cream, preceded the sound and light show.

A thousand people came to watch and listen. Peabody's citizens were stunned by the size

6.30 *Many of Peabody's MainStreet structures are built of Kansas limestone, which adds texture and color as well as a distinctly regional cast to the architecture. During the summer of 1988, these buildings were the backdrop for a sound and light show, an evening of theater which dramatized the town's buildings and history. Courtesy Peabody (Kansas) MainStreet Association*

of the crowd and thrilled that their downtown was dramatically showcased. The sound and light show will probably become an annual event, perhaps combined in future years with a craft and home fair.

Within a period of a few months, five facade improvements have been completed. People drive downtown to look at them; they are clearly an attraction. The downtown district is not yet on the National Register, but an architectural survey and nomination will be completed soon. With National Register designation, federal tax credits will be available for rehabilitation work, which may encourage additional owners to make improvements. As in many other towns, the local bank is resistant to low-interest loans for facade work, and the merchants do not want to borrow the money anyway.

Peabody's municipal government provides approximately half of the MainStreet Program's $20,000 annual budget. The rest must be raised privately. Faced with this requirement, the Main-

Street board came up with an inspired solution: they appeal to their "alumni," the high school graduates of years past who now live in other parts of the country. These 1500 or more former Peabody residents not only send financial support, they are the greatest enthusiasts for the revitalization of the town's historic resources, and their enthusiasm has rubbed off on Peabody's permanent residents. Julie Eberhard's office mails a quarterly newsletter and an annual Christmas appeal for funds to all alumni and Friends of Peabody.

The national marketing firm that advises Peabody's MainStreet Program recommended that the town make the most of local crafts by promoting a cottage industry retail trade in which quilters, carvers, carpenters, spinners, and other handicraftsmen would demonstrate and sell their creations from a home and studio setting. Daytrippers from Wichita and other nearby cities would be attracted to specialty shopping of this kind. Gary and Marilyn Jones, owners of a sheep farm outside of town, have already developed a business patterned along these lines. They have become experts on the wool operations of the world and offer spinning classes that attract people from around the country. Mayesville Mercantile in downtown Peabody has recently been renovated by the Joneses, who intend to use it for demonstrations, for the sale of their own woolen wares, and for leasing to other craftsmen.

A second Peabody business, Baskets Beautiful, offers an intriguing possibility as a prototype for western small-town entrepreneurship. In 1985, Larry and Susan Larsen began to line wicker baskets with decorative fabrics and sell them in their gift shop in nearby Marion. They have opened a wholesale business in Peabody, employing five full-time workers and several other Peabody residents who do piecework in their homes. The baskets are now sold in thirty-five states as well as in the Larsens's Peabody retail outlet. Wholesale business now accounts for 90 percent of their income. The Larsens have the advantage of operating in a low-cost business environment, living in a small town, and yet not having to be confined to the limited amount of retail trade generated within Peabody. Developing a national or global market may be the answer for other mountain and plains towns that have lost their local base of trade because of population declines.

The leaders of Peabody's budding MainStreet Program have allowed themselves three to five years to accomplish their goals. They have achieved a great deal in only a few months, but progress sometimes seems slow to Julie Eberhard: "We need to learn to work together—to set goals, adopt procedures, and then be disciplined enough to follow them. It's hard."

One of their goals is to recruit eight to ten new businesses within their five-year time frame. Their first recruit, a school of dance, will lease an upper floor of one of the renovated buildings, which is often a difficult location to rent. In addition, it is hoped that parents will shop in the nearby stores while their children take dance lessons.

Eberhard believes that the trick is to keep a balance among all the required ingredients for success: design, economic development (especially the recruiting of businesses), special events, and fund raising. A concentration on one or two at the expense of the others jeopardizes the overall strength of the program.

Reflecting on their activities to date, Eberhard could just as well be speaking for all MainStreet towns: "We're not done with ourselves yet, but we're really proud of what we've accomplished so far."

7.1 *Many buildings in Cripple Creek, Colorado, one of the West's largest gold camps, have burned or have been moved or torn down. The town's boom days started in 1893, and by 1900, more than 50,000 people lived in Cripple Creek. The population was down to about 1000 by the 1970s. Courtesy Myron Wood*

Saving the West's Mining Towns

O f all the historic sites in the mountains and plains West, none are more fascinating than the collection of mining camps and towns scattered throughout the Black Hills and the Rocky Mountains. Their appeal is universal. Westerners fancy their ghost towns with the same avidity as that shown by the long-distance tourists who flock to see them. In particular, the region's early gold and silver camps evoke a sense of risk and excitement. They recall an intensity of experience and high times that once set them apart from ordinary life.

Mining towns present special problems for preservationists. Many were founded a century or more ago and abandoned shortly thereafter. They are continually exposed to the elements. Without care, the wooden buildings decay and fall, especially when roofs collapse under the load of heavy winter snows. Fire—mischievous or accidental—has claimed hundreds of individual buildings and even entire towns. With these stresses, it is no wonder that much of the physical evidence of nineteenth-century mining disappeared long ago. Nonetheless, the period before World War II was a relatively safe one for western ghost towns. In those days, fewer people went to out-of-the-way places in the mountains. It was not unusual for an occasional hiker climbing in the back country to come upon a deserted miner's cottage with the furniture still in place. After World War II, when Americans had access to four-wheel-drive vehicles that could take them anywhere, ghost towns became fair game for scavanging. Abandoned build-

7.2   In 1896, after two devastating fires, Cripple Creek rebuilt its business district on Bennett Avenue, and it is intact today. Courtesy Myron Wood

ings that had withstood a hundred years of hostile winter weather suddenly fell victim to souvenir hunters and vandals.

Paul Putz of South Dakota's historic preservation office is pessimistic about the future of most Black Hills mining camps. "Deserted ghost towns are prey to vandals, many of them otherwise law-abiding citizens who cannot resist picking off weathered boards and antique fixtures. And we're helpless to stop them."

In the mid-1970s, as South Dakotans watched their ghost towns disappear, they took the first steps toward preserving the towns' histories by making a record of existing buildings. The state's preservation office, working with the Historic American Engineering Record (HAER), began a study of mining districts in the Black Hills. The HAER surveyors prepared maps and sketches of important sites and then photographed individual buildings and described their histories. These documents form a valuable permanent record for research. By 1985, the South Dakota preservation office had developed and published a standard methodology for surveying mining sites. Other

7.3   The Masonic Temple in Victor, Colorado.
Although mining towns typically began as col-
lections of makeshift buildings, the successful,
established mining camps produced a serious,
lasting architecture. Courtesy Myron Wood

*7.4   Two churches in Victor, Colorado, with
a mining headframe on the hillside overhead.
Victor boomed alongside Cripple Creek. Leveled
by fire in 1899, the town rebuilt with brick.
Courtesy Myron Wood*

western states have completed similar studies of
their mining towns, buildings, equipment, and
paraphernalia.

What is being done to save these remnants
of western mining history? Mining-town preservation has a peculiar history of its own. Nearly
all late nineteenth century mining towns developed similarly after their founding—first a chaotic
camp of tents and shacks, then a more organized
phase of frame and log buildings followed by a
stage of permanent masonry buildings, and for
a few, culminating in an urban industrial era.
Because of the boom and bust nature of the
industry, a mining town might have been abandoned at any of these stages. As a complication,
the economies of mining towns sometimes veered

7.5   Last Chance Gulch was the hub of gold-mining activity in Helena, Montana. These Victorian commercial buildings are part of a pedestrian mall and park, which celebrates Helena's bonanza days.

off in a totally new direction. Silver City, New Mexico, became an agricultural market; in Montana, Helena's famous Last Chance Gulch became engulfed by development related to the city's role as the state capital; more recently, many Colorado mining towns boomed a second time as ski resorts. The differences that existed among mining communities a century ago have become more marked as time passes.

Although many nineteenth-century mining towns did have a distinctive look that penetrates our mind's eye when we hear the term "ghost town," in reality, the western mining legacy is more varied than this stereotype suggests. The preservation solutions for mining towns are equally varied. Each of four early mining camps—

St. Elmo, Colorado; South Pass City, Wyoming; Ashcroft, Colorado; and Bannack, Montana—has been stabilized and preserved in a different fashion. Aspen, Colorado, and a dozen other high-country ski resorts have been struggling to retain their vernacular architecture as property values soar, creating pressures to build anew. Deadwood, South Dakota, a popular tourist mecca since the 1920s, is reinventing itself now to recapture its authentic early mining history, much of it buried beneath layers of commercialized Wild West myth-making. Finally, Butte, Montana, an urban copper capital, continues a long fight to retain its urban and industrial heritage.

St. Elmo, Colorado

Ghost towns stand the best chance of enduring when they have a sufficient number of concerned residents to ward off vandals, but few enough people to alter the town's original character. It is difficult to strike the proper balance. Under the watchful eye of a handful of old-time families, the small gold-mining camp of St. Elmo, high in Colorado's Sawatch Mountains, has survived handsomely into our own time.

Although many historic mining camps get high marks for picturesque charm, St. Elmo ranks as a special favorite. The town stands at 10,000 feet above sea level near the end of Chalk Creek Canyon at the continental divide. Aspen and spruce forests cover the mountain slopes and fill the gulches that spread out like fingers into the high country. A jeep road leads out of town, ascending a 12,000-foot pass and then continuing to Tincup, one of several mining camps in the surrounding terrain.

Today, a dozen faded frame buildings stand along Main Street. Others are spread about in the heavy brush across Chalk Creek. An abandoned two-story false-front store, formerly Pat Hurley's

saloon, faces on Main Street across from the stone ruins of an old mill. Next door, new owners have renovated the Miners' Exchange, a small clapboard-covered structure that first housed a bank, later a saloon.

The Home Comfort Hotel, another notable Main Street building, is now boarded up, its wood siding stained brown from years of exposure to the weather. For many years following World War I, as the town's prosperity began to wane, Annabelle Stark and her two brothers, Tony and Roy, ran the Home Comfort and the local post office. After a while everyone left town, the brothers died, and Annabelle became more and more reclusive. Reportedly, she greeted strangers with a shotgun and ran them off. Her quintessentially Wild West solution to unwanted strangers probably saved St. Elmo from vandalism during the years when it was virtually deserted.

During the 1970s and early 1980s, Priscilla Hartman ran a general store in the center of town on Main Street. It was the only business left in St. Elmo. She had come to town out of curiosity twenty years before to search for a distant relative's grave in the gold fields. She stayed, opened the store, and helped to oversee the town along with fellow members of the St. Elmo Fire and Protection Association. The town's population by then consisted of three households who lived there year-round and another fifteen families who owned cabins and came up occasionally in the summer.

In 1978, St. Elmo was listed as a district on the National Register of Historic Places, but the town still had no formal preservation program. A few property owners began to fix up their buildings, but mostly they watched visitors to make sure that windows were not broken or boards removed. From the vantage of her Main Street store, Priscilla Hartman kept an eye on outsiders and reprimanded those who trespassed or damaged property, like the woman who kicked down the front door of an empty store across the street, or the couple who wandered uninvited through the kitchen of Priscilla Hartman's own log cabin.

7.6   Vandals and Colorado mountain winters have been hard on St. Elmo's fragile frame buildings, but a small group of residents have started a preservation program.

7.7   In St. Elmo, vandals and thoughtless visitors have necessitated the boarding up of entries and storefronts.

Then, in 1986, the general store burned down. Rather than rebuild, Priscilla Hartman decided it was time to retire. She moved to Buena Vista, twenty miles away. Local property owners did not know what to do; without Hartman's vigilant eye, would vandals have their way in St. Elmo? Might some entrepreneur come to town and build a large, garish new store on Main Street?

A group of St. Elmo residents decided it was time to take action. As they saw it, there were two constant threats: vandalism and new construction. Vandals ruined the old buildings, whereas new buildings might ruin the old look of the town. Throughout the mountain region, more and more summer homes were being built, and it was only a matter of time before additional cabins appeared in St. Elmo. New cabins were likely to be larger than the simple vernacular buildings of the town and to stand out because of their architectural lines and bright, new wooden surfaces. The St. Elmo preservationists wanted to stabilize the town, protecting its sun-browned, weathered, authentic mining-camp appearance. They organized themselves as Historic St. Elmo and got to work.

With a Preservation Services Fund grant from the National Trust for Historic Preservation, Historic St. Elmo began to move ahead with design guidelines and historic district zoning for the town, a process that has yet to be worked out with officials of Chaffee County. In the meantime, while they wait for guidelines, Historic St. Elmo has encouraged property owners not to paint their buildings, but rather to coat them with linseed oil to maintain the natural look of the wood. The Fire and Protection Association has proceeded with a major restoration of the city hall, replacing the weakened foundation with native rock and repairing both roof and floor. The hall stands out among its dark-stained neighbors. Its brightly painted white walls and bell tower form a pleasant pairing with the white steepled schoolhouse on a hill across the creek.

A new general store has opened in the Miners' Exchange building, offering limited refreshments and merchandise to residents and visitors. While holding to a simple and rustic profile, Historic St. Elmo offers tours of the town during a special festival period the first week in July. Long-time residents and descendents of old St. Elmo families are recruited to wear period costumes and guide visitors through the town's historic buildings.

Although there are only a few people to do the work or pay the bills, Historic St. Elmo has managed well. Its members offer care and continuity, always necessary in an effective preservation program. Several buildings have been modestly improved, and the twin threats of new construction and vandalism have been kept at bay. As a result, the fragile historic resources of St. Elmo have been stabilized and strengthened.

South Path City, Wyoming

The preservation program adopted for South Pass City, Wyoming, another nineteenth-century early-stage mining camp, is considerably different from St. Elmo's stabilization solution. South Pass City has been rehabilitated by the Wyoming Recreation Commission, which now operates the town as part of the state's park system. During the preservation process, several badly deteriorated buildings were dismantled and reconstructed. The aim here has been not merely to stop the decay of the buildings, but to return them to their appearance in an earlier time.

South Pass City was a small gold-mining camp that burst on the scene in 1867 but then went into a decline barely a year after its founding. The town was named for the point on the Oregon Trail that marks its highest crossing over the Rocky Mountains. The discovery of gold attracted an influx of miners and other temporary residents to South Pass City, pushing the population to 2000 within a year's time. A total of 1500 mines and lodes—all part of the Sweetwater Mining District—were scattered among the hills surrounding the town.

A classic mining town, South Pass City's Main Street was lined with one- and two-story log buildings, their gable ends disguised by square false fronts. In addition to the mining apparatus and buildings of the nearby gold fields, the town had five hotels, thirteen saloons, a bank, a school, and several stores. It was standard stuff—the basics of life from a miner's point of view.

Within three years, competition from other towns and a disappointing yield from the South Pass City mines led miners elsewhere, and another western boom town went bust. By 1871, a writer for the *Appleton Hand-Book of American Travel* described South Pass City and its boom-town neighbor, Atlantic City, as a largely abandoned collection of some 250 houses, steam mills, and mines. Mining never died out altogether; every decade or so renewed activity—gold, copper, or iron—infused money and energy into the district, although never again close to its 1860s bonanza level. South Pass City remained a stagecoach stop for a time and served the surrounding ranching community as well, which helped to keep the town alive into the twentieth century.

When the Wyoming Recreation Commission took possession of South Pass City around 1970, two of the town's most important structures, the Houghton-Colter Store and the South Pass Hotel, were in a state of ruin and required dismantling and rebuilding. A third structure, a giant underground root cellar known as "The Cave," was deemed unsafe and was rebuilt before it was opened to the public. Other buildings, including the Sherlock Hotel, a 1910 school, and numerous cabins, were in sufficiently good condition to be repaired. Rehabilitation of the twenty-seven buildings in the commission's charge has been stretched over a long period, with a few structures completed at a time. About half of the buildings, all of which were built of logs, are faced with frame false fronts painted white with deep red trim, as they were originally. The logs have been left untouched.

In addition to its twenty-seven historic buildings, the South Pass City Historic Site is the re-pository for 13,000 artifacts, 90 percent of which are original to the town. Many of these items are exhibited in the same places where they were used a century ago.

Curator Tod Guenther believes the artifacts—furnishings, cookware, and tools—and the authentic character of the buildings show visitors what the Old West was really like, a departure from popular movie myths. The interpretation of South Pass City presents the early mining period as an unusual time in western history but not an aberration. The cyclical nature of economic life in the West is a dominant theme, joined with the need for innovation and mobility on the part of the residents.

South Pass City, designated a historic site, is open to the public from mid-May through October 15. Many of the buildings contain exhibits that explain the town's early history from the first boom days of the 1860s and on into the twentieth century.

St. Elmo, Colorado, and South Pass City are different from each other in several respects. St. Elmo comprises privately owned properties, the exteriors of which can be viewed by visitors from the road as they drive or walk through town. The buildings reflect the use and weathering of a century. The city hall and the school are the exceptions; they are cared for in a more conventional way, painted and improved. What St. Elmo "tells" the visitor depends on what the visitor is able to observe and deduce.

South Pass City, as a public site, presents a version of itself using architecture and artifacts in addition to the town's setting. Guides, exhibits, maps, and literature support the message of the physical materials and spaces. South Pass City is more explicit than St. Elmo, more didactic, less impressionistic, less evocative. Its lessons are selective and to the point. South Pass City today is a historic site and a museum, whereas St. Elmo, though largely deserted, still functions as a private community. Both are successful preservation projects.

Whether a building should be stabilized (stop-

7.8 *Bachelors' Row in Bannack, Montana, a collection of frame and log buildings occupied by single miners. Newly arrived prospectors probably spent their first few months sleeping in wagons, tents, or brush shelters and then built a cabin or shack as winter approached. These weathered remnants offer an example of the hands-off preservation approach adopted by Montana's Department of Fish, Wildlife and Parks. The buildings are protected from vandals but few physical improvements have been made. Courtesy Montana Department of Fish, Wildlife and Parks*

ping or slowing its deterioration) or restored (returning it to its original appearance and condition, which may require reconstruction) is debated by preservationists. Sometimes necessity rather than principle dictates a direction of action, i.e., a building may have to be stabilized because there is no money to restore it. On the other hand, it may have to be restored because it is too badly damaged or altered to stabilize. The average visitor probably responds more enthusiastically to a restored building. It looks better than a distressed building and is more explicit in its his-

torical and architectural messages. Because of this response, rehabilitation projects that receive substantial funding from tax dollars are likely to be under greater pressure to restore rather than stabilize. Restored buildings are often quite dazzling in their transformation, pleasing to the eye of the visitor as well as satisfying to the restoration technicians whose skills contribute to their makeover. Nonetheless, preservation professionals today are tilting toward stabilization, conserving the building as they find it rather than as it might have appeared at some earlier time.

Bannack, Montana

In Montana, the ghost town of Bannack, eighty miles south of Butte, exemplifies stabilization at its minimal best. Like St. Elmo, this early camp of wooden buildings dates back to Montana's gold rush days in the 1860s. When the Division of Fish, Wildlife and Parks acquired Bannack in 1950, people were still living there. The last resident left in 1983. The parks division did sufficient repair on the town's sixty log and frame structures to keep them from deteriorating further, but they left the accumulated materials of a century—old linoleum, paper, and paint—on the walls and floors.

Bannack is operated frugally with a minimum staff: a resident manager year-round, assisted by a maintenance worker and four "seasonals" who keep an eye on the property during the summer tourist season. Each year, around 50,000 visitors tour the town. A brochure is available and visitors are free to wander among and through the buildings except for a few rooms that are kept roped off. During Bannack Days at the end of July, costumed volunteers offer craft demonstrations and activities, such as horseback riding and gold panning. One of the houses serves as a visitors' center where slides are sometimes shown. Self-guided tour brochures are available on the front porch. Other than these few visitor amenities, Bannack offers only its buildings, a mountain setting, and mystery.

Marcella Sherfy, Montana's historic preservation officer, regards Bannack as the "ghostliest" of all of the state's preserved and interpreted mining camps, and she admires the restrained approach taken by the Montana parks division. Sherfy inclines toward the "less is more" theory of historic site restoration, believing that the accumulated layers of history are more interesting and honest than a period restoration, which often involves removing or otherwise destroying building fabric, much like the destruction of a prehistoric site by an archeological excavation. A decision to stabilize a historic building, the minimalists would argue, protects the patina of age for future study.

Ashcroft, Colorado

Another variation of stabilization—and a minimalist approach to interpretation—has been adopted by the Aspen Historical Society for Ashcroft, a small community of mining buildings ten miles south of Aspen. Over the years, nine log structures in close proximity had been vandalized and gutted until they were little more than shells. Several roofs had collapsed under heavy winter snows. The U.S. Forest Service owned the Ashcroft buildings and probably would have demolished them, following their standard practice of removing abandoned buildings.

Under a special use permit from the Forest Service, the Aspen Historical Society took responsibility for Ashcroft in 1974. With $40,000 in raised funds, they rehabilitated the buildings, taking them back to what they looked like twenty years earlier, before the roofs began to fall in. The society connected the repaired and stabilized buildings with simple wooden boardwalks and then opened them to the public. In truth, the buildings had been open to the public for decades, with unfortunate results, but now the public was officially welcome to inspect and enjoy them.

The Ashcroft buildings now have protection in the form of a "resident ghost" who guides visitors and watches the property. There are no entrance fees, but visitors are asked for contributions, which have produced sufficient income to make the site self-supporting.

Is there a magic answer, or even an easy answer for mining towns? Much is known about the evolution of mining communities, and this accumulated knowledge has brought greater sophistication to preservation of the mining legacy. During the 1970s and early 1980s, as preservation techniques were being perfected, there was a tendency to standardize, to make the site fit the solution. Today, preservationists are less inclined to intervene with a building's evolution. The knowledge that some mining structures have stood empty for a century may be their most important message, not necessarily a negative one but a reminder that the cultural trappings of the West are often ephemeral, born of economic turbulence.

Colorado Resorts: The New Boom for Mining Towns

After World War II, the ski industry created a second bonanza in slumbering Rocky Mountain mining camps. In Aspen, Colorado, and a dozen other nineteenth-century towns, skiers have brought in new wealth and, along with it, new development that has obscured and destroyed much of the original mining legacy. The surviving historic structures have been overwhelmed by an invasion of condominiums, chalets, restaurants, and shops, and the resulting rise in land values has made it difficult to retain the vernacular buildings—particularly the small miners' cabins—that were at the heart of the original town.

Sky-rocketing real estate values are no friend to historic architecture, whether in Aspen or Santa Fe or Dallas. By the late 1980s, an average little cottage on a 6000-square-foot lot in Aspen was selling for around $400,000. If the cottage itself had only 600 square feet, it would seem to be expensive space, especially if it were a very ordinary miner's home with no redeeming architectural features, or if it had been altered considerably. The buyer in this instance would probably push for demolition to facilitate construction of a large,

comfortable modern home or a building that produced income.

Of the approximately 275 miners' cabins that existed in Aspen in the mid-1980s, fifteen had been lost by the end of the decade. By that time, only twenty-five cottages remained in Aspen's east end, and at least half were threatened because buyers and developers wanted to demolish them. With vacant land at a high premium, there was not even a place to move the cabins.

In response to these pressures, Aspen's city officials have developed a set of incentives, the largest in the state, encouraging property owners to save historic buildings and to respect the small scale of Aspen's original mining community. For instance, the Historic Preservation Commission can grant variances on setbacks and density in order to save a historic building. Construction of a second and larger new building might be allowed near the back property line behind a historic cottage, or a cottage might be moved to the side of a lot to allow a new one of similar size to be built alongside. The city has granted owners of historic residential property the right to operate bed and breakfasts, not otherwise allowed, and as a further incentive to save Aspen's old buildings, the city now makes designation grants of $2000 to property owners who allow their historic buildings to be named local landmarks. These legislative solutions have slowed the demolition process and have encouraged owners to find creative solutions that can coexist with historic buildings.

Development pressures have existed in Aspen since 1945 and show no signs of abating. To be sure, the town holds more in its hand than historic architecture. It also boasts a splendid mountain climate, exceptional scenery, invigorating outdoor recreation, strong cultural offerings, and the personal pleasures of fine dining and shopping. The historic institutional and commercial buildings located downtown are secure and well cared for—the Opera House, for example, and the Pitkin County Courthouse. The question is, will Aspen lose some of its fundamental character when most of its mining era vernacular homes vanish? Most

7.9   *The older commercial and institutional buildings of downtown Aspen have fared well during the town's postwar ski boom, but the small cottages and cabins once ubiquitous in Aspen are in fast retreat. Here, the Aspen Block commands a major downtown corner.*

7.10   *Like many other mining capitals, Aspen built an elegant opera house. A detail of the cornice illustrates fine materials and workmanship.*

7.11   *The bar of Aspen's recently refurbished Jerome Hotel is still a favorite hangout, although the clientele has changed from miners to skiers.*

residents and visitors would probably say "Yes!" But can enough incentives be found to persuade both buyer and seller that small—and old—is beautiful? Ramona Markalunas, a former council member who shaped the town's preservation ordinance, believes Aspen's citizens need a creative solution that is not yet in sight. She would favor a principle such as the transfer of development rights, except that, in Aspen, many people object to increased density in any area of town. As it stands, people who have hung onto their old buildings for years will eventually sell, presumably at a high price, and the buyer will want to have a larger building on the property to justify the investment. Unless new incentives are created, Aspen will continue to lose its vernacular mining heritage.

Aspen may be the most visible of Colorado's mining towns turned ski resorts, but it is not alone in struggling with the issue of preservation and property values. The battle appears to be lost in Breckenridge, which these days evokes very few associations with its mining origins. Telluride, in Colorado's southwestern quadrant, resembles Aspen's situation of a decade ago, according to some local preservation observers, and risks losing its small-town, high-country character if new development continues at its present pace.

Of this endangered mountain species, the town of Crested Butte, a nineteenth-century silver- and coal-mining community, has held its own the most successfully, probably because its ski area is not within arm's reach. In Aspen, Telluride, and Breckenridge, the slopes stretch dizzily up from the town itself; in Crested Butte, the ski area and its surrounding residential village occupy a mountainside three miles away. Rising property values in Crested Butte have created changes, some of them disruptive, but the town retains the look and flavor of its nineteenth-century origins.

Ironically, it was the prospect ten years ago of renewed mining activity near Crested Butte that threatened to bring an end to the town's surviving historic character. A vast complex for molybdenum mining was proposed for the mountains nearby, which might have added a population of up to 10,000 workers, many living in trailer parks. Environmental changes, all to the worse, were feared by most of the town's residents. A great tumult arose—meetings, hearings, and litigation—as the town's citizens squared off against the mining company. Then, a sudden drop in molybdenum prices ended the project. In this case, a mining scheme went bust before it even had a chance to boom. Someday, the molybdenum company may be back. In the meantime, Crested Butte citizens benefitted from a worst-case scenario that prompted them to sort out those qualities of the town worth keeping. Uppermost is its historic architecture.

7.12   Crested Butte, Colorado, preserves its nineteenth-century mining town look better than many ski resorts, perhaps because the ski slopes are several miles away and much of the new construction has occurred there. Courtesy Sandra Cortner

7.13   The Union Congregational Church in Crested Butte is beautifully preserved, still maintaining its original carpentry trim. Courtesy Sandra Cortner

SAVING THE WEST'S MINING TOWNS

Deadwood, South Dakota

During the 1920s, when automobile tourism brought a stream of visitors to enjoy a gold rush drama peopled by such characters as Calamity Jane and Wild Bill Hickok, Deadwood, South Dakota, first embarked on a theatrical and exploitive approach to its own past. Ever since, trinkets, garish signs, and honky-tonk have been a big part of Deadwood's shoot-first persona, an embodiment of Wild West hyperbole and a stage set for bawdy, brawling excess. In the interest of a good story, many Deadwood merchants covered over sturdy late nineteenth century masonry buildings with frontier village false fronts. For years, Deadwood's actual evolution into a mature mining town literally was kept under wraps.

Then, in the late 1980s, Deadwood's citizens voted to legalize gambling. Their hope is to attract a larger number of tourists over an expanded season rather than depend financially on the heavy summer trade. The decision has forced to the forefront issues about design and about community life in general that have implications for the town's historic architecture. Townspeople know there are risks involved with gambling, problems such as unconsidered growth, undesirable businesses, and jarring physical changes, any of which could create an overall negative image. At the same time, they understand that the history of Deadwood has been their bread and butter.

Having put Deadwood on a new course, the town's leaders and citizens now must sort out some basic questions: "What is Deadwood's true character?" "What do we want Deadwood to be?" They must decide which era of the town's history should receive the most attention for practical investments, such as streetscape improvements. Design guidelines have to be prepared and adopted for use by the Historic Preservation Commission. Should Deadwood stick with its tried-and-true but slightly far-fetched Wild West veneer, or should the town pay greater attention to the existing but patently less interesting downtown brick buildings? From South Dakota's preservation office, Paul Putz has advised them that they can do both. By dealing with a longer span of history, they can give the visitor an honest picture of economic evolution in one of the longest-lived gold districts in the country, and at the same time they can reach back for an encore from Calamity Jane, Wild Bill Hickok, and other legendary figures.

Deadwood has yet to sort out the answers, but they have already made one decision: to regulate the quality and nature of their environment. In the process, they are developing a point of view about who they are and how they want to look. They may stick to their guns, as it were, and that wouldn't be all bad. The West, above all, must leave room for rowdy, extravagant experiences such as one finds in the more dramatic moments of life in gold rush capitals, like Central City, Colorado, and Deadwood, South Dakota.

Butte, Montana: A Boom and Bust Survivor

Seventy years ago, nearly 80,000 people lived and worked in Butte, Montana, product of a mining heritage a century and a quarter old. Now reduced to a population of 34,000, and with an economy faltering from a much-diminished mining industry, the city is vastly overbuilt—a city in spirit and memory trying to recapture its place in the sun.

Butte has been a conundrum to preservationists generally and a challenge to the city's own leadership for the past thirty or so years. Despite its severe economic problems, the city has impressive assets. With an intriguing history to draw on—gold, silver, and copper mined within a vast

7.14   The frame building in the center is one of Deadwood's oldest. Courtesy State Historical Preservation Center, South Dakota Department of Education and Cultural Affairs

7.15   A detail of Deadwood's commercial facades illustrates the overload of materials, textures, and messages. Courtesy State Historical Preservation Center, South Dakota Department of Education and Cultural Affairs

7.16 *Shored up by mining wealth and moving rapidly toward a large population, estimated at 80,000 by early in this century, Butte built an urban core of substantial masonry buildings, many of them of considerable architectural style. This is Broadway, shown just before façade and street improvements were underway. Courtesy Historic American Engineering Record, National Park Service; Jet Lowe, photographer*

industrial complex—Butte captures the imagination of anyone interested in America's early twentieth century economic development. The city's surviving physical resources are awesome: a large, high-density urban downtown; strong institutional and public buildings; a distinctive residential fabric of mansions, workers' cottages, and boarding houses all clustered cheek by jowl; and a residue of industrial structures that have always been an intimate part of the community's life.

Looking beyond the impressive buildings and the legacy of a boisterous, hell-raising world of miners, we come upon Butte's long history of troubles. After 125 years of mining, the peril brought by toxic wastes is at crisis stage. Invisible poisons permeate the earth, just as they do in other parts of the mining West, polluting

7.17 *Beginning in the 1930s and continuing after World War II, merchants across the land remodeled storefronts in hopes of keeping up with the times. Glass, metal, plastic, and shake shingles have all been popular. Here, in Butte's Ivanhoe Building, three splendid, decorative brick bays have been totally ignored in the re-fashioning of the store entries. This photo was part of the uptown survey completed in the late 1970s and predates facade preservation work. Courtesy John N. DeHaas, Jr.*

water systems and posing health hazards that lie in wait like a time bomb. More obvious and immediate are the city's financial woes. The mines completely shut down in 1983, cutting jobs for thousands. The recent start-up of some mines under new ownership offers promise but hardly solves the overall economic problems. Attracting new wealth has not been easy. Like all of Montana, Butte is isolated, too distant for easy auto access and outside the well-traveled air corridors.

What will become of Butte? That a solution has not emerged is not for lack of trying. For the past twenty years, city, state, federal, and private funds have underwritten studies, surveys, plans, and a number of successful, active programs. During the 1970s, there was an infusion of fresh blood into the city—young people tied to the counterculture values of environmentalism and attracted by the West's lifestyle, who brought energy and a commitment to solve the city's problems. Many have stayed to provide leadership and a new perspective on Butte's future, but people and programs have not been enough to counteract a failing economy.

What will become of Butte? Some advocates believe the city's unique history has become a resource that can compensate for, if not replace, the dwindling wealth of the mines. Likening Butte to Lowell, Massachusetts, where the National Park Service has created a large industrial urban park to protect historic textile mills and interpret them to the public, preservationists see a new role for Butte as a citadel of western industrial history.

The early mines of Butte were gold and silver; copper became the primary industry in the late nineteenth century and remained so until 1983, when the mines were at least temporarily shut down. (Some were partially reopened in 1986.) In the early days, in order to be close to work, miners built their homes around the steel headframes located above the mine shafts. Immigrant groups (in 1910, 70 percent of Butte's residents were foreign-born or first-generation Americans) kept to their own kind, creating separate ethnic neighborhoods around the mining complexes. The Irish

lived in Centerville, the Austrians and Italians in Meaderville. These neighborhoods, along with East Butte and McQueen, are gone now, swallowed up by the Berkeley Pit, the huge open mine that replaced the shafts and underground mines in the 1950s.

What the pit failed to engulf was threatened anyway by the changing tastes of a more affluent and mobile population. The younger generation, having grown up in the ethnic neighborhoods around the mines, preferred modern houses in the suburbs for their own families. The strength of the traditional neighborhoods began to dissipate after World War II.

For a time in the 1950s, open pit mining renewed Butte's prosperity, but the city's decline had actually begun in the 1920s when cheap imported copper eroded the American market. When mining in the pit became mechanized in the 1970s, many miners lost their jobs. The situation steadily worsened until, in 1980, Atlantic Richfield, having acquired the Anaconda Company four years earlier, announced the closing of the copper smelter in the nearby town of Anaconda. Two years later, mining ceased in Berkeley Pit, and Butte's copper era came to a close.

Butte residents realized long ago that a brighter future depended on new enterprises more reliable than the mining industry, and they began to look elsewhere for new businesses. They saw promise in the rising interest among visitors in learning more about the city's history. At least during the summer season, tourism offers a strong source of income. Each year 300,000 visitors stop at Custer Battlefield in south-central Montana. Glacier National Park on the Canadian border attracts more than 2 million visitors annually. It would be easy enough to divert these travelers to Butte to see the city's historic sites.

Much of Butte was declared a National Historic Landmark in 1962, but it was not until the late 1970s that the first intensive building surveys brought the city's historic resources to public attention. When the Anaconda Company proposed to the city in 1976 that the central business dis-

7.18   Butte's mining wealth created islands of domestic grandeur in what was essentially a working-class town. This chateau was built at the turn of the century for Charles Clark, the son of one of Butte's copper kings. There are no expanses of green lawn or landscaping in Butte; this great house is wedged into a corner lot as though it were in land-scarce New York City. The house is now a community arts center and museum. Courtesy John N. DeHaas, Jr.

7.19 *Butte proved itself to be an industrial and financial center by erecting majestic buildings steeped in history and tradition.*

trict be moved to make way for an expansion of Berkeley Pit, the public protested and efforts began in earnest to find ways to use the existing but largely empty commercial buildings in the district, known as "Uptown." The city hired John DeHaas, an architectural historian at Montana State University, to conduct and publish a survey of Uptown's buildings.

When the Butte–Silver Bow Urban Revitalization Agency was established in 1979 (the city of Butte and Silver Bow County have formed a combined city/county government), its charge was to concentrate on Uptown, strengthening its economic situation and improving its physical stability and appearance. The urban renewal office was headed by Janet Cornish, one of Butte's cadre of talented, energetic newcomers and an advocate for the preservation of Uptown's historic architecture. At the request of the city, the Historic American Engineering Record completed another

inventory of buildings as well as a market analysis and a plan for development.

Of the approximately 4500 buildings in Butte's historic districts, more than 125 are in Uptown. A few of the commercial buildings are stone; most are red or buff brick, built three or four stories high. Several large buildings have six floors. The tallest rises eight stories. Overall, Uptown is a dense urban townscape, and its context is dramatic. Uptown occupies a steep hillside (Uptown and the residential districts were built as close to the mines as possible), and part of that hillside is now the excavated Berkeley Pit.

Preservation-minded citizens in the early 1980s continued to examine the city's historic resources, organizing a comprehensive survey of the historic buildings and sites in the official National Landmark area. Montana's State Historic Preservation Office provided the funding as part of the national mandate for surveys, and the community

7.20   The Silver Bow County Courthouse
in uptown Butte was very much a child of its
time. In the first fifteen years of the twentieth
century, the construction of imposing classical
buildings became every prosperous community's
aspiration. Today, Butte's handsome buildings
offer a chance to attract new businesses as well
as visitors who can enjoy the city's extraordinary
history.

7.21   The dome window of the Silver
Bow County Courthouse. Courtesy John N.
DeHaas, Jr.

7.22   *Miners' cottages, Butte. Courtesy Mark Reavis, Butte–Silver Bow Historic Preservation Office*

increased its commitment to historic architecture and Butte's mining legacy.

At the very time that Butte's place in history was being strengthened, however, its day-to-day economic life was slipping away. In 1983, when Atlantic Richfield closed down Berkeley Pit, and mining ceased, Butte's citizens were in despair. What had been known as "the richest hill on earth" was now a collection of empty buildings, idle machinery, and ugly tailings dumps.

Faced with a devastating economic crisis, Butte's government agencies and business community redoubled their efforts to attract other industry. Don Peoples, a former teacher and coach in Butte's Central High School, had been serving as chief executive of the Butte–Silver Bow city/county government for four years when the min-

ing economy began to collapse. He was to hold the position for more than a decade, projecting an attitude of optimism in the face of nearly overwhelming circumstances and offering practical, active, and hopeful solutions in areas where something could be done.

One of those areas was Uptown. Butte's new strategic plan included public improvements and a program to rehabilitate commercial building facades. Over the next ten years, more than fifty business structures were cleaned and repaired. New signs, entries, and awnings were added. To improve both appearance and convenience, several landscaped parking lots were installed on vacant land in the central business district. To spruce up the area further, the city added period lighting, bus stops, and benches.

Butte's Uptown street improvements were funded through tax-increment financing; as property is improved through new construction and rehabilitation, taxes increase. These additional revenues—the "increment"—can then be directed back into the commercial district for new lights, repaved streets, and so forth, creating a tangible benefit to owners who invest in their buildings, as well as to the general public. By the late 1980s, increment financing was producing between $1 and $1.5 million annually.

Much of this income resulted from the decision of the Montana Power Company and US West, the telephone company, to make a serious investment commitment to Butte. Montana Power has renovated the Hennessey Building, one of the city's largest. US West has invested $7 million in a new building to house advanced digital equipment in anticipation of increased regional needs over the next twenty years. This progressive decision and show of faith constitute a tremendous boost to Butte.

Some of Butte's financing during the 1980s came from the U.S. Department of Commerce in the form of Community Development Block Grants, which support economic development, public improvements, and housing rehabilitation. The city has upgraded and rebuilt more than 200 houses over a ten-year period. The majority are small workers' cottages occupied by low-income owners. In addition to making structural repairs and decorative improvements, the rehabilitation effort replaces worn-out heating and plumbing systems. To aid owners and contractors, the Butte–Silver Bow Historic Preservation Office publishes a guide to house rehabilitation, examining the city's architectural styles and building forms. The guide helps homeowners to sort through their repair problems and outlines appropriate steps for improving everything from roofs to sewer systems while preserving the building's salient historic features. The Montana State Historic Preservation Office, a consistent funder of Butte's architectural projects, supported production of the guide.

THE BUTTE–ANACONDA HISTORICAL PARK SYSTEM

Uptown and the neighborhoods around it were looking better after several years of rehabilitation, but preservationists continued to question the fate of Butte's mining paraphernalia. What about the industrial buildings and features that had created the city in the first place? With the mines completely shut down, no maintenance or care was going into Butte's vast complex of mining structures and related sites. The pumps had stopped operating; both Berkeley Pit and the underground mines were gradually filling with water.

Hoping to set aside at least one of Butte's signature headframes as a focus for a program to interpret the city's mining history to visitors, the Butte Historical Society approached the Anaconda Company with a proposal to preserve the Anselmo Mine and open it to the public. The company had been asked to support several heritage proposals in Anaconda and Butte, and they hesitated to start a piecemeal project. Would the historical society do a master plan of Butte and Anaconda? Would they include a comprehensive analysis of how the closed mining complex could be put to its best use? The company offered to put up money for a study.

Accepting Anaconda's offer, the Butte Historical Society raised other funds from local merchants, preservation advocates in Anaconda, the National Trust for Historic Preservation, and the State Historic Preservation Office. The society then hired the firm headed by Fred Quivik, an architectural historian who had been actively involved since the mid-1970s in recording Montana's industrial history. Quivik's team spent two years studying the Anaconda and Butte sites and then presented an analysis of both the possibilities and the problems, followed by detailed descriptions of how each site could be included in an extended park system and how much each project would cost.

The proposed park—extending from Anaconda's smelter complex thirty miles by rail to

7.23   *Butte's preservation community worked with the Anaconda Company to secure thirteen of the district's headframes, the structures that provide access to the underground copper mines. Plans are underway to create a mining museum around the buildings and headframe of the Anselmo Mine, shown here, just north of uptown. The Anselmo complex is part of a proposed mammoth industrial-historical park that will preserve and interpret the remaining mining buildings, railroad facilities, equipment, and paraphernalia of both Butte and nearby Anaconda.*

Butte's industrial, commercial, and residential core—offers a visionary, integrated solution to what appears on the surface to be a fragmented, chaotic collection of neglected and deteriorating historic sites. Within this comprehensive and inclusive approach, several sites are singled out for attention: in Butte, the Anselmo and the original headframes and associated buildings; and in Anaconda, the smelter stack, the smelter works ruins, and the roundhouse of the Butte, Anaconda and Pacific Railway. All of these sites would be rehabilitated, opened to the public, and interpreted through guided tours given by former miners, smeltermen, and railroaders of the region. Exhibitions, displays, films, and printed materials would also present the area's mining history.

A great deal of interpretation is proposed for the total park system, much of its self-guided by visitors as they stop at scenic overlooks, which would be equipped with weather-proofed text panels and maps explaining a particular vista. Several museum centers would help to orient the visitors, who would be able to ride on trolleys and a train that will connect the sites.

The historical park would emphasize the mining district's sophisticated technology and its massive scale. During the boom years in Butte, equally sophisticated and ambitious financing went along with the modern technology. The Anaconda Company operation was the largest of its kind in the early part of the century. Everything about it is big. One mining shaft is nearly a mile deep; the Berkeley Pit is a mile wide. In their long history, the mines at Butte produced more than 20 billion pounds of copper. To help one comprehend this huge quantity, Fred Quivik likens it to a solid block the size of a football field and rising 750 feet in the air. The miners who produced this wealth organized themselves into a powerful, aggressive labor movement, and for a time, as the Western Federation of Miners, they were a match for management.

The park's planners envision an extensive social history as well, using Anaconda's and Butte's extant architectural resources, both commercial and residential, as a stage for presenting the area's cultural development. The cosmopolitan mix of immigrants and the peculiar patterns of miners working shifts around the clock created a community life of its own. Restaurants catered to ethnic tastes, specializing in the dishes made popular by certain national groups. Cafes, bars, and brothels were open twenty-four hours a day. Miners who lived in boarding houses or in the upper floors of Uptown's commercial buildings sometimes shared their quarters with other workers on different shifts. As one left for work, another arrived home. These are not the rhythms of mainstream American life; they are the signs of a heavily industrialized society imposing itself on a harsh frontier.

Capital, technology, labor, and urban culture are four of the major themes that would serve as the framework for Butte's interpretive history throughout the proposed park system. In his firm's project report, planner Fred Quivik argues that any responsible interpretation of Butte's mining history must include material on the despoiling of the environment by the mining process itself. The Butte and Anaconda areas will soon undergo a massive clean-up under the Environmental Protection Agency's jurisdiction. This project and the ongoing work of reversing the damage of decades of chemical pollution will be part of the Butte story, if Quivik's ideas prevail.

Will this unusual park come to be? A few steps have been taken: the Anaconda Company has agreed to give the Anselmo headframe and mining works to the community, and a short line of the Butte, Anaconda and Pacific Railway is operating as a tour car, equipped with guides who explain the history of the mines along the way.

The proposed park matches the scale of Butte's industry—ambitious, massive, and far-flung. Where will the money come from to rehabilitate and administer a park and on-site museum of this dimension? The solution for Butte's historic resources is likely to follow one of the new collaborative models that are emerging throughout the West—alliances of government agencies, political and corporate leaders, merchants, professional advisers, volunteers, and nonprofit institutions. Fort Worth is organizing this type of collaborative effort to revitalize its Cultural District. Dallas has done the same with its Art Deco fairgrounds and museum enclave, Fair Park. Denver has mobilized its entire power structure to save and revitalize historic Lower Downtown. These examples are in large urban areas, but Butte's history, too, is urban, even if its present circumstances are not. Broad-based collaboration can work in rural or isolated areas as well, although assembling the key people face to face is more difficult. In the Texas Hill Country, the National Park Service has recently involved its dispersed "LBJ Country" sites with a new organization, the LBJ Heartland Council, to encourage participation of nearby residents as well as Texas universities and state agencies. Operations like these are complex, dynamic, difficult, and politically charged, but when they work, they guarantee broad-based support and continuity because everybody is on board.

A full-scale industrial park system for Butte and Anaconda is beyond the means of the Butte Historical Society. Their accomplishments are commendable—the architectural surveys, the industrial park plan, and the saving of Butte's mining headframes are uppermost—and they set the stage for the possibility of creating a comprehensive historical park to attract people from around the world. Making that happen will require an infusion of funds and interest from outside.

Butte's former chief executive Don Peoples sees hope for a coalition and agrees that the scope of the Butte-Anaconda industrial park is beyond the city's carrying capacity. "Going ahead with the Anselmo Mine is the next step. Before we can get outside support, we have to show people what can be done. We need a demonstration project. Even some of our local people need to be convinced that these old mines are worth saving." Initial work on the Anselmo will be supported by around $150,000 in funds from the state's abandoned mine reclamation program.

THE FUTURE FOR BUTTE

One can still ask, What will become of Butte? At the end of the 1980s there was a quiet over the city. A Montana contractor, Dennis Washington, had purchased the Anaconda Company holdings and resumed mining, although at a scale much reduced from that of former days. Butte is a mining town, and when there is mining to be done, people tend not to want to contemplate alternatives. Few believe, however, that Butte will ever be the copper capital again.

Although Butte's leaders are still a long way from their vision of a revitalized city, ten years of hard work since the copper-mining collapse have produced tangible results. The streetscape is healthier, the buildings are more attractive. Throughout the redevelopment programs, there has been a strong commitment to honor the city's historic architecture.

After nearly eleven years in office, Don Peoples, the city's elected chief executive, decided in 1989 to leave government and work in statewide economic development. The optimism about Butte that sustained so many people during his long tenure is still with him. He is pleased with the resumption of mining, and he believes that the two new mining companies are sufficiently technically advanced and realistically structured to last in the difficult world of copper production.

Peoples perceives a dramatic shift in public attitudes toward historic architecture and the possibility of economic gain. Is the community unified? "Now it is. People are behind these ideas. They weren't ten years ago. There was a resentment of other people succeeding. You don't hear

that anymore." He points to the recent renovation of the city's old high school as proof that Butte residents have pride in their heritage and want to protect the vigor of Uptown. The $8.5 million renovation of the high school, which serves 1800 students, was supported with $1.5 million in city funds and will be underwritten eventually with $4.5 million in tax settlements from the Anaconda Company.

The industrial diversity that Peoples and others sought is beginning to fall into place. A Canadian company, Canbra Foods, will produce oil and margarine from canola seeds, a major crop in Canada. Butte offered Canbra tax incentives and provided them with a grocery warehouse, a building appraised at $4.5 million but sold to the company for one dollar. Canbra will start with 60 employees and then increase to 150.

Beyond Butte, the canola oil plant will have a positive impact on Montana's agricultural production. Don Peoples estimates that 100,000 Montana acres will be planted with canola in the near future with a jump to 700,000 acres within five years. Now that this deal has been struck, Butte's economic development leaders will seek other Canadian agricultural producers.

Raw, tough, proud Butte is ready for a comeback and another era of good times. Appearances are often deceiving. Visitors to Butte, having just driven through some of the West's most awesome mountain scenery, often regard the town as ugly and derelict. Yet, Butte has its appeals, and one of them is its singularity as a hard-core industrial town in a region otherwise given over to tourism and agriculture. Only Pueblo, Colorado, a steel city 100 miles south of Denver, matches Butte for a kind of smokestack esthetic of faded redbrick commercial downtowns and grimy industrial structures, slag heaps, and railroad yards. There is a sense of honest work in Butte, of a nononsense blue-collar ethic and style that provides a refreshing balance to the prettified ski resorts of the mountains and a forceful contrast to the wellbehaved blandness of the small towns out on the plains.

Preserving the West's Mining Heritage in the Next Century

The sporadic renewal of mining activity all over the West, bringing new roads, test sites, construction, and excavation, has accelerated the destruction of historic mining camps. In response, South Dakota now requires that mining companies document any buildings or features that are likely to be destroyed by new mining activity. To avoid the delay and expense of a survey, mining company officials sometimes elect to let the old buildings stand. The permit system therefore serves as a de facto preservation tool.

Because historic preservation is more widely accepted today as a community value and ethic, some mining companies are more respectful of historic buildings than they might have been twenty years ago. They are mindful of the negative public response that might come their way if they destroy old mining sites, just as they are cautious about triggering criticism from environmentalists.

Ordinarily, preservationists would applaud the continuation of a region's industry. What better way to ensure economic stability, which is always the best guarantee of architectural conservation? The problems arise because of the cyclical nature of the enterprise. In mining, we have the disruptiveness of boom and bust rather than the gentler forces of gradual economic growth.

The development of surface mining is particularly disquieting from a preservation point of view. In Butte, Montana, the gargantuan maw of Berkeley Pit—now a mile across—swallowed several neighborhoods and an entire city park before a decision was made to contain its growth. Near the historic town of Lead, South Dakota, a new open pit gold mine has quadrupled in size during the last half of the 1980s. Above Colorado Springs, gigantic excavations for gravel have marred the scenic foothills below Pikes Peak. These operations have destroyed historic landscapes and, often, historic buildings along with them.

Where mining activity resumes in a community, preservationists must be prepared to monitor companies and advocate strong protections for historic property. Mining rights, which have extensive guarantees under the law, are not easy to curb. Successes in this area may depend more on citizen action and public opinion than on legal action.

8.1   One of the Galveston Historical Foundation's first success stories was saving the 1839
Samuel May Williams Home, which is open to
the public today as a house museum. Courtesy
Galveston Historical Foundation

Organizing for Urban Preservation

C ommunity preservation organizations often emerge out of a crisis, typically a call to arms when a cherished public building is about to be torn down. When the crisis passes, the rescuing organization may fade along with it. Often, however, a concerned and activated group will take hold, organizing surveys, house tours, and membership events, and getting involved in hands-on restoration. These mobilized and motivated citizens might publish a newsletter, lobby their legislators and city council representatives, raise money, and sponsor preservation conferences. This type of organization might survive for years and then suddenly lose its effectiveness when key leaders move on, or when the economy turns bad and support slips

because members are distracted with other concerns. Keeping a preservation group going year after year requires leadership that can build a strategy of successes and sufficient visibility to keep the public informed and mobilized.

In southern Texas, two organizations have stood the test of time and emerged as two of the West's most effective preservation advocates. They are the Galveston Historical Foundation, led by attorney Peter Brink, and the San Antonio Conservation Society, a women's volunteer group. In their *modus operandi* these two entities are different from one another, but their preservation legacies are similar. Not only have these two titans saved a remarkable number of historic buildings, they have interwoven preservation into the entire fabric of their communities—the arts, politics, the environment, education, and, above all, economics. They have gained power, and they have learned how to use it effectively.

In Denver and Santa Fe, citizens devoted to their community's historic architecture have organized similarly forceful preservation organizations. Historic Denver, Inc., was founded in 1970 as a citywide advocacy and action group with programs that encompass education, building restoration, legislative advocacy, neighborhood revitalization, and publications. Historic Denver and the Galveston Historical Foundation have approached their agendas in similar fashion, although the Galveston effort has had greater focus and continuity, primarily because of Peter Brink's leadership and long tenure. In Santa Fe, responsibility for the city's architectural legacy is shared by many individuals and organizations—an unusual solution, but then Santa Fe is an unusual community. Recognition of Santa Fe's historic buildings and a conscious determination to further that heritage developed nearly a century ago.

These four cities—Galveston, San Antonio, Denver, and Santa Fe—have been powerful forces for the protection of historic architecture, but they are by no means the only successful urban preservation groups in the region. Landmarks, Inc., in Omaha; the Heritage Society in Austin, Texas; the Historic Preservation League in Dallas; Historic Boulder in Colorado; the Lawrence Preservation Alliance in Kansas; and Preservation Tulsa have aggressively promoted and protected historic buildings in each of their communities, and there are many others. Texas alone has more than 600 historical organizations in addition to 254 county historical commissions.

Despite these riches, the mountains and plains overall are not blessed with strong preservation organizations. Why not? Several explanations have been offered: first, the architecture in most of this region is too new to be considered historic; second, many communities are isolated from each other by great distances and therefore do not identify with a national preservation movement;

and third, the myth of rugged individualism dictates against any controls over private property. Another reason may be tied to the turbulent gyrations of the region's economy with its history of booms and busts, or to a tradition of regional history that is scenic and literary, rather than social and material. In other words, the cowboy myth or the gold miner's legend is associated with an idealized, generic landscape rather than with a particular place. Even if a particular place is singled out, such as Dodge City, its importance derives from its role in the myth, not from its broader meaning as a frontier community. The real places become unreal, and they remain disconnected from our own lives.

Preservation as a community value is rooted in stewardship and continuity, and unless these conditions are reinforced by institutionalized advocacy groups, they are not likely to prevail. The achievements in Galveston, San Antonio, Denver, and Santa Fe are an inspiration to other communities to promote and formalize a preservation agenda.

Galveston: Preservation by the Sea

Galveston is no island paradise. It is too frontal for that, swept by gulf waters and winds. While other ports repose behind protective barrier reefs or outlying islands, Galveston meets the sea head on and has often paid the price for it. The 1900 hurricane, the worst natural disaster in American history, killed 6000 Galvestonians, nearly a sixth of the island's population.

This dangerous proximity to the sea also gives Galveston its character. The island lies at the northern rim of the Caribbean, across the gulf from the vast region of jungle and heat that constitutes Central America. If not yet the tropics, Galveston Island comes exceedingly close, tilting toward another hemisphere. A hint of other worlds has always been apparent in its buildings, especially its dwellings. In Galveston we see an exotic, highly decorative residential architecture, many of its cottages set on stilts like shorebirds in a row, the house walls enveloped by verandas embracing the sea air while high, shuttered windows are poised to keep it out.

The island shelters contradictions of wealth and poverty, splendor and desolation. The sea winds that cool the high-ceilinged rooms and filled the ships' sails are the same winds that lay waste the island during a storm. There are hidden threats as well. Salt-laden sea breezes erode paint and eventually destroy steel. On The Strand, the city's wharfside historic financial district, brick and stucco buildings only a half-dozen feet above sea level rest on footings of brick and wood, which leach or rot through time as moisture seeps in and out. Termites add their own devastation, moving easily through Galveston's sandy soil and sometimes ascending buildings as high as five or six stories to feed on structural wood. Restoration architects face a formidable challenge here, working in water below grade on crumbling foundations and from the inside out on the structure proper to correct the ravages of salt, water, and insects. Maintenance and repair are doubly difficult in this seaside environment but are well worth the effort. The Strand, a major nineteenth-century financial enclave, was built to last.

Galveston's preservation community had its work cut out for it when it sought to reverse the damage and indifference the island's buildings suffered during much of this century. Although they faced a daunting prospect in the early 1960s, these preservation enthusiasts started with certain advantages. First, Galveston through the years had retained a large number of historic buildings. Even before surveys were completed, it was obvious that the older parts of town were lined

with hundreds of historic structures, many of them architecturally important as well as visually distinctive. Second, the city had been a center of power and riches for a significant portion of the nineteenth century. Theirs was no trivial or ordinary past. Third, several prominent families—Moody, Kempner, Sealy, and Hutchings—whose wealth emanated from the nineteenth-century sea trade, had maintained their ties to the island and generously supported preservation activity once it was organized. Joining their ranks as major investors and philanthropists were George and Cynthia Mitchell of Houston. Mitchell's Greek immigrant father had settled in Galveston in 1909.

The island's first preservation efforts were episodic, which is often the case. In 1954, the Samuel May Williams House was saved from destruction thanks to the work of several local women. Fearful for other important historic buildings, the group reorganized the city's historical society, founded in 1871, as the Galveston Historical Foundation and expanded its purposes to include an agenda of landmark preservation. An attempt in 1962 to establish a historic district in the East End neighborhood failed, at least temporarily, owing to lack of support from the area's residents.

With the publication of Howard Barnstone's *The Galveston That Was* in 1965, preservation awareness on the island—and in nearby Houston—exploded, and the orchestrated activity of the Galveston Historical Foundation began, slowly at first, then gathering a momentum that has been sustained to this day. With backing from the Moody Foundation, the Galveston Historical Foundation conducted an architectural survey of the city, always an important early step for identifying, saving, and using historic buildings. As a result, forty blocks of the East End neighborhood were declared a local district, complete with demolition and design review, and The Strand was listed on the National Register of Historic Places.

As the decade of the 1960s closed, attention focused on three critically important Galveston buildings: the 1882 Trueheart-Adriance Building by architect Nicholas Clayton, restored by the

8.2   The 1877 barque Elissa *captures the drama and grandeur of Galveston's nineteenth-century sea trade. Although restoration and maintenance of* Elissa *has been costly for the Galveston Historical Foundation, the ship's day sails and longer journeys in the gulf have proven to be publicity bonanzas. Courtesy Galveston Historical Foundation*

Junior League in 1969; a portion of the 1859 Hendley Row business block on The Strand; and the 1859 Italianate Ashton Villa, which became the foundation's showcase house museum.

When Peter Brink became head of the Galveston Historical Foundation in 1973, he concentrated on handling the intricate and demanding finances of The Strand's revitalization and on developing a strategy for historic preservation on the island. The foundation concurred with Brink that a prudent, productive goal was for a preservation plan encompassing all of Galveston, not just a building here and a district there maintained as fragments. Brink and the board of directors decided that a proper interpretation of Galveston's history required going beyond the confines of the island to the sea itself. The sea, after all, was the most important part of the island's heri-

tage. The city's entire economic being in the early days derived from sea trade, and the resplendent architecture that took shape along The Strand, Broadway Boulevard, and elsewhere was a direct result of goods moving in and out of Galveston Harbor.

This allegiance to physical setting, particularly a setting that bears heavily on economic and social development, has given the historic architecture of Galveston greater meaning. Without question, the city's tangible remains are important in and of themselves, but they also evoke the compelling, dangerous era when tall ships sailed across the gulf and into Galveston.

To dramatize Galveston's golden age of the sea, the foundation acquired a nineteenth-century sailing ship. The project created great financial strains on the foundation, but once past the grueling

8.3 *An artist's rendering of the Texas Seaport Museum now under construction in Galveston Harbor. Courtesy Galveston Historical Foundation*

and costly demands of its restoration, the 1877 barque *Elissa* dramatized as nothing else could the early glory of Galveston. With the daring and dynamic *Elissa*, the historical foundation has given the world a grand symbol of the city's debt to its early days of sea trade. To see the ship in full sail is to be transported through one's imagination to another time and place. To board the anchored ship is to begin to understand the realities of what it was like to move goods and passengers around the world a hundred years ago.

The restoration of *Elissa* cost the historical foundation more than $4 million. The annual bill for maintenance and operation is nearly $400,000, but Peter Brink believes that the ship's annual day-long sails and special longer voyages are worth millions of dollars in promotion for Galveston and Texas. In addition to being

a major attraction, essential to the city's tourism industry, *Elissa* announces the foundation's seriousness of purpose as an organization that informs and educates. Even though its architectural restorations throughout the city have been done with care and quality, without *Elissa* and a new maritime museum now under construction, Galveston would risk sliding into a round of superficial tourist invasions—day-trippers who shop and eat and give only cursory attention to the city's nineteenth-century architectural heritage. The city's distinctive maritime legacy gives Galveston an edge in attracting visitors; the interpretive work done for *Elissa* and the wharf redevelopment keeps the effort on a high plane.

The Galveston Historical Foundation acquired, restored, and launched *Elissa* in the early 1980s. The ship was considered phase one of the

8.4 *The Strand's commercial buildings exemplified power and wealth. None did it better than the Hutchings Sealy Building, a commission house that handled produce and goods shipped in and out of Galveston Harbor. Designed by Nicholas Clayton and built in 1895, the Hutchings Sealy Building was renovated in the late 1980s and now houses a restaurant and several retail shops.*

Texas Seaport Museum. By the end of the decade, the foundation had raised another $2 million and started a second phase, building an interpretive center and support facilities near *Elissa*'s pier in order to expand on the visitor's experience of seeing the ship. Audio-visual presentations in a new theater will simulate the experience of sailing on the *Elissa*, and adjoining galleries will exhibit materials that explain Texas maritime history.

The final form of the Texas Seaport Museum will be realized when a major structure—a minimum of 35,000 square feet is proposed—joins the preliminary museum buildings at Piers 20–21. The new facility will tell Galveston's story as a shipping and immigration center during the late nineteenth century when sailing ships and steamers carried cotton out of Galveston to Europe and the American East, returning with manufactured goods for the new frontier. Building materials filled the ships' holds as well—cast iron, lumber, and quarried stone destined for Galveston's new homes and businesses. The effects of trade—of Galveston's rise and its sustained connections with other countries—will be the subject of the maritime museum's ambitious interpretive program. Using a variety of media, the museum will present permanent exhibitions, such as photographic and textual displays of the arrival of immigrants. Visitors will be invited onto observation decks to watch the workings of the modern-day port, which surrounds the museum.

In addition to its own material culture of vessels and docks, shipping created an ancillary commercial architecture. In Galveston this area was called The Strand, a quarter-mile stretch of buildings that housed bankers, brokers, wagon shippers, insurance agents, wholesalers, and other principals who enabled money and goods to flow in and out of the city. Restaurants, saloons, and hotels kept body and soul together as business was carried on.

Buildings on The Strand were serviceable and practical with sufficient ornament to express appropriately the power and wealth they represented. Renaissance detailing and strong color contrasts created dramatic, bold facades, richly textured and elegantly stated. When Galveston Historical Foundation officials began to look at them with an eye toward preservation, they envisioned The Strand as the first stage in the regeneration of all of historic Galveston. Architecturally and historically, The Strand's value was obvious, but how would these distressed buildings—many of them empty—be made to pay their way?

Wisely, the foundation began immediately to develop a market. First, buyers had to be found for the buildings, buyers willing to take on responsibility first for a high-quality restoration and then for operating a successful business where none had been before. Second, the foundation would need to generate a stream of off-island visitors and Galveston shoppers coming to The Strand daily to support these pioneer merchants in their newly restored buildings.

Revitalization of The Strand required money,

salesmanship, and a strategy. The foundation decided that control over the use and appearance of each building was mandatory if the district was to establish quality and maintain it. A meticulous restoration of the Trueheart-Adriance Building in 1969 by the Junior League had set a high standard. Now, the rest of The Strand had to be brought to that same level and kept there. With a grant of $200,000 from the Moody Foundation and another $15,000 from the Harris and Eliza Kempner Fund, both Galveston-based foundations, the Galveston Historical Foundation established a revolving fund in 1973 and quietly began the first of twenty-six real estate transactions that would be consummated over the next decade. Eventually, forty-three buildings on The Strand would be bought and rehabilitated, involving an investment of more than $70 million.

The foundation settled on two requirements that would attract serious buyers committed to historic preservation and strong community values. They required new owners to carry out designated improvements in a given amount of time. This stricture tended to drive off speculators. As soon as a building was restored, it joined the active business ranks on The Strand, which helped everyone by strengthening the market. Revolving fund sales carried deed restrictions requiring that no demolition, exterior changes, or new construction occur without approval. The restrictions also set a standard for routine maintenance and structural safety. Subsequent owners are bound by these requirements. Although the restrictions add costs to each building, they protect the owner's investment over the long run.

Peter Brink has estimated that when he came to Galveston, he spent as much as 80 percent of his time supervising The Strand's revitalization, which is not surprising given the demands of commercial redevelopment. The legal, financial, marketing, and construction problems of these projects create formidable hurdles and require an organized effort carried out by knowledgeable, skilled professionals.

During the ten-year push to revive The Strand,

8.5   *Ashton Villa (1859), a house museum restored and operated by the Galveston Historical Foundation, gives visitors a firsthand look at the island's mid-nineteenth century architectural finery. Courtesy Galveston Historical Foundation*

the Galveston Historical Foundation had many other balls in the air: building a membership of 3000, restoring and operating two house museums (the 1859 Ashton Villa and the 1839 Williams House), managing a neighborhood preservation program, restoring the tall ship *Elissa,* adapting the Hendley Building for the foundation's offices and The Strand Visitors' Center, and producing an annual home tour along with the block-busting Christmas event, Dickens on The Strand. Behind the scenes, Brink and his staff and volunteers were raising money, attracting political support, wooing constituencies in the community, building a national network—and planning.

If one were asked to name the two most definitive qualities of the Galveston Historical Foundation, the answer would surely point to their tireless ability to put on a quality show and their capacity for carrying through long-range plans of great complexity. Event and program planning are not necessarily tied to the same sets of skills, but each requires discipline and organization. The Galveston foundation is long on both.

Peter Brink directs a staff of thirty-five and

8.6   *Dickens in the Strand, Galveston's annual Christmas festival, allows the city to show off its revitalized commercial district while throwing a gigantic party designed for fun . . . and funds. The event attracts 150,000 visitors and pumps $10 million into the local economy. Courtesy Jim Cruz, Galveston Historical Foundation*

oversees a volunteer corps of hundreds. As the organization has become more skilled and experienced, it has leaned toward a more managerial style. "Our volunteer leadership is less sacrificial and less emotional now," Brink observes. "The risks are more calculated." He looks back on the struggles of the 1970s, perhaps a bit wistfully but also with relief. "There is a loss when you no longer have people who give everything, who make the organization their life. But we have moved on to a new stage now, something with greater maturity and a broader range of programs. That's the gain."

Every December, the Galveston Historical Foundation hitches its managerial and administrative talents to a nineteenth-century legend and produces a weekend of street theater attracting nearly 150,000 annually. The weekend gala, Dickens on The Strand, recreates a Victorian London street scene with British food, music, dancing, shopping, and a lively round of performances of all kinds. More than 6000 volunteers—each one in Victorian costume—help to stage the event, which pumps $10 million into the local economy. The Dickensian literary Christmas theme is reinforced by the attendance each year of Cedric Dickens, the British writer's great-grandson, who entertains visitors with anecdotes and book signings.

In 1978, the Dickens on The Strand committee worked with Texas A & M's marketing department to undertake a study of the visitors

8.7   Costumed street vendors dispensing a variety of Christmas treats are one of the attractions of Dickens in the Strand. Courtesy Galveston Historical Foundation

who come to the festival. They learned that the typical visitor is likely to be from Houston, at least 35 years old and earning $35,000 a year or more. Fifty percent or more had been to the Dickens celebration before. What did visitors like best? The costumes, and next to that the historical ambience of The Strand itself, and then the British food and drink. They complained about parking and a lack of conveniently located restrooms. The following year the foundation ran a shuttle bus from Houston and then encouraged visitors to ride the new trolley that runs along The Strand.

Galveston preservationists understand mar-kets, and because they do, they have built an economic base of daily and special visitors whose buying power keeps the enterprise alive. Their marketing achievements give them safeguards and a certain flexibility for coping with setbacks. A severe hurricane in 1983 did only moderate damage to buildings but completely destroyed the tourist season. In the mid-1980s, the immobilizing financial crisis throughout the West caused by a sudden drop in oil prices further handicapped the tourism industry and curbed property investment. At the same time, federal funding for preservation began to drop off considerably.

Galveston was hit from all sides, but because the foundation was well established and positioned, it managed not only to hang on but to grow.

The liveliness and general appeal of the foundation's programs are matched by a determination to inform the public as much as to entertain them. An emphasis on research and a pattern of serious study about Galveston and its place in history provide the intellectual underpinnings that keep the foundation on course. In May 1989 the foundation organized a major scholarly conference at the house museum Ashton Villa, the first to be held there. Museum curators and academicians from around the country spoke on nineteenth-century decorative arts as well as on how one approaches the study of American cultural history.

The level of excitement created by this business of perpetual examination is otherwise hard to achieve. A building can be meticulously and completely restored, but its meanings are not likely ever to be entirely known. The quest to know and understand is almost palpable in Galveston's historical environment. Even the most nonintellectual visitor can appreciate the richness of an interpretive program presented with care and integrity. The fully realized maritime museum near The Strand will be the Galveston Historical Foundation's ultimate expression of that faith in learning and knowing.

San Antonio

If continuity is the first requirement of preservation (longevity and lastingness are implicit in the very idea of "preserve"), then adaptability is surely the second, offering the capacity for dealing with changed circumstances in the interests of saving something of value. The San Antonio Conservation Society, founded in 1924, has mastered both to become a legendary force for historic preservation regionally and nationally. The society has starred in its role as protector of the city's heritage and has done so with adept attention to change.

San Antonio is now the nation's ninth largest city, a tourist mecca and trade center that quietly pulls some of its income from military bases and medical centers. One of the region's oldest cities, it looks back to the early eighteenth century when Jesuit padres established five Spanish missions along the San Antonio River. Although never a colonial stronghold, San Antonio strengthened its otherwise tenuous hold on the formidable Texas plains with the introduction of ranching, brought in from northern Mexico—an industry that allowed the area to emerge as a power when Texas became part of the United States in the middle of the nineteenth century.

Already, San Antonio had established itself as a cosmopolitan city. Germans were settling in the Hill Country and in the city itself by mid-century, joining San Antonio's population of Indian, Mexican, and Anglo residents. At the same time, Alsatians and immigrants from eastern Europe were settling to the east and south of the city.

To this day, it is the San Antonio River that gives the city its special character. Even though little remains of the haciendas and the network of acequias that once were lifelines to the agricultural lands in the valley, the river symbolizes the earlier Spanish, Mexican, and Indian cultures and serves as a defining natural feature in the modern city.

During the 1920s, following two disastrous floods, San Antonio's civic and business leaders proposed that the bend of the river flowing through downtown be cemented over to create parking areas and a storm sewer. A fledgling conservation group—thirteen influential women, most of them artists and historians, who had organized only recently to oppose demolition of a historic and architecturally distinctive stone building, the old Market House—took up the cause and defended the river. They called on the mayor and commissioners with handmade puppets and an original script based on the story of the goose

8.8   *Paseo del Rio—The River Walk. Visitors can paddle or ride the river through downtown San Antonio past restaurants and shops. Bridges connect the walkways on either side. Courtesy San Antonio Convention and Visitors Bureau*

8.9   *San Jose Mission, part of the San Antonio Missions Historical Park and one of many preservation projects supported by the San Antonio Conservation Society. Courtesy National Park Service*

CHAPTER EIGHT

8.10 *The San Antonio Conservation Society occupies this ashlar limestone house, formerly the Anton Wulff home (ca. 1870), located at the edge of the King William Historic District. This light native limestone is ubiquitous in central Texas. Courtesy San Antonio Conservation Society*

that laid the golden egg, and invited them to tour the river. This determined group of women convinced the city leaders to approve a storm channel bypassing the downtown river bend. The portion thus saved became in time a landscaped walkway, now the famous Paseo del Rio, a source of enjoyment for residents and a great attraction to visitors. This successful bout of civic activity gave birth not only to the Paseo del Rio but to the San Antonio Conservation Society, which would become a national leader in historic preservation.

Today the society has 3500 members, a substantial annual budget, and several historic properties, all run by a volunteer governing board and a small support staff. From time to time the society purchases endangered properties and resells them to buyers who are willing to respect historic property deed restrictions. In 1965 they bought the Ursuline Academy (1851–85), a girls' school, saving it from demolition. With private donations and a grant from the federal Economic Development Agency, they restored this complex

8.11   *Now a house museum, Edward Steves Homestead (1876), King William Historic District, San Antonio, is one of several properties owned and operated by the San Antonio Conservation Society. Courtesy San Antonio Conservation Society*

of buildings and then sold it to a not-for-profit arts and crafts center. In 1979, again to head off demolition, the society purchased a pair of late nineteenth century brick business buildings in the heart of downtown on Commerce Street and sold them later to a developer sympathetic to preservation.

The society owns and operates eight historic sites, several of which are in the King William Historic District. The Anton Wulff House (1870), built of Texas limestone, serves as the society's main office. Three blocks away is the Edward Steves Homestead (1876), which is open daily as a house museum. The term *homestead* is misleading in this instance. The Steves house is no pioneer log cabin; it is a grand, eclectic Victorian mansion built of ashlar limestone, its third-story mansard roof decorated with iron cresting. Texas and Mexico architect Alfred Giles is thought to have executed the design. Several outbuildings on the property—carriage house, servants' quarters, and natatorium—have also been restored. The property is noted for its landscaping of laurel gardens as well as pecan, cypress, magnolia, palm, black walnut, and anaqua trees.

Society members are quick to point out that their concern is as much for the natural and cultural landscape as it is for the built environment. They launched their organization by saving the river, and they have fought equally hard for park lands in and around the city. In 1937 they purchased lands surrounding the only remnant of a Spanish colonial water system, the Espada Aqueduct, and gave it to the National Park Service in 1983 to become part of the San Antonio Missions National Historical Park.

The conservation society keeps going back to the river in the same way that the Galveston Historical Foundation always keeps an eye on the sea. The river gave the original settlement its form and physical definition, and it provided the economic underpinnings for the area's survival.

The centrality of the San Antonio River is a recurring theme in conversations with the city's leaders. Architect Boone Powell asserts that the river, even though it is small, dominates everything in San Antonio. "It is the city's most important feature. It's the thread that pulls everything together."

Powell believes that history, which the river represents, provides a measure and a context for the city's planning. "In issue after issue, the question is always asked: 'Is this good for the community? How will this affect the river?'" Powell perceives a general respect for the past, which has helped historic San Antonio to survive growth. "You must have a sense of who you are."

Boone Powell's own rendezvous with history embraces many of the state's most important older buildings, including much of the restoration of Galveston's historic Strand. His firm has done the last two preservation plans for the Alamo and worked extensively on conservation of the city's four missions. They are embarked now on the state's largest preservation project ever: the Texas state capitol in Austin, which will be expanded and restored at a cost of $150 million.

Powell was a partner of the late O'Neil Ford, who was the most renowned architect in Texas and a man greatly influenced by the region's rural buildings and particularly by the stone heritage of the Texas Hill Country. "O'Neil paid attention to scale and local materials—not in a literal way—but to establish design principles that emphasized a sense of place."

For both men, history has been a touchstone, something to turn back to, but not imitate. Powell sees San Antonio as comfortable with its history, at ease with a mix of cultures and classes in its historic district, not rigid or overly archeological in its building rehabilitations.

Architects may be more sensitive to context than most people, but San Antonians as a whole are extremely conscious of setting. Visitors to the city share with the natives an enthusiasm for this pervasive sense of place. John Mosty, who headed the city's convention bureau during the 1980s, cites research showing the Alamo as the big draw for visitors initially, but they leave "*loving* the river."

8.12 *The San Antonio Conservation Society purchased the Otto Bombach House in 1950 and then restored and leased it for use as a restaurant. The rubble limestone structure, thought to have been built around 1855, is located in La Villita Historic District. Courtesy San Antonio Conservation Society*

As a tourism professional, Mosty is aware of the power of tourism but also of the problems it creates. "Preservationists must always fight to maintain the integrity of an area." Property values along the river are very high, and pressures exist to open operations with a high return from tourists. Legislation has kept cheap bars and tourist traps out. "San Antonio has protected the river from this kind of opportunistic development," says Mosty.

Mosty credits the conservation society with instilling in San Antonians a possessive regard for the city's downtown. "San Antonio saved its downtown for itself first. It wasn't done just for tourists. That's its strength. Everybody cares about it. When people who live here have out-of-town guests, they take them downtown."

Downtown San Antonio, in a project supported by the conservation society, is undergoing a major facelift. By 1991, seventy-three blocks will have new utilities, streets, sidewalks, lights, bus stops, benches, and landscaping. The area around the Alamo has been paved with stone as part of these improvements. San Antonio's new look in the inner city is certain to please tourists, but it also keeps San Antonians coming downtown, just as the historic buildings, the river, and the annual festivals do.

The recurring notion that whatever gets done in San Antonio needs to make sense first for the city is expressed by Conrad True, executive director of the conservation society during the 1970s, a period of great change as the society moved from a focus on house museums to a larger and more mainstream position. True, like John Mosty, sees downtown as a common ground for residents and visitors, maintaining its traditional role as a city center. From that vantage, the miles of new street projects just completed represent not only a tangible improvement for San Antonians but a statement of value.

San Antonio has a powerful pull on Texans, True believes. It's like a second home town. This unusual fusion strengthens the argument of "what's good for San Antonio is good for tourism," because most visitors feel they are at home in the city.

Conversations in San Antonio about historic preservation always circle back to the conservation society. Outsiders as well as members take pride in telling stories about the "ladies" in the early days who, with permission from their husbands, cashed in annuities and insurance policies to underwrite the purchase of threatened buildings. To further their preservation goals, they have been trading in real estate since the 1920s. They became historic property buyers early on, not just because they had the means and could afford it, but because they were women of action who understood that owning a building meant controlling it and therefore saving it. Bankers always take them seriously and treat them with respect. In more cases than not throughout their 65-year history, they have resold a rescued site to a sympathetic buyer, thus increasing the number of properties saved. Because of what the society has accomplished, according to Boone Powell,

"Historic preservation now is institutionalized in San Antonio. There is an age and patina here that is successful."

Success has not made life any easier for the society. Mary Ann Castleberry, a former society president and now a National Trust advisor, points to the new pressures of doing business. "The biggest change has been the complexity of the politics and finances. The operations are complicated. We have to know so much more." Their 1988 purchase of the downtown Aztec Theater is a case in point. This 1920s movie palace along with two others, the Empire and the Majestic, form a theater enclave in the middle of downtown. The conservation society has worked with several arts groups, investors, and the city to devise a complicated formula to provide for performing arts and film in the theaters and for residential units to be built in the floors above. With hard times in Texas, neither the investors nor the banks have been able to sustain the necessary financing. A solution has yet to be found. In the meantime, the society has formed a subsidiary company, Aztec Conservation, Inc., which operates the Aztec as a movie theater until the entire theater/housing package can be assembled.

Castleberry believes that circumstances in preservation and in the city itself may require changes in the society. The continuing growth of the city and the expansion of tourism drive property values up, which nearly always threatens historic properties. How can the society best deal with these pressures? Are they as streamlined and prepared as they need to be to deal with fast-breaking property transactions and the political maneuvering that goes with them? Just as preservationists have found in Santa Fe and Denver, locking energy and resources into individual properties over the long run can become a diversion from preservation action. The society may be at a point where they need to concentrate on revolving funds, which allow acquisition of property, followed by a quick turnover, as a strategy that is more practical than owning and operating historic sites.

8.13 To save the Aztec Theater, the San Antonio Conservation Society bought it and then started a corporation to continue running it as a movie theater until the right buyer could be found. Courtesy San Antonio Conservation Society

In the interests of exercising all its options, will the society increase its use of professional staff, or will it remain an essentially volunteer organization with a productive but cumbersome bureacracy? Will the society's board of directors remain a female preserve, or will men, who now can be nominated for membership, be eligible for service on the board? The San Antonio Conservation Society has been a force in the city's political and financial life, it wields real power, and it has remained true to its principles and goals. The society has repeatedly mobilized thousands of members and volunteers to stage some of the largest festival events in the world—"A Night in Old San Antonio" attracts 100,000 participants and earns enough money each year to pay for all of the society's operating expenses. These notable accomplishments are carried out by a premier preservation group, one that will be watched and emulated across the country. Their success at influencing political action and public policy will be the test of their effectiveness in the 1990s.

8.14 *The Molly Brown House, Historic Denver's first major preservation project. Courtesy Historic Denver, Inc.*

Historic Denver

In 1988, when Denver's city council, after a two-year period of struggle and controversy, voted historic district designation for Lower Downtown, the city's oldest commercial area, Historic Denver, Inc., could count itself as only one of many civic organizations behind the campaign. It had been a collaborative effort, following years of work by downtown business and civic leaders, neighborhoods, and advocacy groups, including preservationists. But in a certain sense Historic Denver could boast of being parent to the child; if it were not for Historic Denver's previous eighteen years of saving buildings and getting people to appreciate and use them, the opportunity for Lower Downtown would not even have existed. As things were going, by 1988 this old commercial district would have been sufficiently rebuilt to have lost its historic character altogether.

8.15 *Historic Denver undertook the rescue and restoration of this block-long collection of Victorian homes in Auraria, the first part of Denver to be settled in the 1860s. Frame houses from the nineteenth century are a rarity in Denver because after several devastating fires the city adopted an ordinance restricting wood construction. These homes were restored by Historic Denver, and the street was developed into a grassy park. The buildings are now used as offices by the university complex that surrounds them, but they would have been demolished had not Don Etter, then a trustee of Historic Denver, proposed that these delicately styled homes with their lacy iron cresting be kept as a permanent and palpable tribute to Denver's beginnings. Courtesy Don Etter*

The ability to maneuver politically and financially within the realm of economic development is the measure of any effective urban preservation group. Historic Denver's influence on the outcome of Lower Downtown reflects positively on the organization's credibility and sophistication. Having paid their dues, they are able to take part in the major decisions and actions that shape the city.

Like many preservation groups, Historic Denver was founded to meet a crisis. In 1970 the loss of one building, the Moffat Mansion, was imminent, and a second home needed rescuing—the Molly Brown House, once owned by the forceful, ebullient lady whose heroism during the sinking of the *Titanic* was celebrated in the Broadway musical and Hollywood movie, "The Unsinkable Molly Brown."

Encouraged by Ann Love, wife of the incumbent governor of Colorado, eight concerned citizens organized Historic Denver, Inc., and began to raise funds to rehabilitate the Molly Brown House as a house museum. For several years after that, the Molly Brown House was almost entirely a volunteer project, and an extremely popular one. Molly Brown had been a colorful and engaging character, and her home reflected her extravagant but conventional tastes. People were drawn to her story and amused by it. Long before the restoration was completed, Historic Denver began to give tours of the Molly Brown House to a large and appreciative audience. A highly visible and heartwarming project, the Molly Brown House offered a perfect launching pad for Historic Denver.

At the time, certain obstacles seemed insurmountable. Securing bank financing for the Molly Brown House was not merely a difficult task, it was impossible. Reflecting on the mortgage situation a decade later, in 1980, the *Historic Denver News* said:

> *"A measure of how far the preservation movement has come in the last ten years is the reluctance of financial institutions in 1970 to finance the Molly Brown House project.*

> *Although Historic Denver approached several banks, none of them would loan the project money because it was considered too much of a risk."*

A solution was found when the owner, who wanted the house saved, offered to carry the loan for Historic Denver.

As soon as the Molly Brown House project was off and running, Historic Denver in 1974 turned to a block-long collection of small Victorian homes that was about to be demolished to make room for a new university campus near downtown. The two rows of houses soon became "Ninth Street Historic Park," restored by Historic Denver and then presented to the state of Colorado for use as administrative offices in the new educational complex. Historic Denver raised more than $1 million from almost 900 sources to restore the fourteen houses, which were completed in 1976.

Looking back on Ninth Street in 1981, Elizabeth Schlosser, who was then executive director of Historic Denver, was convinced of the project's major impact on public perceptions. "This was a broad-based effort, a real community effort, and it raised awareness in Denver about what we can do with historic preservation. Ninth Street was an important step for Historic Denver toward working on larger projects and entire neighborhoods."

In the meantime, Historic Denver had been improving and expanding its organizational agenda by training volunteers, attracting members, and producing special events. Several members made a trip to Texas to observe "A Night in Old San Antonio," organized by that city's conservation society. By 1974, Historic Denver's own "Night in Old Denver" was netting $65,000.

Historic Denver sponsored the publication of several books about historic architecture in Denver during its early years, and its volunteer corps took part in a citywide architectural inventory sponsored by the Junior League. Historic Denver's work was continually before the public.

In the mid-seventies, Historic Denver took

8.16 *Curtis Park, one of Denver's earliest streetcar suburbs, became Historic Denver's focus in the late 1970s. Close to downtown, Curtis Park was attractive to the new breed of urban pioneers wanting to live in the city. To keep the area from becoming gentrified, Historic Denver developed several innovative programs to help low-income residents to rehabilitate their homes. Courtesy Don Etter*

8.17 *Ironwork, wood carpentry trim, and decorative brickwork dress up this modest Curtis Park home. Courtesy Don Etter*

CHAPTER EIGHT

on the daring but difficult task of rehabilitating Curtis Park, one of the city's oldest neighborhoods. An interesting mix of large homes and modest cottages, Curtis Park had deteriorated to a depressing state, a victim of absentee landlords, crime, poverty, and permissive zoning. Some houses in the neighborhood had been burned out; others, irretrievably damaged, had been condemned and soon would be demolished. Only the neighborhood's richly detailed architecture signaled hope for a better future. Fortunately, Curtis Park's proximity to downtown, combined with the possibilities for renovation, attracted a large number of urban pioneers to move into the area. They began to restore dilapidated houses and became neighborhood residents.

Sensitive to the criticism generated in other cities that gentrification displaces the poor, Historic Denver was determined to build a neighborhood that allowed not only a mix of races but of social classes. With help from the National Trust, Historic Denver established a revolving fund to buy abandoned houses, reselling them with low-interest loans to buyers willing to renovate. A second program, "Face Block," allowed homeowners up to $20,000 for renovation. Awards were restricted to low-income families already living in the neighborhood. On request, Historic Denver arranged for architects to redesign exteriors in keeping with their original appearance. After three years, fifty homes had been refurbished inside and out. Under "Project Infill," three small cottages were moved from another part of the city onto vacant lots in Curtis Park, where they were rehabilitated and sold to moderate-income owners. These projects protected the economic mix of this integrated neighborhood.

Although many Curtis Park homes are much improved, the neighborhood remains fragile. Heavy traffic enroute to the airport cuts through the heart of the neighborhood. The energy slump in the middle 1980s resulted in foreclosures and abandonment, but Historic Denver has reaffirmed its interest in the district. President Jennifer Moulton believes that designating an area as a historic district is not the culmination of an effort but the beginning. Designation, she maintains, is a declaration of civic value and of an intent to protect a neighborhood from damaging encroachment. "Historic districts don't thrive without active nurturing," Moulton has said. For Historic Denver, Curtis Park is more than a project. It has required patient monitoring and a capacity for intervention when city agencies fall back into treating the neighborhood like a slum.

Citing a recent resurgence of interest in restoration and hoping to attract new buyers, Curtis Park's block council organized a tour of the neighborhood in June of 1989.

Historic Denver's fourth major agenda item has been the restoration of the Paramount Theater, a 1929 Art Deco movie palace on Sixteenth Street in downtown. The Paramount became a central cause just about the time that Historic Denver began focusing its energies on downtown. Three million dollars were raised, some of it borrowed, to restore the theater, which was then turned over to the Historic Paramount Foundation, a separate nonprofit organization that operates the building and manages the bookings. The foundation presents several concert series each year, both evening and noon hour, and produces a major fund-raising event annually. To generate additional income, the theater is rented for annual meetings or private events, such as a series of subscription jazz concerts. The Paramount is regarded by the preservation community as one of the most important historic sites on Denver's revitalized Sixteenth Street in the heart of downtown.

Other Denver buildings have benefitted from Historic Denver's attentions—the Grant-Humphreys Mansion, the Four-Mile House, the Tramway Building, and more—but the four projects described here have kept public attention drawn to historic preservation in Denver for long periods of time. Historic Denver's actions have been positive, aggressive, and highly public. The group has moved quickly from one project to another, and it frequently has had several complicated transactions underway at once.

8.18 *As Historic Denver became more adept and seasoned in shoring up the city's architectural legacy, it turned its attention downtown, purchasing and restoring the 1929 Paramount Theater, which combined Art Deco lighting with huge murals and extravagantly styled plant motifs in bas-relief. Courtesy Roger Whitacre*

8.19 This 1979 view of Sixteenth Street shows
just how dismal Denver's downtown had become. The Kittredge Building on the corner has
since been rehabilitated and the Paramount
Theater totally restored. Most important, Sixteenth Street has been entirely refashioned into
a landscaped mall with new lighting, landscaping, paving, and a wealth of eateries, many
of which have sidewalk seating. Lower Downtown lies behind the Daniels and Fisher Tower
in the background. Few communities have
had success with pedestrian malls, but this one
has worked well for Denver. Courtesy Roger
Whitacre

8.20 *Historic Denver was one of several organizations that helped to find new uses for the Grant-Humphreys mansion on Capitol Hill. For a time, its headquarters were located here. The mansion, completed in 1902, made lavish use of terra cotta—a molded, fired clay material—that became a popular substitute for stone in the early twentieth century. The entryway columns and all decorative surfaces shown here are terra cotta.*

The advantages of this strategy have been twofold: first, the projects selected have informed and persuaded the public about the value of Denver's historic architecture, and second, Historic Denver has been able to educate its membership and leaders about every aspect of preservation, including—especially—the finances. All preservation projects have a bottom line. Although a few projects in any community justifiably can be supported by tax dollars, most must generate support through earned income and private gifts. His-

toric Denver's leadership has become expert at discerning both the limits and the opportunities in preservation economics. All the answers are not yet evident, but the organization can now, with some confidence, recommend to the community just how a historic building or district can be successfully integrated into Denver's physical and economic fabric.

A high public profile has helped Historic Denver to fulfill its mission. The constancy of its leadership has also been a big part of its

300

root strength. Even though its board chairpersons and presidents have come and gone—the tenures for both have been short—most of them have remained part of the Denver preservation circle. Ann Love, one of the founding members, now serves on the board of the Historic Paramount Foundation. Elizabeth Schlosser, who once headed the staff at Historic Denver, later became executive director at the Paramount. Attorney Don Etter, former chairman of Historic Denver and the author of several books on the city's historic architecture, now heads Denver's parks department and has undertaken a new program to restore the city's historic parks and roadways. Dana Crawford, one of the group's founders and former chairwoman, was the driving force behind the development of Larimer Square and remains a major investor in historic properties. Barbara Sudler, who headed Historic Denver in its formative days, later assumed the directorship of the Colorado Historical Society, where she also serves as the state's historic preservation officer. Many others have taken a big role, and many of the same people who started the organization eighteen years ago are still supporting it. "People are the most important part of preservation," Ann Love maintains. "It's dedication. We've had a strong core who have stayed involved, and when there's a call to arms, they respond."

What lies ahead for Historic Denver? Interestingly, Ann Love has identified a problem that has also been a concern voiced by spokespersons of the San Antonio Conservation Society and the Historic Santa Fe Foundation—what to do about owning and operating historic properties. It makes sense for preservation societies to buy threatened properties, and to restore them, and perhaps even to operate them for a time, as Historic Denver did with Ninth Street and the Paramount. But do they want to own and run the Molly Brown House, or Four-Mile House, forever?

Historic properties need constant care. They are labor intensive and require a bureaucratic and highly structured administration to keep them

going. But is this the best use of a preservation group's resources? Ann Love believes that Historic Denver must remain ready to deal with crises and to play a role in the politics and planning of the city. This requires a dynamic, unencumbered, politically astute organization prepared to jump in and cope with complexity and change, hardly the same set of skills needed for stewardship. Perhaps it is time for urban preservation groups to form separate property trusts for their historic buildings. With that accomplished, the leaders of Historic Denver and similar organizations can spend their time in a more active mode, shaping the look and destiny of their cities.

Santa Fe, New Mexico

The citizens of Santa Fe as a whole, not just its preservation community, place a high value on the city's adobe architectural heritage, an expression derived from centuries of Pueblo and Spanish colonial building in New Mexico. Preservationists here work through fifteen different statewide and citywide private organizations dedicated to the region's traditional material culture, including architecture. A few of these groups are highly specialized: the Acequia Madre Ditch Association, for example, maintains and operates Santa Fe's centuries-old irrigation ditch, and the Guadalupe Historic Foundation preserves the eighteenth-century Guadalupe Church. In addition to these fifteen state and local private groups, preservation advocates call on the services of the National Trust for Historic Preservation as well as eight local, state, and federal public historical agencies based in Santa Fe and Albuquerque. For a city with a population of 50,000, Santa Fe has linked itself to an extraordinary number of historical resources.

Long a retreat for expatriate easterners and self-exiled artists, Santa Fe has a history of concern for its historic buildings. Critical of Victorian

8.21 *This adobe building in central Santa Fe, purported to be the city's oldest house, shows the simple, fluid lines of adobe construction. Because fresh earth plaster is applied every few years, an uneven and unique surface develops. The lower-level course of vigas, the wooden cross beams, have been dated to the mid-nineteenth century, but the house is believed to be older than that. The second story is twentieth century, replacing an earlier version.*

intrusions into traditional Southwestern architecture, and fearful that native building crafts would be lost, Anglo newcomers began in the early twentieth century to revive Spanish colonial and Pueblo building features and, in doing so, created the Santa Fe style, a combination of flat roofs, adobe walls, wood trim, *portals* (open porches), and courtyards. The Spanish–Pueblo Revival buildings of this century are reminiscent of the Don Severino Martinez hacienda at Taos,

the village church in Las Trampas, or any of a dozen Indian pueblos. This highly romantic architectural revival produced many fine homes, such as the Carlos Vierra house on Old Pecos Trail, built in 1919. The style was adopted for large commercial and public buildings as well, including La Fonda Hotel (1920) and the Museum of New Mexico, Museum of Fine Arts (1917).

A second revival—this one of the nineteenth-century Territorial style—flourished after World

8.22   *The Pinckney R. Tully House (1851)*
is a premier example of the Territorial style.
Elements of Greek Revival—pediment-shaped
windows, a formalized portal, symmetry, and
dentil-like decoration at the roofline—are com-
bined with flat-roofed adobe construction. The
house was built just after the war with Mexico
and at the same time that Fort Union, also
built in the Territorial style, was being con-
structed in the northeastern corner of the state.
Note the traditional canales, rainspouts, which
drain water from the flat roof and away from
the walls. This adobe house is painted red. The
mortar lines are actually white paint applied by
hand to achieve the effect of brick.

8.23   In the late nineteenth century, the railroads brought Victorian architecture to Santa Fe, including this Italianate brick house, which later became La Posada (The Resting Place, or The Inn) near downtown. As the revival of traditional adobe architecture took hold in the twentieth century, the house was coated with stucco. Various wings and cottages were added, all designed with pueblo features. Other Santa Fe Victorian buildings underwent a similar transformation.

War II alongside the continuing popular revivals of Spanish colonial and Pueblo forms. Territorial Revival buildings, like the others, were executed primarily in adobe. Territorial styling rests in spartan, flat-roofed buildings incorporating features of Greek Revival, an architectural style dominant in the South and along the eastern seaboard in the early nineteenth century. Coming west with the U.S. Army during the Indian Wars, the Territorial style introduced window pediments (shallow, peaked wooden ornaments over the lintel, which suggest the front of a Greek temple), square porch posts, brick parapets, and a taste for symmetry—in short, Neoclassical features. John Gaw Meem, a prominent New Mexico architect, shaped a major portion of the Territorial Revival in the Southwest. The original nineteenth-century Territorial style had included pitched metal roofs, but these were spurned by the revivalist designers.

The reaffirmation by Santa Fe residents of their Pueblo, Spanish colonial, and Territorial architectural heritage has created some peculiar building hybrids. The old First National Bank, designed in 1912 in the formal Neoclassical style, was completely remodeled in 1957 in the Spanish–Pueblo Revival adobe tradition. Its transformation into an indigenous form is only approximate, at best. A similar change has been wrought on the large Victorian Italianate house that anchors La Posada, an inn east of the plaza. After World War II, this brick house was surfaced with brown stucco. At the same time, traditional adobe cottages and service areas were attached to the house or erected on the grounds as guest quarters. The overall effect of La Posada is Santa Fe style until one's eyes wander up to the Italianate brackets under the hipped roof. Today, Victorian architecture has a respected place of its own within Santa Fe's building history. These odd adaptations are not likely to happen again.

When Santa Fe designated several historic neighborhoods in addition to its traditional downtown area, the city's modest and newer vernacular structures began to come into their own as well. The Guadalupe District near downtown contains small adobe homes, stores, and scattered warehouse buildings associated with the Atchison, Topeka and Santa Fe station, still in service, and the Denver and Rio Grande station, now a restaurant. The district is named after its most distinguished landmark, the eighteenth-century Guadalupe Church, recently restored for use as a performing arts hall. During the first decade of the 1900s, the Don Gaspar neighborhood, a middle- to upper-class enclave, reflected the influence of an architectural invasion brought by the railroads. Mission Revival and Craftsman brick cottages became a popular alternative to the traditional Santa Fe adobe, but not for long. By the 1920s and 1930s, Spanish, Pueblo, Mediterranean, and Territorial styling was back in demand, much of it adapted to the bungalow size and plan. The Guadalupe and Don Gaspar districts expand the definition of Santa Fe's historic architecture by including buildings that are comparatively recent and are representative of the working and middle classes.

Although imported Anglo designs enticed builders for a brief period, the revivals of Spanish-Pueblo and Territorial architecture have dominated building in Santa Fe in this century. During the 1950s, fearful that a postwar building boom would destroy this singular legacy, preservation advocates succeeded in passing an ordinance that requires design review for new construction and renovation within designated historic districts. Under the ordinance, adobe or a visual equivalent is required for exterior surfaces. Styling must remain within the range of Spanish-Pueblo, Territorial, and their revivals, which discourages pitched metal roofs, a nearly ubiquitous feature of northern New Mexico adobe village architecture from the late nineteenth century onward. Exterior wall colors under the ordinance are confined to an earth-tone palette, with a larger choice of color for wood trim.

The controversy surrounding this legislation continues to this day, particularly over the issue of building heights, which should be limited depending on the context of the building, but often

8.24   *The Inn at Loretto, named after the nineteenth-century Gothic chapel (1878) behind it, has been the most successful of Santa Fe's new large hotels in accommodating the adobe tradition. Using an elaborate system of setbacks and asymmetrical tiers suggestive of the pueblo at Taos, the architect has managed to enclose a substantial amount of space without creating a monumental building at streetside.*

are not. Even two stories is too much in some areas of Santa Fe. Recently, several hotels have built comparatively massive structures, which are softened by setbacks—a stepped, building-block approach not unlike the multistoried pueblo at Taos. Despite accommodations made to the design review ordinance, these buildings are out of scale with their surroundings and have been subject to criticism. A basic conflict between the historic styles ordinance and the zoning ordinance has yet to be resolved. Just because a building meets the zoning code's requirements for size, setbacks, and height does not necessarily make it compatible with the historic character of a neighborhood. A few protruding logs and an adobelike covering are not enough to cover the excesses of an out-of-scale Spanish–Pueblo Revival hotel.

Santa Fe's design review process is not likely to become any easier for the city's leaders in the near future. The city has been going through an economic transition, making it difficult to retain the traditional folk village appearance and atmo-

8.25   *La Fonda Hotel has erected what is surely one of the best-looking parking ramps in the country. One could argue that a parking garage has no business aspiring to be a Spanish colonial church, but it does succeed in keeping a lot of automobiles out of sight in the heart of Santa Fe.*

sphere for which it is famous. The recent changes have been driven by tourism and development money. The city's leaders are debating the changes and trying to find a balance.

Dale Zinn, a young architect on the design review board, grew up in Santa Fe and has observed the city's transformation from a small city both arty and agrarian in tone to a high-priced tourist destination. About fifteen years ago property values began to climb, and many downtown stores were priced out of the mar-

ket. "Until around 1980, the ordinary Santa Fe resident could still shop downtown. There were shoe stores, a hardware store, clothing stores . . . things that people need." Today, expensive galleries and specialty shops have crowded out the necessities, trading instead to the wealthy tourist dollar. Zinn estimates that downtown retail space climbed from $6 to $35 a square foot within a ten-year period beginning in 1975.

Rising property values always pose a threat to small, scattered historic buildings. The village tra-

8.26 *Americans in the post-railroad days had a great influence on Santa Fe's architecture. So did Bishop Lamy, a French cleric who arrived in Santa Fe in 1851 shortly after the war with Mexico. A powerful religious leader who revived the long-neglected Catholic Church in New Mexico, Lamy imposed his French tastes on architecture and art, building this large Romanesque Cathedral of St. Francis a short distance from the seventeenth-century central plaza.*

8.27 *The insistence on openness, human scale, and landscaping in Santa Fe is no more evident than in Sena Plaza, a courtyard surrounded by restaurants, offices, and shops. This peaceful, pleasing space across from St. Francis Cathedral and only a block away from the bustle and traffic of the main plaza, is historic Santa Fe at its best.*

dition of Santa Fe—detached one-story houses, yards, and trees—becomes increasingly difficult to maintain because property income must match investment, an impossibility for small buildings on expensive land. The economics push for taller, bigger buildings, which are not compatible with the Santa Fe landscape or architectural tradition. The design review board is faced with fitting a behemoth into a setting meant for something small. "You have a stucco box pumped up," Zinn says.

"It may meet the letter of the ordinance but it doesn't look like a Santa Fe building."

Even though problems of density and scale are hard ones to solve, Zinn thinks the Santa Fe ordinance is a good one. "There is a commitment here to the adobe tradition." He believes that architects will come up with new adaptations that are appealing and successful. "It has happened before."

In Santa Fe's hot real estate and tourism mar-

8.28   *The portal at the edge of Sena Plaza.*

ket, there will be more new buildings and more debates over what form they should take. There are debates as well over existing landmarks and whether they must all be saved. Santa Fe's top tier of significant landmarks are not in danger, owing to the city's consensus on the value of historic architecture, but those older buildings farther down the list—the ordinary Territorial house, the modified bungalow, the deteriorated barn—are in jeopardy now that rising land values have proclaimed the death of the ordinary. It will be harder now, Dale Zinn realizes, to hang onto the modest and imperfect architectural examples from the past.

The design review board is the stage on which preservation debates and decisions take place today, but its authority and power have been decades in the making. Its capacity to exercise real control over development during a time of intense economic pressures springs from a century

of devotion to a venerable architectural tradition. Individuals and organizations during all those years have affirmed the region's earth architecture, making it easier for city officials and regulatory boards to insist that the chain not be broken.

Santa Fe's formal preservation groups organized early; first the Old Santa Fe Association was founded in 1926 as an advocacy and political organization, then the Historic Santa Fe Foundation in 1961 to receive donations, administer property, and carry out educational programs. In 1979, the foundation completed restoration of the Pinckney R. Tully House (1851), an excellent example of Territorial architecture. Both organizations have been centrally involved in dealing with the problems created by the intense development pressures of the past fifteen years.

The economic benefits of tourism in historic districts are often used to justify the fuss over saving old buildings, but a community's history and its architecture have a higher value than as a commercial lure to outsiders. The look of a city should please its residents first, then its visitors. Tourists will follow anyway in the wake of a citizenry that loves its city and takes pride in its history.

The staying power of Santa Fe's historic architecture rests in maintaining loyalty to the look of the city's pre-twentieth century Pueblo-Spanish adobe buildings and combining that loyalty with a tolerance for interpretative variations. Visitors come to Santa Fe to partake of what the residents enjoy year-round. If the balance is reversed, everybody loses.

For preservation to work, people have to agree on the basics. In Santa Fe, the bottom line is adobe architecture. Other communities have their own fundamentals. San Antonio citizens and officials appraise every new major proposal on the basis of what effect it will have on the river. In Denver, preservationists have pounded home the idea that downtown historic buildings are the essential, not an optional, element in the cityscape. The Galveston Historical Foundation continually affirms the city's nineteenth-century maritime legacy. Perhaps the greatest achievement of these powerful private preservation groups is not their restorations or revolving funds or dazzling events, but their success at selling their fellow citizens on one simple idea.

9.1 *Union Station at the northwest end of Seventeenth Street, serves as a powerful anchor for Denver's Lower Downtown. The granite, glass, and terra-cotta station was designed in the Renaissance Revival style by Denver architects Aaron Gove and Thomas Walsh during the City Beautiful era, a time of formal and monumental building in this Queen City of the Plains. Courtesy Roger Whitacre*

Cities:
A New Look at
the Old

During the late nineteenth century, the far-flung cities of the West—Omaha, San Antonio, Denver, Bismarck, and a dozen other large railroad and trade centers—expressed their commercial and civic aspirations through architecture. They built block after block of Second Empire and Renaissance business buildings in the 1870s and 1880s, great Romanesque warehouses and offices a decade later, and Neoclassical train stations and public buildings in the years before World War I.

Many western downtowns grew rapidly during the 1920s, getting higher as well as larger, their most prominent landmarks creating a skyline visible for miles. By 1930, a large portion of the Victorian era buildings were gone, torn down and replaced by larger and newer structures—hotels, department stores, theaters, banks, and office towers. During the money-scarce years of the Depression and World War II, however, few buildings were added. In most cities during that period, the downtowns stood still until after the war, and then they rapidly lost ground to the suburbs.

During the postwar years, western cities began to grow and prosper from tourism, new industry (gas, oil, uranium, and electronics), agriculture (water from new irrigation systems had turned the Great American Desert green), and the expansion of military bases. Little of that new wealth went into the historical city centers; the lifeblood of the city was flowing outward along the new expressways to shopping centers and subdivisions.

Planners and investors started complaining about inner-city blight and the need for new, modern construction. In response, city leaders, aided by federal funds, tore down most of what was left from the late nineteenth century, hoping that the cleared land in downtown areas would beckon builders with the same force attracting them to the open fields at the edge of town. It was a dreary time for many cities: cars and traffic everywhere, superficial remodelings of old buildings, and acres of parking lots. As urban renewal proceeded, many downtowns began to look like bombed-out war zones.

By the late 1960s, people began to think positively about downtown again. After years of neglect and demolition, downtowns were thought to be worthy of investment, not only of money but of personal energy. Many citizens, shocked and saddened at the irretrievable loss of familiar landmarks, and bolstered by passage in 1966 of the National Historic Preservation Act, began to demand that historic architecture be saved.

Each downtown had its own special problems and possibilities. A few small cities—Helena, Montana, and Galveston, Texas, among them—still had most of their historic buildings intact, more than they had any good use for. They needed to build a healthy economy around an architecturally important legacy of buildings. In contrast, the fast-growing larger cities—Denver, Omaha, Albuquerque, Houston, Oklahoma City, Tulsa, and Dallas—had already demolished most of their historic buildings to make room for the new. There were notable exceptions. San Antonio, prodded by its preservation-minded conservation society in the late 1920s, had made a significant effort to honor its history, accomplished by creating the Paseo del Rio, a landscaped development of restaurants, hotels, and shops along a river canal that wound through the middle of downtown. For the others, a way had to be found to protect what historic architecture remained, a task made doubly difficult by sky-rocketing property values that left smaller, older buildings economically untenable. In the long run, historic preservation had to become cost effective, contributing to the financial health and economic life of these cities.

Because each mature city has its own character and identity, it must seek its own preservation design solutions. Denver has focused its attention on creating the Sixteenth Street Mall along the city's main retail street as well as protecting and revitalizing its "Lower Downtown," a district of late nineteenth and early twentieth century supply houses and commercial buildings. In Dallas, several significant landmarks have been rehabilitated and a large warehouse area has been redeveloped as a restaurant, office, and retail district. Omaha has refurbished such important landmarks as its Orpheum Theater, the Omaha Building, and The Old Market District, but recently the city has sacrificed Jobbers Canyon, a large concentration of warehouses. Increasingly, urban preservationists are finding ways to highlight the distinctive qualities of historic buildings in order to keep them competitive with new construction.

Denver, Colorado

After thirty years of work in the field, Denver's historic preservationists have paid their dues. Today, the preservation movement is credible and organized, able to wield power and to influence the cultural and economic life of the city. Progress has been uneven, but the cumulative effort is impressive. The contribution of the movement to Denver's new downtown plan demonstrates the positive effect of a mature, diversified preservation constituency able to exercise leadership and maintain continuity. Denver today is a thoroughly modern city but one that still retains its past in tangible form, thanks to its preservation forces.

From the vantage of the freeway that circles its western edge, downtown Denver appears to be entirely a creation of the space age. At the center, skyscrapers rise as high as seventy stories,

9.2   *Trinity Methodist-Episcopal Church, de-*
signed by Denver architect Robert Roeschlaub
in 1887, holds its own amid the city's oil-boom
skyscrapers. Its heavily textured stonework and
grand spire offer a pleasant counterpoint to late
twentieth century glass and metal facades.

9.3   The palazzo lines of the Equitable Building (1890; architects: Andrews, Jacques and
Rantoul) offered dignity and distinction to
Denver's emerging Seventeenth Street financial
district. Courtesy Donald Etter

9.4   Tiffany-designed windows in the Equitable Building. Courtesy Donald Etter

9.5 Denver's premier architect, Frank E. Edbrooke, designed The Navarre in 1880 and ten years later completed the Brown Palace, considered by many to be his finest building. The Navarre became sadly derelict in the 1970s, and then was rehabilitated as a western art museum.

creating a startling and sudden vertical thrust from out of the flatness of the plains. These tightly clustered new office towers in a dozen materials and colors—black, gray, red, violet, and many shades of white and shimmering silver—express modern architectural tastes ranging from the spare regularity of the international style to the unpredictable, extravagant forms of postmodern design.

From a distance it all looks new, a product of the 1970s energy boom. Viewed at closer range, from within the business district, however, Denver's historic buildings stand out amid the new towers, providing a welcome counterpoint to the dominant contemporary image. Union Station (1911), a neoclassical building in the Beaux Arts mode, closes the lower end of Seventeenth Street, home of the city's banks, law offices, and broker-

*9.6   The Brown Palace's great atrium lobby
ca. 1950. Courtesy Brown Palace Hotel*

age houses. A few passenger trains still move in and out of Union Station, but most of its spacious interior is now empty or used for offices and restaurants. A block away stands the Oxford Hotel (1891), designed by Denver's foremost nineteenth-century architect, Frank Edbrooke.

In the boom years of the 1870s and 1880s, the area surrounding Union Station and The Oxford was the heart of Denver's downtown, a lively hodge-podge of banks, stores, and warehouses mixed with saloons, gambling halls, horse corrals, and stagecoach offices. Market Street at that time gained notoriety as the city's red-light district. Elegant bordellos, such as The House of Mirrors, existed alongside tiny one-room "cribs" on the street from which prostitutes solicited customers. By the turn of the century, as downtown businesses moved southeast along Sixteenth and Seventeenth streets, wholesale merchants had taken over most of the blocks near the railroad station.

Southeast of Union Station along Seventeenth Street, Denver's financial district, several important landmarks remain from the time when Denver came of age as a major city of the West. The Boston Building (1889), a masterpiece of smooth red sandstone and classic lines, and the Equitable Building (1890), an Italian Renaissance palazzo designed by the Boston architectural firm of Andrews, Jacques and Rantoul, were among the distinctive designs that put Denver on the map at the turn of the century. Both have been renovated and maintain their eminence among the city's prestigious buildings.

Today, the silver-toned Amoco Building, a new skyscraper resembling a giant streamliner turned on end, anchors the far end of Seventeenth Street, its modernism tempered by several nearby nineteenth-century landmarks: The Brown Palace (1890), a premier hotel noted for its huge, handsome atrium lobby; Trinity Methodist Church (1888), built of light-gray granite and crowned with a magnificent corner spire; and The Navarre (1880), a small brick hotel recently restored as a museum of western art. Particularly for pedes-trians, these historic buildings present a welcome variation of design, texture, and scale.

Around the corner on Sixteenth Street, the downtown scene changes suddenly. In the late 1970s, Sixteenth Street was redesigned as a pedestrian shopping mall. The street has been closed to all traffic except buses. Trees, benches, flowers, and new lighting now occupy the ground formerly covered with asphalt and concrete. Shoppers and tourists move along the mall past stores and restaurants. At noon each day the area is crowded with workers from the surrounding office towers who pour into neighborhood restaurants or sit on benches in the open mall to eat sack lunches and watch people go by.

Several historic buildings add to the character of the new mall, including the Kittredge Building (1891), the Masonic Temple (1889), and the recently vacated Denver Dry Goods Store (1894), which is being adapted for mixed residential and commercial use. Farther down the street the Daniels and Fisher Tower (1911) stands like a sentinel, the only surviving feature of Denver's second major department store and probably the city's most famous landmark. Its 23-story tower, modeled after the campanile in Venice's St. Mark's Square, was renovated in 1980 for offices. The tower is a stone's throw from Larimer Square, where Denver's downtown preservation movement originated in the mid-1960s after a handful of Denver residents began to respond to the wholesale demolition of the inner-city's historic architecture.

The rehabilitation of individual structures is typically a long, complicated, and expensive process, but revitalizing an entire downtown is daunting almost beyond comprehension. Denver's effort reflects nearly three decades of intensive work by an army of individuals from both the private and public sectors. Along the way, key projects like Larimer Square shaped the destiny of downtown.

Larimer, a block of Victorian buildings architecturally pleasing and rich in lore, makes up in significance what it lacks in size. Along with Blake

9.7 *The appealing scale and texture of buildings like the Kittredge (late 1880s; architect: Morris Stuckert) are responsible for much of the success of Denver's Sixteenth Street Mall. Courtesy Roger Whitacre*

CHAPTER NINE

*9.8 Only the tower (1911) of the old Daniels
and Fisher department store remains on Sixteenth Street. It was the city's tallest downtown
structure until 1953 and still serves as a unique
and important landmark, one that was nearly
lost during the 1960s when urban renewal demolished much of Denver's historic architecture.
Courtesy Roger Whitacre*

9.9 *The face of Larimer Street is famous for exuberantly decorative buildings like the Crawford (1875), executed in the Second Empire style.*

and Market streets, Larimer had been at the core of Denver's original settlement. Mining wealth flowed in from the mountains in the 1870s and through the 1880s, fattening fortunes and creating a building boom of brick and stone Italianate commercial palaces distinguished by magnificent window moldings and grand cornices. Then, in the 1890s, Denver's downtown shifted southeast toward the new state capitol. Larimer and the warehouse district below it suddenly moved from the center of the city's drama to its fringes and remained there as Denver solidified its claim as a modern trade center and regional capital.

The twentieth-century demise of the old downtown district seemed irrevocable. By the end of World War II, Larimer Street had been transformed into a skid row, a disheartening world of derelict buildings. Some of the light-industrial and wholesalers' operations around Union Sta-tion kept going, but the area no longer drew a general public, and many people said "good riddance" whenever Lower Downtown buildings were torn down. In the early 1960s, when demolition claimed the Tabor Opera House (1880) and the Windsor Hotel (1880)—both sumptuous Second Empire designs and foremost among the city's early buildings—it became clear that the wrecking ball was serving as a death knell for Denver's historic center.

The destruction of the Windsor Hotel jolted at least a few people to action. A group of private investors led by Dana Crawford, then a free-lance public relations consultant, banded together to save the last intact block of Larimer Street. Motivated by a desire to preserve historic buildings, they were also determined to create a lively and successful shopping area to draw people downtown in the evening as well as the daylight hours. Denied financial support from skeptical local bankers, the newly formed Larimer Associates negotiated a series of loans and began renovation of the rows of Victorian buildings that faced each other along one block of Larimer Street. In addition to cleaning, painting, and renovating a total of eighteen structures, the owners added new spaces to the old buildings in the form of arcades, courtyards, sunken patios, and covered passageways.

Larimer Square's first tenants included restaurants, food shops, galleries, clothiers, and a theater. Professionals in such fields as architecture, geology, and law occupied the seventy offices on the upper floors. Vigorously marketed and managed, Larimer soon became known nationally as a successful renovation project attractive to tourists and Denver residents alike. Annual celebrations— a Christmas Walk and a German Oktoberfest— kept the square in the public eye. Music festivals and other performances continually attracted visitors, who stayed on to shop and dine in Larimer's forty stores and nine restaurants. Among the most popular has been The Market on the first floor of the 1873 Gallup-Stanbury Building, a gourmet food market and restaurant offering special coffee blends and fresh pastries baked on the premises. Single, centralized ownership of the Larimer properties meant that the tenant mix and overall marketing strategy was carefully orchestrated and controlled. Crowded with Denver's young movers and shakers, The Market accomplished Dana Crawford's goal of recapturing the "gay and boisterous spirit of Denver's youthful era."

Aware that the success and durability of Larimer was tied to downtown Denver's future, Dana Crawford threw her energies into related urban causes. She helped to start the city's landmark group, Historic Denver, Inc., and sat on the board of the Colorado Historical Society. Later, she became a vice-president of Downtown Denver, Inc., a group of merchants, architects, bankers, and developers shaping the Sixteenth Street Mall, the revitalized heart of the downtown shopping area. With the leadership of Richard C. D. Fleming, president of Downtown Denver, Inc., preservationists and planners argued successfully that building an environment on a human scale—lively, safe, accessible, and attractive—was best accomplished by saving and highlighting the downtown's historic buildings. Because of their work, such buildings as the Daniels and Fisher Tower, the Kittredge Building, and the Brown Palace Hotel are recognized today as vital ingredients of a distinctive downtown. Success was seen in 1983 when, after a damaging fire, the Masonic Building, next door to the Kittredge on Sixteenth Street, was shored up rather than being demolished. A new structure was built inside the old walls, retaining the building's original exterior appearance.

Certainly a great deal of synergy is required in preservation redevelopment. The evolving historic districts help each other. Larimer Square's impact on its neighbors has been positive. In the 1970s, when a new university complex was built in Auraria, an old section of Denver across Cherry Creek from Larimer, a cluster of nineteenth-century homes was saved and restored with help from Historic Denver. The restored houses, known as Ninth Street Historic Park and used as university offices, form an important cultural centerpiece for a neighborhood that has been almost entirely rebuilt. Larimer has also been a positive force in the development of what is now called Lower Downtown, the original heart of the city.

Because successful preservation tends to be contagious, spilling over into nearby historic areas, a few of Denver's merchants and investors in the 1970s began to see possibilities in the blocks adjacent to Larimer. Against the advice of their bankers and friends, several young urban pioneers bought historic buildings in Lower Downtown. Architect Peter Dominick, Jr., renovated a three-story brick building that had seen better days, creating an open, high-tech interior, which he rented out except for the space occupied by his own architectural firm. Dominick's firm, housed in the Wazee Exchange, named in honor of the street alongside, was one of many architectural

9.10 *Denver's skyscrapers were on the march in the 1970s and 1980s, a threat to Market Street and other historic blocks in Lower Downtown. Demolition restrictions and design review in 1988 finally offered protection to older buildings in "LoDo." Courtesy Roger Whitacre*

offices moving into the neighborhood. His colleague William Saslow had earlier renovated the Market Street Mall and then converted a two-story nineteenth-century brick storefront to condominium units, occupying one of them with his family. Other investors searching for an alternative to the high-rises of downtown made similar moves, and the old buildings of Lower Downtown continued to exchange their cast-off look for a refurbished facade.

In the early 1970s, Dominick, Saslow, and another associate, attorney Alan Reiver, sought a change from the existing industrial code in Lower Downtown. The city of Denver responded by creating a complicated special zone that would encourage a mixture of uses, including residences and small-scale buildings that would offer a pleasant counterpoint to the megaliths next door in downtown. A spectacular rise in property values later in the 1970s threw the plan askew. With office space in demand, bigger became better and the distinctive historic architecture of Lower Downtown lost out. (The eventual loss was substantial; between 1979 and 1987, 20 percent of the buildings in Lower Downtown were demolished.)

In the early 1980s, under the urging of The Denver Partnership and Historic Denver, the ordinance was once again amended with the intention of giving greater protection to the district's historic architecture. Inadvertently, the new zoning allowed for the development of half-block packages with room enough on the site for a large office tower of sixteen stories, and the rest—more than half of the property—given over to a parking ramp of four or five stories.

Three of these projects were completed by the early 1980s, during Denver's energy boom. Preservationists watched in disgust as historic buildings fell, only to be replaced by towering brick walls with large expanses of reflective glass totally at odds with the original human dimension of the area. The new zoning legislation, designed to give a break to owners of small historic properties, was actually being used to cannibalize the district. Denver's largest remaining collection of historic commercial buildings was being eaten up in a rush of new construction.

This volatile situation made everyone uncomfortable. Property owners wanting to make the most of their investment were nervous about the likelihood of strong prohibitive measures emanating from the historic preservation community. The latter, in turn, were worried about being branded as antibusiness obstructionists who would be isolated as pariahs and eventually defeated, bringing the district's historic architecture down with them. In their own interest, a few property owners began to meet every week or so with a few preservationists. Out of this alliance grew a remarkable preservation and economic development structure, nearly a decade in the making, which made history as a landmark in urban planning.

The recent success of Denver's citizens in securing historic district status for Lower Downtown is testimony to the coming of age of the city's preservation movement. Hundreds of people were involved in the process, but one veteran preservationist, Lisa Purdy, saw the district project through from beginning to end, providing a perspective and understanding that was as valuable at the time as it is in retrospect.

In 1981, Purdy moved from a job with Historic Denver to become a development specialist for the Denver Partnership, an organization of civic and business leaders charged with improving the cultural appeal and economic performance of downtown. She had just finished lobbying for successful passage of an ordinance on the transfer of development rights for Denver's central business district. This new legislation, which has been adopted in other cities as well, offers owners of small historic buildings a chance to sell the space above their buildings as real property to owners of new buildings nearby who are seeking greater height allowances than the zoning ordinances would otherwise allow. The principle behind the arrangement is that the sale or transfer of rights makes up in part for the loss of potential income from property on which a small historic building is located, lessening the likelihood of its demolition. In turn, the property owners who purchase the rights can build larger buildings, thereby realizing the full value of their property. This transfer was one of a number of solutions sought by Denver leaders to keep the city's surviving historic buildings intact.

Purdy became part of the small group of preservationists and property owners in Lower Downtown who were trying to mesh history with economic development. At the time, a new convention center was being proposed for an area adjacent to Lower Downtown. Property owners in favor worried about opposition from Denver's preservation forces. A few of them sat down together in a long series of informal meetings, trying to figure out how they could make the convention center work for this historic commercial neighborhood. Could they take advantage of the economic boost but still protect the buildings? They explored the trade-offs and dangers involved, but before long the convention center issue was defeated by Denver voters. The ad hoc group stopped meeting, but the issue of preservation *versus* economic development had been turned around to involve discussions of preservation *and* economic development. The seeds were planted.

A few months later, in 1982, Richard Fleming—later to head the Chamber of Commerce but at that time president of the Denver Partnership—entered a joint venture with the Planning Office of the City and County of Denver to bolster downtown. As a start, Mayor Frederico Peña appointed a committee of twenty-eight citizens charged with creating a downtown area plan.

Purdy had by then started her own firm as a real estate development consultant. Several of the city's preservation entities asked her to represent them on the downtown area plan committee—as the only designated preservation advocate—and she began a volunteer stint that would absorb a large portion of her time for the next four years. She was a trustee on the board of Historic Denver at the same time.

Although Denver preservationists were interested in the entire downtown area, they were particularly keen on pulling Lower Downtown into the overall downtown plan so it would no longer be a stepchild, a peripheral neighborhood of aging buildings apart from the mainstream. Purdy was pleasantly surprised to find a considerable amount of appreciation for Lower Downtown on the committee. Members recognized that it contributed to Denver's identity because it offered tangible evidence of the city's early history as a cow town, a mining town, and a railroad center. The reasoning was, "If you want character in this city—something that no other city can claim—you'd better save Lower Downtown." They saw the neighborhood as unique, giving Denver a competitive edge in the battle with the suburbs for more business.

While the committee deliberated, historic buildings were being demolished in Lower Down-

town to make room for new, larger structures that were threatening to change the area totally. Preservation advocates on the committee kept asking, "Do you really think Lower Downtown is vital to Denver's future?" Invariably, members answered, "Yes!" Purdy and her allies persisted: "If you do, then we've got to have legislation with teeth. We need demolition review and design review and height limitations." Old buildings should stand, the reasoning went, and new, infill buildings should be made to fit in. The committee agreed, strongly supporting special district status for Lower Downtown as part of the downtown area plan adopted in 1986.

Once the plan was passed, work began on the special district ordinance. It was a very tough fight, lasting for two years. Some owners of historic buildings in Lower Downtown had intended to demolish them and erect larger structures. They complained to the city council of a "taking" of their property rights. The press, picking up on the conflict, emphasized the "preservation versus progress" argument, but the approach adopted by the downtown area plan committee had worked toward a more positive balance of promoting the district and at the same time protecting historic buildings. The true economic value of Lower Downtown, according to much of the city's leadership, was directly tied to its tangible history. To them, Lower Downtown's old buildings were like the goose with the golden eggs.

As discussion of Lower Downtown's future progressed, the historic district advocates found that they lacked hard economic data from other cities. They could point to Seattle's Pioneer Square or Dallas's West End Warehouse District or Baltimore's waterfront redevelopment as obvious successes, but they lacked integrated, analytical information that would prove to any skeptic the economic value of commercial, urban historic architecture. Statistical research on potential economic gains would have helped to shore up the anecdotal and physical evidence.

As the arguments before the council heated up, Historic Denver mobilized support from the city's neighborhoods, following a strategy that Lower Downtown was of citywide importance. Leaders from a dozen nearby neighborhoods responded by sending letters to council members and making statements at hearings in support of a Lower Downtown special district.

Jennifer Moulton, a young architect who was later to become president of Historic Denver, headed up that group's preservation committee during the hearings on Lower Downtown. Tough-minded and articulate, she spoke effectively before city council, making a strong case for Lower Downtown's worth to the city as a unique historic resource tied directly to the Sixteenth Street Mall. These special areas were described as a critical part of the pedestrian draw, those lively and human-scale streetscapes that make a city hum.

Denver's design community lined up behind the historic district proposal. Local chapters of the American Institute of Architects (AIA) spoke in favor of the district plan, as did the Urban Design Forum, a citywide design group particularly interested in topical issues of urban environment. Several members of the AIA had recently developed design guidelines for Speer Boulevard, a three-mile historic parkway that runs along the southwestern edge of Lower Downtown. Simultaneously, a plan was being developed for restorative work on Civic Center Park at the upper end of downtown. These parallel new commitments to traditional cityscape features reinforced the proposal for district status for Lower Downtown because, together, they reaffirmed Denver's early history.

Support for special district status began to converge from all sides, moving the Lower Downtown project far beyond a "save the buildings" stance to a forward-looking concern for the city's style and substance. As the city council review of the issue progressed during the summer and fall of 1987, the League of Women Voters voiced their approval of a special district, adding their considerable credibility to the cause. The business community, already represented by property owners and the Denver Partnership, registered further support through the Chamber of Commerce.

Clark Strickland, director of Denver's National Trust Regional Office, described the Lower Downtown campaign as a tour de force in local policy making and planning. The trust had lobbied hard for strengthening the district and poured substantial support into the effort, including a $25,000 grant in 1981 for a planning study, a second grant four years later to help to mediate differences that had emerged during the formal downtown area plan procedures, and finally, a $200,000 loan for facade improvements on the district's buildings.

Throughout the six-year struggle for Lower Downtown, the Denver media either opposed special district status outright or cast a negative shadow on the planning process by highlighting the property owner–preservationist conflict. *The Rocky Mountain News* signaled thumbs down from the beginning. At *The Denver Post*, senior editor William Hornby, a member at large on the downtown area plan steering committee, backed the historic district ordinance, but the paper's editorial board steered clear of commitment until close to the final count. *The Post's* architectural and urban design writer, Joanne Ditmer, who is a long-time Denver preservation advocate, supported the Lower Downtown historic district from the start.

Handling television news stretched the talents of Denver's preservation community as they worked to build public support. The time constraints of television news formats limit the reporting of a complicated story. The concept of whether old buildings stand or fall is easy enough to communicate quickly, but the tools of preservation economics are often complex and even arcane. If you have fifteen seconds to make a point about property values in a historic district, you had better not start a discussion of a transfer of development rights or facade easements or floor-area ratios—even though it is these very technical tools that can make a preservation project successful—because the time is too short to explain the problem fully, and the average viewer is not interested in these issues to begin with. When dealing with the evening news during the two years of hearings on Lower Downtown, preservationist Lisa Purdy chose to let the buildings speak for themselves by using them as a backdrop when she was invited by the press to make a statement or answer questions. She believed that the tangible history shown was likely to be as strong a message as anything she said into the microphone.

On March 7, 1988, Denver's city council voted eight to five to establish a special historic district for Lower Downtown, requiring demolition and design review and restricting building heights. Claiming the vote as a victory for Denver's future as well as its past, the city's preservationists were well aware that district designation was only the beginning. Lower Downtown's economy was weak and uneven (Denver itself was just beginning to pull free from a wrenching energy-related collapse), and the area's property owners and businesses had yet to establish themselves as a unified, effective force. Many historic buildings had been lost during the previous decade. These sites in some instances were now vacant lots or were occupied by new buildings totally out of character with the original historical context. The possibilities for Lower Downtown now that protective legislation had been passed offered great hope, but the district's problems, including that of inertia, had to be faced and solved. Lower Downtown's regeneration was not about to take care of itself.

The key players in the long planning process—the Denver Partnership, the city's planning office, Historic Denver, and Lower Downtown's property owners—continued to meet to decide on an agenda for the district's redevelopment. During formulation of the downtown plan, everyone had agreed that the new district should continue to star as Denver's design industry hub, home to architects, interior designers, showrooms, and suppliers. They also agreed that Lower Downtown offered an attractive solution to Denver's

need for downtown housing. Loft units in some of the area's converted warehouses, when combined with small-scale new apartment houses, would appeal to a growing Denver population looking for homes that are entirely urban without being encased in high-rise towers. Finally, the Lower Downtown package would continue to serve residents and visitors alike with restaurants, bars, galleries, and specialty stores.

Having determined "who" and "what," the support teams now turned their attention to "how." A revolving loan fund was created to support restorative construction work on historic buildings. Denver's planning office proceeded with a National Register nomination to enable owners of eligible historic buildings to apply for tax credits on the improvements they made.

Before the historic district was put in place, the Denver Partnership had opened a Lower Downtown business support office to help businesses that were starting up, expanding, or reorganizing. Their support services included office "incubator" facilities featuring shared clerical personnel and equipment, plus below-market rents. To further tout Lower Downtown, an illustrated quarterly, *Directions*, was launched by The District Collaborative, a nonprofit, membership organization representing the area's design and business community.

After years of waiting and the exhausting exercise of hammering out a workable plan, Lower Downtown owners and advocates were ready for positive action. In 1988, shortly after district designation, the city authorized $1.8 million in immediate street improvements: period street lights, special paving at intersections, gateway markers, outdoor furnishings, metal railings around parking lots, paint, and new parking meters. Several controversial and unsightly viaducts, which feed traffic into the district, are to be removed. At the district's edge, historic Larimer Square is undergoing a major facelift, having weathered more than thirty years of heavy customer traffic. A second boundary area, Cherry Creek and Speer Boulevard, is in the planning stage for a land-

9.11   Lower Downtown is home now to Denver's design community. This former refrigerated warehouse on Wynkoop Street has been adapted for designer showrooms. Architects, artists, and design retailers have also relocated to Lower Downtown, providing a specialized but varied use for storage and commodities buildings in this historic area.

scaped linear pedestrian park that will add both a view and a vastly improved promenade for Lower Downtown's citizens and visitors.

As an entertainment and shopping area, Lower Downtown will draw tourists, as it should, but an essential point of the district's development is that it was organized to be first and foremost an attractive area for Denverites, not just an overlay of quaint Old West shops for out-of-town visitors. Tourists will be drawn to Lower Downtown for the same reasons its residents are attracted to it— the scale, the texture, the variety of architectural detail, and a special mix of unusual shops and services. This kind of development is the healthiest and the most enduring, because Denver's citizens care about it.

Mayor Frederico Peña was aware from the start that Lower Downtown's future touched all of Denver's citizens, and his persistence in seeing the issue through gave strength to the ordinance at a point when even preservationists were beginning to waffle. Peña believes strongly that Denver's parks, downtown, and nearby neighborhoods are the three tangible ingredients that give the city distinction. For several years, Peña had watched the erosion of Lower Downtown. Knowing that several compromise solutions in the past had failed to protect the district's historic architecture, he took a firm stand on the need for design and demolition review. He let it be known that he would veto an ordinance that was watered down, and he called a press conference the night before the council vote to express again his commitment to a protective ordinance. The mayor's position was consistently supported by council members Dave Doering and Debbie Ortega, who represents the portion of Denver that includes Lower Downtown.

The campaign for Lower Downtown provided a valuable opportunity for Denver preservationists to increase the public's appreciation of the city's architecture. Today, the city's landmarks commission has greater visibility and the city council has a strengthened commitment to Denver's unique history.

It is instructive to remember that Lower Downtown gained historic district status because Denver's business community thought it was a good idea. In the early years in Denver and around the country, the historic preservation movement was isolated and defensive, rescuing a single threatened building here and there. Action was often *reaction* to developers. For the past ten years in Denver, however, preservation advocacy has more often been part of the development process, not an obstacle to it. During the two years in which Lower Downtown's district status was being organized and reviewed, a similar historic district 500 miles away in Omaha, Nebraska, was being demolished, and among the city's leaders hardly a voice was raised against the action, although Omaha's preservation community fought the destruction. Historic buildings, so often viewed in the past as irrelevant and expendable, have a new lease on life in Denver because they attracted not only popular support but the commitment of the city's most powerful corporate and government leaders.

Dallas, Texas

When you think of historic urban architecture, Dallas does not immediately come to mind. Nearly all of its nineteenth-century buildings are gone. Money and energy in Dallas go into making the new, not protecting or restoring the old. Compared to the celebration of historic buildings in Galveston or San Antonio or Santa Fe, there's not much here to get excited about.

Why should preservationists, then, take seriously a city that has demolished much of its old urban core and for the most part is proud of it? There are at least two good reasons for paying attention to preservation in Dallas, despite the city's boom-town, new-look ways. First, Dallas is one of the great western urban centers and as such

9.12   The entire country seemed alive with "Union" train stations beginning around the time of World War I. Dallas in 1914 built this restrained but elegant Neoclassical station on the west end of downtown. It now houses the city's visitors center and offers a wide variety of dining in its grand lobby. Union Station is still an active train terminal. *Courtesy Doug Tomlinson*

is an expansive, aspiring example of how cities in this region develop and evolve. What Dallas has done with its tangible past is very much the same as what Oklahoma City, Amarillo, Albuquerque, and Colorado Springs have done, as have dozens of other smaller cities in the Southwest that grew quickly after World War II—embraced the promise of freeways and urban renewal, and demolished most of their old downtown buildings and nearby residential areas as well. As impressive as San

Antonio is—and Galveston—and Santa Fe—they are not realistic role models for western cities whose historic resources have been sacrificed. The historical have-nots must look to each other and find a way of integrating and magnifying the architectural and cultural treasures that survive.

Second, Dallas preservationists have scored some important victories with significant clusters of buildings. They understand the importance of neighborhoods, the appeal of human scale, the

9.13 *"Old Red," the Richardsonian Roman-*
esque courthouse designed in 1892 by architects
Orlopp and Kusener of Little Rock, appears as
a mere postscript to its towering new neighbor,
NCNB Plaza, formerly First RepublicBank
Plaza (1985; architects: JPJ, Dallas). From a
distance, Dallas's glossy glass skyscrapers domi-
nate the skyline, just as they do in Houston
and Denver. But close up, the red sandstone
courthouse assumes an air of importance as
one of several low but monumental buildings
circling downtown, including city hall, the
Dallas Museum of Art, and several vintage
structures: Guadalupe Church, Cumberland
School, and the Majestic Theater. Courtesy
Doug Tomlinson

9.14　From a stone's throw away, Old Red wears a comfortable cloak of institutional authority, looming large just as it did in the nineteenth century. The red sandstone building was restored in the 1980s. Courtesy Doug Tomlinson

need for variety, and the realities of the market. They have always been sophisticated organizers and politicians.

At the end of the 1980s everything was on hold in Dallas. The economy had soured in Texas and throughout the Southwest. With rates of new construction down, no one was knocking over old buildings to make room for something new. When life stirs again in Dallas, however, will the advocates for historic architecture be heard above the din?

Dallas, like Denver, takes pride in its corporate riches and cosmopolitan image. Both cities have ridden the boom-and-bust roller coaster several times in the past century, and like other energy-dependent communities in the West, they have learned how to pick up the pieces after a bad fall.

Dallas hides its history. From a distance, its downtown appears to be totally a modern city of glass and office towers. Indeed, coming in from the Dallas–Fort Worth airport on the Stemmons Expressway, a visitor is dazzled first by the new

9.15 *The Beaux Arts decorations crowning the Adolphus Hotel are well above eye level, but even from afar, the building's copper roof and high-relief stone arches mark it as an exceptional and costly design. The Adolphus, designed in 1912 by a St. Louis firm, was renovated in the 1980s. Courtesy Doug Tomlinson*

Hyatt-Regency Hotel, all sheathed in reflective glass, and then the seventy-story NCNB Plaza (formerly First RepublicBank Plaza), a shimmering tribute to the building boom of the early 1980s. Assorted skyscrapers of varying heights are lined up behind it. The only landmark in town appears to be the Hyatt's fifty-story Reunion Tower, named after La Reunion colony, whose members settled near the site in 1855.

There is more historic architecture in down-

town Dallas than meets the eye from the city's edge. Physically and visually, the expressways surrounding downtown Dallas act as a concrete moat, containing and defining its dimensions and its character. Inside these barrier walls the modern monoliths that dominate from a distance recede a bit, and the city's historic landmarks—albeit far too few—take on greater significance.

The older buildings in downtown date to the early twentieth century, a period of explosive

*9.16   The Magnolia Building (1922; archi-
tect: Alfred C. Bossom) is one of Dallas's most
famous landmarks. Its neon-lit Flying Red
Horse has been a Dallas symbol for years.
Courtesy Doug Tomlinson*

growth in Dallas. Nothing remains of its Victorian commercial architecture. Near the new Hyatt towers, the gleaming white walls of Union Station (1916) introduce a strong statement from the City Beautiful era, a time of municipal reform and monumental architecture. Recently, the Woodbine Corporation renovated the station, organizing its interior into a complex of shops and restaurants along with a visitors' center for the Dallas Chamber of Commerce.

Directly north of Union Station stands one of the city's few surviving nineteenth-century buildings, the Dallas County Courthouse (1890), popularly known as "Old Red." Texas is famous for its courthouses, and Old Red is one of the state's finest, although slightly diminished from the loss years ago of its original 200-foot clock tower. Its reddish rough-cut sandstone exterior, styled in Romanesque Revival with a strong salute to H. H. Richardson, offers a pleasant counterpoint to the slick, high-tech surfaces of downtown's office towers. In 1988, Old Red was restored, returned to its original appearance except for the large panes of tinted window glass that had been installed during an earlier remodeling. This intrusion mars both the color and line of the building. Perhaps one day the offending panes will be replaced with clear glass set in window sash of the period. After an interlude of several decades, a tricolor slate roof again crowns the courthouse, an expensive but beautiful improvement.

Along Commerce Street a half-dozen blocks east of the courthouse stands one of the city's preeminent historic buildings, the Adolphus Hotel (1912), a richly decorated Beaux Arts structure designed by St. Louis architects Barnett, Haynes, and Barnett for Adolphus Busch, the brewer. Every feature of the Adolphus has been refurbished, from its first-floor dining rooms to the top of its green-tinted copper mansard roof.

The elegance of the Adolphus is echoed across the street in the Magnolia/Mobil building, which was the city's tallest skyscraper for a full two decades after its construction in 1922. The 29-story twin-tower building designed by English architect Alfred C. Bossom became a revered Dallas landmark recognized from miles away for its distinctive sign—a three-story, neon-lit revolving Pegasus, the "flying red horse." Mobil Oil donated the Magnolia to the city of Dallas in 1977, and after some anxious moments in the ensuing attempt to find a sympathetic buyer, the building was renovated in the early 1980s by San Francisco preservation developers Herbert McLoughlin and Edward Conner and is again considered a premier office address in downtown Dallas.

The Wilson Building (1902) adds further architectural interest to the Dallas main street and is regarded by many preservationists as the city's most beautiful structure. Its lavish ornamentation suggests an Italian palazzo and is one of only a few expressions of turn-of-the-century classicism left in the city. The Wilson outshines its reserved neighbor, the Neiman-Marcus Department Store (1914; addition and present facade, 1928), more renowned for its upscale merchandising than for the restrained quality of its seven-story Renaissance facade, although the delicately carved stonework around the store's entry arches offers a welcome decorative detail not usually found in today's designs.

This enclave of six splendid buildings by no means represents the entirety of historic architecture in downtown Dallas. The Kirby Building, a 1913 Gothic office tower, was recently refurbished for office and commercial space; the Municipal Building (1914), a monumental Classic Revival limestone structure, originally served as city hall; the Majestic Theater, a John Eberson design, was built in 1922; and the Egyptian-styled Dallas Power and Light Building (1930) was designed in an Art Deco mode by the city's most important architectural firm, Lang and Witchell. Several historic churches remain in the inner city: First Presbyterian (1912), Guadalupe Cathedral (1898), and First Baptist (1891), along with one old school, the Cumberland (1888), renovated in 1980 by SEDCO Corporation for its headquarters.

On the northwest border of downtown Dallas,

9.17   *Like the Brandeis Building in Omaha,
the Wilson Building exudes a rock-solid urban
confidence and would certainly have proved to
turn-of-the-century Dallas residents and visitors alike that the city was well on its way as a
capital of commerce. Sanguinet and Staats of
Fort Worth designed the Wilson, built in 1902.
Courtesy Doug Tomlinson*

9.18 *Dallas's warehouse area, now the West End Historic District, assembled an architecture of practicality, but these functional buildings were not without design distinction. The Kingman-Texas Building (1905), a farm implement warehouse, with its graceful arches, is a stripped-down cousin to the Beaux Arts Wilson Building a few blocks away. With the benefit of federal tax incentives, the warehouse has been rehabilitated and is occupied by two restaurants on the ground floor and offices above. Courtesy Doug Tomlinson*

not far from Union Station and Old Red, fifteen square blocks of warehouses now form the West End Historic District. Some of the surrounding streets and nearly all of the district's forty-five buildings are red brick. From two to eight stories tall, these boxy structures are simple and functional, designed in the early part of the century to store farm implements, sewing machines, groceries, furniture, and other manufactured goods. Spacious and flexible, these old commercial buildings have adapted easily to new uses. The county government and the city's transit authority are two major tenants in newly renovated office space.

The West End has become the downtown's restaurant district, attracting workers from nearby office buildings and conventioneers from downtown hotels. The cheery, earthy brick tones and comfortable scale of the architecture create a welcome atmosphere for pedestrians who crowd into the district during the noon hour, after work, and into the evening. By 1989, with a total of thirty-seven restaurants in the district, some preservationists worried that the area was disappointingly one-dimensional and rested on a fickle and trendy economic base. With a glut of office space in Dallas at the decade's end, the West End's long-term situation can only be guessed. A developer of one of the district's successful office buildings believes that the area's overall mixture of owners and tenants will soon expand to include housing and that within another few years the West End will be one of several successful and distinctive inner-city districts, each reinforcing the other and the cumulative whole enhancing all of downtown.

Private investors in the West End have taken advantage of special city and federal tax incentives available for historic buildings. The city has poured several million dollars into the district, most of it underground for new water and sewage lines but a significant portion for new sidewalks, landscaping, signs, and other amenities to create a parklike context for the buildings. The city of Dallas actively promotes the district, working closely with the West End Association, a group of building owners and tenants.

Preservation history is full of irretrievable losses, but in the case of the West End, circumstances of an emerging preservation movement in the early 1970s combined with a slow real-estate picture in downtown, which gave West End advocates an opportunity to push for protection under a historic preservation ordinance. Another five years, and development pressures from the new construction surge in downtown would have precluded setting the West End aside as a low-density, restricted historic area. It was a propitious moment, and one that served Dallas well.

Anonymity best characterizes the West End's architecture. Functional brick boxes of commerce tend not to draw attention to themselves—with one exception. From the sixth floor of the West End's most famous structure, the Texas School Book Depository (formerly the Southern Rock Island Plow Company Building), Lee Harvey Oswald allegedly fired the shots that killed President John F. Kennedy on November 22, 1963. Since that day, millions of Americans and foreign visitors as well have walked onto Dealy Plaza to examine a scene imprinted long ago by the media coverage of that tragedy. They search out the grassy knoll and underpass, tracing the route of the motorcade and pointing to the corner window where Oswald is believed to have stood waiting for the president to pass on the street below in an open limousine.

Kennedy's assassination has been a heavy burden on Dallas, and for more than a quarter of a century citizens have debated a solution for the offending building. "Tear it down," some said. "Interest in the site will subside," they argued. But the millions who came negated that argument. Something more was called for, a tangible, informative commemoration to acknowledge openly a dark moment in history and tie it to a larger national experience.

Dallas County bought the depository in 1977. With funding from the National Endowment for the Humanities, the county studied the site and recommended that the entire sixth floor be turned into an educational exhibition about the Kennedy

9.19　Fair Park, one of the nation's largest collections of Art Deco and Moderne buildings, houses several Dallas museums and is the site of the Texas state fair. The park has been reorganized to improve its visitor attractions, and many of its stylish twentieth-century buildings are being renovated. Located about a mile and a half from downtown, Fair Park is one of several nearby areas—including the West End, Uptown, Deep Ellum, and the Arts District—that can be connected through transportation systems and visual cues to strengthen Dallas's urban core. This sculpture is part of the Plant Engineering Building built in the mid-1930s for the Texas Centennial Exposition honoring the one-hundredth anniversary of the state's independence from Mexico. Courtesy Doug Tomlinson

tragedy. The remainder of the building would be adapted for county offices. During the 1980s, the newly formed Dallas County Historical Foundation took as its agenda the tasks of developing the exhibition's design and of raising the $3.5 million needed to pay for it. With plans for the sixth floor underway, the county proceeded with restoration of the exterior and renovation of the first two floors.

In 1989 the Sixth-Floor Exhibit opened, serviced by a new visitors' center adjacent to the depository. An exterior elevator carries visitors to the sixth floor where they see films, photographs, artifacts, and other displays that chronicle the events surrounding the president's death. Exhibition organizers and county officials predict an annual visitation of 500,000. Not surprisingly, the Sixth-Floor Exhibit generated controversy. Preservationists unanimously applauded restoration of the building, but some criticized the exhibit as morbid, the visitors' center and elevator as architecturally intrusive, and the half-million visitors a year as an excessive number to be absorbed within the modest scale of the historic West End. On the other side, organizers of the exhibition have argued that November 22, 1963, is a fact of life in both Dallas and the nation and should not be ignored or underplayed. Lindalyn Adams, chairman of the Dallas County Historical Foundation, points to the requirements of history, noting that President Kennedy himself had described history as the "memory of a nation."

The site has been a compelling one; there is no argument about that. The Historical Foundation has retained highly qualified and discerning designers to create the exhibition. Only time will reveal whether this solution is the right one for Dallas. Visitors to the Kennedy exhibit will arrive on the scene positively disposed toward learning about a historic event, and they will be motivated to see other historic areas of the city before they leave. John Crain of the Dallas Historical Society has observed a reawakening within the city of an interest in the past, an interest reinforced by the preservation activity of the past twenty years. A reflective presentation on the Kennedy tragedy can only add to an appreciation of Dallas as a mature city with a richly woven historical fabric.

The larger question for Dallas is what will happen to the remaining historic buildings downtown when the next boom comes and real estate values heat up again. If the free market cannot support the city's old buildings (high land costs will create a demand for taller, larger structures), can they be subsidized? Within the past decade the Wolff Building has been demolished, and the Kress, and the Volks Brothers Department Store. What will be next? The Magnolia with its flying red horse? Or Neiman-Marcus? No one can ask an individual investor to lose money, but Dallas as a community can invest in its downtown by creating financial solutions that protect its shrinking number of historic buildings. Dallas preservation activists and the city's planners salvaged a significant portion of the inner city in the 1970s by organizing historic residential neighborhoods, along with Fair Park and the commercial districts of Deep Ellum and

the West End. Their challenge now is to convince the business community that the landmarks left in downtown Dallas are history's gift to the city—irretrievable and irreplaceable.

Omaha: Wins and Losses

As downtown Omaha moved into the 1980s, it still retained many of its most attractive and important historic buildings. The city's Richardsonian post office had been demolished in the 1960s after considerable public outcry, but the Douglas County Courthouse (1912) had survived, along with Central High School (1912) and the Public Library (1892). Among commercial building stock, the Fontenelle Hotel (1914) and the Woodmen of the World Life Insurance Company Building (1912) had succumbed, but many fine examples remained, including McKim, Mead, and White's New York Life Building (1889, later called the Omaha Building), a granite palazzo of considerable distinction. Other notable surviving structures were the Brandeis Department Store (1905); City National Bank (1910), which incorporated the Orpheum Theater; and the Kirkendall Building (1889), an example of the Richardsonian Romanesque style. All of these buildings occupy Omaha's central business district. Not far afield are two outstanding buildings of modernistic design, the Joslyn Memorial Art Museum (1931) and the Union Pacific Terminal (1931).

In addition to these individual landmarks, Omaha in the early 1980s boasted two intact historic warehouse districts on the edge of downtown—Jobbers Canyon and an adjacent four-block area known as the Old Market. In 1988, following a wrenching civic struggle, Jobbers Canyon was demolished. In contrast, the Old Market, with buildings dating from the 1890s, has evolved into one of the country's most appealing and successful commercial historic districts.

9.20 *Brandeis and Sons Department Store (1905; architect: John Latenser) was one of several major Omaha buildings designed in the classical mode. The store was vacated by the Brandeis Company around 1980 and rehabilitated with the assistance of federal tax credits to offer retail and commercial services on the first floor and office space on the upper stories. Courtesy Lynn Meyer*

9.21   Central High School, built between 1900 and 1912 on a hill near Omaha's downtown, is another of the city's monumental salutes to classicism. Courtesy Lynn Meyer

9.22   The New York Life Building, built in 1889 and now known as the Omaha Building, was the city's first skyscraper. The prestigious New York firm of McKim, Mead, and White designed the structure. The first three floors are built of granite, with brick and terra cotta used for the stories above. Denver's Equitable Building, built at the same time, follows a similar palazzo form. Courtesy Lynn Meyer

9.23 Brick streets provide a pleasant harmony with the buildings in Omaha's Old Market Historic District. The canopies, which once sheltered produce, now offer shade and protection from rain and snow for the visitors who frequent this popular restaurant and retail area near downtown. Wooden planters at the edge of the canopies hold petunias and other bright flowers during the mild seasons and evergreen boughs in winter.

OMAHA'S OLD MARKET HISTORIC DISTRICT

Through inheritance and purchase, several blocks of produce and warehouse buildings were acquired in the late 1960s by members of the Mercer family, descendents of Dr. Samuel D. Mercer, a surgeon who had established the city's first hospital and founded a streetcar company. The family formed Mercer Management and set about to revive this once lively market area. Mark Mercer and his cousin, Nicholas Bonham Carter, two of the company's principals, have carried the lion's share of the district's management.

When Mercer Management began in the early 1970s to search out new enterprises for the Old Market area, they were handicapped by the run-down and grimy condition of the buildings. The stone-trimmed brick structures obviously had life left in them, however, and the original brick streets were in good repair. Huge roof overhangs resting on steel posts reached out from the building facades to shelter the wide sidewalks. With time and work, the buildings would brighten.

Today, vines climb the support posts, and bright petunias cascade over the edges of the canopies. In winter, garlands of evergreens take their place. The 100-foot-wide brick streets provide a spacious court for the specialty shops and restaurants that make up the Old Market. Fresh paint, new signs, and inviting window displays have transformed the streetscape.

Like Denver's Larimer Square, the Old Market benefits from its single ownership. The Mercer family takes full control over choosing the signs, architectural designs, and perhaps most important, the merchants who do business there.

Mercer Management tries for an atmosphere that is convivial and inviting, sophisticated but not too slick, and cosmopolitan without being snobbish or pretentious. They avoid franchises and chain stores. They are more likely to respond to an enterprise perceived to be compatible with existing tenants rather than one with impeccable market credentials. They experiment, and they start businesses themselves in order to get what they want, such as good food in a sophisticated setting. They opened a French restaurant and a second continental eatery, V. Mertz, both of which quickly gained a reputation for fine dining. In the upper stories of several buildings, they built lofts and apartments because they believed at least a few of Omaha's residents should live downtown.

Mercer Management's inventiveness and diligence were rewarded by animosity from much of Omaha's mainstream, at least in the early stages. "People thought it was too hippie," Mark Mercer recalls. "Health inspectors always seemed to be around, and building inspectors and other bureaucrats." In part because of this reaction, Mercer and his family partners were wary of nomination of the market area to the National Register of Historic Places, or of local district designation. The partners objected to the prospect of anyone else having control over building use or

design, and they feared a situation in which a certain kind of academic historicism might be forced upon them. It was only after Joseph Wood, head of the historic landmarks commission, convinced Mercer and Carter that the character of their highly personalized and flexible enterprise would be respected that they agreed to participate in the formation of a local historic district for the Old Market.

Mercer Management's greatest architectural achievement is not even a building, but rather a passageway—a "found" space that captures the essence of Old Market ambience. This nine-foot-wide space between two nineteenth-century brick buildings has been covered with a skylight grid, and the front and back are enclosed with glass. By excavating the basement level, a narrow, brick-covered courtyard has been created. The windows on the original exterior walls have been opened up to form an arcade on each floor, connected with a stairway and bridge at the upper two levels. The effect is one of surprise and contradiction; the space is narrow and enclosing, and at the same time it is high and aspiring. The skylight creates a greenhouse look. Vines and potted plants hang from the brick walls, and a huge bougainvillea brightens the windows at the entry. In summer, the little alley is a cool, quiet retreat from Omaha's humidity; in winter, it offers a bright and cozy refuge from the city's gloomy skies. Restaurants, shops, and offices occupy the passageway's extremities.

The success of Omaha's Old Market could have been the benchmark for commercial revivals throughout the city, and it still may. Other warehouse and industrial buildings south of the market have potential for pedestrian-oriented, small-scale, design-conscious development. The area of greatest promise, however, Jobbers Canyon, is out of the running. Through time, Jobbers Canyon might have made the transition to a specialized retail and residential area in the same thoughtful, incremental, straightforward way developed by the Mercers for their Old Market. The destruction of Jobbers Canyon removes that possibility for-

9.24   *The passageway in the Old Market is a delightful space in any season. Mercer Management, owners and developers of the market, covered the space between two buildings and turned the windowed walls into arcades. Interior walkways parallel the windows and give access to shops and offices on the second and third floors. Like Dallas's West End, the Old Market has developed a thriving restaurant business and is a favored destination of residents as well as out-of-town visitors. Courtesy Lynn Meyer*

ever, a discouraging reminder that without community investment, historic sites are perpetually at risk.

OMAHA'S JOBBERS CANYON

> "Sooner or later in this preservation business, it becomes unpleasant and you have to draw the line."—*George Haecker, Omaha architect and founder of Landmarks, Inc.*

Surprise. Shock. Disbelief. Denial. These were the reactions of Omaha's preservationists in the summer of 1987 when rumblings were first heard around town that Jobbers Canyon, a National Register district of early twentieth century warehouses, would be torn down to meet the design requirements for a new corporate headquarters on adjacent land. Two years later, as the final five of twenty-two historic buildings in Jobbers Canyon fell to the wrecking ball following a tough court fight, preservationists were still traumatized and incredulous over the devastation. Could this loss have been avoided? Can this defeat be turned around to benefit the city's remaining historic architecture?

Omaha's preservation community had maintained high hopes for Jobbers Canyon, a six-square-block collection of brick buildings that had traditionally housed goods shipped in by rail until "jobbers" could deliver them to suppliers farther west. In the mid-1980s, at the time of National Register designation, the warehouses were in sound condition, many of them still occupied by thriving businesses. The district employed about 500 people in eight active companies.

These were large buildings—sturdy, symmetrical, and square—some of them eight stories high. The district's oldest buildings were designed in the Richardsonian Romanesque style, but the larger portion expressed the Renaissance Revival with decorative elements on the entries and cornices, yet rather plain facades overall. Brick streets in and around the district added continuity and texture to the deep red surfaces of the buildings.

The Jobbers Canyon district, nominated to the National Register only a year before demolition talk began, was located on the edge of downtown Omaha close to the Missouri River and adjacent to an earlier warehouse area, the Old Market, which had been successfully adapted to accommodate restaurants, shops, apartments, and offices. The Old Market, a popular spot for Omaha residents, had also been named a favorite tourist destination. A large new urban park, Central Park Mall, ran alongside the Old Market and Jobbers Canyon. Eventually this collection of pedestrian-oriented areas was to connect downtown Omaha to the Missouri River. When that happened, Jobbers Canyon would be ideally situated for development in much the same manner as the Old Market. The canyon was more than holding its own, and its future seemed bright.

The shift in circumstances that killed the warehouse district was economically driven and fueled by fear. In 1985 a major corporation left Omaha to relocate in Texas, taking with it 2000 jobs and a reputation as a civic-minded company that would be hard to replace. During the same period, two other corporations trimmed back their work forces. Omaha's business community was scared, and when ConAgra, a food-processing conglomerate, started looking around the country for a new home, Nebraska's business and political leadership determined to keep them in the state. The legislature passed a law extending tax credits to companies making substantial investments within the state, and several Nebraska communities began to vie for ConAgra's headquarters.

Omaha—its Chamber of Commerce, development foundation, municipal government, and the city's major newspaper, *The Omaha World-Herald*—urged ConAgra to consider a fifty-acre vacant site near the river and adjacent to Jobbers Canyon. The city's civic and business leaders had spent the better part of twenty years planning a riverfront development, linking it to a large regional plan that included Council Bluffs, Iowa, and several smaller communities. They envisioned marinas, parks, recreational areas, and urban de-

9.25 *Spacious warehouses, brick streets, railroad tracks, and raised loading docks were hallmarks of Jobbers Canyon, a National Register historic district until it was demolished in 1988 to accommodate a new corporate campus. Courtesy Lynn Meyer*

9.26 *Taken from the same vantage point as Figure 9.25, this photograph illustrates the scope of demolition in Jobbers Canyon. Buildings on the right were subsequently removed.*

velopment. A ConAgra corporate campus near the river would supply a big piece of an emerging plan that would benefit the city overall and be of particular help to downtown.

ConAgra liked the proposed location, but found the site confining. Charles M. Harper, ConAgra's chief executive officer, insisted that buildings in Jobbers Canyon be cleared to create a more compatible context for the company's planned low-rise suburban complex. Harper dismissed claims of architectural or historical distinction for the warehouse district, describing the canyon as "some big, ugly red brick buildings," a remark that was to be quoted frequently during the year ahead.

Omaha's city planners cautioned ConAgra against demolition. The city itself had nominated the district to the National Register of Historic Places just the year before. Planning director Marty Shukert defended the canyon's value to the city and then argued that, if it were taken down, costs for demolition and relocation of existing businesses would be prohibitive. Whether the canyon's buildings *could* be demolished was open to question. National Register properties are offered no protection against demolition unless federal funds are involved. Omaha's preservationists thought they saw such a connection. The ConAgra project was to be privately funded, but it was part of the larger riverfront development in which several federal agencies were involved. Planning in these earlier stages had included Jobbers Canyon, and for this reason Omaha's planners and preservationists were reasonably certain that the warehouse district would stand. Under that assumption, ConAgra's architects proceeded with a design that confined the corporate campus to the proposed fifty acres, with only a slight incursion into Jobbers Canyon.

The prospect of old brick buildings looming over the new corporate headquarters was unacceptable to Harper and ConAgra. By the summer of 1987 the company was wavering in its commitment to Omaha and threatening to take its $50 million development elsewhere. The business community rallied, convinced the city planners to give in on the demolition of Jobbers Canyon, and pledged the money it would take to level the district and relocate existing businesses. A deal was struck early in January of 1988, and ConAgra proceeded with plans to build on the proposed riverfront site, which would be accessed and buffered by the cleared land of Jobbers Canyon. The subsidy of private and public funds to accomplish the project totaled nearly $40 million.

Over the summer, Omaha's preservationists hesitated, certain that the warehouses would somehow be spared. When the city lined up behind ConAgra and the Omaha Development Corporation began raising money to demolish Jobbers Canyon and relocate businesses, the preservation community understood that the peril was real and imminent. But the power of the developer's alliance had itself created an immobilizing and dividing force.

The twenty-year-old Landmarks, Inc., organized in 1966 after Omaha lost its ca. 1890 Richardsonian post office, began an agonizing appraisal of its options. Would a spirited defense of Jobbers Canyon irrevocably alienate Omaha's business community? Were there legal grounds on which to fight? If saving the canyon meant the sacrifice of badly needed economic development, was the price too high?

Dismayed by the equivocation among the board of directors, a portion of the landmarks group broke away to join other activists in a new advocacy organization, PROUD (People for Responsible Omaha Urban Development). Led by a young attorney, Mark Himes, PROUD spent a few weeks in early 1988 organizing itself and raising funds, and then it filed a law suit demanding that the city allow more time for review of the ConAgra riverfront agreement. They argued that a formal review was required under federal law because a National Register district was involved in a project associated with several federal agencies. The National Trust for Historic Preservation joined PROUD in its suit. A decision in PROUD's favor would buy some time and trigger

9.27   *These cherubs, who appear to be carrying produce to market, adorned the Sullivanesque arched entryway to Fairbanks, Morse and Company, dealers in machinery, boilers, and windmills. This 1893 warehouse was one of twenty-two large historic buildings demolished in Jobbers Canyon. Courtesy Lynn Meyer*

a review process that might be beneficial to the historic properties.

Demolition proceeded through the summer and fall. Explosives, wrecking balls, and bulldozers began to attack and level the warehouses in Jobbers Canyon. Inside the courtroom, the case moved slowly. Judges at the state and federal level struck down the litigation brought by PROUD and its allies, but finally, in March of 1989, an appellate court issued a temporary injunction against further demolition on five of the

remaining buildings until the court could rule on the issue of federal involvement. In June, the court removed the injunction and declared that no cause had been found for federal review.

With that decision, the remaining five buildings were lost. In all, six square blocks, twenty-two buildings, and 1.7 million square feet of nationally significant historic architecture literally bit the dust.

Could it have been otherwise? It is easy enough with benefit of hindsight to fault Omaha's preservationists, and without a doubt, they have been very hard on themselves. Looking back over the two-year fight, these conclusions are clear: they reacted too late with too little. They were shocked to learn how shallow the support for historic architecture was in their community. They were ill-prepared organizationally and financially to take on a battle of this magnitude. More seriously, they equivocated about their basic obligation to protect Omaha's significant architecture.

Even if they had acted with greater speed and focus, it is hard to say whether the result would have been different. On the other side of the aisle, the developers hardly presented an exemplary case study. ConAgra's campuslike design scheme with its free-standing low-rise buildings in a kind of vague salute to Frank Lloyd Wright is not a good fit for the dense character of an urban downtown area. Architect George Haecker, looking at the project from a planner's view, has pointed to one clumsy circumstance after another: the necessity for condemnation of property, massive demolition, expensive relocations, the disruption of business, and the destruction of historic architecture. Nonetheless, the developers prevailed. Given this scorched earth approach to victory, one wonders about the quality of the aftermath. Will there be peace and prosperity? Has this episode been good for the citizens of Omaha?

Jobbers Canyon's worth to the city had been brought into question during a period of economic uncertainty, usually a time of peril for historic landmarks. The business community put enormous resources and commitment into persuading ConAgra to build in downtown Omaha. To rally public opinion, they harnessed the support of the city's daily newspaper. These are formidable weapons. Landmarks, Inc., was at a disadvantage. One does not want to be in an adversarial position under these circumstances.

Landmarks, Inc., had been a constructive but relatively powerless group within the Omaha business community in the 1980s. Its membership at around 300 was strong for the size of the city (population 350,000), and its good works

included publications, tours, and projects that heightened public awareness of the city's architectural heritage. It had not been a major player, however, because it lacked the economic clout of the San Antonio Conservation Society or the political savvy of Historic Denver. The landmarks group was not positioned for a win against the odds they faced, and they were caught off guard. No Omaha preservationist would ever have imagined the wholesale demolition of Jobbers Canyon.

A second preservation force in Omaha was the city's historic preservation staff, part of the planning department and certainly one of the strongest in the region. Because few western cities or towns have effective private preservation organizations, much of the burden for protecting historic architecture has fallen on the planning departments of counties and municipalities. They have taken the initiative to conduct surveys of historic sites, publish illustrated reports of their findings, nominate significant properties to the National Register, administer preservation ordinances, and assist owners in taking advantage of tax credits for the rehabilitation of buildings. In most cities, including Omaha, the historic preservation staff provides nearly all of the day-to-day structure and activity needed to protect and enhance the community's old buildings. In a politically volatile confrontation, however, they are immobilized. When city officials take a stand antithetical to preservation, planners are silenced, as they were in the Jobbers Canyon situation. Government planners are not free agents, and private citizens should think twice about expecting city or county employees to operate effectively or successfully in a highly charged political arena. George Haecker's observation that sooner or later the preservation business gets unpleasant is a timely reminder to preservation activists of the continual need for citizen leadership.

While the case was in court, and demolition was underway, attorney Thomas White, a founder of PROUD, wrote "Lessons from the Loss of Omaha's Jobbers Canyon" for *Preservation Forum* quarterly, reflecting on the city's loss and offer-

9.28   The Burlington Building, plain but
handsome, survived the destruction of its neighbors in Jobbers Canyon. Rehabilitated and
occupied now by offices, the Burlington abuts
award-winning Central Park Mall, which has
been developed in the past decade as a landscaped park and pedestrian space adjacent
to downtown. The Burlington was built in
1879 and then remodeled in 1899. Courtesy
Lynn Meyer

ing advice to other advocacy groups. Stressing a need for preparation and organization, White cautioned preservationists to identify potential allies early on and put them to work. Community support, or the lack thereof, may have been the most important variable in this fight, and it may explain the negative Jobbers Canyon outcome as compared to a recent successful battle against a proposed expanded and intrusive freeway in downtown Fort Worth, or the positive gains made by preservationists in Denver's Lower Downtown. In both instances, a large portion of the business community supported preservation principles and action.

Musing over the antipreservation, prodevelopment attitudes of Omaha's business community, George Haecker notes, "In the 1940s and 1950s here, during the period following World War II, we had big contractors and architects—corporate leaders—who were seen as the wave of the future. They were *builders*. They were tearing down the old and building the new. Historic preservation was sissy stuff. *Real men build*. They don't fix up. They start over and leave their mark."

Will egocentric and destructive attitudes like the ones to which Haecker refers—and which still are embraced in portions of the mountains and plains West—be replaced with a more pluralistic view of architecture and community life, or will the loss of Jobbers Canyon be part of a larger urban pattern in Omaha?

For preservationists, terrible losses can be great energizers. Very likely, Landmarks, Inc., and PROUD will reorganize and emerge as bigger and better advocates for Omaha's historic buildings and landscapes. They will want to lead the promotion of historic sites as economic resources and as important cultural attributes that give the community a special character, just as the Old Market does now. The guiding principle behind urban historic preservation is that street life should be safe, textured, lively, diverse, and enjoyed on a human scale. Preservation of these attractive qualities helps a city to achieve its economic goals.

10.1   *These three shingled Craftsman houses in the North End of Colorado Springs, probably designed by a single builder, exemplify the varied but harmonious quality of many American neighborhoods. Similar materials, scale, and forms, along with standardized setbacks from the street, accommodate both a sense of individuality and a need for order.*

CHAPTER TEN

Neighborhoods and Residential Preservation

The renaissance of neighborhoods in the past twenty years has been preservation's brightest star. If not the city's heart, neighborhoods most surely constitute its soul. The social fabric of a neighborhood, woven of habits and myriad patterns and created from closely held values, supplies the personal force that in turn shapes public, collective experience.

The regeneration of an area of older homes is an important achievement in its own right as well as a source of strength for nearby downtown commercial districts. Residential neighborhoods surround and define the historic core. Healthy inner-city residential neighborhoods shore up downtowns economically and transform them visually.

Old neighborhoods have been a proving ground for preservation since the 1960s, when urban renewal and expanding businesses began to invade inner-city residential areas. Often, the result was a kind of no man's land of houses converted to apartments and businesses, or replaced altogether with small commercial buildings surrounded by a sea of asphalt-surfaced parking lots. In the process, fine old homes were lost.

The change had actually started earlier. Wartime housing shortages in many cities had encouraged homeowners to add apartments in basements or upper floors. These makeshift units solved an immediate housing need but changed the character of neighborhoods and gradually contributed to their decline.

After the war, veterans benefits and federal

subsidies beckoned home buyers to the suburbs. The new financial incentives included new houses at low interest rates and with no down payment. Bolstering this attractive financial arrangement was a pervasive desire to build anew and to put aside the sufferings and deprivations associated with the Great Depression and World War II. The suburbs became the mecca for single-family home buyers as the mood of the country turned modern, embracing the dream of new houses equipped with the most advanced appliances.

Not everyone wanted to flee to the suburbs, however. Some preferred proximity to downtown and welcomed the ambience of a settled area, or they chose to stay in an old neighborhood because they had always lived there. It was home.

As the postwar changes accelerated in the 1960s, impinging on the inner city, residents in some older neighborhoods began to fight back. Historic preservation was not yet an issue in the West. Most residents knew little of their area's history or architecture. They simply knew that

10.3   *Rowhouses were never as popular in the*
heartland as they were in the cities of the East.
Individualized, detached homes were the norm
in most neighborhoods. This apartment house
in Topeka is an exception. The repeated forms
are pleasing to the eye. Courtesy Bern Ketchum,
Topeka-Shawnee County Kansas Metropolitan
Planning Commission

10.4 *These identical cottages in the Tennessee Town neighborhood of Topeka were part of an 1880s settlement of 500 black immigrants from the South. Courtesy Bern Ketchum, Topeka-Shawnee County Kansas Metropolitan Planning Commission*

their neighborhoods were settled, comfortable, and convenient. The call to arms early on was to protect the residential character of the neighborhood; the use of historic preservation as a rationale and a rallying cry came later.

The Neighborhoods Fight Back

Much of the neighborhood advocacy that emerged in the 1960s was directed against the introduction of commercial enterprises into residential areas. The business developers were motivated by the low cost of residential property compared to land zoned for commercial uses. Operating from a nearby residential neighborhood, a business could benefit from proximity to downtown without paying a premium for high-cost land.

The local zoning codes became the neighborhood battleground. Most western communities (Houston is a notable exception) had adopted zoning ordinances by mid-century to control growth and change. A city's highest and purest residential zone typically would be coded "R-1" for single-family residences. There would be several categories of "mixed uses" and, finally, a series of business and industrial zones. Within each category, variances or exceptions were allowed under certain circumstances. Amended and revised versions of these zoning ordinances are still in place in most communities.

The problem with residential zones during the pressure period of business expansion in the 1960s—and still true today—was that once they were "cracked," they were fair game for all other business projects that came along. It becomes politically difficult for a zoning commission to turn down an applicant for commercial use of residential property if a similar use has already been granted to someone else. The "all or nothing" character of zoning decisions ultimately creates an unfortunate rigidity in neighborhood life because all intrusions, no matter how beneficial to residents, must be fought off or a flood of commercial development will overwhelm the area.

Not all zoning change requests involve businesses. Small institutions looking for low-cost facilities or wanting to operate in the comfort of a residential setting often seek zoning changes. Foster-care homes, drug-treatment centers, halfway houses, and health clinics are examples. These requests can create divisiveness in a neighborhood because many residents want to support the social agency involved. Sometimes the new home or organization is not compatible with the rest of the neighborhood, however, and even if it is, the domino effect from zoning changes is just as threatening from a halfway house as it is from a hot dog stand.

Many historic neighborhoods owe their health to homeowners who, during the 1960s, fought one zoning battle after another. Many architecturally distinctive residential districts were stabilized at that time by the strength of citizen advocacy. In many instances the neighborhood was then "down-zoned," i.e., the zoning was changed from R-2 or R-3 to the more desirable R-1, or single family, to reflect the improving character of the area.

As historic preservation became an organized movement with planning tools of its own, older neighborhoods were given added protection. By the early 1970s, aided and encouraged by state historic preservation offices, many older neigh-

borhoods were listed on the National Register of Historic Places. Local governments were apt to take a neighborhood more seriously if the state and local government considered it historically important, and National Register nomination unfailingly raised neighborhood pride.

There are compelling sagas of preservation battles successfully waged and won in the historic neighborhoods of the West. Unlike the revitalization of commercial areas, where deals are consummated by professionals trained in law, finance, real estate, and the marketplace, neighborhood preservation advocacy has been carried out by volunteers who devote themselves for months and even years to ensure the security and future of their family homes. Typically, the task is thrust on them when they hear a piece of neighborhood news that signals a potential problem with zoning or another disruption. The school principal sends out a notice saying that a portion of the neighborhood school's playground will be swept up by a proposed freeway ramp, or a realtor at the door announces the imminent construction of an out-patient motel, ancillary to a nearby hospital, which will replace the remaining houses in the block.

In response, neighborhood volunteers must educate themselves and begin to organize the local residents to fight back. More often than not, these volunteers are women. Men get involved, too, but because these threats often erupt overnight and demand great amounts of time, housewives have traditionally taken the responsibility for defending their neighborhoods. In the process, they are likely to become experts in zoning and traffic law, preservation financing, and historic architecture. They may have to attend all zoning board and city council sessions for the duration. To win their cause, they must inform and motivate their neighbors to sign petitions and attend all public meetings involving the impending intrusion on the neighborhood.

As a result of these citizen stands, many historic neighborhoods have been saved and strengthened in the past twenty years. Fortu-

10.5 *Capitol North, a neighborhood close to downtown Cheyenne, has had a running battle with the state's capitol over parking and expansion. This National Register Historic District has had little legislative protection locally and depends on citizen advocacy to maintain its residential integrity. Courtesy Richard Collier, State Historic Preservation Office, Wyoming Department of Archives, Museums and History*

nately, the battle won has often meant the beginning of a unified homeowners' association and general improvements in the neighborhood, followed by increased property values. Today, neighborhood groups have power and are to be reckoned with. Even communities that lack broad-based historic preservation groups, as many western cities do, are likely to have strong neighborhood associations capable of uniting in a common cause. Oklahoma City's neighborhood coalition, long a national model, advocates historic preservation as well as other quality-of-life issues. Denver's neighborhoods recently rallied to protect a section of the city's old downtown. In most western cities, neighborhood organizations have changed the balance of political power.

After a neighborhood has held its own in the zoning wars, created a neighborhood association, and achieved listing on the National Register, its residents may seek a local historic district designation and an ordinance to preserve the area's historic character. Usually ordinances are communitywide, with regulations and guidelines customized for individual historic districts. Typi-

10.6   *The West Side in Helena, Montana,
is home to an extraordinary number of beautifully appointed mansions. This house was
built in 1888 by Louis Kaufman, a prominent
rancher.*

cally a preservation ordinance requires building owners to submit proposed design changes for approval. Renovations—perhaps even exterior paint colors—must remain in keeping with the dominant, or significant, materials and visual qualities of the neighborhood. Historic preservation ordinances sometimes require permits and waiting periods for demolition.

Cheyenne, Wyoming, following this trail, first completed a survey in the late 1970s, then nominated three districts to the National Register, and in 1985 adopted a historic preservation ordi-

nance. As ordinances go, this one is little more than window-dressing. There are no requirements for owner compliance on building renovation or demolition. The legislation provides only the bare minimum to qualify Cheyenne as a Certified Local Government, which enables it to receive historic preservation funds channeled through the state from the U.S. Department of the Interior. A dozen other Wyoming towns have a similar administrative structure. The framework of support that exists for historic districts has little substance, and therefore the strength of the state's historic neighborhoods depends on citizen interest and advocacy.

Cheyenne's three historic districts include Capitol North, a collection of 115 early twentieth century homes located near downtown and adjacent to the state capitol. Capitol North's loosely knit neighborhood association is visible and vocal and has successfully fought off most of the commercial enterprises that have tried to move into this residential area. They have been less successful in staving off their imperial neighbor, the state of Wyoming, which has demolished several homes in past years for building expansion and parking. Still, it is a stable neighborhood with the advantages of strong housing stock, an effective advocacy group, and historic district designation. For these reasons, and because the West's energy-related economy has been on a downslide for several years, putting a brake on development, Capitol North has held its own, as hundreds of other mountain and plains neighborhoods have successfully done in the past decade.

The West Side in Helena, Montana, a large neighborhood of huge homes, is another example of a stabilized historic district operating within a laissez-faire environment offering virtually no legal protection. The West Side's architecture is well-known in the community, and its historic value is acknowledged. Helena's older residences are extraordinary for a city of 24,000. A wealthy mining boom town at the end of the 19th century, Helena became the state capital and forged a new life for itself after the gold boom collapsed. Out of that initial gilt-edged affluence emerged a collection of stone and brick mansions, and some frame Italianate and Queen Anne homes as well, occupying the hill overlooking Last Chance Gulch, the hub of the original mining camp.

When Last Chance Gulch was revitalized in the late 1960s, the West Side exhibited some fraying at the edges, but the greater portion of the neighborhood has remained intact, and there are few commercial pressures today. The West Side was nominated to the National Register of Historic Places in 1972 as part of a district that included the older portions of downtown.

The Helena Old House Club watches over the West Side and the city's other historic neighborhoods, holding its membership meetings in a different historic home each month. The West Side's longevity may be threatened eventually by the large size of most of its homes—three stories, front and back stairways, servants' quarters, oversized lawns, and carriage houses. They are expensive to heat and costly to repair. But for now, a former president of the Old House Club, Carla Cronholm, believes that owners of West Side houses expect some financial sacrifice and are willing to make it for the experience of living there. "People do it out of love. It's a conscious decision. You expect to put a lot of work and money into these homes."

There is a strong ethic still in the West that says "a man's property is his to do with as he pleases," without the government or anyone else interfering. As in Cheyenne, Helena, and many other of the region's communities, the residents and city officials of fast-growing Albuquerque are loathe to impose protective restrictions on historic property. The city has seven neighborhoods on the National Register, but only one, Huning-Highlands, is a locally designated district with design and review standards. In addition, the area known as "Old Town"—Albuquerque's original seventeenth-century settlement—has been designated a special historic zone whose buildings are subject to controls over use and design.

Albuquerque's historic preservation planner, Mary Davis, believes there are trade-offs on the ordinance control issue. "The principle is 'if it ain't broke, don't fix it.' Why spend money and energy creating a locally controlled historic district—which is a lot of work at the outset, plus a bureaucracy which must be funded—when the neighborhood is maintaining well without the legal regulation?" On the other hand, Davis recognizes that the constant threat of demolition or disruption is always there, prompting residents to be more favorably inclined toward a protective ordinance. But she is quick to point out that

10.7   *This Helena, Montana, house was built in 1890 by a Virginian who made, and then lost, a fortune in gold in Last Chance Gulch. In 1900 Conrad Kohrs, Montana's most prominent cattle baron, bought the house as an anniversary present for his wife, Augusta.*

10.8 *A projecting gable, narrow eaves, a Palladian window, and a "stretched" shingle surface identify this house as part of the American Shingle style. This style had been popular for at least a decade when, in 1897, merchant Edward Babcock built this home for his family in Helena's West Side.*

the intrusions in a historic neighborhood are not always architectural. In Albuquerque, Davis explains, freeways, major arteries, and one-way streets have created more damage to residential neighborhoods than commercial development. Automobiles move fast along one-way streets because traffic lights are timed to avoid stops and because there are more than the usual number of lanes for passing. Speeding automobiles, however, are not a good fit with a quiet neighborhood of family homes. "And once a historic district is seriously compromised by traffic, it's nearly impossible to recapture its earlier character."

Even though an appreciation for historic architecture has vastly increased in the region's communities over the past twenty years, westerners are likely to continue to view historic preservation ordinances with suspicion. Protection of control

10.9 Like many western neighborhoods,
Albuquerque's Huning-Highlands Historic
District is listed on the National Register of
Historic Places. Close to the University of New
Mexico, the neighborhood's spacious late nine-
teenth century housing has been attractive to
the academic community and others who enjoy
the area's traditional qualities.

10.10 Residents of historic neighborhoods
worry not only about commercial intrusions,
freeways, and one-way streets, but also about
the quality of institutions in their midst.
Huning-Highlands has been aggravated for
years over the existence at its borders of a sadly
deteriorated high school, a target of vandalism
and other crime. When this building—a strong
and attractive example of an early twentieth
century revival of Elizabethan styling—is rehabilitated, the entire neighborhood will be
buttressed.

NEIGHBORHOODS AND RESIDENTIAL PRESERVATION

over personal property is important, but when development pressures are intense, there may be no other way to save a building or district. A strong neighborhood organization is a powerful tool for preservation, but it is not always adequate to deflect a threat of demolition or disruptive change. A historic preservation ordinance can offer added protection.

Neighborhoods are complicated organisms, and no two are alike. Because they exist at the heart of daily life, however, they have similar needs and problems. In their ways of coping they are widely divergent. Three western cities, one in Colorado and two in Texas, offer three entirely different neighborhood environments. In Colorado Springs, the historic North End—a healthy, intact district much like Cheyenne's Capitol North—has adopted a basically reactive survival technique, fighting off zoning changes and maintaining the status quo. Dallas's Swiss Avenue Historic District, in contrast, has aggressively battled its way back up from a serious decline to regain its place as a premier residential area. Galveston, led by its powerful Historical Foundation, has adopted a citywide campaign to save, rebuild, and preserve all of its residential neighborhoods. These three stories have different plots but common ingredients—vigilance, leadership, and organization.

COLORADO SPRINGS: THE NORTH END

Founded in 1871 as a fashionable resort, Colorado Springs became a mining and financial capital in the 1890s when gold was discovered thirty miles away in Cripple Creek on the "back" side of Pikes Peak. New riches triggered new growth. The mining millionaires and their functionaries moved to the North End, a new suburb a mile from downtown.

Bordered on one side by Fountain Creek, on another by the campus of Colorado College, and on a third by the grounds of a tuberculosis hospital, the North End exemplified the garden suburb ideals of the late nineteenth and early twentieth centuries. The neighborhood architectural choices embraced Neoclassical styling as well as popular English derivatives and a few examples of American Shingle style. After World War I, a sudden burst of bungalows marked the arrival of middle-class families without servants. Most North End houses are of frame construction faced with wooden shingles or clapboard siding. Cast-iron fences manufactured in a local foundry surround many yards.

The North End held its own through the years, fading a bit during the dislocations caused by the Depression and World War II when many of the larger homes were subdivided into apartments. Then, in the 1950s, the old Glockner-Penrose Sanitorium, having evolved into a general hospital, elected to build a large, modern facility, a decision that would bring permanent changes to the North End. A few property owners nearby, foreseeing the impact of a 12-story hospital on the neighborhood, organized the North End Home Owners Association to challenge the expansion.

The association was headed by a neighborhood resident, Jean Szymanski, an iron-willed lady recognized for her integrity and forthrightness, and for her devotion to the idea that residential neighborhoods are not to be tampered with. The organization had no social or promotional role, unlike many neighborhood associations. The North End group met formally once a year to elect officers. The rest of the time, Szymanski kept her eye on the neighborhood and monitored the proceedings of the planning commission, which reviewed all zoning requests.

As its first test, the new North End group argued that a large hospital was incompatible with a neighborhood of single-family homes. A new hospital, they reasoned, would unleash a flood of related enterprises, particularly doctors' offices. Residents also worried about traffic and parking. Their fears were borne out. Before the new hospital was in place, a group of doctors requested a zoning variance to build an office complex across the street. The neighborhood again mobilized to protest the change. After many hear-

10.11 *The North End in Colorado Springs is a middle-class neighborhood with a few mansions; many substantial large homes, cottages, and bungalows; and square frame houses like this one with classical details.*

10.12 *The carpentry detailing on older homes is the source of much of their appeal, as on this large frame home in Colorado Springs's North End.*

ings and appeals, the issue went to the Colorado Supreme Court, which decided in the doctors' favor. Within months, a brick office building appeared on the corner of a block otherwise filled with private homes.

Over the years, the hospital built more additions. Parking problems worsened; the neighborhood was perpetually agitated. The hospital bought two adjoining blocks, removed the houses, and made parking lots for their employees, which temporarily eased the parking problem but greatly altered the character of the neighborhood.

At a stand-off with the hospital, the North

End advocates turned their attention—with greater success—to stopping other threats to the neighborhood. During the 1960s, as Colorado Springs began to grow rapidly, pressures grew with it to build businesses and apartment houses in the North End. During a thirty-year period beginning in the late 1950s, neighborhood organizers in the North End fought off more than one hundred requests for variances or other zone changes.

Jean Szymanski monitored all of them. Fully informed about every nuance of the city's zoning ordinance, she sometimes quelled a request

10.13 Neighborhoods sometimes have features that unify disparate architectural styles. In the North End, iron fences, which were popular in the late nineteenth century, play that role. Most of the neighborhood's fences were manufactured locally at the Hassell Ironworks. Although treasured today, the fences fell out of fashion fifty years ago. More would have been removed except for the fact that they are extremely difficult to dig up.

before it got to the public hearing of the planning commission by dissuading a realtor or his client from pursuing the application. If a battle became full-blown and a show of force by the neighborhood was required, she would meet with the executive committee and the residents closest to the proposed project. Together, they would develop a strategy for the hearing. The affected neighbors were encouraged to be as subjective as they wished. After all, they were the victims of the proposed new enterprise, and the commissioners were likely to sympathize with them. The homeowners' spokesmen, in contrast, were cool, professional, and to the point, always sticking to a first principle: "The North End is a *residential* neighborhood."

As many as three hundred North End residents would pack the small city council chambers to protest zoning changes. Nearly always, their strategy and show of force worked. They were able to shut the door to dozens of business enterprises—beauty parlors, insurance agencies, and apartment blocks—to the point where realtors began to steer prospective business clients away from the area.

Coexisting with institutions has turned out to be more difficult for the North End than fending off commercialism. Homeowners can make a persuasive argument that convenience stores and filling stations have no place on a quiet residential street, but this argument loses some of its force against a hospital, a church, or a college, all of which have claims on community values. North End residents have a commitment to Penrose Hospital. It is the city's largest medical facility. Most people in the neighborhood go there when they need medical care, and many hospital staff members live in the North End. When the hospital reaches out for more neighborhood space, the North End can flex its considerable muscle, but the influential hospital board is equally powerful. The choices are confusing and muddied, the resolution often unsatisfactory to all parties. For the neighborhood, a demolished historic house is a terrible loss no matter how exemplary the institution that replaces it.

The National Register of Historic Places named the North End a historic district in 1982. In 1988, the Colorado Springs City Council adopted a historic preservation ordinance. Architectural guidelines were later developed for the North End. These preservation devices have helped the neighborhood to consolidate its gains.

The recent history of the North End is an instructive lesson on the importance of leadership and the need for strong neighborhood organizations. In the late 1980s, a church in the heart of the district sought permission to demolish two buildings, one of them a historic home, to build a parking lot. As attractive and historically important as this neighborhood had always been, there obviously were many people in the community who were ready to sacrifice it. Fortunately, the North End had Jean Szymanski, who reminded everyone once again that "this is a *residential* neighborhood."

GALVESTON'S HISTORIC NEIGHBORHOODS

More than anything, Galveston's experience of the past three decades proves what can be accomplished when a disciplined, energetic preservation organization sets its sights on improving a community's homes and neighborhoods. Thirty years ago, Galveston was an isolated seacoast island with exceptional historic buildings—many of them badly deteriorated—and a generally depressed economy. Through the Galveston Historical Foundation, preservationists created a climate for improvement, first with positive, well-publicized activities: annual tours of homes, demonstration projects, publications, house museums, and nominations to the National Register of Historic Places; and second, with the provision of such resources as revolving loans, building materials, technical services, and federally financed neighborhood improvements. In the process, hundreds of houses have been rehabilitated, many of them completely restored. Against great odds, Galveston preservationists have achieved a remarkable transformation of the city's neighborhoods.

Galveston's physical circumstances on the Texas coast are different than those of other towns of the mountains and plains region, but the preservation community's approach and solutions form a strong model nonetheless.

Galveston's historic homes have a different look about them. Here are surviving High Victorian and Greek Revival mansions among the palm trees and live oaks of Broadway Boulevard, an abundance of spacious frame houses, and everywhere a collection of cottages and diminutive homes, many of them graced with elaborate porches and carpentry decoration. Vulnerable to hurricanes and flooding rains, the city's houses are set high off the ground on piers of brick, often disguised with coverings of latticework, cypress siding, or pickets. This additional elevation—anywhere from three to eight feet—gives even a modest cottage an air of importance and is one of the hallmarks of Galveston's residential areas.

The city's homes reflect its economic history: enormous wealth and power through the nineteenth century, a decline in the early twentieth century, areas of intractable poverty developing during the Depression, widespread neglect and haphazard destruction of the historic fabric after World War II, and a regeneration of neighborhood vitality and appearance during the 1970s and '80s after the Galveston Historical Foundation accomplished its work. During all these years, conscientious owners kept their homes in fine condition, but overall, many structures were allowed to deteriorate and a number were lost.

The achievements of the Galveston Historical Foundation are doubly impressive when they are measured against the financial and physical problems that have been endemic to the island in this century. Recent improvements, although extensive, still fall short of the mark. There is too much left to be done, too many decrepit buildings in counterpoint to the houses that have been carefully restored in the past twenty years. As uneven as the progress has been, however, there is a sense in Galveston's residential enclaves of past glory and grandeur and a determination to seek comfort

10.14   The Joel B. Wolfe House (1886), Galveston. For protection against gulf storms, Galveston homes typically have shutters. On calm summer days, sea breezes are enjoyed on balconies, wrap-around verandas, and porches, which often are decorated with elaborate carpentry trim. Courtesy Jim Cruz, Galveston Historical Foundation

10.15 The J. F. Smith House (1885), a large Italianate home, was part of Galveston's Fifteenth Annual Historic Homes Tour in 1989. Courtesy Jim Cruz, Galveston Historical Foundation

and civility within this exposed setting and what has often been a punishing climate.

Galveston's neighborhoods have always reflected an economic, social, and racial mix. Today, you might find an empty, unpainted frame house two and one-half stories tall next to a superbly kept cottage. Several historic districts of exceptional quality have been designated: the Silk Stocking District and the East End, both National Historic Landmarks, and Kempner Park. Close by, however, as one moves around the island from block to block, are vacant lots and abandoned structures, some of them burned out or simply decaying and sagging under their own weight. Dilapidated buildings are found in most cities. The unusual thing about Galveston is the existence of these derelicts in nearly every neighborhood. They are a testimony to the island's uncertain

10.16 *Galveston's moist salt-laden air is hard on painted surfaces. To encourage owners to paint their homes regularly, the Galveston Historical Foundation in 1981 began to offer free paint to homeowners. By the end of the decade more than 450 homes had been repainted through the Paint Partnership Program. Courtesy Jim Cruz, Galveston Historical Foundation*

economy during the past eight decades when property became increasingly difficult to maintain but impossible to sell, particularly when encumbered by years of back taxes and general neglect. These sad buildings, troubled enough already, are preyed upon by transients who litter the landscape, vandalize the interior, and occasionally set the houses on fire.

The Galveston Historical Foundation, working with the city, has put together an ambitious program to improve and preserve the island's unique stock of houses. Coping with 1500 structures, many of them in distressed condition, the foundation wisely chose to organize programs that would encourage owners to make certain protective changes, preferably changes that would be visible, easily accomplished, and of modest cost. The cheapest, easiest improvement, of course, is paint. In 1981, with funding from the Eliza and Harris Kempner Fund, the foundations residential program began to offer free paint to the island's homeowners. Eight years later, "Paint Partnership" could point to 450 houses with new exterior paint jobs. Discovering that free paint

was not always a sufficient incentive, the foundation added "Paint Pals" to the package, providing volunteer labor from the Jaycees and other service clubs for owners who were unable to do the work themselves.

When owners are ready to restore their homes, the residential program offers "used parts" sold through the foundation's salvage warehouse. Materials are donated by local residents and are to be used only on historic homes in Galveston. Prices range from a $2 wooden spindle to $100 for cast-iron columns. For help with the hands-on work, the residential program advisers run rehabilitation workshops, distribute "how-to" literature, meet with neighborhood groups and individual owners, present "We Did It Ourselves" preservation awards, and provide lists of local contractors and craftsmen.

The foundations active field work is complemented by lobbying for housing legislation at all levels and then working with owners to implement government programs. Low-interest loans, tax credits, and neighborhood street improvements are among the benefits available to owners of historic homes. Because of the magnitude of the task, the idea behind all of these programs from the foundation's point of view is one of triage. They've asked the question, "How can we make the greatest gains for preservation with the least investment of resources?" Theirs is a disciplined program run by deeply committed people, both staff and volunteers, and if the need thus far has outstripped their valiant efforts, it still remains a positive approach that has visibly strengthened the residential fabric of Galveston.

Throughout Galveston's neighborhoods, the historical foundation monitors what it calls "endangered properties," abandoned and dysfunctional houses that are falling apart. The residential program staff keeps a notebook of several dozen threatened properties, promoting them to local realtors and occasionally advertising them in special national listings of historic sites. Using a revolving fund established for the city's residential areas in 1982, the foundation may purchase a particularly derelict but important house. Acquisition enables them to secure it against entry and to make emergency repairs, usually on the roof, to halt further damage from the elements. A buyer is sought and deed restrictions are put in place requiring the new owner to maintain the house as a historic property.

The foundation leaves no stone unturned to find a buyer for one of its endangered buildings. In 1986 they acquired the Darragh House (1886), a spacious frame house of uncertain style perhaps best described as coastal Italianate—large, columned and bracketed porches uniting towers at either end—designed by a local architect of note, Alfred Mueller. The house, situated on a large corner property, is surrounded by a high, ornate iron fence. When the foundation bought the house, they spent $40,000 reconstructing the roof and making other repairs. Then they boarded the windows of the empty house to secure it. Hardware and fireplace mantles had been removed by vandals during the years the house stood abandoned and open.

By 1989, because the Darragh House had still not been sold, the foundation decided to place it on the Fifteenth Annual Tour of Homes along with nine fully restored historic homes. To the foundation's leaders, putting this shabby cousin alongside several showcase homes on a tour route made good sense. The annual housewalk, in addition to raising funds and providing a pleasurable event for visitors, provides educational outreach and is a time-honored lure for bringing new investors to the island. No buyers came forward during the tour, but perhaps a seed was planted. In 1987, the dilapidated Egert house, virtually a shell, found a buyer when it was included on the annual tour of homes.

Once the decision had been made to put the Darragh house on tour, the foundation invested another $30,000 in the structure, restoring its grand double-gallery porch, repairing the interior stairway, and replacing plywood window covers with glass to let in natural light. The foundation, by offering the house for $120,000, will take a considerable loss (an additional $350,000 could easily be spent on restoration by the new owner), but saving this showy and historically significant large corner property is regarded as the cost of doing business for a responsible preservation group.

In addition to temporarily acquiring homes through the revolving fund, the foundation owns two houses it operates as museums: Ashton Villa, an 1859 Italianate mansion built by James Brown, a Galveston financial and social leader; and the 1839 Samuel May Williams House, an early Texas adaptation of Greek Revival built by one of the territory's most accomplished entrepreneurs and politicians. A third Galveston house, the Bishop's Palace, now owned by the Catholic diocese, is also open daily to visitors. Truly a grand mansion, the highly decorative "palace" is one of the West's most spectacular houses, especially noted for its colorful stone exterior, carved woodwork, and stained glass. Together these house museums offer the Galveston visitor an example of high living during the island's financial heydays of the nineteenth century.

10.17 *Workmen painted and repaired the two-story front porch of the Darragh House to prepare it for Galveston's annual home tour.*

10.18 *With its porch repaired, windows installed, and facade freshly painted, the J. L. Darragh House (1886) was ready for the 1989 Annual Historic Homes Tour in Galveston. The deserted and derelict Darragh House is one of several endangered properties the Galveston Historical Foundation has taken under its wing in hopes of finding a buyer. Courtesy Galveston Historical Foundation*

10.19   *The Frederick W. Beissner House
(1886) is one of Galveston's most sumptuous
frame homes. Courtesy Jim Cruz, Galveston
Historical Foundation*

Galveston's cottages get their share of attention, too. They are always included in the annual home tour and promoted by the foundation's residential program. As part of the American bicentennial celebration in 1976, Ellen Beasley, a preservation consultant based in Galveston, prepared a special photographic exhibition of the island's small houses. She noted that examples of early houses were likely to be Greek Revival, as one would expect in any western city settled as early as Galveston. She described wooden shotgun houses, known locally as "commissaries," which are found in similar form in many other parts of the country. They are small narrow houses, the gable end to the street, one room opening onto another in linear fashion. Early records showed that small houses were likely to be rental properties and, as they are today, were less well cared for and often overlooked. The Galveston Historical Foundation offers help to owners of these small dwellings to facilitate restorative work honoring the original lines and materials.

Galveston's residential preservationists spend most of their time in the trenches, but on one occasion each year they go on parade—during the annual tour of historic homes held for two successive weekends each May. More than 1700 volunteers are mobilized to manage the event, acting as house chairmen, hosts, guides, ticket takers, and traffic controllers. Although the house walk is a fund raiser, its main purpose is to showcase Galveston's best buildings and bring people over to the island for an immersion in history and architecture. A half-dozen houses are shown, and the tour typically includes one or two other important historic buildings (and occasionally a distressed house like the Darragh). In 1988, visitors toured the Grand Opera House, which had just undergone an $8 million restoration, while the Junior League showed off their prize-winning restoration of the Trueheart Building, designed by Nicholas Clayton and recognized as a tour de force of ornamental brickwork.

Since 1974, when the foundation began its annual house walk, more than 100 homes have been opened to the public. Home tour customers are encouraged to visit the island's attractions and museums as well, including the 1877 barque *Elissa*, which is anchored near The Strand, Galveston's revitalized commercial district. All in all, the annual tour of homes is a giant celebration, and the foundation wants its guests to enjoy the ambience of the island as well as the intimacy of the half-dozen special and often spectacular homes that are opened for the occasion.

One of the great gifts offered to the island by the historical foundation is continuity. Not only do they do good works, they never let go. They have set out to make Galveston's neighborhoods attractive through historically documented regeneration. They also aim for the neighborhoods to be safe and sound, in the simplest understanding of those words. Preserving the architecture is paramount because that is Galveston's special hold on history, but the process of living day to day in these neighborhoods is always on their minds. Hildegard Johns, a historic homeowner with old family ties to the Galveston area, and who served recently as chairman of the residential program, describes the foundation as a galvanizing force, a tenacious preservation corps that keeps everyone

going year after year, adjusting to the market, the weather, and the vagaries of life itself.

SWISS AVENUE: THE BIRTH OF HISTORIC PRESERVATION IN DALLAS

Among the region's neighborhood rehabilitation success stories, Swiss Avenue remains a frontrunner. The speed of its recovery and its overall unblemished good health set it off as a special case. Admittedly, it has enjoyed a few advantages while fighting its way out of the urban doldrums. Although by 1970 most Dallas residents probably dismissed Swiss Avenue as a declining neighborhood and were willing to write it off, the area had never become a hard-core slum. Even during the dog days of the sixties, this architecturally intact neighborhood retained its majestic bearing.

Swiss Avenue, in addition to containing splendid historic resources, has also been blessed with an energetic, persuasive group of activists who, while fighting for their homes, set the stage for the city's preservation movement. Sympathetic city planners stood by to help them, and there were times when the planners took the lead.

One senses in the Swiss Avenue story a tremendous amount of directed energy and great momentum. The small band of people who first organized the neighborhood were neophytes at preservation. Dallas had no precedent at that time to guide them, but they were successful and competent people adept at organizing and particularly skilled in the art of persuasion. They knew when to seek outside help and where to find it, a vital key to overcoming obstacles. Throughout their struggle, they understood the economics of preservation. They realized that Swiss Avenue had to make sense financially—that rhetoric alone would not save it. By promoting the district's real estate, they created a market where there had been none. As a result, a home on Swiss Avenue tempted buyers because the neighborhood once again had a future.

Dallas's leading citizens built Swiss Avenue— part of the Munger Place subdivision—between

10.20   *Swiss Avenue homes are imposing in part because of raised front lawns and deep setbacks, which tend to exaggerate building size. Homes in affluent areas are often hidden behind walls, fences, and shrubbery, but on Dallas's Swiss Avenue, the architecture is highly visible, all the more reason why the district's postwar decline was devastating. There were no buffers against blight, and there was no place to hide. Courtesy Doug Tomlinson*

1900 and 1925, an era of rapid growth for the city. The street itself is proof of the neighborhood's quality: a wide boulevard divided by a landscaped center park. Imposing stone gates announce the entry to Swiss Avenue. Front lawns are raised four feet above street level to ensure proper drainage and to enhance a vista of large, commanding homes. Set back seventy feet from the curb, the substantial houses two and one-half stories tall are widely spaced from each other. Most are built of brick; many have tile or slate roofs. Although the architectural styles vary—Neoclassical, Mission, Prairie, Mediterranean, and Tudor, typical of the period—common features unify the designs: large entries, often with glass doors surrounded by sidelights and a transom; hipped roofs extending far over the walls to form wide eaves; enclosed sun porches; and *porte-cochères* (carports—the roofed automobile drive-throughs that preceded attached garages).

10.21 The strong horizontal lines of this Swiss Avenue house are reinforced by porch wings, porte-cochères, extending eaves, and balustrades. In the early years of the century—as Swiss Avenue was being developed—the long, low Prairie House was becoming popular in the upper Midwest. Although it seems an odd marriage, several Swiss Avenue houses combine formalism with the modernistic lines of Prairie architecture. Courtesy Doug Tomlinson

Swiss Avenue houses are large to begin with, but their set-back placement along a wide street and their oversized architectural details combine to make them appear even larger. Together, the houses form an elegant, rhythmic pattern that signals a collective grandeur while at the same time manages to accentuate individual expression.

Swiss Avenue's auspicious beginnings did not save it from a fate common to other American inner-city neighborhoods. As early as 1930, leading Dallas families were looking northward to the new suburbs of Highland Park and University Park. Gradually, the large homes on Swiss Avenue and in other parts of East Dallas were turned into apartments, a process accelerated by the housing shortages of World War II. Each decade brought new problems. In the 1950s, the Central Expressway cut East Dallas off from downtown. In the 1960s, high-rise zoning ushered in apartment towers. Nearby streets became loaded with heavy traffic.

Swiss Avenue's days were numbered. Large homes that had held single families were now divided into apartments. As more people and cars crowded the neighborhood, the traditional security and quiet of Swiss Avenue disappeared. Even though many responsible owners continued to keep up their homes, the neighborhood houses and yards overall were deteriorating.

It takes heroic action to turn a neighborhood around. Swiss Avenue owes its renewal to the cooperative work of an initial small group of homeowners, the city's planning director, and the National Trust for Historic Preservation. Together, they were eventually able to involve hundreds of other preservationists and to bring Swiss Avenue's rebirth to the attention of the entire city.

The founding group of nine Swiss Avenue residents began to meet in the spring of 1972 with the idea that designating the neighborhood a historic district might solve some of its problems. They were steered in this direction by the city's planning staff, which had already started an architectural survey of the area. One of the homeowner group's leaders, Virginia Talkington McAlester, describes their early rescue work in the neighborhood as a quick study in public relations and high finance. Most people in the community were skeptical about Swiss Avenue's future. To succeed in turning the neighborhood around, the preservationist core needed to convince their neighbors, the banks, the city council, the real estate industry, and future residents that Swiss Avenue was worth rebuilding as a prestigious family neighborhood. Following the advice of preservation leaders elsewhere, the Swiss Avenue "gang of nine" organized themselves as the Historic Preservation League of Dallas. To make the biggest impact possible, they designated every member an officer and ordered the best letterhead stationery they could afford.

Having gained clout and credibility by forming the league, Swiss Avenue's advocates began talking—on the telephone, over the fence, at cocktail parties, at work, while picking up kids at school. They talked with bankers and real estate agents. They spoke at neighborhood meetings and public hearings. When they weren't talking, they were writing. They produced brochures that praised Swiss Avenue's fine homes. They published an occasional newsletter, and whenever local papers printed an editorial or news story about historic preservation or the neighborhood, the league volunteers immediately reprinted and enclosed them with their own newsletter. They circulated petitions, posted flyers, and mailed copies of correspondence with city officials to everyone in the neighborhood. League officials cultivated the press and began to advertise Swiss Avenue properties in the real estate pages of the newspapers. Whenever an opportunity arose, they quoted national preservation experts, architectural historians, urban planners, and other authorities whose opinions might lend credibility to the idea of a revitalized Swiss Avenue.

One of the league's first victories was a restraining order preventing the construction of a high-rise apartment building in the middle of the neighborhood. Under the zoning then in place, high-rises were allowed. By convincing officials that the neighborhood was on the verge of a turnaround, the Swiss Avenue advocates succeeded in squelching the apartment building, which was tantamount to a public declaration of the neighborhood's improving health. In early 1973, the league began a drive to have Swiss Avenue declared a local historic district. After months of emotion-filled hearings and presentations, the Dallas City Council obliged them with the appropriate legislation. A short time later, Swiss Avenue was named a district on the National Register of Historic Places. Having secured the imprimatur of both the city of Dallas and the federal government, Swiss Avenue had arrived as a bona fide historic area and could begin to reap the benefits of historic designation, which included not only greater status and credibility but increased protection as well.

Meanwhile, the league set its sights beyond Swiss Avenue and Munger Place to greater East Dallas. Block by block, they circulated petitions to homeowners, building support for changing the area's zoning back to single-family residential. They began to advertise the entire area and published an illustrated booklet urging people to buy a home in East Dallas. They gave slide presentations to groups all over the city and wrote articles about East Dallas for the newspapers.

Within a year after their promotion began, more than $750,000 had been invested in East Dallas neighborhoods. The turnaround had come. Property values went up, and houses returned to single-family use as new owners moved into the neighborhood and improved their properties.

The changes on Swiss Avenue came swiftly—not because they were easily accomplished, but because a group of determined homeowners campaigned hard to make them happen. An articulate Historic Preservation League leadership demonstrated great skill at getting their story out and around. They understood the value of informing their fellow homeowners—an aroused neighborhood could be counted on to write letters, attend hearings, and take petitions door to door. Their hard work paid dividends. All in all, the Swiss Avenue entrepreneurial spirit created a new and positive market for neighborhood improvement.

The Historic Preservation League also had important institutional support. The city's planning department, at that time directed by Weiming Lu, had initiated talk of a district in the early seventies and had started an architectural survey. The planners were in a position to advise the city council on the benefits of neighborhood preservation. From the start, neighborhood leaders were on the phone with preservationists and planners in other cities. This decision to find out what other neighborhoods were doing saved the Dallas group time and effort. They knew what to do, and they could back up their actions by pointing to the successes of neighborhoods in other parts of the country. Not least in assistance was the National Trust, which involved itself from the start with advice, technical services, and funds.

The National Trust was particularly helpful in the rejuvenation of Munger Place, a residential district adjoining Swiss Avenue and historically a part of the original development. When the preservation league turned its attention to Munger

Place, they expected their hard-hitting, energetic promotional campaign to be as successful in this more modest neighborhood as it had been along the elegant sweep of Swiss Avenue. The league courted realtors and ran ads in local newspapers, trying to attract buyers just as they had done a few blocks away, but Munger Place, with its low owner-occupancy and high vacancy rates, failed the test.

Although the deterioration of Swiss Avenue had seemed bad enough, conditions in Munger Place were much worse. Older homes were interspersed with apartment houses built during the 1960s. The area had become a revolving door for "in-migrants," new to Dallas, who lived in Munger Place for a few days or weeks while they searched out a permanent residence. Most residents, therefore, had little investment in the neighborhood. The only investment came through absentee owners waiting to sell their properties to developers. Upkeep was minimal and marginal. The banks had red-lined the area, resulting in credit requirements beyond the reach of young middle-class families. The league felt that its hands were tied.

A National Trust official touring the neighborhood encouraged the league to start a revolving fund to buy up some of the available properties and get the ball rolling. Backed by a line of credit from the trust, the league first recruited neighborhood investors as co-signers and then negotiated with a local bank to establish a revolving loan fund. With this backing, the league bought twenty-four homes in the Munger Place district and arranged a short time later for a well-publicized urban pioneer sale. They sold all of the available houses during the first weekend. Most of the financing for the project was accomplished in two stages, the local Lakewood Bank providing the initial rehabilitation loans and Fannie Mae (Federal National Mortgage Association) allotting $5 million to carry the neighborhood's long-term mortgages.

Dallas preservationists turned Munger Place from a crime-ridden neighborhood of transients into a stabilized district of owner-occupied historic homes. What happened to the transients? Most of them found homes in other parts of the city, as had been their intention when they came to East Dallas. The preservation league worked with the East Dallas Tenant Alliance to relocate about a dozen families, allowing them free rent during their tenure in Munger Place, and providing furniture, moving expenses, and the first month's deposit for their new quarters.

After a decade of revitalization, most Munger Place homes are in good condition, some of them meticulously restored to their original appearance. A few pockets of neglect still exist, and the neighborhood has to live with the intrusive presence of apartment houses built during the zoning lapses after World War II. Occasional vacancies can be blamed on the economic downturn that immobilized Dallas in the late eighties. Even in the best of times, Munger Place can never match the uncompromised elegance of Swiss Avenue. Still, this rejuvenated area earns high marks as an inner-city neighborhood enterprisingly preserved.

Historic House Restoration

For the historic preservation movement, the rehabilitation of neglected, deteriorated buildings is the proof of the pudding. This is where the real hands-on preservation work takes place, and this is the time when owners and contractors find out what their building is really like. The hidden surprises—rotten roof beams, rusty sewer lines, structural damage in the foundations—are invariably expensive, time-consuming, and generally disheartening. Compound these hazards with the fact that many house restorers are amateurs at construction, and the situation is one in which it seems miraculous that historic residential neighborhoods have made it this far. That thousands of

this region's homeowners have endured the financial, physical, and emotional costs of renovation is a tribute to the human spirit and an acknowledgment of the inherent appeal of historic homes.

The terms *renovate, rehabilitate, remodel,* and *restore* are used loosely here, as they are by most people who do the actual work of refurbishing an old house. Few people "restore" a home if they intend to live in it. Of necessity, they usually install modern bathrooms and kitchens and often make other accommodations to comfort and safety. The term *restore* is more accurately applied to house museums, and even in these cases a modern bathroom and kitchen may be added for staff and visitors. In most communities, substantial building code requirements necessitate changes in structures built fifty or more years ago, another reason why a literal restoration rarely happens. *Remodel* is a term that sends up red flags because of its association with the renewal work of the 1950s, when original building fabric and lines were torn out or obscured. *Renovate* and *rehabilitate* are the most useful terms of the lot, suggesting significant improvement coupled with respect for the home's original materials and appearance.

Probably most people who renovate a house live in it themselves. The work is too much a labor of love to want to do it for the benefit of anyone else. Restoration contractors and craftsmen redo old houses for a living, of course, but they account for only a fraction of the homes in America that have been reconstituted in the past twenty years.

By modern standards, many old houses are large, sometimes much too large for couples or singles who want the experience of renovating, owning, and living in a historic house but find it too expensive to maintain as a single residence. For these would-be preservationists, one solution is to adapt their chosen big old house into a bed and breakfast inn, thus satisfying their need both to possess a renovated historic home and to survive financially. The bed and breakfast solution also enables the owners to show off their handiwork to appreciative guests.

Today, more than 5000 bed and breakfasts are

officially listed in this country, and probably many more operate anonymously and independently. Most are in historic houses, sometimes in a community's largest and most significant residence. The transition of a historic house from a lived-in family home to a bed and breakfast has the drawback of interrupting the original and traditional role of the structure as a private home, but the change often means that the house has been saved from demolition. In addition, the house becomes open to the public as an inn and can be enjoyed and experienced by people who appreciate historic architecture.

HELENA, MONTANA: THE SANDERS

When a real estate agent showed Bobbi Uecker and Rock Ringling the old Sanders House high above Last Chance Gulch in historic Helena, they knew they had found the right place for a bed and breakfast inn. The house was located in the area of Helena most closely associated with Montana's early gold mining history, which would be appealing to tourists, but it was also close enough to the state capitol to attract visitors on official business.

Wilbur Sanders, a lawyer, had been among Montana's most important citizens in the early history of the state, arriving there in 1863 as the first gold strikes were being made. He served as the state's first U.S. Senator and founded the Montana Bar Association and the Montana Historical Society. Harriet Sanders, his wife, had emmigrated to Montana via wagon train across the Oregon Trail, keeping a daily diary of her experience. Together, as leaders of Helena society, the Sanderses shaped much of Montana's early social and cultural life.

Their commodious home, built in 1875, was designed by Billings architects Paulsen and McConnell in the Queen Anne style. The large brick-and-shingle house was fashionable but unpretentious, certainly less ambitious than other Helena homes of the time. The city claimed more millionaires per capita than any other city in the country, its wealth derived from mining

and ranching. Within the residential opulence of Helena, the Sanders House would have held its own but was not extraordinary.

Like many late nineteenth century homes, the Sanders residence was richly appointed on the interior. Oak, fir, and cherry woodwork, incised with stylized leaves and floral patterns, covered large portions of the walls and floors, including the sitting room fireplace mantle, front hall staircase and paneling, dining room china closet, and window and door surrounds in all rooms. In the sleeping rooms upstairs, bedsteads and bureaus had been built to match the woodwork.

Fortunately for Uecker and Ringling when they took possession of the house in 1986, most of the woodwork had never been painted and—miraculously—much of the furniture was still there. The furniture was the pièce de résistance in their decision to buy. Even Sanders's collections of ore samples and of relics from the Custer battlefield were intact. The house revealed ample evidence of its early history.

Once underway, the new owners worked with astonishing speed. They started construction work in May 1987 and were finished by August. They acted as their own contractor, hiring laborers first to remove walls (the house had been subdivided into apartments), flooring, a chimney, and other cast-off materials. By the end of the summer they had hauled away 30,000 pounds of trash. Uecker and Ringling kept their full-time jobs over the summer, working on the house early each morning and for several hours each evening.

They were able to move along quickly during the construction phase in large part because they had spent the previous year planning and preparing. They made a commitment to purchase the house in the summer of 1986, and the sale was finalized in December of that year. During the intervening months, they learned what they could about the innkeeping business and carried out basic market research. Why did visitors come to Helena? How long did they stay? What were the hotel and motel occupancy rates? With a location close to spectacular mountain scenery and with a

10.22 *The corner china cupboard and wainscotting in the dining room of The Sanders, a recently restored bed and breakfast inn in Helena, Montana, had never been painted and required only a thorough cleaning. Courtesy The Sanders*

10.23 *Decorated tile, brass, and wood, were used in the corner fireplace of The Sanders's sitting room. Courtesy The Sanders*

lively mining history to show off, Helena seemed a good candidate for a bed and breakfast. They incorporated all this information into a business plan to get a loan from the bank.

Uecker and Ringling talked with other bed and breakfast owners, learning the basics of the business. Cleanliness, personal service, and "better than average" food were the three requirements most often mentioned. Guests want an environ-ment designed especially for them, not someone's extra bedroom, and most visitors do not want to feel as though they are in an old boarding house.

Before they bought the house, Uecker and Ringling checked out every requirement for oper-ating a bed and breakfast, including building codes, fire control, health department regulations, and zoning laws. All were manageable, although requirements that all bathrooms (they have eight) be vented directly to the roof gave them some bad moments.

Every renovation project has at least one dreadful surprise. At The Sanders, it was the plumbing. One day early in the summer, after construction was underway, Bobbi Uecker was working at the kitchen sink. Not a drop of water would come out of the faucet. She could see that the neighbors below had their sprinkler on, so she knew the water wasn't turned off. When the plumbers arrived and started digging they discovered that the connecting pipe to the street was full of holes; therefore, during periods of high use, such as a hot summer day, everyone else in the neighborhood (the house is at the top of a hill) got the water first. To correct this problem, the pipe to the main line under the street had to be dug up and replaced.

There were pleasant surprises as well. After old carpet and linoleum were removed, workmen found narrow-cut fir and maple floors that had never been refinished. The dirty but protected wood responded well to light sanding and varnishing. The owners were pleased, too, with the resourcefulness of their work force. At each stage, the head carpenter would scope out the problems, describe them in simple terms to Uecker and Ringling, discuss the options, and tell them what each option would cost. As construction novices, the owners appreciated the quality and cost control that this approach gave them. Their electricians were similarly helpful. Wiring an old house is difficult without the use of surface conduit, which is unsightly. The electricians managed to hide all the wiring in the walls and at the same time design a completely up-to-date system.

Guests at The Sanders have access to two front parlors and the dining room, where each morning Rock Ringling produces an ample breakfast of freshly ground coffee, bacon, and a Ringling speciality, such as traditional Montana sourdough pancakes or blueberry and walnut flapjacks. The wrap-around front porch is an option as the setting for the morning's last cup of coffee.

Rock Ringling confesses to one major mistake in the renovation of The Sanders. Eager to get the guest rooms and kitchen ready, they avoided gutting and redoing their own apartment on the third floor, a task that remains to be done. They abhor the thought of tearing out walls and starting the construction process all over again. "The dust, it's awful . . . but someday. . . ."

HOUSE MUSEUMS

House museums have come on hard times in historic preservation circles. Often they are regarded with disdain or disinterest, which is a pity because one of the great pleasures for a visitor to a strange city is to walk slowly through a grand mansion under the tutelage of a devoted volunteer tour guide. The visitor can try to imagine what life was like when the West's richest citizens surrounded themselves with crystal chandeliers, silk damask wall coverings, parquet floors, ornamental brass hardware, and carved woodwork from floor to high ceiling, not to mention all the extra features of conservatories, paneled libraries, butler's pantries, music rooms, wrap-around verandas, gazebos, and huge carriage houses. To visit one of these exemplars of high style and the high life is invariably a pleasure and sometimes a revelation.

Why, then, does the preservation community look down its nose at a historic house museum? Actually, there are valid reasons for the disdain. When preservation activity gained momentum all over the country in the 1960s and 1970s, one of the first objects of concern in many towns and cities was the biggest, oldest, and grandest house, which very likely had been owned and occupied by the wealthiest and most powerful family. For most people, those reasons were enough to justify preservation. In addition to having lofty status and imperial size, these houses are usually breathtaking to behold—majestically set back on a half-block or more of landscaped property, heaped with decorative detail realized in costly materials, and designed within an august architectural tradition. In most neighborhoods and towns, these aspiring houses stand apart—they represent a cul-

10.24   *Amelia Earhart's birthplace in Atchison, Kansas, combines a Gothic gable with classic features on the porch and entry. Atchison has many grand homes in the hills overlooking the Missouri River, but it would be hard to match the charm and pleasing proportions of this modest frame house. Courtesy Kansas State Historical Society, Historic Preservation Department*

ture different from the more modest bourgeois and worker homes around them.

It was this very specialness—not only standing apart, but standing *above*—that got traditional house museums into trouble with preservationists. They complained that saving the nation's architectural heritage meant more than preserving a few grand houses of the rich. To linger at that stage meant to settle for isolated buildings separated physically, economically, and socially from the mainstream of history. House museums

were elitist and, even worse, irrelevant. Historic preservation must take into account the larger picture, these advocates argued, by improving the building fabric of entire commercial districts and residential neighborhoods. Everyday settings, not shrines, deserve attention.

Their arguments are well taken. It *is* essential to concentrate preservation action on a sufficiently large environment to make a significant difference in how we live and work—a rehabilitated neighborhood, a revitalized downtown, a restructured

10.25 Atchison's McInteer Villa, now a house museum. Courtesy Kansas State Historical Society, Historic Preservation Department

industrial area, a re-landscaped park. Nevertheless, can't we give these princely homes their due, enjoy them more, forgive their hauteur? After all, many preservation groups were first formed in an attempt to save these great houses. In communities all across the country, the mansion of a local business baron offered the first lesson in what it means and what it takes to save and share a tangible piece of history.

There are more than 700 house museums in the mountain and plains states, and to be truthful,

not all of them are grand mansions. Amelia Earhart's childhood home in Atchison, Kansas, is a small gothic cottage of clapboard siding and carpenter trim. In Colorado Springs, Henry McAllister's brick cottage, a stylish but small house built by one of the city's founders, offers visitors a look at one of the few remaining structures from the city's early settlement. In Taos, New Mexico, the adobe home and studio of artist Ernest Blumenschein reveals the intimate world of that area's famous art colony.

10.26   The Oklahoma Historical Society owns
the 1903 Overholser Mansion, which has been
restored for the public by the state chapter of
the American Institute of Architects. Courtesy
Oklahoma Historical Society

10.27   Several former governor's mansions
have been restored and opened to the public,
including this large frame house in Bismarck,
North Dakota. Courtesy Bonnie J. Halda, State
Historical Society of North Dakota

For the most part, however, historic house museums are large. The West has some opulent examples. The 42-room home of Marcus Daly, the copper king, near Hamilton, Montana, has just been acquired by the state of Montana and will be operated as a public facility by the Daly Mansion Preservation Trust. This Georgian Revival mansion was built in 1890. In Sheridan, Wyoming, Trail End (1908), the home of John B. Kendrick, a nineteenth-century cattleman and U.S. Senator, is now a museum. Other western cities have opened the doors of equally luxurious homes: the Overholser Mansion (1903) in Oklahoma City; the Thatcher home (Rosemont; 1892) in Pueblo, Colorado; and the McInteer Villa in Atchison, Kansas. Former governor's homes in Wyoming, Montana, and North Dakota are now museums. These grand houses, and others like them, enable visitors to see how the rich and powerful lived during the region's formative years.

THE MOSS MANSION IN BILLINGS

In Billings, Montana, the rose sandstone Moss Mansion was acquired recently on behalf of the state of Montana and the city of Billings. The home's new caretakers and administrators, the Billings Preservation Society, have worked their way through a series of steps that appear to have become quite standard for organizations intent on rescuing a mansion. First is the matter of acquisition, then stabilization to protect the house against weather damage and its own structural failure, then an administrative program to interpret and maintain the building, and finally a long-range plan to secure it physically and financially.

The Moss home is unusual in that only one family had lived in it for a period of nearly ninety years and, with few exceptions, the rooms had never been redecorated. Even the curtains and tablecloths are thought to be original. In most rooms, the first wall coverings are still intact, including a delicate Art Nouveau stenciling in the sitting room.

Around 1900, P. B. and Mattie Moss commissioned New York architect Henry Hardenbergh, who designed the Plaza Hotel, to develop plans for their Billings home. Moss was owner and president of the First National Bank and a partner in the city's Northern Hotel. In true western frontier style, he had a hand in several leading financial projects, including the local utility company and *The Billings Evening Journal*. The Mosses had six children. Their middle daughter, Melville, lived in the house until her death in 1984.

The Billings Preservation Society raised $450,000 in private, city, and state funds to purchase the mansion, no small sum for a community of 80,000. With acquisition behind them, they were immediately faced with repair and improvements needed to stabilize the building. They have had substantial help from Montana's Cultural and Esthetics Trust Fund, which dispenses tax revenues earned from coal production. The awards must be matched three to one. When the house was first acquired, a grant of $25,000 from the trust fund was matched with $75,000 raised by the society to fund exterior repairs. In addition to these funds, the society invested $38,000 in the repair of the home's clay-tile roof. Recently, they have restored the conservatory, again with help from the Montana trust fund.

During their start-up period, the Billings Preservation Society has performed well on earned income. Revenues for 1988, their first year in full swing, totaled nearly $55,000 from admissions, bookstore sales, events, and memberships. Except for one staff person, a full-time executive director, all activities at the Moss Mansion are carried out by a volunteer corps numbering more than 200. At present, they sponsor one major event a year, a special Christmas tour, which has been a popular attraction for Billings residents.

The society has published a small illustrated book about the mansion and, with help from Montana tourism agencies, distributes a handsomely designed color brochure to promote visitation. They have produced a booklet on the Moss family and mansion as a resource for local fourth-

10.28   *The square Moss Mansion in Billings is nearly the same on all four sides. When New York architect Henry Hardenbergh designed the turn-of-the-century Chateauesque home, he planned for windows at two levels near the corner shown here on the left, but a last-minute change in the furniture plan resulted in the window space being filled in with stone.*

grade teachers and are planning a study guide to prepare the bus loads of school children who come to visit from across the state.

For museum novices, the Moss Mansion group has proceeded professionally and at a fast pace. They are sensitive to the particular requirements of preserving a fragile heritage at the same time that it is kept accessible to the public. With the aid of consultants, they intend to examine all features and materials in the house and to develop a conservation plan for repair and maintenance.

The Moss Mansion leadership credits the national network of house museums and historic districts for backup provided to the Billings group. Former board president Judy McNally cites conversations with "everyone from Charleston to the Molly Brown House in Denver. They've been through it all, and they can tell us what to do next and where to go for help." The society would like to form a regional council of house museums to provide an on-going exchange of ideas and assistance.

Keeping up a great house requires time, care, and distressing amounts of money. It also requires some difficult sorting through of conservation policy issues. Simply put, at what rate is one allowed to wear out the house and its furnishings? The question is even more difficult when a historic house comes equipped with original furnishings and decoration. Textiles are particularly sensitive to light, and the society wisely has installed ultraviolet filters on the windows. Even so, sunlight and artificial lights will continue to do their damaging work. Should the delicate Belgian lace curtains in the living room be reproduced and the originals stored for safekeeping? Similar choices exist for the carpeting. The Moss Mansion is blessed with beautiful Oriental rugs, some of them a part of the original family furnishings. Should visitors be allowed to walk on them? Should they be covered with unsightly protective plastic coverings? Should the rugs be moved aside and the rooms roped off? With a newly acquired house filled with furnishings and textiles in good condition, this question of use is not yet a pressing issue, but it will become one before long, just as it does for all house museums. The responsibility of preserving a building in perpetuity removes it from the familiar maintenance customs of personal housekeeping and is one of the major reasons why the upkeep becomes inordinately costly. The idea behind a historic house museum, after all, is that it should last forever.

HISTORIC HOUSES: FINDING NEW USES

Institutions, particularly colleges and churches, are often asked to accept or purchase nearby historic houses. These acquisitions can be a mixed blessing. In the 1960s, the Colorado Springs School acquired an estate in the Broadmoor neighborhood—The Trianon, a 1907 white terra-cotta Neoclassical residence—to use as its central meeting and administration building. The house is derivative of the Grand Trianon at Versailles and closely resembles its American contemporary, Rosecliffe, in Newport, Rhode Island.

Maintaining this luxurious building has been a drain on the school, which has its educational agenda to think of first. A separate capital fund now being considered may offer some relief, but the financial solution for the Trianon thus far has eluded the school's board of trustees, just as it has many other historic property owners. Opening the building to the public is not an option because of neighborhood restrictions. Owing to the special costs involved in rehabilitation and maintenance, many organizations today are requiring that an endowment fund accompany gifts of property. Unfortunately, this was not possible for the Colorado Springs School. They must look elsewhere for a solution.

In Omaha, the Joslyn Castle, for several years the administrative offices of the Omaha public school system, will be put to a new use following a state-sponsored feasibility study. Through time, school officials have found the building to be impractical, and the offices have been moved. Restrictive covenants on the property placed by the original owner, Sarah Joslyn, require that it be used for education, broadly defined. To find a satisfactory new use and to assist the transition, an advisory coalition has been formed representing the landmarks commission along with the city's business, arts, and preservation communities. The castle is a great favorite of Omaha's citizens, and interest runs high in keeping it well-maintained and accessible.

The mansion dates to 1903 and was designed in the chateauesque style by local architect John McDonald. The 35-room house is predictably endowed with extravagant materials and decoration; crystal, Spanish mahogany, and other rich-toned woods, along with marble and etched glass, highlight the interior. The house and land occupy four city blocks surrounded by a fence of wrought iron and stone. The estate has always been known for its beautiful grounds, which contain nearly fifty varieties of trees.

A historic house does not have to be a century old to be a valued landmark. In 1985 the University of Oklahoma accepted the gift of Shin'enKan,

10.29   Although many opulent western mansions were "behind the times" when they were measured against the homes in the more fashionable East, the Baldwin estate in Colorado Springs, now called The Trianon, captured the moment in High Style design. The terra-cotta mansion, derivative of the Grand Trianon at Versailles, now houses a private boarding and day school.

10.30   A terra-cotta detail on The Trianon.

10.31   Detailing on the keystone of an entry arch, The Trianon. Although expensive, terra-cotta facing is far less costly than carved stone. It was widely used in the early twentieth century for large houses and commercial buildings.

10.32   Major George Washington Littlefield, a prominent Texas cattleman and banker, built this lavish Victorian castle in 1894. It was later incorporated into the University of Texas campus. The public rooms on the main floor have been kept in their original state. The upper floors are used for offices. The two-story porch has columns of blue granite. Courtesy David Glover/Camerawork

10.33   Another castle, this one with crenellations and huge corner towers, answered the fantasies of Omaha's Joslyn family, who built the 35-room house in 1903. The castle was given to the local school system many years ago; a new use is now being sought. Courtesy Lynn Meyer

10.34   The Great Plains legacy of house museums includes this modern work designed by
Bruce Goff over a period of twenty years for Joe
Price in Bartlesville, Oklahoma. Now owned by
the University of Oklahoma, the Price House
(1956–76) is considered one of Goff's most
important works.

10.35   The Price House exhibits highly intricate details, such as this colored glass and metal
decoration on the tower windows.

10.36   Anthracite coal and glass cullets form
the surface of the Price House walls.

10.37 *A variety of commercial uses have extended the lives of large old homes throughout the country. The patina of age and the appeal of luxurious materials creates a setting particularly appropriate for dining. The Whipple House, near downtown Cheyenne, Wyoming, is a popular restaurant. Courtesy Richard Collier, State Historic Preservation Office, Wyoming Department of Archives, Museums, and History*

a highly personalized and expressionistic country house designed by architect Bruce Goff for Joe Price in Bartlesville, Oklahoma. The house was built in three stages, first in 1956 as a bachelor's quarters for young Joe Price, then expanded in 1966 for Price when he married and began to collect Japanese art, and a third time in 1976 after the birth of the two Price daughters.

Price had grown up in Oklahoma in a progressive and entrepreneurial family. His father, owner of a pipeline construction company, had commissioned Frank Lloyd Wright to design an office tower in Bartlesville, which became the Price Tower (1955). Wright also designed a house for Harold Price, Joe's older brother. Goff was an admirer of Wright and a modernist, but his own vision of architecture dramatically prevailed in his conception of Shin'enKan—"home of the faraway heart." The house was a collaborative project; Joe Price set down very particular requirements and offered many design suggestions.

The most striking feature of this highly unusual house is the material Goff chose for the facing of the support walls inside and out. He combined anthracite coal with blue-green "cullets" (large chunks of waste glass) from the Liberty Glass Plant near Okmulgee, Oklahoma. A two-story tower rises above the black coal and green glass walls.

Inside, in the living room, a white wool shag carpet covers the floor as well as sunken built-in banquettes that form the room's seating. In another part of the house, shag carpet covers the walls and ceiling as well as the floors. Goff added extraordinary details for effect: in the skylight pyramid over the living room, goosefeathers have been glued in place to diffuse the light and enhance the acoustics. Shiny metal and glass are used throughout. The roofs are gold-anodized aluminum.

The master bedroom, which also serves as a gallery for Japanese paintings, is dominated by a hexagonal fountain lined with glass. It acts as a skylight to the Japanese bath on a lower floor directly below it, which is lined with ceramic tiles in brilliant hues of orange, gold, and platinum.

Shin'enKan is an inward-looking house, as Joe Price requested. Most windows are small, and some are above eye level. The grounds, spacious and attractively landscaped, are best enjoyed outside the house. They are not incorporated into the interior design in the modern American way.

Shin'enKan, Goff's largest and costliest house, stands along with the Bavinger House in Norman and Boston Avenue Methodist Church in Tulsa as his most distinguished and innovative designs. Goff's work offers a welcome and fascinating counterpoint to Oklahoma's more conventional buildings, which were essentially copies of styles developed in other parts of the country. Although the mountains and plains region developed a large body of vernacular architecture, there was little originality among High Style designers. Most architecture here was derivative, heavily influenced by designers in the Midwest and on either coast. Bruce Goff was an exception, and the region is richer for his singularity.

The architecture school of the University of Oklahoma oversees the Price House, reserving it for receptions and seminars except for one day a week when the public is invited to tour the house and grounds.

MANSIONS IN THE MARKETPLACE

Hundreds of other western houses have been recycled for commercial uses. They make admirable professional offices, and architects and lawyers seem especially drawn to them. The gracious spaces and decor of large old homes also adapt well for restaurants. The Whipple House in Cheyenne, Wyoming, has been converted to a restaurant, and probably the grandest example is the mansion on Turtle Creek in Dallas, formerly the Sheppard King House (1925), an eclectic confection of Moorish, Mission, and Spanish colonial architecture that has been adapted as a gourmet restaurant.

11.1   The ruins of Cliff Palace, Mesa Verde
National Park, are dramatic evidence that
a carefully crafted, permanent architecture
existed in the region long before Europeans
explored the continent. A scale model of the
ruins enchanted visitors to the 1893 Columbian
Exposition in Chicago and influenced passage
of the protective American Antiquities Act of
1906. Credit: National Park Service

CHAPTER ELEVEN

Archeology

The arena of responsibility for historic preservation has always included archeology. In fact, action by the federal government to protect prehistoric archeological materials preceded similar action on behalf of historic sites by more than half a century.

The Southwest's fragile prehistoric ruins captured the American imagination very early, while the region was still a frontier. At the Columbian Exposition in Chicago in 1893, a scale model of the cliff dwellings at Mesa Verde awakened the country to the extraordinary ruins then being discovered and excavated in Colorado and New Mexico. Heightened awareness of archeological sites led to passage of the Antiquities Act of 1906, the country's first preservation legislation, and to the designation of Mesa Verde, in Colorado,

and Chaco Canyon, in New Mexico, as national preserves.

Mesa Verde's awesome ruins dramatize the role of prehistoric inhabitants in America and reveal a well-developed agricultural civilization. During a 700-year occupation beginning around A.D.600, the area's inhabitants—the Anasazi, or "ancient people," in an Anglicized version of a Navajo term—built communal homes and increasingly complex water-control systems. They moved from pithouses dug into the ground to occupy the tops of mesas—the flat tablelands that rise over the Southwest deserts—and the terraces above rivers, where they built houses of jacal and mud. Some of these residences were built individually or in small clusters; others were attached in long curving rows. By the year 1000, stone masonry had begun to replace mud construction, and within another 100 years, the Anasazi were erecting two- and three-story buildings containing as many as fifty rooms. Around 1200, they moved down from their mesa-top homes to build south-facing stone apartment structures in the overhangs of canyon walls, creating the remarkable cliff dwellings for which Mesa Verde—now a National Park—is famous.

This golden age endured little more than a century. The Anasazi abandoned the region in the early 1300s. Some prehistorians conjecture that severe drought in an already arid region made life at Mesa Verde intolerable, forcing the cliffdwellers to migrate south and east to the Rio Grande Valley, where they became part of an existing Pueblo Indian culture. The Anasazi cliff houses stood silent and empty until they were "discovered" by two American cattlemen in the late 1880s.

Although Mesa Verde has been the Southwest's best known archeological site in this century, Chaco Canyon in northwestern New Mexico has captured increased public attention in the past few years as its history is revealed through new research. A portion of these Chacoan sites have been set aside as a National Historic Park protected and interpreted by the National Park Service, which has become the principal administrator of western archeological resources open to the public.

The Chacoan peoples were similar in many ways to the cliffdwellers of Mesa Verde a hundred miles away. Foragers and farmers, they irrigated fields with floodwater and built small dams and reservoirs to capture runoff. They, too, built magnificent pueblo dwellings, first of mud and rock, later of masonry. The largest contained 700 rooms and were five stories high, the tallest structures in America until the 1870s when New York City's first skyscrapers were built.

The largest pueblos, or villages, contained round, roofed ceremonial rooms called *kivas* in which the members of the pueblo convened. During Chaco Canyon's classic period in the late 1000s, these kivas grew to be huge structures, with that at Casa Rinconda measuring nearly 64 feet in diameter.

In addition to these village compounds, the Chacoans built great public works—elaborate road and water-management systems—spreading for miles through the canyon and beyond. They carried on a lively trade with neighboring villages and with Indians far to the south in Mexico. If conjecture is correct—that their population doubled from 3000 to 6000 in a fifty-year period between 1050 and 1100—the Chacoans were an early example of the "boom and bust" pattern that was to become commonplace later in the nineteenth-century West. Around the mid-1100s, probably because of drought, the grand era of the Chacoans closed, just as the Mesa Verde golden age would do a century later. Perhaps the inhabitants of Chaco moved away toward the Rio Grande. Within a few decades, Chaco Canyon was deserted.

The federal government designated Chaco Canyon a National Monument in 1907. During the 1920s, archeologist Neil Judd completed seven summers of excavations sponsored by National Geographic and the Smithsonian Institution. The sites were worked intermittently until 1970 when the National Park Service and the University of New Mexico began to collaborate on large-scale surveys and excavations using aerial and satellite photography to gather new information about a prehistoric road system that fanned through the Chaco pueblo complex.

Archeologists surveying Chaco also looked closely at the surrounding lands of the San Juan Basin. They identified seventy additional Chacoan sites, designating about half as "protection" sites, a Park Service procedural step that acknowledges their importance and paves the way for more protective measures later on. Meanwhile, the canyon had been elevated in status from a National Monument to a National Historic Park. The areas preserved contain about 3500 ruins and sites, but archeologists estimate that the entire San Juan Basin, of which Chaco Canyon is the center, contains thousands more, perhaps tens of thousands.

The aura of ancient Chaco lingers today within

11.2 *Casa Rinconada, the Great Kiva of Chaco Canyon, New Mexico, was built in the last half of the 11th century. Kivas, subterranean structures with a flat roof, were a center of religious and community life. Credit: National Park Service*

11.3 *This small pueblo site in Chaco Canyon is near the kiva Casa Rinconada. The pueblo contains several kivas in addition to storage and living areas. Credit: National Park Service*

the canyon walls in subtle sounds and smells and, more strikingly, in the great color-charged vistas that mark the desert Southwest. On the final thirty miles toward the canyon, only the telephone lines along the hard-packed clay road give reminders that this is the twentieth century. Miles away, low-lying, treeless buttes recede into shadows of deep blue and gray, their colors taken from afternoon storm clouds—ominous, giant thunderheads that fill the sky in late summer. Red clay soil underlies a sparse cover of grass. Desert shrubs—rabbit and sagebrush, chamisa, greasewood, and soapbush—form an uneven blanket of muted blue-greens and grays.

At the canyon's edge, large striated stone formations signal a change of terrain, and the earth suddenly gives way as a fissure in the rock walls opens up to a narrow valley below, framed by brown sandstone cliffs. Shrubs cover the canyon floor, cut by a deep, dry creek bed lined with dying cottonwood trees. Compared to the monumental landscapes just above the canyon, the sun-baked cliffs of Chaco seem warmly confining. One feels sheltered, at home. Here, at a time when the river flowed nearly year-round and the slopes were dotted with trees, the prehistoric Chacoans built their villages.

At intervals along the rock faces one comes upon the Chacoan "apartment" houses, or pueblos. They are marvels of masonry, their stone rubble walls faced on either side with delicate, shaped sandstone pieces—some barely more than slivers—intricately fitted together as in a mosaic. The Chacoans covered these artfully crafted stone walls with adobe plaster, sloughed off years later by wind and rain.

Above the canyon on flat mesas stand other pueblo remains, accessible only along footpaths. Alone at noon on a sandy trail, one hears the buzz of insects and the cheerful sound of wrens, fly-catchers, and mockingbirds. High above the surrounding mesas, ravens glide slowly and silently. Swallows bank and dive toward the rock cliffs. On the ground, lizards stir, darting from shadow to shadow, avoiding the hot summer sun. At trail's end the ruins seem haunted and vaguely threatening, great shells of stone shrouded in mystery.

Today, the National Park Service assists visitors to comprehend not only Chaco Canyon's dramatic ruins but the patterns of life that existed there a millennium ago. Because of its limited accessibility, Chaco tends to draw people interested in history who are already knowledgeable about the Anasazi. There are few casual visitors or passers-by, although new information about the sites, publicized by television and magazines, has generated a wider public in the past ten years.

The canyon has been a testing ground for new archeological techniques: analyses of pollen and bones, carbon-dating of wood remains, and various remote-sensing devices used in aerial photography. The latter were especially helpful in revealing an immense road system that served Chaco and its outlying pueblos. The carefully engineered, 30-foot-wide roads are a puzzle to everyone. Why would an ancient people with neither vehicles nor beasts of burden construct a highway system? Were these ceremonial roads, or were they of some practical use, yet undiscovered?

Present-day archeologists approach Chaco from the broad perspective of human behavior and environmental change. They are more likely to be interested in the rhythms of daily life than a single tangible architectural ruin, however spectacular. "Years ago, archeologists themselves took a narrow view," explains Ken Mabery, formerly the chief ranger at Chaco. "They excavated the big ruins, took out all the artifacts, and hauled them back to museums in the East." It was a form of sanctioned plunder, far more destructive than anyone realized at the time. Archeological sites when carelessly excavated and recorded are sadly limited for future study. The 10-year project completed at Chaco in 1981, which used aerial photography and other new techniques along with traditional excavations, produced more data than all the previous archeological efforts there put together.

Blessed with new tools, Southwest archeologists struggle against new threats—large-scale development of energy and mineral resources on nearby lands. A quarter of the nation's strip-mine coal reserves lie buried in northern New Mexico, along with oil, natural gas, and rich deposits of uranium. One day, the pristine world of Chaco Canyon may be surrounded by industrial activity that threatens to bulldoze ruins, pollute the air, and destroy the natural landscape. Federal restrictions on strip mining, protective of the environment, apply not only to public or Indian lands but also to private owners seeking federal licensing. The laws are in place. What is needed is the serious commitment of finances and personnel by the state and federal agencies to require compliance with existing regulations. In the face of recession and the energy crises, as well as lobbying on the part of the energy companies, this level of commitment is often lacking.

Mining and exploration cause great damage to archeological areas. So do the pipelines, power plants, and highways built to move and use the resources. These industries are extremely unstable. Coal is in demand, for example, when petroleum and gas prices are high, because it then becomes a comparatively inexpensive source of fuel. Uranium, not many years ago, was being mined at fever pitch near the town of Grants, New Mexico, just southeast of Chaco Canyon. Then prices fell, production ceased, and the town's economy went into a tailspin. It is this boom-bust cycle so familiar in the West that hinders preservation because future conditions, both physical and economic, are uncertain. Without continuity, preservation planning becomes a trivial exercise.

Because of these economic uncertainties and the sheer scope of prehistoric materials, archeologists in the Southwest and throughout the region have their work cut out for them. Vast expanses of land have yet to be intensively surveyed. Often the money for this type of study is made available only because an area is about to be developed, at which point federal law requires that it be done. When energy companies are ready to begin mining or drilling on new lands, archeologists face a nearly overwhelming task of hurriedly surveying and salvaging prehistoric materials that are about to be disturbed or destroyed.

Archeology in the Southwest, however, involves more than vanished civilizations. Important sites remain from the early period of contact between the indigenous peoples and the Spanish colonizers. One such site to the east of Santa Fe, Pecos, is a bridge from southwestern prehistory to the historical period. Pithouses dating to around A.D. 800 have been excavated at Pecos, and a multi-storied pueblo is known to have been in place by 1450. The pueblo village survived into the early nineteenth century. A hundred years later it gained recognition as a major archeological treasure and, in 1965, was named a National Monument.

Historians had known about Pecos all along. Not only was the pueblo part of the written historical record, but its ruins were there for everyone to see. From 1915 to 1919, the noted Southwest archeologist Alfred Kidder worked at Pecos in what was the largest archeological undertaking in North America up to that time. In the first modern excavation that paid strict attention to strata, Kidder worked through layer after layer of remains, uncovering six different settlements and an extraordinary number of artifacts. He summoned his colleagues to Pecos in 1927 to devise the first workable chronology for southwestern prehistory. Because of Kidder's work, Pecos has been a key site in the history and evolution of archeological techniques within the region and throughout the Americas.

Pecos has continued to yield significant materials. In 1965 the National Park Service began new excavations, uncovering the ruins of a fortress church constructed in 1620 by Spanish friars. During the 1680 Pueblo Revolt, an uprising of the native peoples against the Spaniards, the church was destroyed. A smaller church was erected in the early 1700s after the Spaniards regained control of the region. Recent excavations have uncovered water-management systems, ninth-century pithouses, and rock art.

Although the Southwest's archeological sites are the best known, there are important historical

11.4   Ruins of an eighteenth-century adobe Spanish church at Pecos Pueblo, an intriguing New Mexico site which marks a transition from prehistory to a Spanish mission and modern pueblo. In many ways, Pecos has been a laboratory for southwestern archeology, continually revealing new information. As recently as 1967, archeologists discovered rock and adobe fragments marking the foundation of an earlier fortress church on this site.

and prehistoric materials throughout the region, many of them discovered during excavations conducted prior to the construction of large public works. These projects tend to be localized, such as the installation of huge dams on the Missouri River in North and South Dakota during the 1940s. The National Park Service joined forces with the Smithsonian Institution, the U.S. Army Corps of Engineers, and the Bureau of Reclamation to excavate, recover, and examine prehistoric and historical sites along the Missouri River in the two Dakotas. Many museums and universi-

ties were involved in the effort, which operated through the 1960s as the Missouri Basin Project. Most of the excavated sites were subsequently inundated when the dams were built and the river valleys were turned into reservoirs.

Several of the most intact villages from this Missouri Basin culture of Mandan, Hidatsa, and Arikara Indians are now administered by the National Park Service at the Knife River Indian Village, sixty-five miles north of Bismarck, established as a National Historic Site in 1974.

The Knife River sites were inhabited by

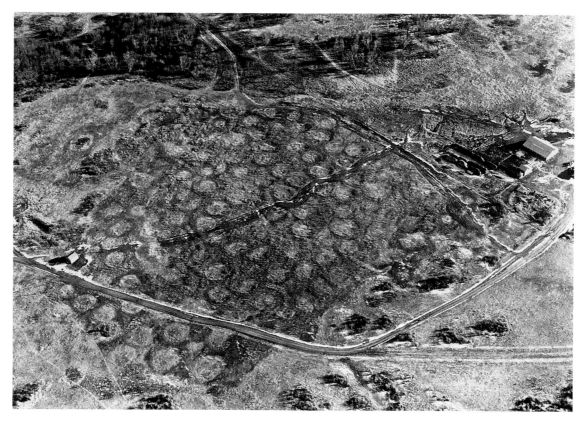

11.5   Big Hidatsa Village at Knife River Indian Villages National Historic Site where 113 earth lodge depressions can be distinguished. The village was settled by the Hidatsa in approximately 1600 and abandoned in 1845. Credit: North Dakota State Highway Department

Hidatsa Indians who arrived there in the 1600s, probably from the East, to engage in agriculture, hunting, and fishing. Archeological evidence indicates occupation of this area by other inhabitants for at least 3500 years and perhaps as far back as 8000 years. The Hidatsa built circular earth lodges, the collapsed ruins of which are evident today. The Hidatsa became adept at trading in the early 1800s, emerging as prosperous middlemen in trade between the Plains Indians and the tribes to the north and west. Lewis and Clark stopped here in 1804, and both Carl Bodmer and George

Catlin painted the village some thirty years later. During these years, probably more people were living along this portion of the Missouri River than do so today.

Decline came swiftly and tragically to the Hidatsa and their Arikara and Mandan neighbors when a smallpox epidemic swept through the villages in 1837. More than half of the population perished, and by 1845, residents of the Knife River sites had abandoned their villages.

When the National Park Service assumed ownership of the Knife River property they

11.6　*The Anasazi Heritage Center in south-western Colorado interprets prehistory to visitors and houses a computerized research library and museum. Some 1600 archeological sites were identified in the vicinity as part of the giant Dolores Reclamation Project which created the McPhee Reservoir shown here. The Escalante Dominquez Ruins lie above the center. Credit: J. Fleetman, U.S. Bureau of Reclamation*

undertook minor excavations, but essentially the villages were left as they were found. The site, which is open to the public year-round, offers the visitor a total community environment in addition to an understanding of how individual earth lodges were built and used from the sixteenth and into the nineteenth centuries.

Large reclamation projects are both a blessing and a bane to preservationists. Construction and subsequent flooding either destroys or inundates precious prehistoric materials and historical sites as well. On the other hand, these public works projects trigger mammoth archeological excavations, providing an opportunity to uncover and study sites that would not otherwise be accessible, primarily because funding is not available. Development of previously undisturbed land has become a fact of life, despite the cultural losses.

Now at least there are educational benefits to be had, thanks to state and federal legislation requiring that threats to archeological sites be "mitigated," i.e., sites are surveyed, excavated, and examined, and the artifacts are removed for safekeeping, future research, and public benefit.

In the Southwest, several federal agencies have collaborated on an Anasazi exhibition and research center built to house and interpret materials excavated in the early 1980s from the Dolores River area in southwestern Colorado near Mesa Verde. This project, like the earlier Missouri River surveys, was accomplished prior to the construction of a dam by the Bureau of Reclamation. Archeologists from the University of Colorado, Washington State University, and many other institutions located and recorded 1600 sites during the project, the largest archeological contract ever awarded in this country.

After the sites were excavated, the Bureau of Reclamation built a large museum to house the two million artifacts taken from the sites. The museum, the Anasazi Heritage Center, is operated by the Bureau of Land Management. These two federal agencies worked with the Forest Service, the National Park Service, and myriad local and state entities to forge a model program of modern archeology. Far too often, excavations yield artifacts that gather dust on a shelf and reports that may be as fragmented as the material they describe. At Dolores, with dispatch, the sites were excavated and the artifacts collected, documented, catalogued, and curated. Many items are displayed or interpreted through photos, illustrations, and simulations. For example, an Anasazi pithouse has been re-created, and several hands-on demonstrations, such as weaving and corn grinding, provide insight into the daily patterns of living. Much of the collection is reserved for research and includes computerized data bases, archives, and a library.

Archeology for most people means ancient sites and prehistory, and until recently this was the case. Around twenty years ago historical archeologists started examining western sites, including early Spanish occupations in New Mexico and

Texas but also later structures, such as forts and trading posts on the plains and even late nineteenth century urban buildings. This convergence of fields has been of great value. Historians have learned how to examine and "read" a building or site with technical precision, and archeologists have participated in the fuller context of recent history, which is closer to home and more personal. In turn, the public benefits because the interpretation of structures and sites is now richer, fuller, and more directly related to the tangible evidence.

The very sophistication and success of techniques in historical archeology have led to controversy over whether ruined, collapsed structures should be rebuilt. The National Park Service wrestles with this issue continually, and indeed the question permeates preservation policy across the board. Is it more important to protect a nearly destroyed but original site than to re-create it?

The National Park Service operates many small, specialized sites that relate directly to nineteenth-century western settlement—military forts, such as Larned in Kansas and Laramie in Wyoming; Custer's battlefield in Montana; Scott's Bluff on the Oregon Trail; the Spanish Missions at San Antonio; and the Homestead Site in Nebraska. In each instance the Park Service must decide what to do with existing buildings and ruins and how best to interpret the site's history to the public. Many structures are badly deteriorated by the time a property enters the park system. If that is the case, the Park Service might elect to "stabilize" the site, repairing and maintaining it to stave off further damage. A new foundation or roof might be added to a damaged building. An overhead shield or a moisture-proof coating might be used to protect eroded adobe walls.

On occasion, the Park Service has rebuilt a destroyed historic structure. At Bent's Fort in Colorado, a private trading post dating to 1833, the Park Service decided to reconstruct the original adobe fort, which had been in ruins for more than a century—only fragments of eroded walls were visible on the surface. In preparation for

11.7 *Bent's Fort, an early nineteenth-century trading post along the Arkansas River in Colorado, was rebuilt in the 1970s by the National Park Service. The reconstruction of ruined sites remains a controversial issue within the preservation community. Credit: Catherine Taylor*

reconstruction, Park Service architects and historians gathered information from a contemporary drawing, written records, and an archeological excavation site report. The rebuilt fort, standing in the bottomland along the Arkansas River in southeastern Colorado, presents a theater of early life and trading on the plains, but the fact remains that it is a highly conjectural simulation.

Reconstruction of this kind is controversial within the preservation community and within the Park Service itself. Critics maintain that expensive fabrications are as likely to mislead as to inform, and that the money should be spent instead to save existing historic buildings. Some Park Service curators and architects are more inclined today to follow the principle of "ghosting"—using symbols, fragments, or ruins to evoke a mood or to suggest an association. The visi-

tor's imagination must do the rest. One might argue that this approach requires a trained eye or a sound background in the site's history and therefore is too abstract and too incomplete for the average visitor. If that visitor has access to nearby models, displays, books, photographs, and films, which extend the experience of being in the actual building, then the site itself is relieved of some of the burden of interpretation.

The Park Service chose to reconstruct Fort Union (the northernmost of the two forts with the same name), located at the juncture of the Yellowstone and Missouri rivers near the boundary between Montana and North Dakota. The site was excavated and the wooden palisade walls and stone fortress towers rebuilt on the foundations of the original site, essentially destroying the archeological material remaining. Reconstructions are very costly. Excavating, documenting, and rebuilding projects easily runs to several million dollars. An alternative would be to carry out limited excavations on the original site and then, in the vicinity, to build a full-scale model of the original structure, which together with a visitors' center and interpretive programs, would offer a great deal of information, cost less, and keep most of the archeological material intact for the future.

A case in point is Custer's battlefield in the Big Horn Mountains of southern Montana, a land of big sky and far horizons. It is one of the most evocative of the National Park Service properties. A visitors' center occupies a rise near the Little Bighorn River. A few small stones mark the graves of soldiers. These are the only intrusions on the open landscape.

Because there were no white survivors at this "last stand," an aura of mystery and isolation surrounds the site. The most compelling aspect of a walk through the battlefield arises out of the distant vistas and the rolling hills covered with tall golden grasses on which one imagines the drama of mounted cavalry and victorious costumed warriors of the plains. The terror of the story is softened by a sense of sadness from knowing that this summary encounter marked an end not only for Custer's troops, but for a vulnerable and collapsing Indian nation.

The National Park Service carries a big load in operating publicly accessible western archeological sites, both historical and prehistoric. For a first-hand look at sites, artifacts, and a wealth of educational material, the Park Service offerings at places like Mesa Verde cannot be rivaled. These experiences tend to be passive, however. The Park Service presents, and the visitor looks and listens. Granted, they are first-rate "look and listen" experiences, but what of the individual who wants to learn more and to participate directly in digging up the past?

To help interested laymen learn more about archeology and to assist them in connecting with organizations that welcome volunteers in field work, the National Park Service in 1987

established a clearinghouse of national projects, the Listing of Education in Archeology Projects (LEAP). Within two years, LEAP had collected more than 1200 examples of techniques used by museums, universities, and agencies to publicize programs in archeology, including opportunities for field work. The rationale for the clearinghouse is that an involved and informed public will protect the nation's antiquities.

One of the best public archeology programs in the country is operated jointly by the Kansas State Historical Society and the Kansas Anthropological Association, which welcomes amateur members. Each summer, professional archeologists and as many as 150 volunteer amateurs meet at a selected Kansas site for two weeks of training, excavations, and laboratory work. Volunteers can work for as little as one four-hour stretch or for the entire sixteen-day field school. Probably a third of the corps have been coming every summer for the past ten years.

Walter and LaVerna Ernst from near Abilene are charter members of the Kansas Archeology Training Program. They heard a lecture on prehistory at the local Mud Creek chapter of the Kansas Anthropological Association in 1975 and decided to try the annual field school. The first dig took place in Scott County in the western part of the state. The Ernsts helped to excavate El Cuartelejo, a small one-story stone and adobe pueblo built by refugees who were escaping the Spanish occupation of New Mexico. Like all new members of the program, they took an orientation course and a training session on archeological techniques. Other prehistory classes run concurrently with the excavation, and volunteers are encouraged to attend.

For Walter and LaVerna Ernst, archeology has brought a fascinating, enriching new interest rather late in their lives. At first they were wary. "What are we doing here under the hot Kansas sun?" LaVerna asked. But the appeals of the actual hands-on work swept away any reservations. They treasure the annual experience for themselves and recognize the importance of the program for

11.8   During an annual summer field school, Kansas archeologists train and supervise volunteers to work on excavations. This project in Norton County uncovered evidence of a culture dating to A.D. 1100. Credit: Kansas State Historical Society

11.9   Kansas archeology volunteers inspect a tiny artifact from the 1985 field school project in Franklin County—the Jotham Meeker farmstead at the Ottawa Baptist Mission. Credit: Kansas State Historical Society

preserving the state's antiquities. Much of this heritage had already been destroyed by farming, reclamation, and energy development over the past half-century.

Walter Ernst credits archeology for opening his eyes to the achievements of the Plains Indians. "They lived here and survived. It was a successful life. They had a communications system, trade routes, trails." Walter Ernst believes the invading Americans and Europeans should have paid more attention to how the Indians lived on the Plains. "Instead, we destroyed a whole culture." Discerning Indian living patterns on the basis of the archeological evidence is what interests Ernst most in the excavations. He enjoys the strict parameters of careful measurements and field documentation. "I'm a good field man," he says.

Verna Detrich, another charter member of the Kansas field school, became so interested in the hands-on aspects of archeology that she volunteered to work in the anthropology laboratory at the State Historical Society in Topeka, eighty miles from her home. Later she applied for a job as a technician in the laboratory. She spends two weeks each year at the field school excavation, and she hasn't missed a dig since they started in 1975. Her enthusiasm matches that of the Ernsts. She believes that working with artifacts and participating in field work has heightened her awareness and has made her a more accomplished observer overall, not just in archeology.

Beyond the personal satisfactions, which obviously are keenly felt by the Kansas participants, the annual field school has created a responsible corps of preservationists who protect the state's archeological resources. Many of these amateurs do surface surveys in their locales, reporting their finds to the state archeologist. By example and through their advocacy, they create a public awareness that archeological materials should not be vandalized, removed arbitrarily, or unnecessarily disturbed. These amateurs began as students, and now they have become educators to their peers.

Advocacy and vigilance. These stances can never be abandoned for long because the materials from the past are continually under threat. In the summer of 1989, J. Jackson Walter, president of the National Trust for Historic Preservation, testified before a United States Senate panel in favor of establishing the Petroglyph National Monument on the West Mesa escarpment outside of Albuquerque, New Mexico. More than 15,000 petroglyphs—prehistoric and historical drawings on rock—have been documented in a seventeen-mile stretch of the West Mesa, prompting the National Trust to place the area on a list of the eleven most endangered nationally significant sites. The proposal had broad support and was realized a year later.

Even though the West Mesa petroglyph preserve is large, it represents only a tiny fraction of New Mexico's archeological resources, which are scattered throughout the state, just as they are in every state. Keeping a meaningful portion of this heritage in place is the charge of numerous government agencies but is the responsibility of every citizen as well. There is too much here to legislate, although legislation is an essential part of the equation.

Thomas Merlan, New Mexico's historic preservation officer, believes that stewardship, day in and day out, is the only hope for both ancient and historical resources, but he is skeptical about society's capacity to sustain the tedious and unglamorous task of quietly maintaining something. "Maintenance is identifying and taking care of the little problems. Preservation requires delicacy and respect for the environment. Don't let it deteriorate." In 1989 Merlan lobbied successfully for burial protection legislation, which has been a controversial issue throughout the country. "Unfortunately, we have an attitude in this country that's exploitative and destructive. Or at least the Euro-Americans have. Their instinct is to dig it up and make off with it. The Navajos, for example, don't dig up sites. They don't desecrate graves. The best protection for a Chacoan site is for it to be in proximity to a Navajo outfit." The New Mexico legislation specifically protects burials, but because valuable items often were placed

11.10　Pueblo Bonito in Chaco Canyon was the largest building in North America until the 1870s when New York's skyscrapers were built. Archeological materials are treasured resources in the mountains/plains region. Prehistoric Chacoan sites alone are scattered over more than 50 million acres in New Mexico and beyond. Courtesy National Park Service

in graves, the bill will do far more than protect human physical remains.

Merlan presides over a preservation domain that includes prehistoric sites, Spanish colonial buildings, Indian pueblos, small towns, ranches, and twentieth-century cityscapes, all of it covered with millions of pot sherds. Prehistoric Chacoan sites alone are scattered over more than 50 million acres, some of them beyond New Mexico's borders. "The material is so ubiquitous," Merlan asserts, "that the only practical solution is to deal with it as part of the way we live, accepting the general idea and practice of conservation." He quotes Jerry Rogers, keeper of the National Register of Historic Places: "You must believe that conservation is a good in itself."

Most historic sites open to the public offer brochures or booklets, which are valuable sources of information. Typically, these materials are only available locally. City and county planning offices frequently publish surveys and master plans of historic districts, and state and local historical societies invariably sell local histories in their bookstores. The following references were particularly helpful during the writing of this book.

Abele, Deborah, 1981, *The West Side: An Introduction to Its History and Architecture,* City of Colorado Springs.

Adams, Robert, 1970, *White Churches of the Plains,* Colorado Associated University Press, Boulder.

———, 1974, *The Architecture and Art of Early Hispanic Colorado,* Colorado Associated University Press and Colorado Historical Society, Denver.

———, 1978, *Prairie,* Denver Art Museum, Denver, Colorado.

Andrist, Ralph K., 1964, *The Long Death: The Last Days of the Plains Indians,* Macmillan, New York.

Appleton Publishing, 1871, *Appleton's Hand-Book of American Travel: Western Tour,* Appleton, New York.

Archdiocese of Santa Fe, 1987, *Report of the Select Committee on the Preservation of New Mexico Churches,* Archdiocese of Santa Fe, Albuquerque.

Atherton, Lewis, 1967, *The Cattle Kings,* University of Indiana Press, Bloomington.

Barnard, Edward, ed., 1977, *Reader's Digest Story of the Great American West,* The Reader's Digest Association, Pleasantville, New York.

Baucus, Jean, 1976, *Helena: Her Historic Homes,* Vol. I, J-G Publications, Helena, Montana.

———, 1979, *Helena: Her Historic Homes,* Vol. II, J-G Publications, Helena, Montana.

Beck, Warren A., and Ynez D. Haase, 1969, *Historical Atlas of New Mexico,* University of Oklahoma Press, Norman.

Bennett, Mildred R., 1951, *The World of Willa Cather,*

Dodd, Mead and Company, New York.

Berry, Wendell, 1977, *The Unsettling of America: Culture and Agriculture,* Avon Books, New York.

Billington, Ray, ed., 1966, *The Frontier Thesis,* Holt, Rinehart and Winston, New York.

Bird, Isabella, 1980, *A Lady's Life in the Rocky Mountains,* a Comstock Edition published by arrangement with the University of Oklahoma Press, Sausalito, California.

Blackburn, Bob L., Arn Henderson, and Melvena Thurman, n.d., *The Physical Legacy: Buildings of Oklahoma County, 1889 to 1931,* Southwestern Heritage Press for the Oklahoma County Historical Society, Oklahoma City.

Blouet, Brian W., and Frederick C. Luebke, eds., 1979, *The Great Plains Environment and Culture,* University of Nebraska Press, Lincoln.

Blumenson, John J.-G., 1977, *Identifying American Architecture: A Pictorial Guide to Styles and Terms, 1600–1945,* American Association for State and Local History, Nashville.

Boorstin, Daniel J., 1973, *The Americans: The Democratic Experience,* Random House, New York.

Bormann, Ernest G., 1980, *Homesteading in the South Dakota Badlands, 1912,* privately published by the author, Stickney, South Dakota.

Brettell, Richard R., 1973, *Historic Denver: The Architects and the Architecture, 1858–1893,* Historic Denver, Inc., Denver.

Brown, Dee, 1972, *Bury My Heart at Wounded Knee: An Indian History of the American West,* Bantam Books, New York.

Bunting, Bainbridge, 1964, *Taos Adobes: Spanish Colonial and Territorial Architecture of the Taos Valley,* Fort Burgwin Research Center and Museum of New Mexico Press, Santa Fe.

———, 1976, *Early Architecture in New Mexico,* University of New Mexico Press, Albuquerque.

Burkholder, Mary V., 1977, *The King William Area: A History and Guide to the Houses,* King William Association, San Antonio, Texas.

Business Research Bureau, University of South Dakota, and the State Historical Preservation Center, 1980, *Historic Sites of South Dakota: A Guidebook,* Modern Press, Sioux Falls.

Butte-Silver Bow Historic Preservation Office, 1989, *Butte's Historic Homes,* Butte-Silver Bow Historic Preservation Office, Butte, Montana.

Caswell, Jon, ed., 1986, *A Guide to the Older Neighborhoods of Dallas,* Historic Preservation League, Dallas.

Cather, Willa, 1941, *O Pioneers!,* reprint edition, The Riverside Press, Sentry Edition, Cambridge, Massachusetts.

———, 1954, *My Antonia,* reprint edition, The Riverside Press, Sentry Edition, Cambridge, Massachusetts.

———, 1972, *A Lost Lady,* reprint edition, Vintage Books/Random House, New York.

Cohen, Judith Singer, 1988, *Cowtown Moderne: Art Deco Architecture of Fort Worth, Texas,* Texas A & M University Press, College Station.

Coles, Robert, with photographs by Alex Harris, 1973, *The Old Ones of New Mexico,* University of New Mexico Press, Albuquerque.

Crawford, Stanley, 1988, *Mayordomo: Chronicle of an Acequia in Northern New Mexico,* University of New Mexico Press, Albuquerque.

Dallas Chapter, American Institute of Architects, 1978, *Dallasights: An Anthology of Architecture and Open Spaces,* American Institute of Architects, Dallas.

DeHaas, John N., Jr., 1977, *Historic Uptown Butte,* survey report for Butte-Silver Bow Urban Revitalization Agency, Butte, Montana.

Delahanty, Randolph, and E. Andrew McKinney, 1985, *Preserving the West,* Pantheon Books, New York.

DeLong, David G., 1988, *Bruce Goff: Toward an Absolute Architecture,* MIT Press, Cambridge, Massachusetts.

DeVoto, Bernard, ed., 1953, *The Journals of Lewis and Clark,* Riverside Press, Cambridge, Massachusetts.

DeWitt, Susan, 1978, *Historic Albuquerque Today: An Overview Survey of Historic Buildings and Districts,* second revised edition, Historic Landmarks Survey of Albuquerque.

Dick, Everett, 1954, *The Sod-House Frontier,* University of Nebraska Press, Lincoln.

Dickey, Roland F., 1970, *New Mexico Village Arts,* University of New Mexico Press, Albuquerque.

Dorsett, Lyle, and G. Michael McCarthy, 1986, *The Queen City,* Pruett, Boulder, Colorado.

Douglas County Historical Society, 1977, *Douglas County Historic Building Survey,* Douglas County Historical Society, Lawrence, Kansas.

Drumm, Stella M., ed., 1962, *Down the Santa Fe Trail and into Mexico: The Diary of Susan Shelby Magoffin, 1846–1847,* University of Nebraska Press, Lincoln, by arrangement with Yale University Press.

Engelbrecht, Lloyd C., and June-Marie F. Engelbrecht, 1981, *Henry C. Trost: Architect of the Southwest,* El Paso Public Library Association, El Paso, Texas.

Erdoes, Richard, 1979, *Saloons of the Old West,* Alfred A.

Knopf, New York.

Etter, Don D., 1972, *Auraria: Where Denver Began,* Colorado Associated University Press, Boulder.

———, 1974, *University Park, Denver,* Graphic Impressions, Denver.

———, 1977, *Denver Going Modern,* Graphic Impressions, Denver.

Farr, William E., and K. Ross Toole, 1978, *Montana: Images of the Past,* Pruett, Boulder, Colorado.

Federal Writers' Project, WPA, 1938, *North Dakota: A Guide to the Northern Prairie State,* Knight Printing, Fargo, North Dakota.

Ferguson, William M., and Arthur H. Rohn, 1987, *Anasazi Ruins of the Southwest in Color,* University of New Mexico Press, Albuquerque.

Ferris, Robert G., ed., 1968, *Explorers and Settlers,* National Survey of Historic Sites and Buildings, National Park Service, Washington, D.C.

———, 1971, *Soldier and Brave,* National Survey of Historic Sites and Buildings, National Park Service, Washington, D.C.

Fite, Gilbert C., 1966, *The Farmer's Frontier, 1865–1900,* Holt, Rinehart and Winston, New York.

Frantz, Joe B., and Julian Choate, Jr., 1955, *The American Cowboy: The Myth and the Reality,* University of Oklahoma Press, Norman.

Frazer, Robert W., 1965, *Forts of the West,* University of Oklahoma, Norman.

Frazier, Ian, 1989, *Great Plains,* Farrar, Straus and Giroux, New York.

Frink, Maurice, W. Turrentine Jackson, and Agnes W. Spring, 1956, *When Grass Was King,* University of Colorado Press, Boulder.

Garland, Hamlin, 1910, *Other Main-Travelled Roads,* Harper and Brothers, New York.

———, 1956, *Main-Travelled Roads,* reprint edition, Harper and Brothers, New York.

Goetzmann, William, 1966, *Exploration and Empire,* Alfred A. Knopf, New York.

Grant, H. Roger, and Charles W. Bohi, 1988, *The Country Railroad Station in America,* revised edition, Center for Western Studies, Augustana College, Sioux Falls, South Dakota.

Greiff, Constance M., 1974, *Lost America: From the Mississippi to the Pacific,* Pyne Press, Princeton, New Jersey.

Gutman, Richard J. S., and Elliott Kaufman, in collaboration with David Slovic, 1979, *American Diner,* Harper and Row, New York.

Hale, Douglas, 1980, *The Germans from Russia in Oklahoma,* University of Oklahoma Press, Norman.

Hart, John Fraser, ed., 1972, *Regions of the United States,* Association of American Geographers, Harper and Row, New York.

Hart, Katherine, 1970, *19th-Century Austin,* Austin Heritage Foundation, Austin, Texas.

Hassrick, Peter, 1977, *The Way West: Art of Frontier America,* Harry N. Abrams, New York.

Historic Santa Fe Foundation, 1982, *Old Santa Fe Today,* third edition, University of New Mexico Press, Albuquerque.

Jackson, John Brinckerhoff, 1980, *The Southern Landscape Tradition in Texas,* Amon Carter Museum, Fort Worth, Texas.

Jacobs, Jane, 1961, *The Death and Life of Great American Cities,* Random House, New York.

Jenkins, Myra Ellen, and Albert H. Schroeder, 1974, *A Brief History of New Mexico,* University of New Mexico Press, Albuquerque.

Jones, Billy M., 1967, *Health-Seekers in the Southwest, 1817–1900,* University of Oklahoma Press, Norman.

Jordan, Terry G., 1978, *Texas Log Buildings: A Folk Architecture,* University of Texas Press, Austin.

Junior League of Tulsa, 1980, *Tulsa: An Architectural Era,* The Junior League of Tulsa, Inc., Tulsa, Oklahoma.

Kauffman, Henry J., 1975, *The American Farmhouse,* Hawthorn Books, New York.

Kay, Jane Holz, with Pauline Chase-Harrell, 1986, *Preserving New England,* Pantheon, New York.

Kennedy, Roger G., 1982, *American Churches,* Steward, Tabori and Chang, New York.

Klamkin, Charles, 1979, *Barns: Their History, Preservation and Restoration,* Bonanza Books, New York.

Koop, Michael, and Stephen Ludwig, 1984, *German-Russian Folk Architecture in Southeastern South Dakota,* State Historical Preservation Center, Vermillion, South Dakota.

Kramer, Jane, 1977, *The Last Cowboy,* Pocket Books/Simon and Schuster, New York.

Kubler, George, 1974, *The Religious Architecture of New Mexico,* reprint edition (originally published by the Colorado Springs Fine Arts Center, 1941), University of New Mexico Press, Albuquerque.

Kurelek, William, 1973, *A Prairie Boy's Winter,* Houghton Mifflin, Boston.

Kutsche, Paul, and John R. Van Ness, 1981, *Cañones: Values, Crisis, and Survival in a Northern New Mexico Village,* University of New Mexico Press, Albuquerque.

Lamar, Howard R., ed., 1977, *The Reader's Encyclopedia*

of the American West, Harper and Row, New York.

Landmarks, Inc., and the Junior League of Omaha, 1977, *Omaha City Architecture,* Landmarks, Inc. and the Junior League, Omaha, Nebraska.

Laramie County Chapter, Wyoming Historical Society, 1976, *Cheyenne Landmarks,* 1976, Wyoming Historical Society, Cheyenne.

Larson, Paul Clifford, ed., with Susan M. Brown, 1988, *The Spirit of H. H. Richardson on the Midland Prairies,* University Art Museum, University of Minnesota, Minneapolis, and Iowa State University Press, Ames.

Lehmer, Donald J., 1971, *Introduction to Middle Missouri Archeology,* National Park Service, Washington, D.C.

Lingeman, Richard, 1980, *Small-Town America,* Houghton Mifflin, Boston.

Loth, Calder, and Julius Trousdale Sadler, Jr., 1975, *The Only Proper Style: Gothic Architecture in America,* New York Graphic Society, Boston.

Luchetti, Cathy, in collaboration with Carol Olwell, 1982, *Women of the West,* Antelope Island Press, St. George, Utah.

Madson, John, 1982, *Where the Sky Began: Land of the Tallgrass Prairie,* Houghton Mifflin, Boston.

Maguire, Jack, ed., 1973, *A President's Country: A Guide to the LBJ Country of Texas,* Shoal Creek Publishers, Austin, Texas.

McAlester, Virginia, and Lee McAlester, 1984, *A Field Guide to American Homes,* Alfred A. Knopf, New York.

———, 1988, *Discover: Dallas and Fort Worth,* Alfred A. Knopf, New York.

McCracken, Harold, 1959, *George Catlin and the Old Frontier,* Bonanza Books, New York.

McDonald, William L., 1978, *Dallas Rediscovered: A Photographic Chronicle of Urban Expansion, 1870–1925,* Dallas Historical Society, Dallas, Texas.

McKee, Russell, 1974, *The Last West: A History of the Great Plains of North America,* Thomas Y. Crowell, New York.

Meinig, D. W., 1969, *Imperial Texas: An Interpretive Essay in Cultural Geography,* University of Texas Press, Austin.

Meredith, Howard L., and Mary Ellen Meredith, eds., 1980, *Of the Earth: Oklahoma Architectural History,* Oklahoma Historical Society, Oklahoma City.

Miller, Donald C., 1975, *Ghost Towns of Montana,* Pruett, Boulder, Colorado.

Moholy-Nagy, Sibyl, 1957, *Native Genius in Anonymous Architecture,* Horizon Press, New York.

Momaday, N. Scott, 1969, *The Way to Rainy Mountain,* Ballantine Books, New York.

Morris, Wright, 1969, *The Home Place,* University of Nebraska Press, Lincoln.

Muilenburg, Grace, and Ada Swineford, 1975, *Land of the Post Rock,* University Press of Kansas, Lawrence.

Museum of Fine Arts, 1975, *Frontier America: The Far West,* Museum of Fine Arts, Boston.

Nash, Gerald D., 1973, *The American West in the Twentieth Century,* Prentice-Hall, Englewood Cliffs, New Jersey.

Nebraska State Historical Society, 1989, "Historic Places: The National Register for Nebraska," *Nebraska History* (special issue) 70(1).

Neill, Peter, ed., 1988, *Maritime America: Art and Artifacts from America's Great Nautical Collections,* Balsam Press in association with Harry N. Abrams, New York.

New Mexico State Planning Office, 1974, *Lincoln, New Mexico: A Plan for Preservation and Growth,* New Mexico State Planning Office, Santa Fe.

Nichols, John, 1974, *The Milagro Beanfield War,* Ballantine Books, New York.

———, with photographs by William Davis, 1979, *If Mountains Die,* Alfred A. Knopf, New York.

———, 1982, *The Last Beautiful Days of Autumn,* Holt, Rinehart and Winston, New York.

Noble, Allen G., 1984, *Wood, Brick and Stone: The North American Settlement Landscape,* Vol. 2: *Barns and Farm Structures,* University of Massachusetts Press, Amherst.

Noel, Thomas J., and Barbara S. Norgren, 1987, *Denver: The City Beautiful,* Historic Denver, Inc., Denver.

Novak, Barbara, 1980, *Nature and Culture: American Landscape and Painting, 1825–1875,* Oxford University Press, New York.

Office of Archeology and Historic Preservation, National Park Service, 1974, *Texas Catalog, Historic American Buildings Survey,* Trinity University Press, San Antonio, Texas.

Omaha City Planning Department, 1980, *A Comprehensive Program for Historic Preservation in Omaha,* Landmarks Heritage Preservation Commission, Omaha.

———, 1984, *Patterns on the Landscape: Heritage Conservation in North Omaha,* Landmarks Heritage Preservation Commission, Omaha.

Pare, Richard, ed., and Phyllis Lambert, director, 1978, *Court House: A Photographic Document,* Horizon, New York.

Parkman, Francis, with a foreword by A. B. Guthrie, Jr., 1950, *The Oregon Trail*, reprint edition, The New American Library, New York.

Paul, Rodman W., 1963, *Mining Frontiers of the Far West, 1848–1880*, Holt, Rinehart and Winston, New York.

Phillips, David R., ed., 1973, *The West: An American Experience*, Henry Regnery, Chicago.

Plowden, David, 1972, *Floor of the Sky: The Great Plains*, Landform Book/Sierra Club, San Francisco and New York.

Pomeroy, Earl, 1957, *In Search of the Golden West*, Alfred A. Knopf, New York.

Ramsey, Ronald, 1975, *Fargo-Moorhead: A Guide to Historic Architecture*, Fargo-Moorhead Board of Realtors, Fargo, North Dakota.

Redford, Robert, 1978, *The Outlaw Trail*, Grosset and Dunlap, New York.

Reeve, Agnesa Lufkin, 1988, *From Hacienda to Bungalow: Northern New Mexico Houses, 1850–1912*, University of New Mexico Press, Albuquerque.

Renewable Technologies, Inc., 1985, *The Butte-Anaconda Historical Park System Master Plan*, Butte Historical Society, Butte, Montana.

Reps, John W., 1965, *The Making of Urban America: A History of City Planning in the United States*, Princeton University Press, Princeton, New Jersey.

Rifkind, Carole, 1977, *Main Street: The Face of Urban America*, Harper and Row, New York.

———, 1980, *A Field Guide to American Architecture*, New American Library, New York.

Rolvaag, O. E., 1929, *Giants in the Earth*, reprint edition, Harper and Brothers, New York.

Rothstein, Arthur, 1981, *The American West in the Thirties*, Dover, New York.

Rudofsky, Bernard, 1987, *Architecture without Architects*, by arrangement with Doubleday and Company, University of New Mexico Press, Albuquerque.

Sando, Joe S., 1976, *The Pueblo Indians*, The Indian Historian Press, San Francisco.

Sandoval, Judith Hancock, 1986, *Historic Ranches of Wyoming*, Mountain States Lithography, Casper, Wyoming, distributed by University of Nebraska Press, Lincoln.

Sandoz, Mari, 1953, *Cheyenne Autumn*, Avon Books, New York.

Sanford, Mollie Dorsey, with introduction and notes by Donald F. Danker, 1976, *Mollie, the Journal of Mollie Dorsey Sanford in Nebraska and Colorado Territories, 1857–1866*, University of Nebraska Press, Lincoln.

Schmitt, Peter J., 1969, *Back to Nature*, Oxford University Press, New York.

Scully, Vincent J., Jr., 1955, *The Shingle Style and the Stick Style*, Yale University Press, New Haven.

Sheppard, Carl D., 1988, *Creator of the Santa Fe Style: Isaac Hamilton Rapp, Architect*, University of New Mexico Press, Albuquerque.

Smith, Duane A., 1974, *Rocky Mountain Mining Camps: The Urban Frontier*, Bison Book Edition, University of Nebraska Press, Lincoln, by arrangement with Indiana University Press.

———, 1988, *Guide to Historic Durango and Silverton*, Cordillera Press, Evergreen, Colorado.

Smith, G. E. Kidder, 1976, *A Pictorial History of Architecture in America*, American Heritage, New York.

Smith, Lucinda, 1980, *Movie Palaces*, Clarkson N. Potter, New York.

Spears, Beverley, 1986, *American Adobes: Rural Houses of Northern New Mexico*, University of New Mexico Press, Albuquerque.

Starck, Robert, and Lynn Dance, 1977, *Nebraska Photographic Documentary Project*, University of Nebraska Press, Lincoln.

Steinbeck, John, 1939, *The Grapes of Wrath*, Modern Library, New York.

Stewart, Elinore Pruitt, 1961, *Letters of a Woman Homesteader*, University of Nebraska Press, Lincoln.

———, 1979, *Letters on an Elk Hunt by a Woman Homesteader*, University of Nebraska Press, Lincoln.

Stokes, Samuel N., with A. Elizabeth Watson, 1989, *Saving America's Countryside: A Guide to Rural Conservation*, Johns Hopkins University Press, Baltimore, for the National Trust for Historic Preservation.

Stratton, Joanna L., 1981, *Pioneer Women: Voices from the Kansas Frontier*, Simon and Schuster, New York.

Texas Historical Commission, 1984, *A Catalog of Texas Properties in the National Register of Historic Places*, Texas Historical Commission, Austin.

Topeka-Shawnee County Metropolitan Planning Commission, 1974, *Remembrances in Wood, Brick, and Stone: Examples from the Architectural Heritage of Shawnee County, Kansas*, Topeka-Shawnee County Metropolitan Planning Commission, Topeka, Kansas.

Tyler, Ron, 1983, *Visions of America: Pioneer Artists in a New Land*, Thames and Hudson, New York.

University of Kansas Museum of Art, 1975, *No Mountains in the Way*, University of Kansas, Lawrence.

Utley, Robert, 1969, *Custer Battlefield,* National Park Service, Washington, D.C.

Vieyra, Daniel I., 1979, *"Fill 'er Up": An Architectural History of America's Gas Stations,* Collier Macmillan, New York.

Warren, Nancy Hunter, 1987, *Villages of Hispanic New Mexico,* School of American Research Press, Santa Fe.

Webb, Walter Prescott, 1931, *The Great Plains,* Grosset and Dunlap, New York.

Whiffen, Marcus, 1969, *American Architecture Since 1980: A Guide to Styles,* MIT Press, Cambridge, Massachusetts.

Whittemore, Loren R., 1967, *An Illustrated History of Ranching in the Pikes Peak Region,* Dentan-Berkeland, Colorado Springs.

Wood, Nancy, 1978, *The Grass Roots People,* Harper and Row, New York.

Woodall, Ronald, and T. H. Watkins, 1977, *Taken by the Wind: Vanishing Architecture of the West,* New York Graphic Society, Boston.

Worster, Donald, 1979, *Dust Bowl: The Southern Plains in the 1930s,* Oxford University Press, New York.

Wrenn, Tony P., and Elizabeth D. Mulloy, 1976, *America's Forgotten Architecture,* Pantheon, New York, for the National Trust for Historic Preservation.

Wyoming Recreation Commission, 1976, *Wyoming: A Guide to Historic Sites,* Big Horn Book Company, Basin, Wyoming.

Young, Otis E., Jr., 1970, *Western Mining,* University of Oklahoma Press, Norman.

McDonald, John, 300

MacDonald, William, *Dallas Rediscovered*, 79–80

McInteer Villa, Atchison, *386*

McIntosh County, N.Dak., 51, 121

McKenzie, Kenneth, 31–32

McKim, Mead, and White (architects), 72, 79, 341, 343

McLaughlin, Don, 110

McLoughlin, Herbert, 336

McNally, Jude, 389

McPhee reservoir, *404*

Magee-Cather House, Red Cloud, *217*

Magnolia Building, Dallas, 335–36, *335*, 341

Magoffin, Susan, 15, 30–31; *Along the Santa Fe Trail*, 17

MainStreet program, 208, 227–43

main streets, *72, 73*; preservation of, 227–43; remodeled, 96–97, *96. See also* downtown districts

maintenance: of ancient sites, 409, 411; of historic properties, 301, *372*, 389–90

Majestic Theater, Dallas, 332, 336

managers: of Bannack, Mont., 255; MainStreet, 228–29, 231, 233, 241–43

Mandan, N.Dak., 20

Mandan Indians, 7, 13, 20, 402–3

Manhattan, Kans., 134

mansions, governors', 387–88

Markalunas, Ramona, 258

Martinez, Antonio Severino, 160

Martinez, Jerome, 191, 201; quoted, 189–90, 193–94

Marysville, Kans., *116*

Masonic Temple, Denver, 319

Masonic Temple, Victor, *247*

Masterson JY Bunkhouse, Ranching Heritage Center, Texas Tech University, *164*

May, David, 79

May Company, 79

Mayfield Dugout, Briscoe County, *46*

Medallion, The, 127–28

Medora, N.Dak., 156–57

Meeker, Jotham, Farmstead, Franklin County, *408*

Meem, John Gaw, 149, 305

Memorial Building, Topeka, *80*

Mennonites, 119

Mercer, Mark, 344–45

Mercer, Samuel D., 79

Mercer Management, 344–46

Merlan, Thomas, 101, 184, 199, 236; quoted, 409, 411

Mesa Verde National Park, *8*, 22, 99, *396*, 397–98, 407

Mexicans, and adobe tradition, 24

Mexico, 8; architecture in, 17; independence of, 26

migration: Indian, 5, 21; westward, 15–17. *See also* westward expansion; settlement

Miller, Alfred Jacob, 11, 13

mining, 36–44; and archeological sites, 401; current, 272–73; and industrial preservation, 269–73; pollution from, 262, 264; surface, 273; and western settlement, 45–46

mining camps, 36, 38–42, 46, 245–47, 249–52; destruction of, 273; supplies for, 150

mining towns, 39–46, 245–50, 252–56, 260, 264, 268–70; abandoned, 44. *See also names of towns*

Minnehaha County Courthouse, Sioux Falls, *71*, 113

mission outposts, Spanish, 26–27

Mission Revival style, *235*, 305

Mission San Antonio de Valero. *See also* Alamo, the

Mission San Jose y Miguel de Aguayo, Tex., *27*

Missouri Basin Project, 402–4

Missouri River, 5, 7, 36, 64, 68, 78; historical sites on, 402–3

mobility, and western life, 14, 16–17, 19, 44–45, 79

Moderne style, *90–91*, 113, 340

modernism, 341; and western cities, 88–95, 97

Moffat Mansion, Denver, 295

Molly Brown House, Denver, *293*, 295

Montana: agricultural population of, 139; historic preservation in, 110–11, 254–55, 260, 262–73, 388–90; industrial preservation in, 269–73; mining in, 38–39, 42–43; rural preservation in, 146–47, 149–55. *See also place names*

Montana Cultural and Esthetics Trust Fund, 388

Montana Department of Fish, Wildlife and Parks, 254–55

Montana Post, quoted, 150

Montezuma Hotel, Las Vegas, *234*, 236

Moody, Tex., *83*

Moody Foundation, 276, 281

Mora County, agricultural population of, 181

moradas, *25, 26*, 61, 184

Mora Valley, N.Mex., 124, 131, 177–82, *178–81*

Mores, Marquis de, 156–57

Mormon Trail, 143

Moss, P. B., 388

Moss Mansion, Billings, 388–90, *389*

Mosty, John, quoted, 289–90

Moulton, Jennifer, 327; quoted, 297

Mueller, Alfred, 373

Mueller, W. E. (Jim), 157

Mueller Ranch, in Colorado, 157–60, *159*

Mullenburg, Grace, *Land of the Post Rock*, 133

murals, Moderne, 97

Murphy, David, 123; quoted, 127

Museum of Fine Arts, Santa Fe, *75*, 302

Museum of New Mexico, Santa Fe, 76, 197, 220, 223

museums: in Galveston, 278–82; house, *274*, 373, 384–90, 393–95. *See also names of museums*

myth, western, 14–15

National Endowment for the Humanities, 339

National Geographic, 398

National Grange, 138

National Historic Landmarks, 264, 266, 371

Wright, Frank LLoyd, 84, 86, 97, 394–95
writers: and historical preservation, 128–37; and preservation projects, 209; and West, 9, 13
Wulff, Anton, Home, San Antonio, 287–88, *287*
Wyoming: agricultural population of, 140; historic preservation in, 252–54; rural sites in, 143–45; vernacular architecture in, 124–25, *125*
Wyoming Recreation Commission, 252–53

XIT Ranch, Texas Tech University, 164

Young, Otis F., *Western Mining*, 38

Z-Bar Ranch, in Kansas, 162–63
Zinn, Dale, 310; quoted, 307, 309
zoning: and downtown preservation, 324–25; high-rise, 378–79; and residential preservation, 358–60, 381